THOMAS C

C H A R T I S M

PAST AND PRESENT

Elibron Classics
www.elibron.com

CHARTISM.

PAST AND PRESENT.

BY

THOMAS CARLYLE.

LONDON:
CHAPMAN AND HALL, 193 PICCADILLY.
M.DCCC.LVIII.

LONDON:
PRINTED BY LEVEY, ROBSON, AND FRANKLYN.
Great New Street and Fetter Lane.

CONTENTS.

CHARTISM.

PAST AND PRESENT.

BOOK I.—PROEM.

BOOK II.—THE ANCIENT MONK.

BOOK III.—THE MODERN WORKER.

BOOK IV.—HOROSCOPE.

CHARTISM.

———

"It never smokes but there is fire."—*Old Proverb.*

CHARTISM.

CHAPTER I.

CONDITION-OF-ENGLAND QUESTION.

A FEELING very generally exists that the condition and disposition of the Working Classes is a rather ominous matter at present; that something ought to be said, something ought to be done, in regard to it. And surely, at an epoch of history when the 'National Petition' carts itself in wagons along the streets, and is presented 'bound with iron hoops, four men bearing it,' to a Reformed House of Commons; and Chartism numbered by the million and half, taking nothing by its iron-hooped Petition, breaks out into brickbats, cheap pikes, and even into sputterings of conflagration, such very general feeling cannot be considered unnatural! To us individually this matter appears, and has for many years appeared, to be the most ominous of all practical matters whatever; a matter in regard to which if something be not done, something will *do* itself one day, and in a fashion that will please nobody. The time is verily come for acting in it; how much more for consultation about acting in it, for speech and articulate inquiry about it!

We are aware that, according to the newspapers, Chartism is extinct; that a Reform Ministry has 'put down the chimera of Chartism' in the most felicitous effectual manner. So say the newspapers;—and yet, alas, most readers of newspapers know withal that it is indeed the 'chimera' of Chartism, not the reality, which has been put down. The distracted incoherent embodiment of Chartism, whereby in late months it took shape and became visible, this has been put down; or rather has fallen down and gone asunder by gravitation and law of nature: but the living essence of Chartism has not been put down. Chartism means the

bitter discontent grown fierce and mad, the wrong condition therefore or the wrong disposition, of the Working Classes of England.
It is a new name for a thing which has had many names, which
will yet have many. The matter of Chartism is weighty, deep-
rooted, far-extending; did not begin yesterday; will by no means
end this day or tomorrow. Reform Ministry, constabulary rural
police, new levy of soldiers, grants of money to Birmingham; all
this is well, or is not well; all this will put down only the embodiment or 'chimera' of Chartism. The essence continuing, new
and ever new embodiments, chimeras madder or less mad, have
to continue. The melancholy fact remains, that this thing known
at present by the name Chartism does exist; has existed; and,
either 'put down,' into secret treason, with rusty pistols, vitriol-
bottle and match-box, or openly brandishing pike and torch (one
knows not in which case _more_ fatal-looking), is like to exist till
quite other methods have been tried with it. What means this
bitter discontent of the Working Classes? Whence comes it, whither goes it? Above all, at what price, on what terms, will it probably consent to depart from us and die into rest? These are
questions.

To say that it is mad, incendiary, nefarious, is no answer. To
say all this, in never so many dialects, is saying little. 'Glasgow
Thuggery,' 'Glasgow Thugs;' it is a witty nickname: the practice
of 'Number 60' entering his dark room, to contract for and settle
the price of blood with operative assassins, in a Christian city,
once distinguished by its rigorous Christianism, is doubtless a fact
worthy of all horror: but what will horror do for it? What will
execration; nay at bottom, what will condemnation and banishment to Botany Bay do for it? Glasgow Thuggery, Chartist
torch-meetings, Birmingham riots, Swing conflagrations, are so
many symptoms on the surface; you abolish the symptom to no
purpose, if the disease is left untouched. Boils on the surface
are curable or incurable,—small matter which, while the virulent
humour festers deep within; poisoning the sources of life; and
certain enough to find for itself ever new boils and sore issues;
ways of announcing that it continues there, that it would fain not
continue there.

Delirious Chartism will not have raged entirely to no purpose,
as indeed no earthly thing does so, if it have forced all thinking
men of the community to think of this vital matter, too apt to be
overlooked otherwise. Is the condition of the English working
people wrong; so wrong that rational working men cannot, will
not, and even should not rest quiet under it? A most grave case,
complex beyond all others in the world; a case wherein Botany

Bay, constabulary rural police, and such like, will avail but little. Or is the discontent itself mad, like the shape it took? Not the condition of the working people that is wrong; but their disposition, their own thoughts, beliefs and feelings that are wrong? This too were a most grave case, little less alarming, little less complex than the former one. In this case too, where constabulary police and mere rigour of coercion seems more at home, coercion will by no means do all, coercion by itself will not even do much. If there do exist general madness of discontent, then sanity and some measure of content must be brought about again, —not by constabulary police alone. When the thoughts of a people, in the great mass of it, have grown mad, the combined issue of that people's workings will be a madness, an incoherency and ruin! Sanity will have to be recovered for the general mass; coercion itself will otherwise cease to be able to coerce.

We have heard it asked, Why Parliament throws no light on this question of the Working Classes, and the condition or disposition they are in? Truly to a remote observer of Parliamentary procedure it seems surprising, especially in late Reformed times, to see what space this question occupies in the Debates of the Nation. Can any other business whatsoever be so pressing on legislators? A Reformed Parliament, one would think, should inquire into popular discontents *before* they get the length of pikes and torches! For what end at all are men, Honourable Members and Reform Members, sent to St. Stephen's, with clamour and effort; kept talking, struggling, motioning and countermotioning? The condition of the great body of people in a country is the condition of the country itself: this you would say is a truism in all times; a truism rather pressing to get recognised as a truth now, and be acted upon, in these times. Yet read Hansard's Debates, or the Morning Papers, if you have nothing to do! The old grand question, whether A is to be in office or B, with the innumerable subsidiary questions growing out of that, courting paragraphs and suffrages for a blessed solution of that: Canada question, Irish Appropriation question, West-India question, Queen's Bedchamber question; Game Laws, Usury Laws; African Blacks, Hill Coolies, Smithfield cattle, and Dog-carts,—all manner of questions and subjects, except simply this the alpha and omega of all! Surely Honourable Members ought to speak of the Condition-of-England question too. Radical Members, above all; friends of the people; chosen with effort, by the people, to interpret and articulate the dumb deep want of the people! To a remote observer they seem oblivious of their duty. Are they not there, by trade, mission, and express appointment of themselves and others, to speak for the good of the British Nation? Whatsoever great British interest can the least speak for itself, for that beyond all they are called to speak. They are either speakers for that great dumb toiling class which cannot speak, or they are nothing that one can well specify.

Alas, the remote observer knows not the nature of Parliaments: how Parliaments, extant there for the British Nation's sake, find that they are extant withal for their own sake; how Parliaments travel so naturally in their deep-rutted routine, commonplace worn into ruts axle-deep, from which only strength, insight and courageous generous exertion can lift any Parliament or vehicle; how in Parliaments, Reformed or Unreformed, there may chance to be a strong man, an original, clear-sighted, greathearted, patient and valiant man, or to be none such;—how, on the whole, Parliaments, lumbering along in their deep ruts of commonplace, find, as so many of us otherwise do, that the ruts *are* axle-deep, and the travelling very toilsome of itself, and for the day the evil thereof sufficient! What Parliaments ought to have done in this business, what they will, can or cannot yet do, and where the limits of their faculty and culpability may lie, in regard to it, were a long investigation; into which we need not enter at this moment. What they have done is unhappily plain enough. Hitherto, on this most national of questions, the Collective Wisdom of the Nation has availed us as good as nothing whatever.

And yet, as we say, it is a question which cannot be left to the Collective Folly of the Nation! In or out of Parliament, darkness, neglect, hallucination must contrive to cease in regard to it; true insight into it must be had. How inexpressibly useful were true insight into it; a genuine understanding by the upper classes of society what it is that the under classes intrinsically mean; a clear interpretation of the thought which at heart torments these wild inarticulate souls, struggling there, with inarticulate uproar, like dumb creatures in pain, unable to speak what is in them! Something they do mean; some true thing withal, in the centre of their confused hearts,—for they are hearts created by Heaven too: to the Heaven it is clear what thing; to us not clear. Would that it were! Perfect clearness on it were equivalent to remedy of it. For, as is well said, all battle is misunderstanding; did the parties know one another, the battle would cease. No man at bottom means injustice; it is always for some obscure distorted image of a right that he contends: an obscure image diffracted, exaggerated, in the wonderfullest way, by natural dimness and selfishness; getting tenfold more diffracted by exasperation of contest, till at length it become all but irrecognisable; yet still the image of a right. Could a man own to himself that the thing he fought for was wrong, contrary to fairness and the law of reason, he would own also that it thereby stood condemned and hopeless; he could fight for it no longer. Nay independently of right, could the contending parties get but accurately to discern one another's might and strength to contend, the one would peaceably yield to the other and to Necessity; the contest in this case too were over. No African expedition now, as in the days of Herodotus, is fitted out *against the South-wind*. One expedition was satisfactory in that department. The South-wind Simoom continues blowing occasionally, hateful as ever, maddening as ever; but one expedition was enough. Do we not all submit to Death? The highest sentence of the law, sentence of death, is passed on all of us by the fact of birth; yet we live patiently under it, patiently undergo it when the hour comes. Clear undeniable right, clear undeniable might: either of these once ascertained puts an end to battle. All battle is a confused experiment to ascertain one and both of these.

What are the rights, what are the mights of the discontented Working Classes in England at this epoch? He were an Œdipus, and deliverer from sad social pestilence, who could resolve us fully! For we may say beforehand, The struggle that divides the upper and lower in society over Europe, and more painfully and notably in England than elsewhere, this too is a struggle which will end and adjust itself as all other struggles do and have done, by making the right clear and the might clear; not otherwise than by that. Meantime, the questions, Why are the Working Classes discontented; what is their condition, economical, moral, in their houses and their hearts, as it is in reality and as they figure it to themselves to be; what do they complain of; what ought they, and ought they not to complain of?—these are measurable questions; on some of these any common mortal, did he but turn his eyes to them, might throw some light. Certain researches and considerations of ours on the matter, since no one else will undertake it, are now to be made public. The researches have yielded us little, almost nothing; but the considerations are of old date, and press to have utterance. We are not without hope that our general notion of the business, if we can get it uttered at all, will meet some assent from many candid men.

CHAPTER II.

STATISTICS.

A WITTY statesman said, you might prove anything by figures.
We have looked into various statistic works, Statistic-Society Reports, Poor-Law Reports, Reports and Pamphlets not a few, with a
sedulous eye to this question of the Working Classes and their
general condition in England; we grieve to say, with as good as
no result whatever. Assertion swallows assertion; according to
the old Proverb, ' as the *statist* thinks, the bell clinks!' Tables
are like cobwebs, like the sieve of the Danaides; beautifully reticulated, orderly to look upon, but which will hold no conclusion.
Tables are abstractions, and the object a most concrete one, so
difficult to read the essence of. There are innumerable circumstances; and one circumstance left out may be the vital one on
which all turned. Statistics is a science which ought to be honourable, the basis of many most important sciences; but it is not to
be carried on by steam, this science, any more than others are; a
wise head is requisite for carrying it on. Conclusive facts are inseparable from inconclusive except by a head that already understands and knows. Vain to send the purblind and blind to the
shore of a Pactolus never so golden: these find only gravel; the
seer and finder alone picks up gold grains there. And now the
purblind offering you, with asseveration and protrusive impor-
tunity, his basket of gravel as gold, what steps are to be taken with
him?—Statistics, one may hope, will improve gradually, and become good for something. Meanwhile it is to be feared, the crabbed
satirist was partly right, as things go: ' A judicious man,' says he,
'looks at Statistics, not to get knowledge, but to save himself from
having ignorance foisted on him.' With what serene conclusive-
ness a member of some Useful-Knowledge Society stops your
mouth with a figure of arithmetic! To him it seems he has there
extracted the elixir of the matter, on which now nothing more
can be said. It is needful that you look into his said extracted
elixir; and ascertain, alas, too probably not without a sigh, that
it is wash and vapidity, good only for the gutters.

Twice or three times have we heard the lamentations and pro-
phecies of a humane Jeremiah, mourner for the poor, cut short by
a statistic fact of the most decisive nature: How can the condition
of the poor be other than good, be other than better; has not the
average duration of life in England, and therefore among the most
numerous class in England, been proved to have increased? Our
Jeremiah had to admit that, if so, it was an astounding fact;

whereby all that ever he, for his part, had observed on other sides of the matter, was overset without remedy. If life last longer, life must be less worn upon, by outward suffering, by inward discontent, by hardship of any kind; the general condition of the poor must be bettering instead of worsening. So was our Jeremiah cut short. And now for the 'proof?' Readers who are curious in statistic proofs may see it drawn out with all solemnity, in a Pamphlet 'published by Charles Knight and Company,'¹—and perhaps himself draw inferences from it. Northampton Tables, compiled by Dr. Price 'from registers of the Parish of All Saints from 1735 to 1780;' Carlisle Tables, collected by Dr. Heysham from observation of Carlisle City for eight years, 'the calculations founded on them' conducted by another Doctor; incredible 'document considered satisfactory by men of science in France:'—alas, is it not as if some zealous scientific son of Adam had proved the deepening of the Ocean, by survey, accurate or cursory, of two mud-plashes on the coast of the Isle of Dogs? 'Not to get knowledge, but to save yourself from having ignorance foisted on you!'

The condition of the working man in this country, what it is and has been, whether it is improving or retrograding,—is a question to which from statistics hitherto no solution can be got. Hitherto, after many tables and statements, one is still left mainly to what he can ascertain by his own eyes, looking at the concrete phenomenon for himself. There is no other method; and yet it is a most imperfect method. Each man expands his own handbreadth of observation to the limits of the general whole; more or less, each man must take what he himself has seen and ascertained for a sample of all that is seeable and ascertainable. Hence discrepancies, controversies, wide-spread, long-continued; which there is at present no means or hope of satisfactorily ending. When Parliament takes up 'the Condition-of-England question,' as it will have to do one day, then indeed much may be amended! Inquiries wisely gone into, even on this most complex matter, will yield results worth something, not nothing. But it is a most complex matter; on which, whether for the past or the present, Statistic Inquiry, with its limited means, with its short vision and headlong extensive dogmatism, as yet too often throws not light, but error worse than darkness.

What constitutes the well-being of a man? Many things; of which the wages he gets, and the bread he buys with them, are but one preliminary item. Grant, however, that the wages were the whole; that once knowing the wages and the price of bread,

¹ An Essay on the Means of Insurance against the Casualties of &c. &c. London, Charles Knight and Company, 1836. Price two shillings.

we know all; then what are the wages? Statistic Inquiry, in its present unguided condition, cannot tell. The average rate of day's wages is not correctly ascertained for any portion of this country; not only not for half-centuries, it is not even ascertained anywhere for decades or years: far from instituting comparisons with the past, the present itself is unknown to us. And then, given the average of wages, what is the constancy of employment; what is the difficulty of finding employment; the fluctuation from season to season, from year to year? Is it constant, calculable wages; or fluctuating, incalculable, more or less of the nature of gambling? This secondary circumstance, of quality in wages, is perhaps even more important than the primary one of quantity. Farther we ask, Can the labourer, by thrift and industry, hope to rise to mastership; or is such hope cut off from him? How is he related to his employer; by bonds of friendliness and mutual help; or by hostility, opposition, and chains of mutual necessity alone? In a word, what degree of contentment can a human creature be supposed to enjoy in that position? With hunger preying on him, his contentment is likely to be small! But even with abundance, his discontent, his real misery may be great. The labourer's feelings, his notion of being justly dealt with or unjustly; his wholesome composure, frugality, prosperity in the one case, his acrid unrest, recklessness, gin-drinking, and gradual ruin in the other,—how shall figures of arithmetic represent all this? So much is still to be ascertained; much of it by no means easy to ascertain! Till, among the 'Hill Cooly' and 'Dog-cart' questions, there arise in Parliament and extensively out of it a 'Condition-of-England question,' and quite a new set of inquirers and methods, little of it is likely to be ascertained.

One fact on this subject, a fact which arithmetic *is* capable of representing, we have often considered would be worth all the rest: Whether the labourer, whatever his wages are, is saving money? Laying up money, he proves that his condition, painful as it may be without and within, is not yet desperate; that he looks forward to a better day coming, and is still resolutely steering towards the same; that all the lights and darknesses of his lot are united under a blessed radiance of hope,—the last, first, nay one may say the sole blessedness of man. Is the habit of saving increased and increasing, or the contrary? Where the present writer has been able to look with his own eyes, it is decreasing, and in many quarters all but disappearing. Statistic science turns up her Savings-Bank Accounts, and answers, "Increasing rapidly." Would that one could believe it! But the Danaides'-sieve character of such statistic reticulated documents is too manifest. A few years ago, in regions where thrift, to one's own knowledge, still was, Savings-Banks were not; the labourer lent his money to some farmer, of capital, or supposed to be of capital, —and has too often lost it since; or he bought a cow with it, bought a cottage with it; nay hid it under his thatch: the Savings-Banks books then exhibited mere blank and zero. That they swell yearly now, if such be the fact, indicates that what thrift exists does gradually resort more and more thither rather than elsewhither; but the question, Is thrift increasing? runs through the reticulation, and is as water spilt on the ground, not to be gathered here.

These are inquiries on which, had there been a proper 'Condition-of-England question,' some light would have been thrown, before 'torch-meetings' arose to illustrate them! Far as they lie out of the course of Parliamentary routine, they should have been gone into, should have been glanced at, in one or the other fashion. A Legislature making laws for the Working Classes, in total uncertainty as to these things, is legislating in the dark; not wisely, nor to good issues. The simple fundamental question, Can the labouring man in this England of ours, who is willing to labour, find work, and subsistence by his work? is matter of mere conjecture and assertion hitherto; not ascertainable by authentic evidence: the Legislature, satisfied to legislate in the dark, has not yet sought any evidence on it. They pass their New Poor-Law Bill, without evidence as to all this. Perhaps their New Poor-Law Bill is itself only intended as an *experimentum crucis* to ascertain all this? Chartism is an answer, seemingly not in the affirmative.

CHAPTER III.

NEW POOR-LAW.

To read the Reports of the Poor-Law Commissioners, if one had faith enough, would be a pleasure to the friend of humanity. One sole recipe seems to have been needful for the woes of England: 'refusal of out-door relief.' England lay in sick discontent, writhing powerless on its fever-bed, dark, nigh desperate, in wastefulness, want, improvidence, and eating care, till like Hyperion down the eastern steeps, the Poor-Law Commissioners arose, and said. Let there be workhouses, and bread of affliction and water of affliction there! It was a simple invention; as all truly great inventions are. And see, in any quarter, instantly as the walls of the workhouse arise, misery and necessity fly away, out of sight,—out

of being, as is fondly hoped, and dissolve into the inane; industry,
frugality, fertility, rise of wages, peace on earth and goodwill towards men do,—in the Poor-Law Commissioners' Reports,—infallibly, rapidly or not so rapidly, to the joy of all parties, super-
vene. It was a consummation devoutly to be wished. We have
looked over these four annual Poor-Law Reports with a variety of
reflections; with no thought that our Poor-Law Commissioners
are the inhuman men their enemies accuse them of being; with
a feeling of thankfulness rather that there do exist men of that
structure too; with a persuasion deeper and deeper that Nature,
who makes nothing to no purpose, has not made either them or
their Poor-Law Amendment Act in vain. We hope to prove that
they and it were an indispensable element, harsh but salutary, in
the progress of things.

That this Poor-Law Amendment Act meanwhile should be, as
we sometimes hear it named, the 'chief glory' of a Reform Cabinet,
betokens, one would imagine, rather a scarcity of glory there. To
say to the poor, Ye shall eat the bread of affliction and drink the
water of affliction, and be very miserable while here, required not
so much a stretch of heroic faculty in any sense, as due toughness
of bowels. If paupers are made miserable, paupers will needs decline in multitude. It is a secret known to all rat-catchers: stop
up the granary-crevices, afflict with continual mewing, alarm, and
going-off of traps, your ' chargeable labourers' disappear, and cease
from the establishment. A still briefer method is that of arsenic;
perhaps even a milder, where otherwise permissible. Rats and
paupers can be abolished; the human faculty was from of old adequate to grind them down, slowly or at once, and needed no ghost
or Reform Ministry to teach it. Furthermore when one hears of
' all the labour of the country being absorbed into employment' by
this new system of affliction, when labour complaining of want can
find no audience, one cannot but pause. That misery and unem-
ployed labour should ' disappear' in that case is natural enough;
should go out of sight,—but out of existence? What we do know
is, that ' the rates are diminished,' as they cannot well help being;
that no statistic tables as yet report much increase of deaths by
starvation: this we do know, and not very conclusively anything
more than this. If this be absorption of all the labour of the
country, then all the labour of the country is absorbed.

To believe practically that the poor and luckless are here only
as a nuisance to be abraded and abated, and in some permissible
manner made away with, and swept out of sight, is not an amiable
faith. That the arrangements of good and ill success in this perplexed scramble of a world, which a blind goddess was always

thought to preside over, are in fact the work of a seeing goddess or god, and require only not to be meddled with : what stretch of heroic faculty or inspiration of genius was needed to teach one that? To button your pockets and stand still, is no complex recipe. *Laissez faire, laissez passer!* Whatever goes on, ought it not to go on ; ' the widow picking nettles for her children's din- ' ner; and the perfumed seigneur delicately lounging in the Œil- ' du-Bœuf, who has an alchemy whereby he will extract from her ' the third nettle, and name it rent and law?' What is written and enacted, has it not black-on-white to show for itself? Justice is justice ; but all attorney's parchment is of the nature of Targum or sacred-parchment. In brief, ours is a world requiring only to be well let alone. Scramble along, thou insane scramble of a world, with thy pope's tiaras, king's mantles and beggar's gabardines, chivalry-ribbons and plebeian gallows-ropes, where a Paul shall die on the gibbet and a Nero sit fiddling as imperial Cæsar; *thou art all right*, and shalt scramble even so; and whoever in the press is trodden down, has only to lie there and be trampled broad :—Such at bottom seems to be the chief social principle, if principle it have, which the Poor-Law Amendment Act has the merit of courageously asserting, in opposition to many things. A chief social principle which this present writer, for one, will by no manner of means believe in, but pronounce at all fit times to be false, heretical and damnable, if ever aught was !

And yet, as we said, Nature makes nothing in vain; not even a Poor-Law Amendment Act. For withal we are far from joining in the outcry raised against these poor Poor-Law Commissioners, as if they were tigers in men's shape; as if their Amendment Act were a mere monstrosity and horror, deserving instant abrogation. They are not tigers ; they are men filled with an idea of a theory : their Amendment Act, heretical and damnable as a whole truth, is orthodox and laudable as a *half*-truth ; and was imperatively re- quired to be put in practice. To create men filled with a theory, that refusal of out-door relief was the one thing needful : Nature had no readier way of getting out-door relief refused. In fact, if we look at the old Poor-Law, in its assertion of the opposite social prin- ciple, that Fortune's awards are *not* those of Justice, we shall find it to have become still more unsupportable, demanding, if Eng- land was not destined for speedy anarchy, to be done away with.

Any law, however well meant as a law, which has become a bounty on unthrift, idleness, bastardy and beer-drinking, must be put an end to. In all ways it needs, especially in these times, to be proclaimed aloud that for the idle man there is no place in this England of ours. He that will not work, and save according to

[handwritten margin note: inverting phrase 'laisses faire...' meaning "let them do as they will"]

his means, let him go elsewhither; let him know that for *him* the
Law has made no soft provision, but a hard and stern one; that
by the Law of Nature, which the Law of England would vainly
contend against in the long-run, *he* is doomed either to quit these
habits, or miserably be extruded from this Earth, which is made
on principles different from these. He that will not work according
to his faculty, let him perish according to his necessity : there is no
law juster than that. Would to Heaven one could preach it abroad
into the hearts of all sons and daughters of Adam, for it is a law
applicable to all; and bring it to bear, with practical obligation
strict as the Poor-Law Bastille, on all ! We had then, in good
truth, a 'perfect constitution of society;' and ' God's fair Earth
' and Task-garden, where whosoever is not working must be beg-
' ging or stealing,' were then actually what always, through so
many changes and struggles, it is endeavouring to become.

That this law of No work no recompense should first of all be
enforced on the *manual* worker, and brought stringently home to
him and his numerous class, while so many other classes and persons still go loose from it, was natural to the case. Let it be enforced there, and rigidly made good. It behoves to be enforced
everywhere, and rigidly made good ;—alas, not by such simple
methods as ' refusal of out-door relief,' but by far other and costlier ones ; which too, however, a bountiful Providence is not un-
furnished with, nor, in these latter generations (if we will understand their convulsions and confusions), sparing to apply. Work
is the mission of man in this Earth. A day is ever struggling forward, a day will arrive in some approximate degree, when he who
has no work to do, by whatever name he may be named, will not
find it good to show himself in our quarter of the Solar System ;
but may go and look out elsewhere, If there be any *Idle* Planet
discoverable ?—Let the honest working man rejoice that such law,
the first of Nature, has been made good on him; and hope that, by
and by, all else will be made good. It is the beginning of all. We
define the harsh New Poor-Law to *be* withal a ' protection of the
thrifty labourer against the thriftless and dissolute;' a thing inexpressibly important; a *half*-result, detestable, if you will, when
looked upon as the whole result; yet without which the whole
result is forever unattainable. Let wastefulness, idleness, drunken-
ness, improvidence take the fate which God has appointed them;
that their opposites may also have a chance for *their* fate. Let
the Poor-Law Administrators be considered as useful labourers
whom Nature has furnished with a whole theory of the universe,
that they might accomplish an indispensable fractional practice
there, and prosper in it in spite of much contradiction.

We will praise the New Poor-Law, farther, as the probable preliminary of *some* general charge to be taken of the lowest classes by the higher. Any general charge whatsoever, rather than a conflict of charges, varying from parish to parish; the emblem of darkness, of unreadable confusion. Supervisal by the central government, in what spirit soever executed, is supervisal from a centre. By degrees the object will become clearer, as it is at once made thereby universally conspicuous. By degrees true vision of it will become attainable, will be universally attained; whatsoever order regarding it is just and wise, as grounded on the truth of it, will then be capable of being taken. Let us welcome the New Poor-Law as the harsh beginning of much, the harsh ending of much! Most harsh and barren lies the new ploughers' fallow-field, the crude subsoil all turned up, which never saw the sun; which as yet grows no herb; which has 'out-door relief' for no one. Yet patience: innumerable weeds and corruptions lie safely turned down and extinguished under it; this same crude subsoil is the first step of all true husbandry; by Heaven's blessing and the skyey influences, fruits that are good and blessed will yet come of it.

For, in truth, the claim of the poor labourer is something quite other than that 'Statute of the Forty-third of Elizabeth' will ever fulfil for him. Not to be supported by roundsmen systems, by never so liberal parish doles, or lodged in free and easy workhouses when distress overtakes him; not for this, however in words he may clamour for it; not for this, but for something far different does the heart of him struggle. It is 'for justice' that he struggles; for 'just wages,'—not in money alone! An ever-toiling inferior, he would fain (though as yet he knows it not) find for himself a superior that should lovingly and wisely govern: is not that too the 'just wages' of his service done? It is for a manlike place and relation, in this world where he sees himself a man, that he struggles. At bottom may we not say, it is even for this, That guidance and government, which he cannot give himself, which in our so complex world he can no longer do without, might be afforded him? The thing he struggles for is one which no Forty-third of Elizabeth is in any condition to furnish him, to put him on the road towards getting. Let him quit the Forty-third of Elizabeth altogether; and rejoice that the Poor-Law Amendment Act has, even by harsh methods and against his own will, forced him away from it. That was a broken reed to lean on, if there ever was one; and did but run into his lamed right-hand. Let him cast it far from him, that broken reed, and look to quite the opposite point of the heavens for help. His unlamed right-hand, with the cunning industry that lies in it, is not this defined to be 'the sceptre of our Planet'? He that can work is a born king of something; is in communion with Nature, is master of a thing or things, is a priest and king of Nature so far. He that can work at nothing is but a usurping king, be his trappings what they may; he is the born slave of all things. Let a man honour his craftmanship, his *can-do;* and know that his rights of man have no concern at all with the Forty-third of Elizabeth.

CHAPTER IV.

FINEST PEASANTRY IN THE WORLD.

THE New Poor-Law is an announcement, sufficiently distinct, that whosoever will not work ought not to live. Can the poor man that is willing to work, always find work, and live by his work? Statistic Inquiry, as we saw, has no answer to give. Legislation presupposes the answer—to be in the affirmative. A large postulate; which should have been made a proposition of; which should have been demonstrated, made indubitable to all persons! A man willing to work, and unable to find work, is perhaps the saddest sight that Fortune's inequality exhibits under this sun. Burns expresses feelingly what thoughts it gave him: a poor man seeking *work;* seeking leave to toil that he might be fed and sheltered! That he might but be put on a level with the four-footed workers of the Planet which is his! There is not a horse willing to work but can get food and shelter in requital; a thing this two-footed worker has to seek for, to solicit occasionally in vain. He is nobody's two-footed worker; he is not even anybody's slave. And yet he is a *two*-footed worker; it is currently reported there is an immortal soul in him, sent down out of Heaven into the Earth; and one beholds him *seeking* for this!—Nay what will a wise Legislature say, if it turn out that he cannot find it; that the answer to their postulate proposition is not affirmative but negative?

There is one fact which Statistic Science has communicated, and a most astonishing one; the inference from which is pregnant as to this matter. Ireland has near seven millions of working people, the third unit of whom, it appears by Statistic Science, has not for thirty weeks each year as many third-rate potatoes as will suffice him. It is a fact perhaps the most eloquent that was ever written down in any language, at any date of the world's history. Was change and reformation needed in Ireland? Has Ireland been governed and guided in a 'wise and loving' manner? A government and guidance of white European men which has issued in perennial hunger of potatoes to the third man extant,—ought to drop a veil over its face, and walk out of court under conduct of proper officers; saying no word; expecting now of a surety sentence either to change or die. All men, we must repeat, were made by God, and have immortal souls in them. The Sanspotatoe is of the selfsame stuff as the superfinest Lord Lieutenant. Not an individual Sanspotatoe human scarecrow but had a Life given him out of Heaven, with Eternities depending on it; for once and no second time. With Immensities in him, over him and round him; with feelings which a Shakspeare's speech would not utter; with desires illimitable as the Autocrat's of all the Russias! Him various thrice-honoured persons, things and institutions have long been teaching, long been guiding, governing: and it is to perpetual scarcity of third-rate potatoes, and to what depends thereon, that he has been taught and guided. Figure thyself, O high-minded, clear-headed, clean-burnished reader, clapt by enchantment into the torn coat and waste hunger-lair of that same root-devouring brother man!—

Social anomalies are things to be defended, things to be amended; and in all places and things, short of the Pit itself, there is some admixture of worth and good. Room for extenuation, for pity, for patience! And yet when the general result has come to the length of perennial starvation, argument, extenuating logic, pity and patience on that subject may be considered as drawing to a close. It may be considered that such arrangement of things will have to terminate. That it has all just men for its natural enemies. That all just men, of what outward colour soever in Politics or otherwise, will say: This cannot last, Heaven disowns it, Earth is against it; Ireland will be burnt into a black unpeopled field of ashes rather than this should last.—The woes of Ireland, or 'justice to Ireland,' is not the chapter we have to write at present. It is a deep matter, an abyssmal one, which no plummet of ours will sound. For the oppression has gone far farther than into the economics of Ireland; inwards to her very heart and soul. The Irish National character is degraded, disordered; till this recover itself, nothing is yet recovered. Immethodic, headlong, violent, mendacious: what can you make of the wretched Irishman? "A finer people never lived," as the Irish lady said to us; "only they have two faults, they do generally lie and steal: barring these"—! A people that knows not to speak the truth, and to act the truth, such people has departed from even the possibility of well-being. Such people works no longer on Nature and Reality; works now on Phantasm, Simulation, Nonentity; the result it arrives at is naturally not a thing but no-thing,—defect even of potatoes. Scarcity, futility, confusion, distraction must be perennial there. Such a people circulates not order but disorder, through every vein of it;—and the cure, if it is

c

to be a cure, must begin at the heart: not in his condition only but in himself must the Patient be all changed. Poor Ireland! And yet let no true Irishman, who believes and sees all this, despair by reason of it. Cannot he too do something to withstand the unproductive falsehood, there as it lies accursed around him, and change it into truth, which is fruitful and blessed? Every mortal can and shall himself be a true man: it is a great thing, and the parent of great things;—as from a single acorn the whole earth might in the end be peopled with oaks! Every mortal can do something: this let him faithfully do, and leave with assured heart the issue to a Higher Power!

We English pay, even now, the bitter smart of long centuries of injustice to our neighbour Island. Injustice, doubt it not, abounds; or Ireland would not be miserable. The Earth is good, bountifully sends food and increase; if man's unwisdom did not intervene and forbid. It was an evil day when Strigul first meddled with that people. He could not extirpate them: could they but have agreed together, and extirpated him! Violent men there have been, and merciful; unjust rulers, and just; conflicting in a great element of violence, these five wild centuries now; and the violent and unjust have carried it, and we are come to *this*. England is guilty towards Ireland; and reaps at last, in full measure, the fruit of fifteen generations of wrong-doing.

But the thing we had to state here was our inference from that mournful fact of the third Sanspotatoe,—coupled with this other well-known fact that the Irish speak a partially intelligible dialect of English, and their fare across by steam is four-pence sterling! Crowds of miserable Irish darken all our towns. The wild Milesian features, looking false ingenuity, restlessness, unreason, misery and mockery, salute you on all highways and byways. The English coachman, as he whirls past, lashes the Milesian with his whip, curses him with his tongue; the Milesian is holding out his hat to beg. He is the sorest evil this country has to strive with. In his rags and laughing savagery, he is there to undertake all work that can be done by mere strength of hand and back; for wages that will purchase him potatoes. He needs only salt for condiment; he lodges to his mind in any pighutch or doghutch, roosts in out-houses; and wears a suit of tatters, the getting off and on of which is said to be a difficult operation, transacted only in festivals and the hightides of the calendar. The Saxon man if he cannot work on these terms, finds no work. He too may be ignorant; but he has not sunk from decent manhood to squalid apehood: he cannot continue there. American forests lie untilled across the ocean; the uncivilised Irishman, not by his strength but by the opposite of strength, drives out the Saxon native, takes possession in his room. There abides he, in his squalor and unreason, in his falsity and drunken violence, as the ready-made nucleus of degradation and disorder. Whosoever struggles, swimming with difficulty, may now find an example how the human being can exist not swimming but sunk. Let him sink; he is not the worst of men; not worse than this man. We have quarantines against pestilence; but there is no pestilence like that; and against it what quarantine is possible? It is lamentable to look upon. This soil of Britain, these Saxon men have cleared it, made it arable, fertile and a home for them; they and their fathers have done that. Under the sky there exists no force of men who with arms in their hands could drive them out of it; all force of men with arms these Saxons would seize, in their grim way, and fling (Heaven's justice and their own Saxon humour aiding them) swiftly into the sea. But behold, a force of men armed only with rags, ignorance and nakedness; and the Saxon owners, paralysed by invisible magic of paper formula, have to fly far, and hide themselves in Transatlantic forests. 'Irish repeal?' "Would to God," as Dutch William said, " *You* were King of Ireland, and could take yourself and it three thousand miles off,"—there to repeal it!

And yet these poor Celtiberian Irish brothers, what can *they* help it? They cannot stay at home, and starve. It is just and natural that they come hither as a curse to us. Alas, for them too it is not a luxury. It is not a straight or joyful way of avenging their sore wrongs this; but a most sad circuitous one. Yet a way it is, and an effectual way. The time has come when the Irish population must either be improved a little, or else exterminated. Plausible management, adapted to this hollow outcry or to that, will no longer do; it must be management grounded on sincerity and fact, to which the truth of things will respond—by an actual beginning of improvement to these wretched brother-men. In a state of perennial ultra-savage famine, in the midst of civilisation, they cannot continue. For that the Saxon British will ever submit to sink along with them to such a state, we assume as impossible. There is in these latter, thank God, an ingenuity which is not false; a methodic spirit, of insight, of perseverant well-doing; a rationality and veracity which Nature with her truth does *not* disown;—withal there is a 'Berserkir rage' in the heart of them, which will prefer all things, including destruction and self-destruction, to that. Let no man awaken it, this same Berserkir rage! Deep-hidden it lies, far down in the centre, like genial central-fire, with stratum after stratum of arrangement, traditionary method, composed productiveness, all built above it, vivified and rendered

fertile by it: justice, clearness, silence, perseverance, unhasting
unresting diligence, hatred of disorder, hatred of injustice, which
is the worst disorder, characterise this people; their inward fire
we say, as all such fire should be, is hidden at the centre.   Deep-
hidden; but awakenable, but immeasurable;—let no man awaken
it!   With this strong silent people have the noisy vehement Irish
now at length got common cause made.   Ireland, now for the first
time, in such strange circuitous way, does find itself embarked in
the same boat with England, to sail together, or to sink together;
the wretchedness of Ireland, slowly but inevitably, has crept over
to us, and become our own wretchedness.   The Irish population
must get itself redressed and saved, for the sake of the English if
for nothing else.   Alas, that it should, on both sides, be poor toiling
men that pay the smart for unruly Striguls, Henrys, Macdermots,
and O'Donoghues!   The strong have eaten sour grapes, and the
teeth of the weak are set on edge.   'Curses,' says the Proverb,
'are like chickens, they return always *home.*'

But now on the whole, it seems to us, English Statistic Science,
with floods of the finest peasantry in the world streaming in on us
daily, may fold up her Danaides reticulations on this matter of the
Working Classes; and conclude, what every man who will take the
statistic spectacles off his nose, and look, may discern in town or
country: That the condition of the lower multitude of English
labourers approximates more and more to that of the Irish competing with them in all markets; that whatsoever labour, to which
mere strength with little skill will suffice, is to be done, will be
done not at the English price, but at an approximation to the
Irish price: at a price superior as yet to the Irish, that is, superior
to scarcity of third-rate potatoes for thirty weeks yearly; superior,
yet hourly, with the arrival of every new steamboat, sinking nearer
to an equality with that.   Half-a-million handloom weavers, working fifteen hours a-day, in perpetual inability to procure thereby
enough of the coarsest food; English farm-labourers at nine shillings and at seven shillings a week; Scotch farm-labourers who,
'in districts the half of whose husbandry is that of cows, taste no
'milk, can procure no milk:' all these things are credible to us;
several of them are known to us by the best evidence, by eyesight.
With all this it is consistent that the wages of 'skilled labour,' as
it is called, should in many cases be higher than they ever were:
the giant Steamengine in a giant English Nation will here create
violent demand for labour, and will there annihilate demand.   But,
alas, the great portion of labour is *not* skilled: the millions are
and must be skilless, where strength alone is wanted; ploughers,
delvers, borers; hewers of wood and drawers of water; menials of

the Steamengine, only the *chief* menials and immediate *body*-servants of which require skill. English Commerce stretches its fibres over the whole earth; sensitive literally, nay quivering in convulsion, to the farthest influences of the earth. The huge demon of Mechanism smokes and thunders, panting at his great task, in all sections of English land; changing his *shape* like a very Proteus; and infallibly at every change of shape, *oversetting* whole multitudes of workmen, and as if with the waving of his shadow from afar, hurling them asunder, this way and that, in their crowded march and course of work or traffic; so that the wisest no longer knows his whereabout. With an Ireland pouring daily in on us, in these circumstances; deluging us down to its own waste confusion, outward and inward, it seems a cruel mockery to tell poor drudges that their condition is improving.

New Poor-Law! *Laissez-faire, laissez-passer!* The master of horses, when the summer labour is done, has to feed his horses through the winter. If he said to his horses: " Quadrupeds, I have no longer work for you; but work exists abundantly over the world: are you ignorant (or must I read you Political-Economy Lectures) that the Steamengine always in the long-run creates additional work? Railways are forming in one quarter of this earth, canals in another, much cartage is wanted; somewhere in Europe, Asia, Africa or America, doubt it not, ye will find cartage: go and seek cartage, and good go with you!" They, with protrusive upper lip, snort dubious; signifying that Europe, Asia, Africa and America lie somewhat out of their beat; that what cartage may be wanted there is not too well known to them. *They* can find no cartage. They gallop distracted along highways, all fenced in to the right and to the left: finally, under pains of hunger, they take to leaping fences; eating foreign property, and—we know the rest. Ah, it is not a joyful mirth, it is sadder than tears, the laugh Humanity is forced to, at *Laissez-faire* applied to poor peasants, in a world like our Europe of the year 1839!

So much can observation altogether unstatistic, looking only at a Drogheda or Dublin steamboat, ascertain for itself. Another thing, likewise ascertainable on this vast obscure matter, excites a superficial surprise, but only a superficial one: That it is the best-paid workmen who, by Strikes, Trades-unions, Chartism, and the like, complain the most. No doubt of it! The best-paid workmen are they alone that *can* so complain! How shall he, the handloom weaver, who in the day that is passing over him has to find food for the day, strike work? If he strike work, he starves within the week. He is past complaint!—The fact itself, however, is one which, if we consider it, leads us into still deeper regions of the

malady. Wages, it would appear, are no index of well-being to the
working man: without proper wages there can be no well-being;
but with them also there may be none. Wages of working men
differ greatly in different quarters of this country; according to the
researches or the guess of Mr. Symmons, an intelligent humane
inquirer, they vary in the ratio of not less than three to one. Cotton-spinners, as we learn, are generally well paid, while employed;
their wages, one week with another, wives and children all working, amount to sums which, if well laid out, were fully adequate
to comfortable living. And yet, alas, there seems little question
that comfort or reasonable well-being is as much a stranger in
these households as in any. At the cold hearth of the ever-toiling
ever-hungering weaver, dwells at least some equability, fixation as
if in perennial ice: hope never comes; but also irregular impatience is absent. Of outward things these others have or might
have enough, but of all inward things there is the fatallest lack.
Economy does not exist among them; their trade now in plethoric
prosperity, anon extenuated into inanition and 'short-time,' is of
the nature of gambling; they live by it like gamblers, now in luxu-
rious superfluity, now in starvation. Black mutinous discontent
devours them; simply the miserablest feeling that can inhabit the
heart of man. English Commerce with its world-wide convulsive
fluctuations, with its immeasurable Proteus Steam-demon, makes
all paths uncertain for them, all life a bewilderment; sobriety,
steadfastness, peaceable continuance, the first blessings of man,
are not theirs.

It is in Glasgow among that class of operatives that 'Number
60,' in his dark room, pays down the price of blood. Be it with
reason or with unreason, too surely they do in verity find the time
all out of joint; this world for them no home, but a dingy prison-
house, of reckless unthrift, rebellion, rancour, indignation against
themselves and against all men. Is it a green flowery world, with
azure everlasting sky stretched over it, the work and government
of a God; or a murky-simmering Tophet, of copperas-fumes, cotton-fuz, gin-riot, wrath and toil, created by a Demon, governed by
a Demon? The sum of their wretchedness merited and unmerited
welters, huge, dark and baleful, like a Dantean Hell, visible there
in the statistics of Gin: Gin justly named the most authentic incarnation of the Infernal Principle in our times, too indisputable
an incarnation; Gin the black throat into which wretchedness or
every sort, consummating itself by calling on delirium to help it,
whirls down; abdication of the power to think or resolve, as too
painful now, on the part of men whose lot of all others would require thought and resolution; liquid Madness sold at ten-pence

the quartern, all the products of which are and must be, like its origin, mad, miserable, ruinous, and that only! If from this black unluminous unheeded *Inferno*, and Prisonhouse of souls in pain, there do flash up from time to time, some dismal wide-spread glare of Chartism or the like, notable to all, claiming remedy from all,—are we to regard it as more baleful than the quiet state, or rather as not so baleful? Ireland is in chronic atrophy these five centuries; the disease of nobler England, identified now with that of Ireland, becomes acute, has crises, and will be cured or kill.

CHAPTER V.

RIGHTS AND MIGHTS.

It is not what a man outwardly has or wants that constitutes the happiness or misery of him. Nakedness, hunger, distress of all kinds, death itself have been cheerfully suffered, when the heart was right. <u>It is the feeling of *injustice* that is insupportable to all men.</u> The brutallest black African cannot bear that he should be used unjustly. No man can bear it, or ought to bear it. A deeper law than any parchment-law whatsoever, a law written direct by the hand of God in the inmost being of man, incessantly protests against it. What is injustice? Another name for *disorder*, for unveracity, unreality; a thing which veracious created Nature, even because it is not Chaos and a waste-whirling baseless Phantasm, rejects and disowns. It is not the outward pain of injustice; that, were it even the flaying of the back with knotted scourges, the severing of the head with guillotines, is comparatively a small matter. The real smart is the soul's pain and stigma, the hurt inflicted on the moral self. The rudest clown must draw himself up into attitude of battle, and resistance to the death, if such be offered him. He cannot live under it; his own soul aloud, and all the Universe with silent continual beckonings, says, It cannot be. He must revenge himself; *revancher* himself, make himself good again,—that so *meum* may be mine, *tuum* thine, and each party standing clear on his own basis, order be restored. There is something infinitely respectable in this, and we may say universally respected; it is the common stamp of manhood vindicating itself in all of us, the basis of whatever is worthy in all of us, and through superficial diversities, the same in all.

As *disorder*, insane by the nature of it, is the hatefullest of things to man, who lives by sanity and order, so injustice is the worst evil, some call it the only evil, in this world. All men sub-

mit to toil, to disappointment, to unhappiness; it is their lot
here; but in all hearts, inextinguishable by sceptic logic, by sorrow, perversion or despair itself, there is a small still voice intimating that it is not the final lot; that wild, waste, incoherent as
it looks, a God presides over it; that it is not an injustice but a
justice. Force itself, the hopelessness of resistance, has doubtless
a composing effect;—against inanimate *Simooms*, and much other
infliction of the like sort, we have found it suffice to produce complete composure. Yet, one would say, a permanent Injustice even
from an Infinite Power would prove unendurable by men. If men
had lost belief in a God, their only resource against a blind No-
God, of Necessity and Mechanism, that held them like a hideous
World-Steamengine, like a hideous Phalaris' Bull, imprisoned in
its own iron belly, would be, with or without hope,—*revolt*. They
could, as Novalis says, by a 'simultaneous universal act of suicide,'
depart out of the World-Steamengine; and end, if not in victory,
yet in invincibility, and unsubduable protest that such World-
Steamengine was a failure and a stupidity.

Conquest, indeed, is a fact often witnessed; conquest, which
seems mere wrong and force, everywhere asserts itself as a right
among men. Yet if we examine, we shall find that, in this world,
no conquest could ever become permanent, which did not withal
show itself beneficial to the conquered as well as to conquerors.
Mithridates King of Pontus, come now to extremity, 'appealed to
'the patriotism of his people;' but, says the history, 'he had
'squeezed them, and fleeced and plundered them, for long years;'
his requisitions, flying irregular, devastative, like the whirlwind,
were less supportable than Roman strictness and method, regular
though never so rigorous: he therefore appealed to their patriotism
in vain. The Romans conquered Mithridates. The Romans, having conquered the world, held it conquered, *because* they could best
govern the world; the mass of men found it nowise pressing to
revolt; their fancy might be afflicted more or less, but in their
solid interests they were better off than before. So too in this
England long ago, the old Saxon Nobles, disunited among themselves, and in power too nearly equal, could not have governed
the country well; Harold being slain, their last chance of governing it, except in anarchy and civil war, was over: a new class of
strong Norman Nobles, entering with a strong man, with a succession of strong men at the head of them, and not disunited, but
united by many ties, by their very community of language and
interest, had there been no other, *were* in a condition to govern it;
and did govern it, we can believe, in some rather tolerable manner, or they would not have continued there. They acted, little

conscious of such function on their part, as an immense volunteer Police Force, stationed everywhere, united, disciplined, feudally regimented, ready for action; strong Teutonic men; who on the whole proved effective men, and drilled this wild Teutonic people into unity and peaceable coöperation better than others could have done! How *can-do*, if we will well interpret it, unites itself with *shall-do* among mortals; how strength acts ever as the right-arm of justice; how might and right, so frightfully discrepant at first, are ever in the long-run one and the same,—is a cheering consideration, which always in the black tempestuous vortices of this world's history, will shine out on us, like an everlasting polar star.

Of conquest we may say that it never yet went by brute force and compulsion; conquest of that kind does not endure. Conquest, along with power of compulsion, an essential universally in human society, must bring benefit along with it, or men, of the ordinary strength of men, will fling it out. The strong man, what is he if we will consider? The wise man; the man with the gift of method, of faithfulness and valour, all of which are of the basis of wisdom; who has insight into what is what, into what will follow out of what, the eye to see and the hand to do; who is *fit* to administer, to direct, and guidingly command: he is the strong man. His muscles and bones are no stronger than ours; but his soul is stronger, his soul is wiser, clearer,—is better and nobler, for that is, has been and ever will be the root of all clearness worthy of such a name. Beautiful it is, and a gleam from the same eternal pole-star visible amid the destinies of men, that all talent, all intellect is in the first place moral;—what a world were this otherwise! But it is the heart always that sees, before the head *can* see: let us know that; and know therefore that the Good alone is deathless and victorious, that Hope is sure and steadfast, in all phases of this 'Place of Hope.'—Shiftiness, quirk, attorney-cunning is a kind of thing that fancies itself, and is often fancied, to be talent; but it is luckily mistaken in that. Succeed truly it does, what is called succeeding; and even must in general succeed, if the dispensers of success be of due stupidity: men of due stupidity will needs say to it, "*Thou* art wisdom, rule thou!" Whereupon it rules. But Nature answers, "No, this ruling of thine is not according to *my* laws; thy wisdom was not wise enough! Dost thou take me too for a Quackery? For a Conventionality and Attorneyism? This chaff that thou sowest into my bosom, though it pass at the poll-booth and elsewhere for seed-corn, *I* will not grow wheat out of it, for it is chaff!"

But to return. Injustice, infidelity to truth and fact and Na-

ture's order, being properly the one evil under the sun, and the
feeling of injustice the one intolerable pain under the sun, our
grand question as to the condition of these working men would
be : Is it just ?   And first of all, What belief have they themselves
formed about the justice of it ?   The words they promulgate are
notable by way of answer ; their actions are still more notable.
Chartism with its pikes, Swing with his tinder-box, speak a most
loud though inarticulate language.   Glasgow Thuggery speaks
aloud too, in a language we may well call infernal.   What kind
of ' wild-justice' must it be in the hearts of these men that prompts
them, with cold deliberation, in conclave assembled, to doom their
brother workman, as the deserter of his order and his order's
cause, to die as a traitor and deserter ; and have him executed,
since not by any public judge and hangman, then by a private
one ;—like your old Chivalry *Femgericht*, and Secret-Tribunal, suddenly in this strange guise become new ; suddenly rising once
more on the astonished eye, dressed now not in mail-shirts but in
fustian jackets, meeting not in Westphalian forests but in the
paved Gallowgate of Glasgow !   Not loyal loving obedience to
those placed over them, but a far other temper, must animate
these men !   It is frightful enough.   Such temper must be wide-
spread, virulent among the many, when even in its worst acme, it
can take such a form in a few.   But indeed decay of loyalty in all
senses, disobedience, decay of religious faith, has long been no-
ticeable and lamentable in this largest class, as in other smaller
ones.   Revolt, sullen revengeful humour of revolt against the upper classes, decreasing respect for what their temporal superiors
command, decreasing faith for what their spiritual superiors teach,
is more and more the universal spirit of the lower classes.   Such
spirit may be blamed, may be vindicated ; but all men must recognise it as extant there, all may know that it is mournful, that
unless altered it will be fatal.   Of lower classes so related to upper,
happy nations are not made !   To whatever other griefs the lower
classes labour under, this bitterest and sorest grief now superadds
itself : the unendurable conviction that they are unfairly dealt
with, that their lot in this world is not founded on right, not even
on necessity and might, is neither what it should be, nor what it
shall be.

Or why do we ask of Chartism, Glasgow Trades-unions, and
such like ?   Has not broad Europe heard the question put, and
answered, on the great scale ; has not a FRENCH REVOLUTION been ?
Since the year 1789, there is now half-a-century complete ; and a
French Revolution not yet complete !   Whosoever will look at
that enormous Phenomenon may find many meanings in it, but

this meaning as the ground of all: That it was a revolt of the oppressed lower classes against the oppressing or neglecting upper classes: not a French revolt only; no, a European one; full of stern monition to all countries of Europe. These Chartisms, Radicalisms, Reform Bill, Tithe Bill, and infinite other discrepancy, and acrid argument and jargon that there is yet to be, are *our* French Revolution: God grant that we, with our better methods, may be able to transact it by argument alone!

The French Revolution, now that we have sufficiently execrated its horrors and crimes, is found to have had withal a great meaning in it. As indeed, what great thing ever happened in this world, a world understood always to be made and governed by a Providence and Wisdom, not by an Unwisdom, without meaning somewhat? It was a tolerably audible voice of proclamation, and universal *oyez!* to all people, this of three-and-twenty years' close fighting, sieging, conflagrating, with a million or two of men shot dead: the world ought to know by this time that it was verily meant in earnest, that same Phenomenon, and had its own reasons for appearing there! Which accordingly the world begins now to do. The French Revolution is seen, or begins everywhere to be seen, ' as the crowning phenomenon of our Mo-' dern Time;' ' the inevitable stern end of much; the fearful, but ' also wonderful, indispensable and sternly beneficent beginning of ' much.' He who would understand the struggling convulsive unrest of European society, in any and every country, at this day, may read it in broad glaring lines there, in that the most convulsive phenomenon of the last thousand years. Europe lay pining, obstructed, moribund; quack-ridden, hag-ridden,—is there a hag, or spectre of the Pit, so baleful, hideous as your accredited quack, were he never so close-shaven, mild-spoken, plausible to himself and others? Quack-ridden: in that one word lies all misery whatsoever. Speciosity in all departments usurps the place of reality, thrusts reality away; instead of performance, there is appearance of performance. The quack is a Falsehood Incarnate; and speaks, and makes and does mere falsehoods, which Nature with her veracity has to disown. As chief priest, as chief governor, he stands there, intrusted with much. The husbandman of ' Time's Seedfield;' he is the world's hired sower, hired and solemnly appointed to sow the kind true earth with wheat this year, that next year all men may have bread. He, miserable mortal, deceiving and self-deceiving, sows it, as we said, not with corn but with chaff; the world nothing doubting, harrows it in, pays him his wages, dismisses him with blessing, and—next year there has no corn sprung. Nature has disowned the chaff, declined growing chaff, and behold now there is no bread! It becomes necessary, in such case, to do several things; not soft things some of them, but hard.

Nay we will add that the very circumstance of quacks in un-usual quantity getting domination, indicates that the heart of the world is *already* wrong. The impostor is false; but neither are his dupes altogether true: is not his first grand dupe the falsest of all,—himself namely? Sincere men, of never so limited intellect, have an instinct for discriminating sincerity. The cunning-est Mephistopheles cannot deceive a simple Margaret of honest heart; 'it stands written on his brow.' Masses of people capable of being led away by quacks are themselves of partially untrue spirit. Alas, in such times it grows to be the universal belief, sole accredited knowingness, and the contrary of it accounted puerile enthusiasm, this sorrowfullest *dis*belief that there is pro-perly speaking any truth in the world; that the world was, has been or ever can be guided, except by simulation, dissimulation, and the sufficiently dextrous practice of pretence. The faith of men is dead: in what has guineas in its pocket, beefeaters riding behind it, and cannons trundling before it, they can believe; in what has none of these things they cannot believe. Sense for the true and false is lost; there is properly no longer any true or false. It is the heyday of Imposture; of Semblance recognising itself, and getting itself recognised, for Substance. Gaping mul-titudes listen; unlistening multitudes see not but that it is all right, and in the order of Nature. Earnest men, one of a million, shut their lips; suppressing thoughts, which there are no words to utter. To them it is too visible that spiritual life has departed; that material life, in whatsoever figure of it, cannot long remain behind. To them it seems as if our Europe of the Eighteenth Century, long hag-ridden, vexed with foul enchanters, to the length now of gorgeous Domdaniel *Parcs-aux-cerfs* and 'Peasants living on meal-husks and boiled grass,' had verily sunk down to die and dissolve; and were now, with its French Philosophisms, Hume Scepticisms, Diderot Atheisms, maundering in the final delira-tion; writhing, with its Seven-years Silesian robber-wars, in the final agony. Glory to God, our Europe was not to die but to live! Our Europe rose like a frenzied giant; shook all that poisonous magician trumpery to right and left, trampling it stormfully under foot; and declared aloud that there was strength in him, not for life only, but for new and infinitely wider life. Antæus-like the giant had struck his foot once more upon Reality and the Earth; there only, if in this Universe at all, lay strength and healing for him. Heaven knows, it was not a gentle process; no wonder that

it was a fearful process, this same ' Phœnix fire-consummation !'
But the alternative was it or death; the merciful Heavens, merciful in their severity, sent us it rather.

And so the ' rights of man' were to be written down on paper;
and experimentally wrought upon towards elaboration, in huge
battle and wrestle, element conflicting with element, from side to
side of this earth, for three-and-twenty years. Rights of man,
wrongs of man? It is a question which has swallowed whole nations and generations; a question—on which we will not enter
here. Far be it from us! Logic has small business with this
question at present; logic has no plummet that will sound it at
any time. But indeed the rights of man, as has been not unaptly
remarked, are little worth ascertaining in comparison to the *mights*
of man,—to what portion of his rights he has any chance of being
able to make good! The accurate final rights of man lie in the
far deeps of the Ideal, where ' the Ideal weds itself to the Possible,' as the Philosophers say. The ascertainable temporary rights
of man vary not a little, according to place and time. They
are known to depend much on what a man's convictions of them
are. The Highland wife, with her husband at the foot of the gallows, patted him on the shoulder (if there be historical truth in
Joseph Miller), and said amid her tears: "Go up, Donald, my
man; the Laird bids ye." To her it seemed the rights of lairds
were great, the rights of men small; and she acquiesced. Deputy
Lapoule, in the *Salle des Menus* at Versailles, on the 4th of August
1789, demanded (he did actually ' demand,' and by unanimous vote
obtain) that the ' obsolete law' authorising a Seigneur, on his return from the chase or other needful fatigue, to slaughter not
above two of his vassals, and refresh his feet in their warm blood
and bowels, should be ' abrogated.' From such obsolete law, or
mad tradition and phantasm of an obsolete law, down to any corn-
law, game-law, rotten-borough law, or other law or practice clamoured of in this time of ours, the distance travelled over is
great!—What are the rights of men? All men are justified in
demanding and searching for their rights; moreover, justified or
not, they will do it: by Chartisms, Radicalisms, French Revolutions, or whatsoever methods they have. Rights surely are right:
on the other hand, this other saying is most true, ' Use every man
according to his *rights*, and who shall escape whipping?' These
two things, we say, are both true; and both are essential to make
up the whole truth. All good men know always and feel, each for
himself, that the one is not less true than the other; and act
accordingly. The contradiction is of the surface only; as in opposite sides of the same fact: universal in this *dualism* of a life we

have. Between these two extremes, Society and all human things must fluctuatingly adjust themselves the best they can.

And yet that there is verily a 'rights of man' let no mortal doubt. An ideal of right does dwell in all men, in all arrangements, pactions and procedures of men: it is to this ideal of right, more and more developing itself as it is more and more approximated to, that human Society forever tends and struggles. We say also that any given thing either *is* unjust or else just; however obscure the arguings and strugglings on it be, the thing in itself there as it lies, infallibly enough, *is* the one or the other. To which let us add only this, the first, last article of faith, the alpha and omega of all faith among men, That nothing which is unjust can hope to continue in this world. A faith true in all times, more or less forgotten in most, but altogether frightfully brought to remembrance again in ours! Lyons fusilladings, Nantes noyadings, reigns of terror, and such other universal battle-thunder and explosion; these, if we will understand them, were but a new irrefragable preaching abroad of that. It would appear that Speciosities which are not Realities cannot any longer inhabit this world. It would appear that the unjust thing has no friend in the Heaven, and a majority against it on the Earth; nay that *it* has at bottom all men for its enemies; that it may take shelter in this fallacy and then in that, but will be hunted from fallacy to fallacy till it find no fallacy to shelter in any more, but must march and go elsewhither; —that, in a word, it ought to prepare incessantly for decent departure, before *in*decent departure, ignominious drumming out, nay savage smiting out and burning out, overtake it! Alas, was that such new tidings? Is it not from of old indubitable, that Untruth, Injustice which is but acted untruth, has no power to continue in this true Universe of ours? The tidings was world-old, or older, as old as the Fall of Lucifer: and yet in that epoch unhappily it was new tidings, unexpected, incredible; and there had to be such earthquakes and shakings of the nations before it could be listened to, and laid to heart even slightly! Let us lay it to heart, let us know it well, that new shakings be not needed. Known and laid to heart it must everywhere be, before peace can pretend to come. This seems to us the secret of our convulsed era; this which is so easily written, which is and has been and will be so hard to bring to pass. All true men, high and low, each in his sphere, are consciously or unconsciously bringing it to pass; all false and half-true men are fruitlessly spending themselves to hinder it from coming to pass.

CHAPTER VI.

LAISSEZ-FAIRE.

FROM all which enormous events, with truths old and new embodied in them, what innumerable practical inferences are to be drawn! Events are written lessons, glaring in huge hieroglyphic picture-writing, that all may read and know them: the terror and horror they inspire is but the note of preparation for the truth they are to teach; a mere waste of terror if that be not learned. Inferences enough; most didactic, practically applicable in all departments of English things! One inference, but one inclusive of all, shall content us here; this namely: That *Laissez-faire* has as good as done its part in a great many provinces; that in the province of the Working Classes, *Laissez-faire* having passed its New Poor-Law, has reached the suicidal point, and now, as *felo-de-se*, lies dying there, in torchlight meetings and such like; that, in brief, a government of the under classes by the upper on a principle of *Let alone* is no longer possible in England in these days. This is the one inference inclusive of all. For there can be no acting or doing of any kind, till it be recognised that there is a thing to be done; the thing once recognised, doing in a thousand shapes becomes possible. The Working Classes cannot any longer go on without government; without being *actually* guided and governed; England cannot subsist in peace till, by some means or other, some guidance and government for them is found.

For, alas, on us too the rude truth has come home. Wrappages and speciosities all worn off, the haggard naked fact speaks to us: Are these millions taught? Are these millions guided? We have a Church, the venerable embodiment of an idea which may well call itself divine; which our fathers for long ages, feeling it to be divine, have been embodying as we see: it is a Church well furnished with equipments and appurtenances; educated in universities; rich in money; set on high places that it may be conspicuous to all, honoured of all. We have an Aristocracy of landed wealth and commercial wealth, in whose hands lies the law-making and the law-administering; an Aristocracy rich, powerful, long secure in its place; an Aristocracy with more faculty put free into its hands than was ever before, in any country or time, put into the hands of any class of men. This Church answers: Yes, the people are taught. This Aristocracy, astonishment in every feature, answers: Yes, surely the people are guided! Do we not pass what Acts of Parliament are needful; as many as thirty-nine for the shooting of the partridges alone? Are there not treadmills, gibbets; even hospitals, poor-rates, New Poor-Law? So answers Church; so answers Aristocracy, astonishment in every feature.—Fact, in the mean while, takes his lucifer-box, sets fire to wheat-stacks; sheds an all-too dismal light on several things. Fact searches for his third-rate potatoe, not in the meekest humour, six-and-thirty weeks each year; and does not find it. Fact passionately joins Messiah Thom of Canterbury, and has himself shot for a new fifth-monarchy brought in by Bedlam. Fact holds his fustian-jacket *Femgericht* in Glasgow City. Fact carts his Petition over London streets, begging that you would simply have the goodness to grant him universal suffrage, and ‘the five points,’ by way of remedy. These are not symptoms of teaching and guiding.

Nay, at bottom, is it not a singular thing this of *Laissez-faire*, from the first origin of it? As good as an *abdication* on the part of governors; an admission that they are henceforth incompetent to govern, that they are not there to govern at all, but to do—one knows not what! The universal demand of *Laissez-faire* by a people from its governors or upper classes, is a soft-sounding demand; but it is only one step removed from the fatallest. ‘*Laissez-faire*,’ exclaims a sardonic German writer, ‘What is this universal cry for ‘*Laissez-faire?* Does it mean that human affairs require no guidance; ‘that wisdom and forethought cannot guide them better than folly ‘and accident? Alas, does it not mean: “*Such* guidance is worse ‘than none! Leave us alone of *your* guidance; eat your wages, and ‘sleep!”’ And now if guidance have grown indispensable, and the sleep continue, what becomes of the sleep and its wages?—In those entirely surprising circumstances to which the Eighteenth Century had brought us, in the time of Adam Smith, *Laissez-faire* was a reasonable cry;—as indeed, in all circumstances, for a wise governor there will be meaning in the principle of it. To wise governors you will cry: “See what you will, and will not, let alone.” To unwise governors, to hungry Greeks throttling down hungry Greeks on the floor of a St. Stephens, you will cry: “Let *all* things alone; for Heaven’s sake, meddle ye with nothing!” How *Laissez-faire* may adjust itself in other provinces we say not: but we do venture to say, and ask whether events everywhere, in world-history and parish-history, in all manner of dialects are not saying it, <u>That in regard to the lower orders of society, and their governance and guidance, the principle of</u> *Laissez-faire* <u>has terminated, and is no longer applicable at all</u>, in this Europe of ours, still less in this England of ours. Not misgovernment, nor yet no-government; only government will now serve. What is the meaning of the ‘five points,’ if we will understand them? What are all popular com-

[Handwritten margin notes at top: "Peterloo Massacre 1819 / crowd demanding suffrage in post- / Napoleonic climate"; "site of gallows in early Paris (wiki)"]

motions and maddest bellowings, from Peterloo to the Place-de-Grève itself? Bellowings, inarticulate cries as of a dumb creature in rage and pain; to the ear of wisdom they are inarticulate prayers: "Guide me, govern me! I am mad and miserable, and cannot guide myself!" Surely of all 'rights of man,' this right of the ignorant man to be guided by the wiser, to be, gently or forcibly, held in the true course by him, is the indisputablest. Nature herself ordains it from the first; Society struggles towards perfection by enforcing and accomplishing it more and more. If Freedom have any meaning, it means enjoyment of this right, wherein all other rights are enjoyed. It is a sacred right and duty, on both sides; and the summary of all social duties whatsoever between the two. Why does the one toil with his hands, if the other be not to toil, still more unweariedly, with heart and head? The brawny craftsman finds it no child's-play to mould his unpliant rugged masses; neither is guidance of men a dilettantism: what it becomes when treated as a dilettantism, we may see! The wild horse bounds homeless through the wilderness, is not led to stall and manger; but neither does he toil for you, but for himself only.

[Handwritten margin note: "dilettante: 'dabbler or amateur'"]

Democracy, we are well aware, what is called 'self-government' of the multitude by the multitude, is in words the thing everywhere passionately clamoured for at present. Democracy makes rapid progress in these latter times, and ever more rapid, in a perilous accelerative ratio; towards democracy, and that only, the progress of things is everywhere tending as to the final goal and winning-post. So think, so clamour the multitudes everywhere. And yet all men may see, whose sight is good for much, that in democracy can lie no finality; that with the completest winning of democracy there is nothing yet won,—except emptiness, and the free chance to win! Democracy is, by the nature of it, a self-cancelling business; and gives in the long-run a net result of *zero*. Where no government is wanted, save that of the parish-constable, as in America with its boundless soil, every man being able to find work and recompense for himself, democracy may subsist; not elsewhere, except briefly, as a swift transition towards something other and farther. Democracy never yet, that we heard of, was able to accomplish much work, beyond that same cancelling of itself. Rome and Athens are themes for the schools; unexceptionable for that purpose. In Rome and Athens, as elsewhere, if we look practically, we shall find that it was not by loud voting and debating of many, but by wise insight and ordering of a few that the work was done. So is it ever, so will it ever be. The French Convention was a Parliament elected 'by the five points,' with ballot-boxes, universal suffrages, and what not, as perfectly as Parliament can hope to be

The Girondins employed with the National Convention to end the revolution but hele resisted the revolution of revolution

in this world; and had indeed a pretty spell of work to do, and did it. The French Convention had to cease from being a free Parliament, and become more arbitrary than any Sultan Bajazet, before it could so much as subsist. It had to purge out its argumentative Girondins, elect its Supreme Committee of *Salut*, guillotine into silence and extinction all that gainsayed it, and rule and work literally by the sternest despotism ever seen in Europe, before it could rule at all. Napoleon was not president of a republic; Cromwell tried hard to rule in that way, but found that he could not. These, 'the armed soldiers of democracy,' had to chain democracy under their feet, and become despots over it, before they could work out the earnest obscure purpose of democracy itself! Democracy, take it where you will in our Europe, is found but as a regulated method of rebellion and abrogation; it abrogates the old arrangement of things; and leaves, as we say, *zero* and vacuity for the institution of a new arrangement. It is the consummation of No-government and *Laissez-faire*. It may be natural for our Europe at present; but cannot be the ultimatum of it. Not towards the impossibility, 'self-government' of a multitude by a multitude; but towards some possibility, government by the wisest, does bewildered Europe struggle. The blessedest possibility: not misgovernment, not *Laissez-faire*, but veritable government! Cannot one discern too, across all democratic turbulence, clattering of ballot-boxes and infinite sorrowful jangle, needful or not, that this at bottom is the wish and prayer of all human hearts, everywhere and at all times: "Give me a leader; a true leader, not a false sham-leader; a true leader, that he may guide me on the true way, that I may be loyal to him, that I may swear fealty to him and follow him, and feel that it is well with me!" The relation of the taught to their teacher, of the loyal subject to his guiding king, is, under one shape or another, the vital element of human Society; indispensable to it, perennial in it; without which, as a body reft of its soul, it falls down into death, and with horrid noisome dissolution passes away and disappears.

But verily in these times, with their new stern Evangel, that Speciosities which are not Realities can no longer be, all Aristocracies, Priesthoods, Persons in Authority, are called upon to consider. What is an Aristocracy? A corporation of the Best, of the Bravest. To this joyfully, with heart-loyalty, do men pay the half of their substance, to equip and decorate their Best, to lodge them in palaces, set them high over all. For it is of the nature of men, in every time, to honour and love their Best; to know no limits in honouring them. Whatsoever Aristocracy *is* still a cor-

poration of the Best, is safe from all peril, and the land it rules is
a safe and blessed land. Whatsoever Aristocracy does not even
attempt to be that, but only to wear the clothes of that, is not
safe; neither is the land it rules in safe! For this now is our
sad lot, that we must find a *real* Aristocracy, that an apparent
Aristocracy, how plausible soever, has become inadequate for us.
One way or other, the world will absolutely need to be governed;
if not by this class of men, then by that. One can predict, without gift of prophecy, that the era of routine is nearly ended.
Wisdom and faculty alone, faithful, valiant, ever-zealous, not pleasant but painful, continual effort, will suffice. Cost what it may,
by one means or another, the toiling multitudes of this perplexed,
over-crowded Europe must and will find governors. ' *Laissez-faire,*
Leave them to do?' The thing they will *do*, if so left, is too frightful to think of! It has been *done* once, in sight of the whole earth,
in these generations: can it need to be done a second time?

For a Priesthood, in like manner, whatsoever its titles, possessions, professions, there is but one question: Does it teach and
spiritually guide this people, yea or no? If yea, then is all well.
But if no, then let it strive earnestly to alter, for as yet there is
nothing well! Nothing, we say: and indeed is not this that we
call spiritual guidance properly the soul of the whole, the life and
eyesight of the whole? The world asks of its Church in these
times, more passionately than of any other Institution any question, "Canst thou teach us or not?"—A Priesthood in France,
when the world asked, "What canst thou do for us?" answered
only, aloud and ever louder, "Are we not of God? Invested
with all power?"—till at length France cut short this controversy
too, in what frightful way we know. To all men who believed in
the Church, to all men who believed in God and the soul of man,
there was no issue of the French Revolution half so sorrowful as
that. France cast out its benighted blind Priesthood into destruction; yet with what a loss to France also! A solution of continuity, what we may well call such; and this where continuity is
so momentous: the New, whatever it may be, cannot now *grow* out
of the Old, but is severed sheer asunder from the Old,—how much
lies wasted in that gap! That one whole generation of thinkers
should be without a religion to believe, or even to contradict;
that Christianity, in thinking France, should as it were fade away
so long into a remote extraneous tradition, was one of the saddest
facts connected with the future of that country. Look at such
Political and Moral Philosophies, St.-Simonisms, Robert-Macair-
isms, and the ' Literature of Desperation'! Kingship was perhaps
but a cheap waste, compared with this of the Priestship; under

which France still, all but unconsciously, labours; and may long
labour, remediless the while. Let others consider it, and take
warning by it! France is a pregnant example in all ways. <u>Aris-
tocracies that do not govern, Priesthoods that do not teach; the
misery of that, and the misery of altering that,—are written in
Belshazzar fire-letters on the history of France</u>.

Or does the British reader, safe in the assurance that ' England is not France,' call all this unpleasant doctrine of ours ideo-
logy, perfectibility, and a vacant dream? Does the British reader,
resting on the faith that what has been these two generations was
from the beginning, and will be to the end, assert to himself that
things are already as they can be, as they must be; that on the
whole, no Upper Classes did ever ' govern' the Lower, in this sense
of governing? Believe it not, O British reader! Man is man everywhere; dislikes to have ' sensible species' and ' ghosts of defunct
bodies' foisted on him, in England even as in France. How much
the Upper Classes did actually, in any the most perfect Feudal
time, return to the Under by way of recompense, in government,
guidance, protection, we will not undertake to specify here. In
Charity-Balls, Soup-Kitchens, in Quarter-Sessions, Prison-Disci-
pline and Treadmills, we can well believe the old Feudal Aristocracy not to have surpassed the new. Yet we do say that the old
Aristocracy were the governors of the Lower Classes, the guides
of the Lower Classes; and even, at bottom, that they existed as
an Aristocracy because they were found adequate for that. Not
by Charity-Balls and Soup-Kitchens; not so; far otherwise! But
it was their happiness that, in struggling for their own objects,
they *had* to govern the Lower Classes, even in this sense of governing. For, in one word, *Cash Payment* had not then grown to
be the universal sole nexus of man to man; it was something
other than money that the high then expected from the low, and
could not live without getting from the low. Not as buyer and
seller alone, of land or what else it might be, but in many senses
still as soldier and captain, as clansman and head, as loyal subject
and guiding king, was the low related to the high. <u>With the supreme triumph of Cash, a changed time has entered; there must
a changed Aristocracy enter</u>. We invite the British reader to meditate earnestly on these things.

Another thing, which the British reader often reads and hears
in this time, is worth his meditating for a moment: That Society
' exists for the protection of property.' To which it is added, that
the poor man also has property, namely, his ' labour,' and the fifteen-pence or three-and-sixpence a-day he can get for that. True
enough, O friends, 'for protecting *property;*' most true: and in-

deed if you will once sufficiently enforce that Eighth Commandment, the whole 'rights of man' are well cared for; I know no better definition of the rights of man. *Thou shalt not steal, thou shalt not be stolen from:* what a Society were that; Plato's Republic, More's Utopia mere emblems of it! Give every man what is his, the accurate price of what he has done and been, no man shall any more complain, neither shall the earth suffer any more. For the protection of property, in very truth, and for that alone! —And now what is thy property? That parchment title-deed, that purse thou buttonest in thy breeches-pocket? Is that thy valuable property? Unhappy brother, most poor insolvent brother, I without parchment at all, with purse oftenest in the flaccid state, imponderous, which will not fling against the wind, have quite other property than that! I have the miraculous breath of Life in me, breathed into my nostrils by Almighty God. I have affections, thoughts, a god-given *capability* to be and do; rights, therefore,—the right for instance to thy love if I love thee, to thy guidance if I obey thee: the strangest rights, whereof in church-pulpits one still hears something, though almost unintelligible now; rights stretching high into Immensity, far into Eternity! Fifteen-pence a-day; three-and-sixpence a-day; eight hundred pounds and odd a-day, dost thou call that my property? I value that little; little all I could purchase with that. For truly, as is said, what matters it? In torn boots, in soft-hung carriages-and-four, a man gets always to his journey's end. Socrates walked barefoot, or in wooden shoes, and yet arrived happily. They never asked him, *What* shoes or conveyance? never, What wages hadst thou? but simply, What work didst thou?—Property, O brother? 'Of my very body I have but a life-rent.' As for this flaccid purse of mine, 'tis something, nothing; has been the slave of pickpockets, cutthroats, Jew-brokers, gold-dust robbers; 'twas his, 'tis mine;—'tis thine, if thou care much to steal it. But my soul, breathed into me by God, my *Me* and what capability is there; that is mine, and I will resist the stealing of it. I call that mine and not thine; I will keep that, and do what work I can with it: God has given it me, the Devil shall not take it away! Alas, my friends, Society exists and has existed for a great many purposes, not so easy to specify!

Society, it is understood, does not in any age prevent a man from being what he *can be.* A sooty African *can* become a Toussaint L'Ouverture, a murderous Three-fingered Jack, let the yellow West Indies say to it what they will. A Scottish Poet, 'proud of his name and country,' *can* apply fervently to 'Gentlemen of the Caledonian Hunt,' and become a gauger of beer-barrels, and tragical immortal broken-hearted Singer; the stifled echo of his me-

lody audible through long centuries, one other note in 'that sacred
Miserere' that rises up to Heaven, out of all times and lands. What
I *can be* thou decidedly wilt not hinder me from being. Nay
even for being what I *could be*, I have the strangest claims on thee,
—not convenient to adjust at present! Protection of breeches-
pocket property? O reader, to what shifts is poor Society reduced, struggling to give still some account of herself, in epochs
when Cash Payment has become the sole nexus of man to man!
On the whole, we will advise Society not to talk at all about
what she exists for; but rather with her whole industry to exist,
to try how she can keep existing! That is her best plan. She
may depend upon it, if she ever, by cruel chance, did come to
exist only for protection of breeches-pocket property, she would
lose very soon the gift of protecting even that, and find her career
in our lower world on the point of terminating!—

For the rest, that in the most perfect Feudal Ages, the Ideal of
Aristocracy nowhere lived in vacant serene purity as an Ideal, but
always as a poor imperfect Actual, little heeding or not knowing
at all that an Ideal lay in it,—this too we will cheerfully admit.
Imperfection, it is known, cleaves to human things; far is the
Ideal departed from, in most times; very far! And yet so long as
an Ideal (any soul of Truth) does, in never so confused a manner,
exist and work within the Actual, it is a tolerable business. Not
so, when the Ideal has entirely departed, and the Actual owns to
itself that it has no Idea, no soul of Truth any longer: at that degree of imperfection human things cannot continue living; they
are obliged to alter or expire, when they attain to that. Blotches
and diseases exist on the skin and deeper, the heart continuing
whole; but it is another matter when the heart itself becomes
diseased; when there is no heart, but a monstrous gangrene pretending to exist there as heart!

On the whole, O reader, thou wilt find everywhere that things
which have had an existence among men have first of all had to
have a truth and worth in them, and were not semblances but
realities. Nothing not a reality ever yet got men to pay bed and
board to it for long. Look at Mahometanism itself! Dalai-Lamaism, even Dalai-Lamaism, one rejoices to discover, may be
worth its victuals in this world; not a quackery but a sincerity;
not a nothing but a something! The mistake of those who believe
that fraud, force, injustice, whatsoever untrue thing, howsoever
cloaked and decorated, was ever or can ever be the principle of
man's relations to man, is great and the greatest. It is the error
of the infidel; in whom the truth as yet is *not*. It is an error

pregnant with mere errors and miseries; an error fatal, lamentable, to be abandoned by all men.

CHAPTER VII.

NOT LAISSEZ-FAIRE.

How an Aristocracy, in these present times and circumstances, could, if never so well disposed, set about governing the Under Class? What they should do; endeavour or attempt to do? That is even the question of questions:—the question which *they* have to solve; which it is our utmost function at present to tell them, lies there for solving, and must and will be solved.

Insoluble we cannot fancy it. One select class Society has furnished with wealth, intelligence, leisure, means outward and inward for governing; another huge class, furnished by Society with none of those things, declares that it must be governed: Negative stands fronting Positive; if Negative and Positive *cannot* unite,—it will be worse for both! Let the faculty and earnest constant effort of England combine round this matter; let it once be recognised as a vital matter. Innumerable things our Upper Classes and Lawgivers might ' do;' but the preliminary of all things, we must repeat, is to know that a thing must needs be done. We lead them here to the shore of a boundless continent; ask them, Whether they do not with their own eyes see it, see strange symptoms of it, lying huge, dark, unexplored, inevitable; full of hope, but also full of difficulty, savagery, almost of despair? Let them enter; they must enter; Time and Necessity have brought them hither; where they are is no continuing! Let them enter; the first step once taken, the next will have become clearer, all future steps will become possible. It is a great problem for all of us; but for themselves, we may say, more than for any. On them chiefly, as the expected solvers of it, will the failure of a solution first fall. One way or other there must and will be a solution.

True, these matters lie far, very far indeed, from the 'usual habits of Parliament,' in late times; from the routine course of any Legislative or Administrative body of men that exists among us. Too true! And that is even the thing we complain of: had the mischief been looked into as it gradually rose, it would not have attained this magnitude. That self-cancelling Donothingism and *Laissez-faire* should have got so ingrained into our Practice, is the source of all these miseries. It is too true that Parliament, for the matter of near a century now, has been able to undertake the adjustment of almost one thing alone, of itself and its own interests; leaving other interests to rub along very much as they could and would. True, this was the practice of the whole Eighteenth Century; and struggles still to prolong itself into the Nineteenth, —which however is no longer the time for it! Those Eighteenth-century Parliaments, one may hope, will become a curious object one day. Are not these same '*Memoires*' of Horace Walpole, to an unparliamentary eye, already a curious object? One of the clearest-sighted men of the Eighteenth Century writes down his Parliamentary observation of it there; a determined despiser and merciless dissector of cant; a liberal withal, one who will go all lengths for the 'glorious revolution,' and resist Tory principles to the death: he writes, with an indignant elegiac feeling, how Mr. This, who had voted so and then voted so, and was the son of this and the brother of that, and had such claims to the fat appointment, was nevertheless scandalously postponed to Mr. That;—whereupon are not the affairs of this nation in a bad way? How hungry Greek meets hungry Greek on the floor of St. Stephens, and wrestles him and throttles him till he has to cry, Hold! the office is thine!—of this does Horace write.—One must say, the destinies of nations do not always rest entirely on Parliament. One must say, it is a wonderful affair that science of 'government,' as practised in the Eighteenth Century of the Christian era, and still struggling to practise itself. One must say, it was a lucky century that could get it so practised: a century which had inherited richly from its predecessors; and also which did, not unnaturally, bequeath to its successors a French Revolution, general overturn, and reign of terror;—intimating, in most audible thunder, conflagration, guillotinement, cannonading and universal war and earthquake, that such century with its practices had *ended*.

Ended;—for decidedly that course of procedure will no longer serve. Parliament will absolutely, with whatever effort, have to lift itself out of those deep ruts of donothing routine; and learn to say, on all sides, something more edifying than *Laissez-faire*. If Parliament cannot learn it, what is to become of Parliament? The toiling millions of England ask of their English Parliament foremost of all, Canst thou govern us or not? Parliament with its privileges is strong; but Necessity and the Laws of Nature are stronger than it. If Parliament cannot do this thing, Parliament we prophesy will do some other thing and things which, in the strangest and not the happiest way, will forward its being done,—not much to the advantage of Parliament probably! Done, one way or other, the thing must be. In these complicated times, with Cash Payment as the sole nexus between man and man, the

Toiling Classes of mankind declare, in their confused but most
emphatic way, to the Untoiling, that they will be governed; that
they must,—under penalty of Chartisms, Thuggeries, Rick-burn-
ings, and even blacker things than those. Vain also is it to think
that the misery of one class, of the great universal under class, can
be isolated, and kept apart and peculiar, down in that class. By
infallible contagion, evident enough to reflection, evident even to
Political Economy that will reflect, the misery of the lowest spreads
upwards and upwards till it reaches the very highest; till all has
grown miserable, palpably false and wrong; and poor drudges hun-
gering 'on meal-husks and boiled grass' do, by circuitous but sure
methods, bring kings' heads to the block!

Cash Payment the sole nexus; and there are so many things
which cash will not pay! Cash is a great miracle; yet it has not
all power in Heaven, nor even on Earth. 'Supply and demand'
we will honour also; and yet how many 'demands' are there, entirely indispensable, which have to go elsewhere than to the shops,
and produce quite other than cash, before they can get their supply! On the whole, what astonishing payments does cash make
in this world! Of your Samuel Johnson, furnished with 'fourpence-
halfpenny a-day,' and solid lodging at nights on the paved streets,
as his payment, we do not speak;—not in the way of complaint:
it is a world-old business for the like of him, that same arrangement or a worse; perhaps the man, for his own uses, had need
even of that and of no better. Nay is not Society, busy with its
Talfourd Copyright Bill and the like, struggling to do something
effectual for that man;—enacting with all industry that his own
creation be accounted his own manufacture, and continue unstolen,
on his own market-stand, for so long as sixty years? Perhaps Society is right there; for discrepancies on that side too may become
excessive. All men are not patient docile Johnsons; some of them
are half-mad inflammable Rousseaus. Such, in peculiar times, you
may drive too far. Society in France, for example, was not desti-
tute of cash: Society contrived to pay Philippe d'Orleans not yet
Egalité three hundred thousand a-year and odd, for driving cabrio-
lets through the streets of Paris and other work done; but in cash,
encouragement, arrangement, recompense or recognition of any
kind, it had nothing to give this same half-mad Rousseau for his
work done; whose brain in consequence, *too* 'much enforced' for a
weak brain, uttered hasty sparks, *Contrat Social* and the like, which
proved not so quenchable again! In regard to that species of men
too, who knows whether *Laissez-faire* itself (which is Sergeant Talfourd's Copyright Bill continued to eternity instead of sixty years)
will not turn out insufficient, and have to cease, one day?—

Alas, in regard to so very many things, *Laissez-faire* ought partly to endeavour to cease! But in regard to poor Sanspotatoe peasants, Trades-Union craftsmen, Chartist cotton-spinners, the time has come when it must either cease or a worse thing straightway begin,—a thing of tinder-boxes, vitriol-bottles, secondhand pistols, a visibly insupportable thing in the eyes of all.

CHAPTER VIII.

NEW ERAS.

For in very truth it is a ' new Era;' a new Practice has become indispensable in it. One has heard so often of new eras, new and newest eras, that the word has grown rather empty of late. Yet new eras do come; there is no fact surer than that they have come more than once. And always with a change of era, with a change of intrinsic conditions, there had to be a change of practice and outward relations brought about,—if not peaceably, then by violence; for brought about it had to be, there could no rest come till then. How many eras and epochs, not noted at the moment; —which indeed is the blessedest condition of epochs, that they come quietly, making no proclamation of themselves, and are only visible long after: a Cromwell Rebellion, a French Revolution, ' striking on the Horologe of Time,' to tell all mortals what o'clock it has become, are too expensive, if one could help it !—

In a strange rhapsodic ' History of the Teuton Kindred (*Geschichte der Teutschen Sippschaft*),' not yet translated into our language, we have found a Chapter on the Eras of England, which, were there room for it, would be instructive in this place. We shall crave leave to excerpt some pages; partly as a relief from the too near vexations of our own rather sorrowful Era; partly as calculated to throw, more or less obliquely, some degree of light on the meanings of that. The Author is anonymous: but we have heard him called the Herr Professor Sauerteig, and indeed think we know him under that name:

' Who shall say what work and works this England has yet to do ? For what purpose this land of Britain was created, set like a jewel in the encircling blue of Ocean; and this Tribe of Saxons, fashioned in the depths of Time, " on the shores of the Black Sea" or elsewhere, " out of Harzgebirge rock" or whatever other material, was sent travelling hitherward ? No man can say: it was for a work, and for works, incapable of announcement in words.

Thou seest them there; part of them stand done, and visible to
the eye; even these thou canst not *name:* how much less the
others still matter of prophecy only!—They live and labour there,
these twenty million Saxon men; they have been born into this
mystery of life out of the darkness of Past Time:—how changed
now since the first Father and first Mother of them set forth,
quitting the tribe of *Theuth,* with passionate farewell, under questionable auspices; on scanty bullock-cart, if they had even bul-
locks and a cart; with axe and hunting-spear, to subdue a portion
of our common Planet! This Nation now has cities and seedfields,
has spring-vans, dray-wagons, Long-Acre carriages, nay railway
trains; has coined-money, exchange-bills, laws, books, war-fleets,
spinning-jennies, warehouses and West-India Docks: see what it
has built and done, what it can and will yet build and do! These
umbrageous pleasure-woods, green meadows, shaven stubble-fields,
smooth-sweeping roads; these high-domed cities, and what they
hold and bear; this mild Good-morrow which the stranger bids
thee, equitable, nay forbearant if need were, judicially calm and
law-observing towards thee a stranger, what work has it not cost?
How many brawny arms, generation after generation, sank down
wearied; how many noble hearts, toiling while life lasted, and wise
heads that wore themselves dim with scanning and discerning,
before this waste *White-cliff,* Albion so-called, with its other Cassi-
terides *Tin Islands,* became a BRITISH EMPIRE! The stream of
World-History has altered its complexion; Romans are dead out,
English are come in. The red broad mark of Romanhood, stamped
ineffaceably on that Chart of Time, has disappeared from the present, and belongs only to the past. England plays its part; England too has a mark to leave, and we will hope none of the least
significant. Of a truth, whosoever had, with the bodily eye, seen
Hengst and Horsa mooring on the mud-beach of Thanet, on that
spring morning of the Year 449; and then, with the spiritual
eye, looked forward to New York, Calcutta, Sidney Cove, across
the ages and the oceans; and thought what Wellingtons, Washing-
tons, Shakspeares, Miltons, Watts, Arkwrights, William Pitts and
Davie Crocketts had to issue from that business, and do their
several taskworks so,—*he* would have said, those leather-boats of
Hengst's had a kind of cargo in them! A genealogic Mythus superior to any in the old Greek, to almost any in the old Hebrew
itself; and not a Mythus either, but every fibre of it fact. An Epic
Poem was there, and all manner of poems; except that the Poet
has not yet made his appearance.'

' Six centuries of obscure endeavour,' continues Sauerteig,
' which to read Historians, you would incline to call mere obscure

slaughter, discord, and misendeavour; of which all that the human memory, after a thousand readings, can remember, is that it resembled, what Milton names it, the "flocking and fighting of kites and crows:" this, in brief, is the history of the Heptarchy or Seven Kingdoms. Six centuries; a stormy spring-time, if there ever was one, for a Nation. Obscure fighting of kites and crows, however, was not the History of it; but was only what the dim Historians of it saw good to record. Were not forests felled, bogs drained, fields made arable, towns built, laws made, and the Thought and Practice of men in many ways perfected? Venerable Bede had got a language which he could now not only speak, but spell and put on paper: think what lies in that. Bemurmured by the German sea-flood swinging slow with sullen roar against those hoarse Northumbrian rocks, the venerable man set down several things in a legible manner. Or was the smith idle, hammering only wartools? He had learned metallurgy, stithy-work in general; and made ploughshares withal, and adzes and mason-hammers. *Castra*, Caesters or Chesters, Dons, Tons (*Zauns*, Enclosures or *Towns*), not a few, did they not stand there; of burnt brick, of timber, of lath-and-clay; sending up the peaceable smoke of hearths? England had a History then too; though no Historian to write it. Those "flockings and fightings," sad inevitable necessities, were the expensive tentative steps towards some capability of living and working in concert: experiments they were, not always conclusive, to ascertain who had the might over whom, the right over whom.'

———

'M. Thierry has written an ingenious Book, celebrating with considerable pathos the fate of the Saxons fallen under that fierce-hearted *Conquistator*, Acquirer or Conqueror, as he is named. M. Thierry professes to have a turn for looking at that side of things: the fate of the Welsh too moves him; of the Celts generally, whom a fiercer race swept before them into the mountainous nooks of the West, whither they were not worth following. Noble deeds, according to M. Thierry, were done by these unsuccessful men, heroic sufferings undergone; which it is a pious duty to rescue from forgetfulness. True, surely! A tear at least is due to the unhappy: it is right and fit that there should be a man to assert that lost cause too, and see what can still be made of it. Most right:—and yet, on the whole, taking matters on that great scale, what can we say but that the cause which pleased the gods has in the end to please Cato also? Cato cannot alter it; Cato will find that he cannot at bottom wish to alter it. Might and Right do differ frightfully from hour to hour; but give them centuries to try it in, they are found to be identical. Whose land was this of Britain? God's who made it, His and no other's it was and is. Who of God's creatures had right to live in it? The wolves and bisons? Yes they; till one with a better right showed himself. The Celt, "aboriginal savage of Europe," as a snarling antiquary names him, arrived, pretending to have a better right; and did accordingly, not without pain to the bisons, make good the same. He had a better right to that piece of God's land; namely a better might to turn it to use;—a might to settle himself there, at least, and try what use he could turn it to. The bisons disappeared; the Celts took possession, and tilled. Forever, was it to be? Alas, *Forever* is not a category that can establish itself in this world of Time. A world of Time, by the very definition of it, is a world of mortality and mutability, of Beginning and Ending. No property is eternal but God the Maker's: whom Heaven permits to take possession, his is the right; Heaven's sanction *is* such permission,—while it lasts: nothing more can be said. Why does that hyssop grow there, in the chink of the wall? Because the whole Universe, sufficiently occupied otherwise, could not hitherto prevent its growing! It has the might and the right. By the same great law do Roman Empires establish themselves, Christian Religions promulgate themselves, and all extant Powers bear rule. The strong thing is the just thing: this thou wilt find throughout in our world;—as indeed was God and Truth the Maker of our world, or was Satan and Falsehood?

'One proposition widely current as to this Norman Conquest is of a Physiologic sort: That the conquerors and conquered here were of different races; nay that the Nobility of England is still, to this hour, of a somewhat different blood from the commonalty, their fine Norman features contrasting so pleasantly with the coarse Saxon ones of the others. God knows, there are coarse enough features to be seen among the commonalty of that country; but if the Nobility's be finer, it is not their Normanhood that can be the reason. Does the above Physiologist reflect who those same Normans, Northmen, originally were? Baltic Saxons, and what other miscellany of Lurdanes, Jutes and Deutsch Pirates from the East-sea marshes would join them in plunder of France! If living three centuries longer in Heathenism, sea-robbery, and the unlucrative fishing of ambergris could ennoble them beyond the others, then were they ennobled. The Normans were Saxons who had learned to speak French. No: by Thor and Wodan, the Saxons were all as noble as needful;—shaped, says the Mythus, "from the rock of the Harzgebirge;" brother-tribes being made of clay, wood, water, or what other material might be going!

A stubborn, taciturn, sulky, indomitable rock-made race of men; as
the figure they cut in all quarters, in the cane-brake of Arkansas,
in the Ghauts of the Himmalayha, no less than in London City, in
Warwick or Lancaster County, does still abundantly manifest.'

———

' To this English People in World-History, there have been,
shall I prophesy, Two grand tasks assigned? Huge-looming
through the dim tumult of the always incommensurable Present
Time, outlines of two tasks disclose themselves: the grand Industrial task of conquering some half or more of this Terraqueous
Planet for the use of man; then secondly, the grand Constitutional
task of sharing, in some pacific endurable manner, the fruit of
said conquest, and showing all people how it might be done.
These I will call their two tasks, discernible hitherto in World-
History: in both of these they have made respectable though un-
equal progress. Steamengines, ploughshares, pickaxes; what is
meant by conquering this Planet, they partly know. Elective
franchise, ballot-box, representative assembly; how to accomplish
sharing of that conquest, they do not so well know. Europe knows
not; Europe vehemently asks in these days, but receives no answer, no credible answer. For as to the partial Delolmish, Benthamee, or other French or English answers, current in the proper
quarters, and highly beneficial and indispensable there, thy disbelief in them as final answers, I take it, is complete.'

———

' Succession of rebellions? Successive clippings away of the
Supreme Authority; class after class rising in revolt to say, "We
will no more be governed so"? That is not the history of the
English Constitution; not altogether that. Rebellion is the means,
but it is not the motive cause. The motive cause, and true secret
of the matter, were always this: The necessity there was for re-
belling?

' Rights I will permit thee to call everywhere " correctly-articulated *mights*." A dreadful business to articulate correctly! Consider those Barons of Runnymead; consider all manner of successfully revolting men! Your Great Charter has to be experimented
on, by battle and debate, for a hundred-and-fifty years; is then
found to *be* correct; and stands as true *Magna Charta*,—nigh cut
in pieces by a tailor, short of measures, in later generations.
Mights, I say, are a dreadful business to articulate correctly!
Yet articulated they have to be; the time comes for it, the need
comes for it, and with enormous difficulty and experimenting it is

got done. Call it not succession of rebellions; call it rather succession of expansions, of enlightenments, gift of articulate utterance descending ever lower. Class after class acquires faculty of utterance,—Necessity teaching and compelling; as the dumb man, seeing the knife at his father's throat, suddenly acquired speech! Consider too how class after class not only acquires faculty of articulating what its might is, but likewise grows in might, acquires might or loses might; so that always, after a space, there is not only new gift of articulating, but there is something new to articulate. Constitutional epochs will never cease among men.'

'And so now, the Barons all settled and satisfied, a new class hitherto silent had begun to speak; the Middle Class, namely. In the time of James First, not only Knights of the Shire but Parliamentary Burgesses assemble, to assert, to complain and propose; a real House of Commons has come decisively into play,— much to the astonishment of James First. We call it a growth of mights, if also of necessities; a growth of power to articulate mights, and make rights of them.

'In those past silent centuries, among those silent classes, much had been going on. Not only had red-deer in the New and other Forests been got preserved and shot; and treacheries of Simon de Montfort, wars of Red and White Roses, Battles of Crecy, Battles of Bosworth, and many other battles been got transacted and adjusted; but England wholly, not without sore toil and aching bones to the millions of sires and the millions of sons these eighteen generations, had been got drained and tilled, covered with yellow harvests, beautiful and rich possessions; the mud-wooden Caesters and Chesters had become steepled tile-roofed compact Towns. Sheffield had taken to the manufacture of Sheffield whittles; Worstead could from wool spin yarn, and knit or weave the same into stockings or breeches for men. England had property valuable to the auctioneer; but the accumulate manufacturing, commercial, economic *skill* which lay impalpably warehoused in English hands and heads, what auctioneer could estimate?

'Hardly an Englishman to be met with but could *do* something; some cunninger thing than break his fellow-creature's head with battle-axes. The seven incorporated trades, with their million guild-brethren, with their hammers, their shuttles and tools, what an army;—fit to conquer that land of England, as we say, and to hold it conquered! Nay, strangest of all, the English people had acquired the faculty and habit of thinking,—even of believing: individual conscience had unfolded itself among them; Conscience, and Intelligence its handmaid. Ideas of innumerable kinds were circulating among these men: witness one Shakspeare, a woolcomber, poacher, or whatever else at Stratford in Warwickshire, who happened to write books! The finest human figure, as I apprehend, that Nature has hitherto seen fit to make of our widely diffused Teutonic clay. Saxon, Norman, Celt or Sarmat, I find no human soul so beautiful, these fifteen-hundred known years;—our supreme modern European man. Him England had contrived to realise: were there not ideas?

'Ideas poetic and also Puritanic,—that had to seek utterance in the notablest way! England had got her Shakspeare; but was now about to get her Milton and Oliver Cromwell. This too we will call a new expansion, hard as it might be to articulate and adjust; this, that a man could actually have a Conscience for his own behoof, and not for his Priest's only; that his Priest, be who he might, would henceforth have to take that fact along with him. One of the hardest things to adjust! It is not adjusted down to this hour. It lasts onwards to the time they call "Glorious Revolution" before so much as a reasonable truce can be made, and the war proceed by logic mainly. And still it is war, and no peace, unless we call waste vacancy peace. But it needed to be adjusted, as the others had done, as still others will do. Nobility at Runnymead cannot endure foul-play grown palpable; no more can Gentry in Long Parliament; no more can Commonalty in Parliament they name Reformed. Prynne's bloody ears were as a testimony and question to all England: "Englishmen, is this fair?" England, no longer continent of herself, answered, bellowing as with the voice of lions: "No, it is not fair!"'

'But now on the Industrial side, while this great Constitutional controversy, and revolt of the Middle Class had not ended, had yet but begun, what a shoot was that that England, carelessly, in quest of other objects, struck out across the Ocean, into the waste land which it named *New* England! Hail to thee, poor little ship Mayflower, of Delft-Haven: poor common-looking ship, hired by common charterparty for coined dollars; caulked with mere oakum and tar; provisioned with vulgarest biscuit and bacon;—yet what ship Argo, or miraculous epic ship built by the Sea-Gods, was other than a foolish bumbarge in comparison! Golden fleeces or the like these sailed for, with or without effect;

thou little Mayflower hadst in thee a veritable Promethean spark; the life-spark of the largest Nation on our Earth,—so we may already name the Transatlantic Saxon Nation. They went seeking leave to hear sermon in their own method, these Mayflower Puritans; a most honest indispensable search: and yet, like Saul the son of Kish, seeking a small thing, they found this unexpected great thing! Honour to the brave and true; they verily, we say, carry fire from Heaven, and have a power that themselves dream not of. Let all men honour Puritanism, since God has so honoured it. Islam itself, with its wild heartfelt "*Allah akbar*, God *is* great," was it not honoured? There is but one thing without honour; smitten with eternal barrenness, inability *to* do or be: Insincerity, Unbelief. He who believes no *thing*, who believes only the shows of things, is not in relation with Nature and Fact at all. Nature denies him; orders him at his earliest convenience to disappear. Let him disappear from her domains,—into those of Chaos, Hypothesis and Simulacrum, or wherever else his parish may be.'

———

'As to the Third Constitutional controversy, that of the Working Classes, which now debates itself everywhere these fifty years, in France specifically since 1789, in England too since 1831, it is doubtless the hardest of all to get articulated: finis of peace, or even reasonable truce on this, is a thing I have little prospect of for several generations. Dark, wild-weltering, dreary, boundless; nothing heard on it yet but ballot-boxes, Parliamentary arguing; not to speak of much far worse arguing, by steel and lead, from Valmy to Waterloo, to Peterloo!'—

'And yet of Representative Assemblies may not this good be said: That contending parties in a country do thereby ascertain one another's strength? They fight there, since fight they must, by petition, Parliamentary eloquence, not by sword, bayonet and bursts of military cannon. Why do men fight at all, if it be not that they are yet *un*acquainted with one another's strength, and must fight and ascertain it? Knowing that thou art stronger than I, that thou canst compel me, I will submit to thee: unless I chance to prefer extermination, and slightly circuitous suicide, there is no other course for me. That in England, by public meetings, by petitions, by elections, leading-articles, and other jangling hubbub and tongue-fence which perpetually goes on everywhere in that country, people ascertain one another's strength, and the most obdurate House of Lords has to yield and give in before it come to cannonading and guillotinement: this is a sav-

ing characteristic of England. Nay, at bottom, is not this the
celebrated English Constitution itself? This *unspoken* Constitution, whereof Privilege of Parliament, Money-Bill, Mutiny-Bill,
and all that could be spoken and enacted hitherto, is not the essence and body, but only the shape and skin? Such Constitution
is, in our times, verily invaluable.'

———

' Long stormy spring-time, wet contentious April, winter chill-
ing the lap of very May; but at length the season of summer does
come. So long the tree stood naked; angry wiry naked boughs
moaning and creaking in the wind: you would say, Cut it down,
why cumbereth it the ground? Not so; we must wait; all things
will have their time.—Of the man Shakspeare, and his Elizabethan
Era, with its Sydneys, Raleighs, Bacons, what could we say? That
it was a spiritual flower-time. Suddenly, as with the breath of
June, your rude naked tree is touched; bursts into leaves and
flowers, *such* leaves and flowers. The past long ages of nakedness,
and wintry fermentation and elaboration, have done their part,
though seeming to do nothing. The past silence has got a voice,
all the more significant the longer it had continued silent. In
trees, men, institutions, creeds, nations, in all things extant and
growing in this Universe, we may note such vicissitudes and budding-times. Moreover there are spiritual budding-times; and
then also there are physical, appointed to nations.
  ' Thus in the middle of that poor calumniated Eighteenth
Century, see once more! Long winter again past, the dead-seem-
ing tree proves to be living, to have been always living; after
motionless times, every bough shoots forth on the sudden, very
strangely:—it now turns out that this favoured England was not
only to have had her Shakspeares, Bacons, Sydneys, but to have
her Watts, Arkwrights, Brindleys! We will honour greatness in
all kinds. The Prospero evoked the singing of Ariel, and took
captive the world with those melodies: the same Prospero can
send his Fire-demons panting across all oceans; shooting with
the speed of meteors, on cunning highways, from end to end of
kingdoms; and make Iron his missionary, preaching *its* evangel
to the brute Primeval Powers, which listen and obey: neither is
this small. Manchester, with its cotton-fuz, its smoke and dust,
its tumult and contentious squalor, is hideous to thee? Think
not so: a precious substance, beautiful as magic dreams and yet
no dream but a reality, lies hidden in that noisome wrappage;—
a wrappage struggling indeed (look at Chartisms and such like) to

[margin note: One is (Churton) natural?]

cast itself off, and leave the beauty free and visible there! Hast thou heard, with sound ears, the awakening of a Manchester, on Monday morning, at half-past five by the clock; the rushing off of its thousand mills, like the boom of an Atlantic tide, ten-thousand times ten-thousand spools and spindles all set humming there,—it is perhaps, if thou knew it well, sublime as a Niagara, or more so. Cotton-spinning is the clothing of the naked in its result; the triumph of man over matter in its means. Soot and despair are not the essence of it; they are divisible from it,—at this hour, are they not crying fiercely to be divided? The great Goethe, looking at cotton Switzerland, declared it, I am told, to be of all things that he had seen in this world the most poetical. Whereat friend Kanzler von Müller, in search of the palpable picturesque, could not but stare wide-eyed. Nevertheless our World-Poet knew well what he was saying.'

' Richard Arkwright, it would seem, was not a beautiful man; no romance-hero with haughty eyes, Apollo-lip, and gesture like the herald Mercury; a plain almost gross, bag-cheeked, potbellied Lancashire man, with an air of painful reflection, yet also of copious free digestion;—a man stationed by the community to shave certain dusty beards, in the Northern parts of England, at a half-penny each. To such end, we say, by forethought, oversight, accident and arrangement, had Richard Arkwright been, by the community of England and his own consent, set apart. Nevertheless, in strapping of razors, in lathering of dusty beards, and the contradictions and confusions attendant thereon, the man had notions in that rough head of his; spindles, shuttles, wheels and contrivances plying ideally within the same: rather hopeless-looking; which, however, he did at last bring to bear. Not without difficulty! His townsfolk rose in mob round him, for threatening to shorten labour, to shorten wages; so that he had to fly, with broken washpots, scattered household, and seek refuge elsewhere. Nay his wife too, as I learn, rebelled; burnt his wooden model of his spinning-wheel; resolute that he should stick to his razors rather;—for which, however, he decisively, as thou wilt rejoice to understand, packed her out of doors. O reader, what a Historical Phenomenon is that bag-cheeked, potbellied, much-enduring, much-inventing barber! French Revolutions were a-brewing: to resist the same in any measure, imperial Kaisers were impotent without the cotton and cloth of England; and it was this man that had to give England the power of cotton.'

'Neither had Watt of the Steamengine a heroic origin, any kindred with the princes of this world. The princes of this world were shooting their partridges; noisily, in Parliament or elsewhere, solving the question, Head or tail? while this man with blackened fingers, with grim brow, was searching out, in his workshop, the Fire-secret; or, having found it, was painfully wending to and fro in quest of a "monied man," as indispensable man-midwife of the same. Reader, thou shalt admire what is admirable, not what is dressed in admirable; learn to know the British lion even when he is not throne-supporter, and also the British jackass in lion's skin even when he is. Ah, couldst thou always, what a world were it! But has the Berlin Royal Academy or any English Useful-Knowledge Society discovered, for instance, who it was that first scratched earth with a stick; and threw *corns*, the biggest he could find, into it; seedgrains of a certain grass, which he named *white* or *wheat!* Again, what is the whole Tees-water and other breeding-world to him who stole home from the forests the first bison-calf, and bred it up to be a tame bison, a milk-cow? No machine of all they showed me in Birmingham can be put in comparison for ingenuity with that figure of the wedge named *knife*, of the wedges named *saw*, of the lever named *hammer*:—nay is it not with the hammer-knife, named *sword*, that men fight, and maintain any semblance of constituted authority that yet survives among us? The steamengine I call fire-demon and great; but it is nothing to the invention of *fire*. Prometheus, Tubalcain, Trip-tolemus! Are not our greatest men as. good as lost? <u>The men that walk daily among us, clothing us, warming us, feeding us, walk shrouded in darkness, mere mythic men.</u>

'It is said, ideas produce revolutions; and truly so they do; not spiritual ideas only, but even mechanical. In this clanging clashing universal Sword-dance that the European world now dances for the last half-century, Voltaire is but one choragus, where Richard Arkwright is another. Let it dance itself out. When Arkwright shall have become mythic like Arachne, we shall still spin in peaceable profit by him; and the Sword-dance, with all its sorrowful shufflings, Waterloo waltzes, Moscow gallopades, how forgotten will that be!'

———

'On the whole, were not all these things most unexpected, unforeseen? As indeed what thing is foreseen; especially what man, the parent of things! Robert Clive in that same time went out, with a developed gift of penmanship, as writer or superior book-keeper to a trading factory established in the distant East.

With gift of penmanship developed; with other gifts not yet developed, which the calls of the case did by and by develop. Not fit for book-keeping alone, the man was found fit for conquering Nawaubs, founding kingdoms, Indian Empires! In a questionable manner, Indian Empire from the other hemisphere took up its abode in Leadenhall Street, in the City of London.

'Accidental all these things and persons look, unexpected every one of them to man. Yet inevitable every one of them; foreseen, not unexpected, by Supreme Power; prepared, appointed from afar. Advancing always through all centuries, in the middle of the eighteenth they *arrived*. The Saxon kindred burst forth into cotton-spinning, cloth-cropping, iron-forging, steamengining, railwaying, commercing and careering towards all the winds of Heaven, —in this inexplicable noisy manner; the noise of which, in Power-mills, in progress-of-the-species Magazines, still deafens us somewhat. Most noisy, sudden! The Staffordshire coal-stratum and coal-strata lay side by side with iron-strata, quiet since the creation of the world. Water flowed in Lancashire and Lanarkshire; bituminous fire lay bedded in rocks there too,—over which how many fighting Stanleys, black Douglases, and other the like contentious persons, had fought out their bickerings and broils, not without result, we will hope! But God said, Let the iron missionaries be; and they were. Coal and iron, so long close unregardful neighbours, are wedded together; Birmingham and Wolverhampton, and the hundred Stygian forges, with their fire-throats and never-resting sledge-hammers, rose into day. Wet Manconium stretched out her hand towards Carolina and the torrid zone, and plucked cotton there; who could forbid her, her that had the skill to weave it? Fish fled thereupon from the Mersey River, vexed with innumerable keels. England, I say, dug out her bitumen-fire, and bade it work: towns rose, and steeple-chimneys;—Chartisms also, and Parliaments they name Reformed.'

Such, figuratively given, are some prominent points, chief mountain-summits, of our English History past and present, according to the Author of this strange untranslated Work, whom we think we recognise to be an old acquaintance.

———

CHAPTER IX.

PARLIAMENTARY RADICALISM.

To us, looking at these matters somewhat in the same light, Reform-Bills, French Revolutions, Louis-Philippes, Chartisms, Revolts of Three Days, and what not, are no longer inexplicable. Where the great mass of men is tolerably right, all is right; where they are not right, all is wrong. The speaking classes speak and debate, each for itself; the great dumb, deep-buried class lies like an Enceladus, who in his pain, if he will complain of it, has to produce earthquakes! Everywhere, in these countries, in these times, the central fact worthy of all consideration forces itself on us in this shape: the claim of the Free Working-man to be raised to a level, we may say, with the Working Slave; his anger and cureless discontent till that be done. Food, shelter, due guidance, in return for his labour: candidly interpreted, Chartism and all such *isms* mean that; and the madder they are, do they not the more emphatically mean, "See what guidance you have given us! What delirium we are brought to talk and project, guided by nobody!" *Laissez-faire* on the part of the Governing Classes, we repeat again and again, will, with whatever difficulty, have to cease; pacific mutual division of the spoil, and a world well let alone, will no longer suffice. A Do-nothing Guidance; and it is a Do-something World! Would to God our Ducal *Duces* would become Leaders indeed; our Aristocracies and Priesthoods discover in some suitable degree what the world expected of them, what the world could no longer do without getting of them! Nameless unmeasured confusions, misery to themselves and us, might so be spared. But that too will be as God has appointed. If they learn, it will be well and happy: if not they, then others instead of them will and must, and once more, though after a long sad circuit, it will be well and happy.

Neither is the history of Chartism mysterious in these times; especially if that of Radicalism be looked at. All along, for the last five-and-twenty years, it was curious to note how the internal discontent of England struggled to find vent for itself through *any* orifice: the poor patient, all sick from centre to surface, complains now of this member, now of that;—corn-laws, currency-laws, free-trade, protection, want of free-trade: the poor patient tossing from side to side, seeking a sound side to lie on, finds none. This Doctor says, it is the liver; that other, it is the lungs, the head, the heart, defective transpiration in the skin. A thoroughgoing Doctor of eminence said, it was rotten boroughs; the want of extended suffrage to destroy rotten boroughs. From of old, the English patient himself had a continually recurring notion that this was it. The English people are used to suffrage; it is their panacea for all that goes wrong with them; they have a fixed-idea of suffrage. Singular enough: one's right to vote for a Member of Parliament, to send one's 'twenty-thousandth part of a master of tongue-fence to National Palaver,'—the Doctors asserted that this was Freedom, this and no other. It seemed credible to many men, of high degree and of low. The persuasion of remedy grew, the evil was pressing; Swing's ricks were on fire. Some nine years ago, a State-surgeon rose, and in peculiar circumstances said: Let there be extension of the suffrage; let the great Doctor's nostrum, the patient's old passionate prayer be fulfilled!

Parliamentary Radicalism, while it gave articulate utterance to the discontent of the English people, could not by its worst enemy be said to be without a function. If it is in the natural order of things that there must be discontent, no less so is it that such discontent should have an outlet, a Parliamentary voice. Here the matter is debated of, demonstrated, contradicted, qualified, reduced to feasibility;—can at least solace itself with hope, and die gently, convinced of *unfeasibility*. The New, Untried ascertains how it will fit itself into the arrangements of the Old; whether the Old can be compelled to admit it; how in that case it may, with the minimum of violence, be admitted. Nor let us count it an easy one, this function of Radicalism; it was one of the most difficult. The pain-stricken patient does, indeed, without effort groan and complain; but not without effort does the physician ascertain what it is that has gone wrong with him, how some remedy may be devised for him. And above all, if your patient is not one sick man, but a whole sick nation! Dingy dumb millions, grimed with dust and sweat, with darkness, rage and sorrow, stood round these men, saying, or struggling as they could to say: "Behold, our lot is unfair; our life is not whole but sick; we cannot live under injustice; go ye and get us justice!" For whether the poor operative clamoured for Time-bill, Factory-bill, Corn-bill, for or against whatever bill, this was what he meant. All bills plausibly presented might have some look of hope in them, might get some clamour of approval from him; as, for the man wholly sick, there is no disease in the Nosology but he can trace in himself some symptoms of it. Such was the mission of Parliamentary Radicalism.

How Parliamentary Radicalism has fulfilled this mission, entrusted to its management these eight years now, is known to all men. The expectant millions have sat at a feast of the Barmecide;

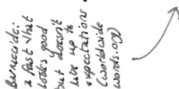

been bidden fill themselves with the imagination of meat. What
thing has Radicalism obtained for them; what other than shadows
of things has it so much as asked for them? Cheap Justice, Justice
to Ireland, Irish Appropriation-Clause, Ratepaying Clause, Poor-
Rate, Church-Rate, Household Suffrage, Ballot-Question 'open' or
shut: not things but shadows of things; Benthamee formulas;
barren as the east-wind! An Ultra-radical, not seemingly of the
Benthamee species, is forced to exclaim: 'The people are at last
wearied. They say, Why should we be ruined in our shops, thrown
out of our farms, voting for these men? Ministerial majorities decline; this Ministry has become impotent, had it even the will to
do good. They have called long to us, "We are a Reform Ministry;
will ye not support us?" We have supported them; borne them
forward indignantly on our shoulders, time after time, fall after fall,
when they had been hurled out into the street; and lay prostrate,
helpless, like dead luggage. It is the fact of a Reform Ministry,
not the name of one that we would support! Languor, sickness
of hope deferred pervades the public mind; the public mind says
at last, Why all this struggle for the *name* of a Reform Ministry?
Let the Tories be Ministry if they will; let at least some living
reality be Ministry! A rearing horse that will only run backward,
he is not the horse one would choose to travel on: yet of all conceivable horses the worst is the dead horse. Mounted on a rearing
horse, you may back him, spur him, check him, make a little way
even backwards: but seated astride of your dead horse, what chance
is there for you in the chapter of possibilities? You sit motionless,
hopeless, a spectacle to gods and men.'

There is a class of revolutionists named *Girondins*, whose fate
in history is remarkable enough! Men who rebel, and urge the
Lower Classes to rebel, ought to have other than Formulas to go
upon. Men who discern in the misery of the toiling complaining
millions not misery, but only a raw-material which can be wrought
upon, and traded in, for one's own poor hidebound theories and
egoisms; to whom millions of living fellow-creatures, with beating
hearts in their bosoms, beating, suffering, hoping, are 'masses,'
mere 'explosive masses for blowing down Bastilles with,' for voting at hustings for *us:* such men are of the questionable species!
No man is justified in resisting by word or deed the Authority he
lives under, for a light cause, be such Authority what it may. Obedience, little as many may consider that side of the matter, is the
primary duty of man. No man but is bound indefeasibly, with all
force of obligation, to obey. Parents, teachers, superiors, leaders,
these all creatures recognise as deserving obedience. Recognised
or not recognised, a man *has* his superiors, a regular hierarchy

above him; extending up, degree above degree, to Heaven itself and God the Maker, who made His world not for anarchy but for rule and order! It is not a light matter when the just man can recognise in the powers set over him no longer anything that is divine; when resistance against such becomes a deeper law of order than obedience to them; when the just man sees himself in the tragical position of a stirrer-up of strife! Rebel without due and most due cause, is the ugliest of words; the first rebel was Satan.—

But now in these circumstances shall we blame the unvoting disappointed millions that they turn away with horror from this name of a Reform Ministry, name of a Parliamentary Radicalism, and demand a fact and reality thereof? That they too, having still faith in what so many had faith in, still count 'extension of the suffrage' the one thing needful; and say, in such manner as they can, Let the suffrage be still extended, *then* all will be well? It is the ancient British faith; promulgated in these ages by prophets and evangelists; preached forth from barrel-heads by all manner of men. He who is free and blessed has his twenty-thousandth part of a master of tongue-fence in National Palaver; whosoever is not blessed but unhappy, the ailment of him is that he has it not. Ought he not to have it then? By the law of God and of men, yea;—and will have it withal! Chartism, with its 'five points,' borne aloft on pikeheads and torchlight meetings, is there. Chartism is one of the most natural phenomena in England. Not that Chartism now exists should provoke wonder; but that the invited hungry people should have sat eight years at such table of the Barmecide, patiently expecting somewhat from the Name of a Reform Ministry, and not till after eight years have grown hopeless, this is the respectable side of the miracle.

CHAPTER X.

IMPOSSIBLE.

"But what are we to do?" exclaims the practical man, impatiently on every side: "Descend from speculation and the safe pulpit, down into the rough market-place, and say what can be done!"— O practical man, there seem very many things which practice and true manlike effort, in Parliament and out of it, might actually avail to do. But the first of all things, as already said, is to gird thyself up for actual doing; to know that thou actually either must do, or, as the Irish say, 'come out of that!'

It is not a lucky word this same *impossible* · no good comes of those that have it so often in their mouth. Who is he that says always, There is a lion in the way? Sluggard, thou must slay the lion then; the way has to be travelled! In Art, in Practice, innumerable critics will demonstrate that most things are henceforth impossible; that we are got, once for all, into the region of perennial commonplace, and must contentedly continue there. Let such critics demonstrate; it is the nature of them: what harm is in it? Poetry once well demonstrated to be impossible, arises the Burns, arises the Goethe. Unheroic commonplace being now clearly all we have to look for, comes the Napoleon, comes the conquest of the world. It was proved by fluxionary calculus, that steamships could never get across from the farthest point of Ireland to the nearest of Newfoundland: impelling force, resisting force, maximum here, minimum there; by law of Nature, and geometric demonstration:—what could be done? The Great Western could weigh anchor from Bristol Port; that could be done. The Great Western, bounding safe through the gullets of the Hudson, threw her cable out on the capstan of New York, and left our still moist paper-demonstration to dry itself at leisure. "Impossible?" cried Mirabeau to his secretary, "*Ne me dites jamais ce bête de mot*, Never name to me that blockhead of a word!"

There is a phenomenon which one might call Paralytic Radicalism, in these days; which gauges with Statistic measuring-reed, sounds with Philosophic Politico-Economic plummet the deep dark sea of troubles; and having taught us rightly what an infinite sea of troubles it is, sums up with the practical inference, and use of consolation, That nothing whatever can be done in it by man, who has simply to sit still, and look wistfully to ' time and general laws :' and thereupon, without so much as recommending suicide, coldly takes its leave of us. Most paralytic, uninstructive : unproductive of any comfort to one! They are an unreasonable class who cry, "Peace, peace," when there *is* no peace. But what kind of class are they who cry, "Peace, peace, have I not *told you* that there is no peace!" Paralytic Radicalism, frequent among those Statistic friends of ours, is one of the most afflictive phenomena the mind of man can be called to contemplate. One prays that *it* at least might cease. Let Paralysis retire into secret places, and dormitories proper for it; the public highways ought not to be occupied by people demonstrating that motion is impossible. Paralytic ;—and also, thank Heaven, entirely false! Listen to a thinker of another sort: 'All evil, and this evil too, is as a nightmare; the instant you begin to *stir* under it, the *evil* is, properly speaking, gone.' Consider, O reader, whether it be not actually so? Evil, once manfully fronted, ceases to be evil; there is ge-

nerous battle-hope in place of dead passive misery; the evil itself
has become a kind of good.

To the practical man, therefore, we will repeat that he has, as
the first thing he can 'do,' to gird himself up for actual doing;
to know well that he is either there to do, or not there at all. Once
rightly girded up, how many things will present themselves as
doable which now are not attemptible! Two things, great things,
dwell, for the last ten years, in all thinking heads in England;
and are hovering, of late, even on the tongues of not a few. With
a word on each of these, we will dismiss the practical man, and
right gladly take ourselves into obscurity and silence again. Universal Education is the first great thing we mean; general Emigration is the second.

Who would suppose that Education were a thing which had
to be advocated on the ground of local expediency, or indeed on
any ground? As if it stood not on the basis of everlasting duty,
as a prime necessity of man. It is a thing that should need no
advocating; much as it does actually need. To impart the gift of
thinking to those who cannot think, and yet who could in that
case think: this, one would imagine, was the first function a government had to set about discharging. Were it not a cruel thing
to see, in any province of an empire, the inhabitants living all mutilated in their limbs, each strong man with his right arm lamed?
How much crueller to find the strong soul, with its eyes still
sealed, its eyes extinct so that it sees not! Light has come into
the world, but to this poor peasant it has come in vain. For six
thousand years the Sons of Adam, in sleepless effort, have been de-
vising, doing, discovering; in mysterious infinite indissoluble communion, warring, a little band of brothers, against the great black
empire of Necessity and Night; they have accomplished such a
conquest and conquests: and to this man it is all as if it had not
been. The four-and-twenty letters of the Alphabet are still Runic
enigmas to him. He passes by on the other side; and that great
Spiritual Kingdom, the toilwon conquest of his own brothers, all
that his brothers have conquered, is a thing non-extant for him.
An invisible empire; he knows it not, suspects it not. And is it
not his withal; the conquest of his own brothers, the lawfully acquired possession of all men? Baleful enchantment lies over him,
from generation to generation; he knows not that such an empire
is his, that such an empire is at all. O, what are bills of rights,
emancipations of black slaves into black apprentices, lawsuits in
chancery for some short usufruct of a bit of land? The grand
' seedfield of Time' is this man's, and you give it him not. Time's

seedfield, which includes the Earth and all her seedfields and pearl-oceans, nay her sowers too and pearl-divers, all that was wise and heroic and victorious here below; of which the Earth's centuries are but as furrows, for it stretches forth from the Beginning onward even into this Day!

> 'My inheritance, how lordly wide and fair;
> Time is my fair seedfield, to Time I'm heir!'

Heavier wrong is not done under the sun. It lasts from year to year, from century to century; the blinded sire slaves himself out, and leaves a blinded son; and men, made in the image of God, continue as two-legged beasts of labour;—and in the largest empire of the world, it is a debate whether a small fraction of the Revenue of one Day (30,000*l.* is but that) shall, after Thirteen Centuries, be laid out on it, or not laid out on it. Have we Governors, have we Teachers; have we had a Church these thirteen hundred years? What is an Overseer of souls, an Archoverseer, Archiepiscopus? Is he something? If so, let him lay his hand on his heart, and say what thing!

But quitting all that, of which the human soul cannot well speak in terms of civility, let us observe now that Education is not only an eternal duty, but has at length become even a temporary and ephemeral one, which the necessities of the hour will oblige us to look after. These Twenty-four million labouring men, if their affairs remain unregulated, chaotic, will burn ricks and mills; reduce us, themselves and the world into ashes and ruin. Simply their affairs cannot remain unregulated, chaotic; but must be regulated, brought into some kind of order. What intellect were able to regulate them? The intellect of a Bacon, the energy of a Luther, if left to their own strength, might pause in dismay before such a task; a Bacon and Luther added together, to be perpetual prime minister over us, could not do it. No one great and greatest intellect can do it. What can? Only Twenty-four million ordinary intellects, once awakened into action; these, well presided over, may. Intellect, insight, is the discernment of order in disorder; it is the discovery of the will of Nature, of God's will; the beginning of the capability to walk according to that. With perfect intellect, were such possible without perfect morality, the world would be perfect; its efforts unerringly correct, its results continually successful, its condition faultless. Intellect is like light; the Chaos becomes a World under it: *fiat lux*. These Twenty-four million intellects are but common intellects; but they are intellects; in earnest about the matter, instructed each about his own province of it; labouring each perpetually, with what partial light can be attained, to bring such province into rationality. From the partial determinations and their conflict, springs the universal. Precisely what quantity of intellect was in the Twenty-four millions will be exhibited by the result they arrive at; that quantity and no more. According as there was intellect or no intellect in the individuals, will the general conclusion they make out embody itself as a world-healing Truth and Wisdom, or as a baseless fateful Hallucination, a Chimæra breathing *not* fabulous fire!

Dissenters call for one scheme of Education, the Church objects; this party objects, and that; there is endless objection, by him and by her and by it: a subject encumbered with difficulties on every side! Pity that difficulties exist; that Religion, of all things, should occasion difficulties. We do not extenuate them: in their reality they are considerable; in their appearance and pretension, they are insuperable, heart-appalling to all Secretaries of the Home Department. For, in very truth, how can Religion be divorced from Education? An irreverent knowledge is no knowledge; may be a development of the logical or other handicraft faculty inward or outward; but is no culture of the soul of a man. A knowledge that ends in barren self-worship, comparative indifference or contempt for all God's Universe except one insignificant item thereof, what is it? Handicraft development, and even shallow as handicraft. Nevertheless is handicraft itself, and the habit of the merest logic, nothing? It is already something; it is the indispensable beginning of everything! Wise men know it to be an indispensable something; not yet much; and would so gladly superadd to it the element whereby it may become all. Wise men would not quarrel in attempting this; they would lovingly coöperate in attempting it.

'And now how teach religion?' so asks the indignant Ultra-radical, cited above; an Ultra-radical seemingly not of the Benthamee species, with whom, though his dialect is far different, there are sound Churchmen, we hope, who have some fellow-feeling: 'How teach religion? By plying with liturgies, catechisms, credos; droning thirty-nine or other articles incessantly into the infant ear? Friends! In that case, why not apply to Birmingham, and have Machines made, and set up at all street-corners, in highways and byways, to repeat and vociferate the same, not ceasing night or day? The genius of Birmingham is adequate to that. Albertus Magnus had a leather man that could articulate; not to speak of Martinus Scriblerus' Nürnberg man that could reason as well as we know who! Depend upon it, Birmingham can make machines to repeat liturgies and articles; to do whatsoever feat is mechanical. And what were all schoolmasters, nay all priests and churches compared with this Birmingham Iron Church! Votes of two millions in aid of the church were then something. You order, at so many pounds a-head, so many thousand iron parsons as your grant covers; and fix them by satisfactory masonry in all quarters wheresoever wanted, to preach there independent of the world. In loud thoroughfares, still more in unawakened districts, troubled with argumentative infidelity, you make the windpipes wider, strengthen the main steam-cylinder; your parson preaches, to the due pitch, while you give him coal; and fears no man or thing. Here *were* a " Church-extension;" to which I, with my last penny, did I believe in it, would subscribe. — — Ye blind leaders of the blind! Are we Calmucks, that pray by turning of a rotatory calabash with written prayers in it? Is Mammon and machinery the means of converting human souls, as of spinning cotton? Is God, as Jean Paul predicted it would be, become verily a Force; the Æther too a Gas! Alas, that Atheism should have got the length of putting on priests' vestments, and penetrating into the sanctuary itself! Can dronings of articles, repetitions of liturgies, and all the cash and contrivance of Birmingham and the Bank of England united bring ethereal fire into a human soul, quicken it out of earthly darkness into heavenly wisdom? Soul is kindled only by soul. To "teach" religion, the first thing needful, and also the last and the only thing, is finding of a man who *has* religion. All else follows from this, church-building, church-extension, whatever else is needful follows; without this nothing will follow.'

From which we for our part conclude that the method of teaching religion to the English people is still far behindhand; that the wise and pious may well ask themselves in silence wistfully, " How *is* that last priceless element, by which education becomes perfect, to be superadded?" and the unwise who think themselves pious, answering aloud, " By this method, By that method," long argue of it to small purpose.

But now, in the mean time, could not by some fit official person, some fit announcement be made, in words well-weighed, in plan well-schemed, adequately representing the facts of the thing, That after thirteen centuries of waiting, he the official person, and England with him, was minded now to have the mystery of the Alphabetic Letters imparted to all human souls in this realm? Teaching of religion was a thing he could not undertake to settle this day; it would be work for a day after this; the work of this day was teaching of the alphabet to all people. The miraculous art of reading and writing, such seemed to him the needful preliminary of all teaching, the first corner stone of what foundation soever could be laid for what edifice soever, in the teaching kind. Let pious Churchism make haste, let pious Dissenterism make haste, let all pious preachers and missionaries make haste, bestir themselves according to their zeal and skill : he the official person stood up for the Alphabet ; and was even impatient for it, having waited thirteen centuries now. He insisted, and would take no denial, postponement, promise, excuse or subterfuge, That all English persons should be taught to read. He appealed to all rational Englishmen, of all creeds, classes and colours, Whether this was not a fair demand ; nay whether it was not an indispensable one in these days, Swing and Chartism having risen ? For a choice of inoffensive Hornbooks, and Schoolmasters able to teach reading, he trusted the mere secular sagacity of a National Collective Wisdom, in proper committee, might be found sufficient. He purposed to appoint such Schoolmasters, to venture on the choice of such Hornbooks ; to send a Schoolmaster and Hornbook into every township, parish and hamlet of England ; so that, in ten years hence, an Englishman who could not read might be acknowledged as the monster, which he really is !

This official person's plan we do not give. The *thing* lies there, with the facts of it, and with the appearances or sham-facts of it ; a plan adequately representing the facts of the thing could by human energy be struck out, does lie there for discovery and striking out. It is his, the official person's duty, not ours, to mature a plan. We can believe that Churchism and Dissenterism would clamour aloud ; but yet that in the mere secular Wisdom of Parliament a perspicacity equal to the choice of Hornbooks might, in very deed, be found to reside. England we believe would, if consulted, resolve to that effect. Alas, grants of a half-day's revenue once in the thirteen centuries for such an object, do not call out the voice of England, only the superficial clamour of England ! Hornbooks unexceptionable to the candid portion of England, we will believe, might be selected. Nay, we can conceive that Schoolmasters fit to teach reading might, by a board of rational men, whether from Oxford or Hoxton, or from both or neither of these places, be pitched upon. We can conceive even, as in Prussia, that a penalty, civil disabilities, that penalties and disabilities till they were found effectual, might be by law inflicted on every parent who did not teach his children to read, on every man who had not been taught to read. We can conceive in fine, such is the vigour of our imagination, there might be found in England, at a dead-lift, strength enough to perform this miracle, and produce it henceforth as a miracle done: the teaching of England to read ! Harder things, we do know, have been performed by nations before now, not abler-

looking than England. Ah me! if, by some beneficent chance, there
should be an official man found in England who could and would,
with deliberate courage, after ripe counsel, with candid insight,
with patience, practical sense, knowing realities to be real, knowing
clamours to be clamorous and to seem real, propose this thing, and
the innumerable things springing from it,—woe to any Churchism
or any Dissenterism that cast itself athwart the path of that man!
Avaunt ye gainsayers! is darkness and ignorance of the Alphabet
necessary for you? Reconcile yourselves to the Alphabet, or depart
elsewhither!—Would not all that has genuineness in England gradually rally round such a man; all that has strength in England?
For realities alone have strength; wind-bags are wind; cant is cant,
leave it alone there. Nor are all clamours momentous: among living
creatures, we find, the loudest is the longest-eared; among lifeless
things the loudest is the drum, the emptiest. Alas, that official
persons, and all of us, had not eyes to see what was real, what was
merely chimerical, and thought or called itself real! How many
dread minatory Castle-spectres should we leave there, with their
admonishing right-hand and ghastly-burning saucer-eyes, to do
simply whatsoever they might find themselves able to do! Alas,
that we were not real ourselves; we should otherwise have surer
vision for the real. Castle-spectres, in their utmost terror, are but
poor mimicries of that real and most real terror which lies in the
Life of every Man: that, thou coward, is the thing to be afraid of,
if thou wilt live in fear. It is but the scratch of a bare bodkin; it
is but the flight of a few days of time; and even thou, poor palpi-
tating featherbrain, wilt find how real it is. ETERNITY: hast thou
heard of that? Is that a fact, or is it no fact? Are Buckingham
House and St. Stephens *in* that, or not in that?

But now we have to speak of the second great thing: Emigration. It was said above, all new epochs, so convulsed and tumultuous to look upon, are 'expansions,' increase of faculty not yet
organised. It is eminently true of the confusions of this time of
ours. Disorganic Manchester afflicts us with its Chartisms; yet is
not spinning of clothes for the naked intrinsically a most blessed
thing? Manchester once organic will bless and not afflict. The
confusions, if we would understand them, are at bottom mere increase which we know not yet how to manage; 'new wealth which
the old coffers will not hold.' How true is this, above all, of the
strange phenomenon called 'over-population!' Over-population is
the grand anomaly, which is bringing all other anomalies to a crisis.
Now once more, as at the end of the Roman Empire, a most confused epoch and yet one of the greatest, the Teutonic Countries

find themselves too full. On a certain western rim of our small Europe, there are more men than were expected. Heaped up against the western shore there, and for a couple of hundred miles inward, the 'tide of population' swells too high, and confuses itself somewhat! Over-population? And yet, if this small western rim of Europe is overpeopled, does not everywhere else a whole vacant Earth, as it were, call to us, Come and till me, come and reap me! Can it be an evil that in an Earth such as ours there should be new Men? Considered as mercantile commodities, as working machines, is there in Birmingham or out of it a machine of such value? 'Good Heavens! a white European Man, standing on his two legs, with his two five-fingered Hands at his shackle-bones, and miraculous Head on his shoulders, is worth something consider-able, one would say!' The stupid black African man brings money in the market; the much stupider four-footed horse brings money. —it is we that have not yet learned the art of managing our white European man!

The controversies on Malthus and the 'Population Principle,' 'Preventive check' and so forth, with which the public ear has been deafened for a long while, are indeed sufficiently mournful. Dreary, stolid, dismal, without hope for this world or the next, is all that of the preventive check and the denial of the preventive check. Anti-Malthusians quoting their Bible against palpable facts are not a pleasant spectacle. On the other hand, how often have we read in Malthusian benefactors of the species: 'The working peo-ple have their condition in their own hands; let them diminish the supply of labourers, and of course the demand and the remunera-tion will increase!' Yes, let *them* diminish the supply: but who are they? They are twenty-four millions of human individuals, scattered over a hundred and eighteen thousand square miles of space and more; weaving, delving, hammering, joinering; each un-known to his neighbour; each distinct within his own skin. *They* are not a kind of character that can take a resolution, and act on it, very readily. Smart Sally in our alley proves all-too fascinating to brisk Tom in yours: can Tom be called on to make pause, and cal-culate the demand for labour in the British Empire first? Nay, if Tom did renounce his highest blessedness of life, and struggle and conquer like a Saint Francis of Assisi, what would it profit him or us? Seven millions of the finest peasantry do not renounce, but proceed all the more briskly; and with blue-visaged Hibernians instead of fair Saxon Tomsons and Sallysons, the latter end of that country is worse than the beginning. O wonderful Malthusian prophets! Millenniums are undoubtedly coming, must come one way or the other: but will it be, think you, by twenty millions of working people simultaneously striking work in that department; passing, in universal trades-union, a resolution not to beget any more till the labour-market become satisfactory? By Day and Night! they were indeed irresistible so; not to be compelled by law or war; might make their own terms with the richer classes, and defy the world!

A shade more rational is that of those other benefactors of the species, who counsel that in each parish, in some central locality, instead of the Parish Clergyman, there might be established some Parish Exterminator; or say a Reservoir of Arsenic, kept up at the public expense, free to all parishioners; for *which* Church the rates probably would not be grudged.—Ah, it is bitter jesting on such a subject. One's heart is sick to look at the dreary chaos, and valley of Jehosaphat, scattered with the limbs and souls of one's fellow-men; and no divine voice, only creaking of hungry vultures, inarticulate bodeful ravens, horn-eyed parrots that do articulate, proclaiming, Let these bones live!—Dante's *Divina Commedia* is called the mournfullest of books: transcendent mistemper of the noblest soul; utterance of a boundless, godlike, unspeakable, implacable sorrow and protest against the world. But in Holywell Street, not long ago, we bought, for three-pence, a book still mournfuller: the Pamphlet of one "Marcus," whom his poor Chartist editor and re-publisher calls the "Demon Author." This *Marcus* Pamphlet was the book alluded to by Stephens the Preacher Chartist, in one of his harangues: it proves to be no fable that such a book existed; here it lies, 'Printed by John Hill, Black-horse Court, Fleet Street, and now reprinted for the instruction of the labourer, by William Dugdale, Holywell Street, Strand,' the exasperated Chartist editor who sells it you for three-pence. We have read Marcus; but his sorrow is not divine. We hoped he would turn out to have been in sport: ah no, it is grim earnest with him; grim as very death. Marcus is not a demon author at all: he is a benefactor of the species in his own kind; has looked intensely on the world's woes, from a Benthamee-Malthusian watch-tower, under a Heaven dead as iron; and does now, with much longwindedness, in a drawling, snuffling, circuitous, extremely dull, yet at bottom handfast and positive manner, recommend that all children of working people, after the third, be disposed of by 'painless extinction.' Charcoal-vapour and other methods exist. The mothers would consent, might be made to consent. Three children might be left living; or perhaps, for Marcus's calculations are not yet perfect, two and a half. There might be 'beautiful cemeteries with colonnades and flower-plots,' in which the patriot infanticide matrons might delight to take their evening walk of contemplation; and reflect what patriotesses they were, what a cheerful flowery world it was. Such is the scheme of Marcus; this is what he, for his share, could devise to heal the world's woes. A benefactor of the species, clearly recognisable as such: the saddest scientific mortal we have ever in this world fallen in with; sadder even than poetic Dante. His is a *no*-godlike sorrow; sadder than the godlike. The Chartist editor, dull as he, calls him demon author, and a man set on by the Poor-Law Commissioners. What a black, godless, waste-struggling world, in this once merry England of ours, do such pamphlets and such editors betoken! *Laissez-faire* and Malthus, Malthus and *Laissez-faire*: ought not *these* two at length to part company? Might we not hope that both of them had as good as delivered their message now, and were about to go their ways?

For all this of the 'painless extinction,' and the rest, is in a world where Canadian Forests stand unfelled, boundless Plains and Prairies unbroken with the plough; on the west and on the east green desert spaces never yet made white with corn; and to the overcrowded little western nook of Europe, our Terrestrial Planet, nine-tenths of it yet vacant or tenanted by nomades, is still crying, Come and till me, come and reap me! And in an England with wealth, and means for moving, such as no nation ever before had. With ships; with war-ships rotting idle, which, but bidden move and not rot, might bridge all oceans. With trained men, educated to pen and practise, to administer and act; briefless Barristers, chargeless Clergy, taskless Scholars, languishing in all court-houses, hiding in obscure garrets, besieging all antechambers, in passionate want of simply one thing, Work;—with as many Half-pay Officers of both Services, wearing themselves down in wretched tedium, as might lead an Emigrant host larger than Xerxes' was! *Laissez-faire* and Malthus positively must part company. Is it not as if this swelling, simmering, never-resting Europe of ours stood, once more, on the verge of an expansion without parallel; struggling, struggling like a mighty tree again about to burst in the embrace of summer, and shoot forth broad frondent boughs which would fill the whole earth? A disease; but the noblest of all,—as of her who is in pain and sore travail, but travails that she may be a mother, and say, Behold, there is a new Man born!

'True thou Gold-Hofrath,' exclaims an eloquent satirical German of our acquaintance, in that strange Book of his,[1] 'True thou Gold-Hofrath: too crowded indeed! Meanwhile what portion of this inconsiderable Terraqueous Globe have ye actually tilled and delved, till it will grow no more? How thick stands your population in the Pampas and Savannas of America; round ancient Car-

[1] *Sartor Resartus*, p. 141.

thage, and in the interior of Africa; on both slopes of the Altaic chain, in the central Platform of Asia; in Spain, Greece, Turkey, Crim Tartary, the Curragh of Kildare? One man, in one year, as I have understood it, if you lend him earth, will feed himself and nine others. Alas, where now are the Hengsts and Alarics of our still glowing, still expanding Europe; who, when their home is grown too narrow, will enlist and, like fire-pillars, guide onwards those superfluous masses of indomitable living Valour; equipped, not now with the battle-axe and war-chariot, but with the steam-engine and ploughshare? Where are they?—Preserving their Game!'

PAST AND PRESENT.

Ernſt iſt das Leben.—Schiller.

PAST AND PRESENT.

———•———

BOOK I.—PROEM.

———

CHAPTER I.

MIDAS.

THE condition of England, on which many pamphlets are now in the course of publication, and many thoughts unpublished are going on in every reflective head, is justly regarded as one of the most ominous, and withal one of the strangest, ever seen in this world. England is full of wealth, of multifarious produce, supply for human want in every kind; yet England is dying of inanition. With unabated bounty the land of England blooms and grows; waving with yellow harvests; thick-studded with workshops, industrial implements, with fifteen millions of workers, understood to be the strongest, the cunningest and the willingest our Earth ever had; these men are here; the work they have done, the fruit they have realised is here, abundant, exuberant on every hand of us: and behold, some baleful fiat as of Enchantment has gone forth, saying, "Touch it not, ye workers, ye master-workers, ye master-idlers; none of you can touch it, no man of you shall be the better for it; this is enchanted fruit!" On the poor workers such fiat falls first, in its rudest shape; but on the rich master-workers too it falls; neither can the rich master-idlers, nor any richest or highest man escape, but all are like to be brought low with it, and made 'poor' enough, in the money sense or a far fataller one.

Of these successful skilful workers some two millions, it is now counted, sit in Workhouses, Poor-law Prisons; or have 'out-door relief flung over the wall to them,—the workhouse Bastille being filled to bursting, and the strong Poor-law broken asunder by a stronger.[1] They sit there, these many months now; their hope of deliverance as yet small. In workhouses, pleasantly so-named, because work cannot be done in them. Twelve hundred thousand workers in England alone; their cunning right-hand lamed, lying idle in their sorrowful bosom; their hopes, outlooks, share of this fair world, shut in by narrow walls. They sit there, pent up, as in a kind of horrid enchantment; glad to be imprisoned and enchanted, that they may not perish starved. The picturesque Tourist, in a sunny autumn day, through this bounteous realm of England, descries the Union Workhouse on his path. 'Passing by the 'Workhouse of St. Ives in Huntingdonshire, on a bright day last 'autumn,' says the picturesque Tourist, 'I saw sitting on wooden 'benches, in front of their Bastille and within their ring-wall 'and its railings, some half-hundred or more of these men. Tall 'robust figures, young mostly or of middle age; of honest coun- 'tenance, many of them thoughtful and even intelligent-looking 'men. They sat there, near by one another; but in a kind of 'torpor, especially in a silence, which was very striking. In si- 'lence: for, alas, what word was to be said? An Earth all lying 'round, crying, Come and till me, come and reap me;—yet we 'here sit enchanted! In the eyes and brows of these men hung 'the gloomiest expression, not of anger, but of grief and shame 'and manifold inarticulate distress and weariness; they returned 'my glance with a glance that seemed to say, "Do not look at us. 'We sit enchanted here, we know not why. The Sun shines and 'the Earth calls; and, by the governing Powers and Impotences 'of this England, we are forbidden to obey. It is impossible, they 'tell us!" There was something that reminded me of Dante's 'Hell in the look of all this; and I rode swiftly away.'

So many hundred thousands sit in workhouses: and other hundred thousands have not yet got even workhouses; and in thrifty Scotland itself, in Glasgow or Edinburgh City, in their dark lanes, hidden from all but the eye of God, and of rare Bene- volence the minister of God, there are scenes of woe and destitu- tion and desolation, such as, one may hope, the Sun never saw before in the most barbarous regions where men dwelt. Compe- tent witnesses, the brave and humane Dr. Alison, who speaks what he knows, whose noble Healing Art in his charitable hands be- comes once more a truly sacred one, report these things for us: these things are not of this year, or of last year, have no reference

---

[1] The Return of Paupers for England and Wales, at Ladyday 1842, is, 'In-door 221,687, Out-door 1,207,402, Total 1,429,089.'—(*Official Report.*)

to our present state of commercial stagnation, but only to the common state. Not in sharp fever-fits, but in chronic gangrene of this kind is Scotland suffering. A Poor-law, any and every Poor-law, it may be observed, is but a temporary measure; an anodyne, not a remedy: Rich and Poor, when once the naked facts of their condition have come into collision, cannot long subsist together on a mere Poor-law. True enough:—and yet, human beings cannot be left to die! Scotland too, till something better come, must have a Poor-law, if Scotland is not to be a byword among the nations. O, what a waste is there; of noble and thrice-noble national virtues; peasant Stoicisms, Heroisms; valiant manful habits, soul of a Nation's worth,—which all the metal of Potosi cannot purchase back; to which the metal of Potosi, and all you can buy with *it*, is dross and dust!

Why dwell on this aspect of the matter? It is too indisputable, not doubtful now to any one. Descend where you will into the lower class, in Town or Country, by what avenue you will, by Factory Inquiries, Agricultural Inquiries, by Revenue Returns, by Mining-Labourer Committees, by opening your own eyes and looking, the same sorrowful result discloses itself: you have to admit that the working body of this rich English Nation has sunk or is fast sinking into a state, to which, all sides of it considered, there was literally never any parallel. At Stockport Assizes,—and this too has no reference to the present state of trade, being of date prior to that,—a Mother and a Father are arraigned and found guilty of poisoning three of their children, to defraud a ' burial-society' of some 3*l*. 8*s*. due on the death of each child: they are arraigned, found guilty; and the official authorities, it is whispered, hint that perhaps the case is not solitary, that perhaps you had better not probe further into that department of things. This is in the autumn of 1841; the crime itself is of the previous year or season. " Brutal savages, degraded Irish," mutters the idle reader of Newspapers; hardly lingering on this incident. Yet it is an incident worth lingering on; the depravity, savagery and degraded Irishism being never so well admitted. In the British land, a human Mother and Father, of white skin and professing the Christian religion, had done this thing; they, with their Irishism and necessity and savagery, had been driven to do it. Such instances are like the highest mountain apex emerged into view; under which lies a whole mountain region and land, not yet emerged. A human Mother and Father had said to themselves, What shall we do to escape starvation? We are deep sunk here, in our dark cellar; and help is far.—Yes, in the Ugolino Hunger-tower stern things happen; best-loved little Gaddo fallen dead on his Father's

knees!—The Stockport Mother and Father think and hint: Our
poor little starveling Tom, who cries all day for victuals, who will
see only evil and not good in this world: if he were out of misery
at once; he well dead, and the rest of us perhaps kept alive? It
is thought, and hinted; at last it is done. And now Tom being
killed, and all spent and eaten, Is it poor little starveling Jack
that must go, or poor little starveling Will?—What a committee of
ways and means!

In starved sieged cities, in the uttermost doomed ruin of old
Jerusalem fallen under the wrath of God, it was prophesied and
said, ' The hands of the pitiful women have sodden their own children.' The stern Hebrew imagination could conceive no blacker
gulf of wretchedness; that was the ultimatum of degraded god-
punished man. And we here, in modern England, exuberant with
supply of all kinds, besieged by nothing if it be not by invisible
Enchantments, are we reaching that? —— How come these things?
Wherefore are they, wherefore should they be?

Nor are they of the St. Ives workhouses, of the Glasgow lanes,
and Stockport cellars, the only unblessed among us. This successful industry of England, with its plethoric wealth, has as yet
made nobody rich; it is an enchanted wealth, and belongs yet to
nobody. We might ask, Which of us has it enriched? We can
spend thousands where we once spent hundreds; but can purchase
nothing good with them. In Poor and Rich, instead of noble
thrift and plenty, there is idle luxury alternating with mean scarcity
and inability. We have sumptuous garnitures for our Life, but
have forgotten to *live* in the middle of them. It is an enchanted
wealth; no man of us can yet touch it. The class of men who
feel that they are truly better off by means of it, let them give us
their name!

Many men eat finer cookery, drink dearer liquors,—with what
advantage they can report, and their Doctors can: but in the
heart of them, if we go out of the dyspeptic stomach, what increase
of blessedness is there? Are they better, beautifuller, stronger,
braver? Are they even what they call 'happier?' Do they look
with satisfaction on more things and human faces in this God's-
Earth; do more things and human faces look with satisfaction on
them? Not so. Human faces gloom discordantly, disloyally on
one another. Things, if it be not mere cotton and iron things,
are growing disobedient to man. The Master Worker is enchanted,
for the present, like his Workhouse Workman; clamours, in vain
hitherto, for a very simple sort of 'Liberty:' the liberty 'to buy
where he finds it cheapest, to sell where he finds it dearest.' With

guineas jingling in every pocket, he was no whit richer; but now, the very guineas threatening to vanish, he feels that he is poor indeed. Poor Master Worker! And the Master Unworker, is not he in a still fataller situation? Pausing amid his game-preserves, with awful eye,—as he well may! Coercing fifty-pound tenants; coercing, bribing, cajoling; doing what he likes with his own. His mouth full of loud futilities, and arguments to prove the excellence of his Corn-law; and in his heart the blackest misgiving, a desperate half-consciousness that his excellent Corn-law is indefensible, that his loud arguments for it are of a kind to strike men too literally *dumb*.

To whom, then, is this wealth of England wealth? Who is it that it blesses; makes happier, wiser, beautifuller, in any way better? Who has got hold of it, to make it fetch and carry for him, like a true servant, not like a false mock-servant; to do him any real service whatsoever? As yet no one. We have more riches than any Nation ever had before; we have less good of them than any Nation ever had before. Our successful industry is hitherto unsuccessful; a strange success, if we stop here! In the midst of plethoric plenty, the people perish; with gold walls, and full barns, no man feels himself safe or satisfied. Workers, Master Workers, Unworkers, all men, come to a pause; stand fixed, and cannot farther. Fatal paralysis spreading inwards, from the extremities, in St. Ives workhouses, in Stockport cellars, through all limbs, as if towards the heart itself. Have we actually got enchanted, then; accursed by some god?—

Midas longed for gold, and insulted the Olympians. He got gold, so that whatsoever he touched became gold,—and he, with his long ears, was little the better for it. Midas had misjudged the celestial music-tones; Midas had insulted Apollo and the gods: the gods gave him his wish, and a pair of long ears, which also were a good appendage to it. What a truth in these old Fables!

CHAPTER II.

THE SPHINX.

How true, for example, is that other old Fable of the Sphinx, who sat by the wayside, propounding her riddle to the passengers, which if they could not answer she destroyed them! Such a Sphinx is this Life of ours, to all men and societies of men. Nature, like the Sphinx, is of womanly celestial loveliness and tenderness; the face and bosom of a goddess, but ending in claws and the body of a lioness. There is in her a celestial beauty,— which means celestial order, pliancy to wisdom; but there is also a darkness, a ferocity, fatality, which are infernal. She is a goddess, but one not yet disimprisoned; one still half-imprisoned,— the articulate, lovely still encased in the inarticulate, chaotic. How true! And does she not propound her riddles to us? Of each man she asks daily, in mild voice, yet with a terrible significance, "Knowest thou the meaning of this Day? What thou canst do Today; wisely attempt to do?" Nature, Universe, Destiny, Existence, howsoever we name this grand unnamable Fact in the midst of which we live and struggle, is as a heavenly bride and conquest to the wise and brave, to them who can discern her behests and do them; a destroying fiend to them who cannot. Answer her riddle, it is well with thee. Answer it not, pass on regarding it not, it will answer itself; the solution for thee is a thing of teeth and claws; Nature is a dumb lioness, deaf to thy pleadings, fiercely devouring. Thou art not now her victorious bridegroom; thou art her mangled victim, scattered on the precipices, as a slave found treacherous, recreant, ought to be and must.

With Nations it is as with individuals: Can they rede the riddle of Destiny? This English Nation, will it get to know the meaning of *its* strange new Today? Is there sense enough extant, discoverable anywhere or anyhow, in our united twenty-seven million heads to discern the same; valour enough in our twenty-seven million hearts to dare and do the bidding thereof? It will be seen!—

The secret of gold Midas, which he with his long ears never could discover, was, That he had offended the Supreme Powers;— that he had parted company with the eternal inner Facts of this Universe, and followed the transient outer Appearances thereof; and so was arrived *here*. Properly it is the secret of all unhappy men and unhappy nations. Had they known Nature's right truth, Nature's right truth would have made them free. They have become enchanted; stagger spell-bound, reeling on the brink of huge peril, because they were not wise enough. They have forgotten the right Inner True, and taken up with the Outer Shamtrue. They answer the Sphinx's question *wrong*. Foolish men cannot answer it aright! Foolish men mistake transitory semblance for eternal fact, and go astray more and more.

Foolish men imagine that because judgment for an evil thing is delayed, there is no justice, but an accidental one, here below. Judgment for an evil thing is many times delayed some day or two, some century or two, but it is sure as life, it is sure as death!

In the centre of the world-whirlwind, verily now as in the oldest days, dwells and speaks a God. The great soul of the world is *just*. O brother, can it be needful now, at this late epoch of experience, after eighteen centuries of Christian preaching for one thing, to remind thee of such a fact; which all manner of Mahometans, old Pagan Romans, Jews, Scythians and heathen Greeks, and indeed more or less all men that God made, have managed at one time to see into; nay which thou thyself, till 'redtape' strangled the inner life of thee, hadst once some inkling of: That there *is* justice here below; and even, at bottom, that there is nothing else but justice! Forget that, thou hast forgotten all. Success will never more attend thee: how can it now? Thou hast the whole Universe against thee. No more success: mere sham-success, for a day and days; rising ever higher,—towards its Tarpeian Rock. Alas, how, in thy soft-hung Longacre vehicle, of polished leather to the bodily eye, of redtape philosophy, of expediencies, clubroom moralities, Parliamentary majorities to the mind's eye, thou beautifully rollest: but knowest thou whitherward? It is towards the *road's end*. Old use-and-wont; established methods, habitudes, *once* true and wise; man's noblest tendency, his perseverance, and man's ignoblest, his inertia; whatsoever of noble and ignoble Conservatism there is in men and Nations, strongest always in the strongest men and Nations: all this is as a road to thee, paved smooth through the abyss,—till all this *end*. Till men's bitter necessities can endure thee no more. Till Nature's patience with thee is done; and there is no road or footing any farther, and the abyss yawns sheer!—

Parliament and the Courts of Westminster are venerable to me; how venerable; gray with a thousand years of honourable age! For a thousand years and more, Wisdom and faithful Valour, struggling amid much Folly and greedy Baseness, not without most sad distortions in the struggle, have built them up; and they are as we see. For a thousand years, this English Nation has found them useful or supportable; they have served this English Nation's want; *been* a road to it through the abyss of Time. They are venerable, they are great and strong. And yet it is good to remember always that they are not the venerablest, nor the greatest, nor the strongest! Acts of Parliament are venerable; but if they correspond not with the writing on the 'Adamant Tablet,' what are they? Properly their one element of venerableness, of strength or greatness, is, that they at all times correspond therewith as near as by human possibility they can. They are cherishing destruction in their bosom every hour that they continue otherwise.

Alas, how many causes that can plead well for themselves in the Courts of Westminster; and yet in the general Court of the Universe, and free Soul of Man, have no word to utter! Honourable Gentlemen may find this worth considering, in times like ours. And truly, the din of triumphant Law-logic, and all shaking of horse-hair wigs and learned-sergeant gowns having comfortably ended, we shall do well to ask ourselves withal, What says that high and highest Court to the verdict? For it is the Court of Courts, that same; where the universal soul of Fact and very Truth sits President;—and thitherward, more and more swiftly, with a really terrible increase of swiftness, all causes do in these days crowd for revisal,—for confirmation, for modification, for reversal with costs. Dost thou know that Court; hast thou had any Law-practice there? What, didst thou never enter; never file any petition of redress, reclaimer, disclaimer or demurrer, written as in thy heart's blood, for thy own behoof or another's; and silently await the issue? Thou knowest not such a Court? Hast merely heard of it by faint tradition as a thing that was or had been? Of thee, I think, we shall get little benefit.

For the gowns of learned-sergeants are good: parchment records, fixed forms, and poor terrestrial Justice, with or without horse-hair, what sane man will not reverence these? And yet, behold, the man is not sane but insane, who considers these alone as venerable. Oceans of horse-hair, continents of parchment, and learned-sergeant eloquence, were it continued till the learned tongue wore itself small in the indefatigable learned mouth, cannot make unjust just. The grand question still remains, Was the judgment just? If unjust, it will not and cannot get harbour for itself, or continue to have footing in this Universe, which was made by other than One Unjust. Enforce it by never such statuting, three readings, royal assents; blow it to the four winds with all manner of quilted trumpeters and pursuivants, in the rear of them never so many gibbets and hangmen, it will not stand, it cannot stand. From all souls of men, from all ends of Nature, from the Throne of God above, there are voices bidding it: Away, away! Does it take no warning; does it stand, strong in its three readings, in its gibbets and artillery-parks? The more woe is to it, the frightfuller woe. It will continue standing for its day, for its year, for its century, doing evil all the while; but it has One enemy who is Almighty: dissolution, explosion, and the everlasting Laws of Nature incessantly advance towards it; and the deeper its rooting, more obstinate its continuing, the deeper also and huger will its ruin and overturn be.

In this God's-world, with its wild-whirling eddies and mad

foam-oceans, where men and nations perish as if without law, and judgment for an unjust thing is sternly delayed, dost thou think that there is therefore no justice? It is what the fool hath said in his heart. It is what the wise, in all times, were wise because they denied, and knew forever not to be. I tell thee again, there is nothing else but justice. One strong thing I find here below: the just thing, the true thing. My friend, if thou hadst all the artillery of Woolwich trundling at thy back in support of an unjust thing; and infinite bonfires visibly waiting ahead of thee, to blaze centuries long for thy victory on behalf of it,—I would advise thee to call halt, to fling down thy baton, and say, "In God's name, No!" Thy 'success? Poor devil, what will thy success amount to? If the thing is unjust, thou hast not succeeded; no, not though bonfires blazed from North to South, and bells rang, and editors wrote leading-articles, and the just thing lay trampled out of sight, to all mortal eyes an abolished and annihilated thing. Success? In few years thou wilt be dead and dark,—all cold, eyeless, deaf; no blaze of bonfires, ding-dong of bells or leading-articles visible or audible to thee again at all forever: What kind of success is that!—

It is true, all goes by approximation in this world; with any not insupportable approximation we must be patient. There is a noble Conservatism as well as an ignoble. Would to Heaven, for the sake of Conservatism itself, the noble alone were left, and the ignoble, by some kind severe hand, were ruthlessly lopped away, forbidden evermore to show itself! For it is the right and noble alone that will have victory in this struggle; the rest is wholly an obstruction, a postponement and fearful imperilment of the victory. Towards an eternal centre of right and nobleness, and of that only, is all this confusion tending. We already know whither it is all tending; what will have victory, what will have none! The Heaviest will reach the centre. The Heaviest, sinking through complex fluctuating media and vortices, has its deflexions, its obstructions, nay at times its resiliences, its reboundings; whereupon some blockhead shall be heard jubilating, "See, your Heaviest ascends!"—but at all moments it is moving centreward, fast as is convenient for it; sinking, sinking; and, by laws older than the World, old as the Maker's first Plan of the World, it has to arrive there.

Await the issue. In all battles, if you await the issue, each fighter has prospered according to his right. His right and his might, at the close of the account, were one and the same. He has fought with all his might, and in exact proportion to all his right he has prevailed. His very death is no victory over him. He dies indeed; but his work lives, very truly lives. A heroic Wallace, quartered on the scaffold, cannot hinder that his Scotland become, one day, a part of England: but he does hinder that it become, on tyrannous unfair terms, a part of it; commands still, as with a god's voice, from his old Valhalla and Temple of the Brave, that there be a just real union as of brother and brother, not a false and merely semblant one as of slave and master. If the union with England be in fact one of Scotland's chief blessings, we thank Wallace withal that it was not the chief curse. Scotland is not Ireland: no, because brave men rose there, and said, "Behold, ye must not tread us down like slaves; and ye shall not,—and cannot!" Fight on, thou brave true heart, and falter not, through dark fortune and through bright. The cause thou fightest for, so far as it is true, no farther, yet precisely so far, is very sure of victory. The falsehood alone of it will be conquered, will be abolished, as it ought to be: but the truth of it is part of Nature's own Laws, coöperates with the World's eternal Tendencies, and cannot be conquered.

The *dust* of controversy, what is it but the *falsehood* flying off from all manner of conflicting true forces, and making such a loud dust-whirlwind,—that so the truths alone may remain, and embrace brother-like in some true resulting-force! It is ever so. Savage fighting Heptarchies: their fighting is an ascertainment, who has the right to rule over whom; that out of such waste-bickering Saxondom a peacefully coöperating England may arise. Seek through this Universe; if with other than owl's eyes, thou wilt find nothing nourished there, nothing kept in life, but what has right to nourishment and life. The rest, look at it with other than owl's eyes, is not living; is all dying, all as good as dead! Justice was ordained from the foundations of the world; and will last with the world and longer.

From which I infer that the inner sphere of Fact, in this present England as elsewhere, differs infinitely from the outer sphere and spheres of Semblance. That the Temporary, here as elsewhere, is too apt to carry it over the Eternal. That he who dwells in the temporary Semblances, and does not penetrate into the eternal Substance, will *not* answer the Sphinx-riddle of Today, or of any Day. For the substance alone is substantial; that *is* the law of Fact: if you discover not that, Fact, who already knows it, will let you also know it by and by!

What is Justice? that, on the whole, is the question of the Sphinx to us. The law of Fact is, that Justice must and will be done. The sooner the better; for the Time grows stringent, frightfully pressing! "What is Justice?" ask many, to whom cruel Fact alone will be able to prove responsive. It is like jesting Pilate asking, What is Truth? Jesting Pilate had not the smallest chance to ascertain what was Truth. He could not have known it, had a god shown it to him. Thick serene opacity, thicker than amaurosis, veiled those smiling eyes of his to Truth; the inner *retina* of them was gone paralytic, dead. He looked at Truth; and discerned her not, there where she stood. "What is Justice?" The clothed embodied Justice that sits in Westminster Hall, with penalties, parchments, tipstaves, is very visible. But the unembodied Justice, whereof that other is either an emblem, or else is a fearful indescribability, is not so visible! For the unembodied Justice is of Heaven; a Spirit, and Divinity of Heaven,—invisible to all but the noble and pure of soul. The impure ignoble gaze with eyes, and she is not there. They will prove it to you by logic, by endless Hansard Debatings, by bursts of Parliamentary eloquence. It is not consolatory to behold! For properly, as many men as there are in a Nation who *can* withal see Heaven's invisible Justice, and know it to be on Earth also omnipotent, so many men are there who stand between a Nation and perdition. So many, and no more. Heavy-laden England, how many hast thou in this hour? The Supreme Power sends new and ever new, all *born* at least with hearts of flesh and not of stone;—and heavy Misery itself, once heavy enough, will prove didactic!—

CHAPTER III.

MANCHESTER INSURRECTION.

BLUSTEROWSKI, Colacorde, and other Editorial prophets of the Continental Democratic Movement, have in their leading-articles shown themselves disposed to vilipend the late Manchester Insurrection, as evincing in the rioters an extreme backwardness to battle; nay as betokening, in the English People itself, perhaps a want of the proper animal-courage indispensable in these ages. A million hungry operative men started up, in utmost paroxysm of desperate protest against their lot; and, ask Colacorde and company, How many shots were fired? Very few in comparison! Certain hundreds of drilled soldiers sufficed to suppress this million-headed hydra, and tread it down, without the smallest appeasement or hope of such, into its subterranean settlements

again, there to reconsider itself. Compared with our revolts in
Lyons, in Warsaw and elsewhere, to say nothing of incomparable
Paris City past or present, what a lamblike Insurrection!—

The present Editor is not here, with his readers, to vindicate
the character of Insurrections; nor does it matter to us whether
Blusterowski and the rest may think the English a courageous
people or not courageous. In passing, however, let us mention
that, to our view, this was not an unsuccessful Insurrection; that
as Insurrections go, we have not heard lately of any that succeeded so well.

A million of hungry operative men, as Blusterowski says, rose
all up, came all out into the streets, and—stood there. What
other could they do? Their wrongs and griefs were bitter, insupportable, their rage against the same was just: but who are they
that cause these wrongs, who that will honestly make effort to
redress them? Our enemies are we know not who or what; our
friends are we know not where! How shall we attack any one,
shoot or be shot by any one? Oh, if the accursed invisible Nightmare, that is crushing out the life of us and ours, would take a
shape; approach us like the Hyrcanian tiger, the Behemoth of
Chaos, the Archfiend himself; in any shape that we could see,
and fasten on!—A man can have himself shot with cheerfulness;
but it needs first that he see clearly for what. Show him the
divine face of Justice, then the diabolic monster which is eclipsing
that: he will fly at the throat of such monster, never so monstrous, and need no bidding to do it. Woolwich grapeshot will
sweep clear all streets, blast into invisibility so many thousand
men: but if your Woolwich grapeshot be but eclipsing Divine
Justice, and the God's-radiance itself gleam recognisable athwart
such grapeshot,—then, yes then is the time come for fighting and
attacking. All artillery-parks have become weak, and are about
to dissipate: in the God's-thunder, their poor thunder slackens,
ceases; finding that it is, in all senses of the term, a *brute* one!—

That the Manchester Insurrection stood still, on the streets,
with an indisposition to fire and bloodshed, was wisdom for it
even as an Insurrection. Insurrection, never so necessary, is a
most sad necessity; and governors who wait for that to instruct
them, are surely getting into the fatallest courses,—proving themselves Sons of Nox and Chaos, of blind Cowardice, not of seeing
Valour! How can there be any remedy in insurrection? It is
a mere announcement of the disease,—visible now even to Sons
of Night. Insurrection usually 'gains' little; usually wastes how
much! One of its worst kinds of waste, to say nothing of the
rest, is that of irritating and exasperating men against each other,

by violence done; which is always sure to be injustice done, for violence does even justice unjustly.

Who shall compute the waste and loss, the obstruction of every sort, that was produced in the Manchester region by Peterloo alone! Some thirteen unarmed men and women cut down,—the number of the slain and maimed is very countable: but the treasury of rage, burning hidden or visible in all hearts ever since, more or less perverting the effort and aim of all hearts ever since, is of unknown extent. "How ye came among us, in your cruel armed blindness, ye unspeakable County Yeomanry, sabres flourishing, hoofs prancing, and slashed us down at your brute pleasure; deaf, blind to all *our* claims and woes and wrongs; of quick sight and sense to your own claims only! There lie poor sallow workworn weavers, and complain no more now; women themselves are slashed and sabred, howling terror fills the air; and ye ride prosperous, very victorious,—ye unspeakable: give *us* sabres too, and then come-on a little!" Such are Peterloos. In all hearts that witnessed Peterloo, stands written, as in fire-characters, or smoke-characters prompt to become fire again, a legible balance-account of grim vengeance; very unjustly balanced, much exaggerated, as is the way with such accounts: but payable readily at sight, in full with compound interest! Such things should be avoided as the very pestilence! For men's hearts ought not to be set against one another; but set *with* one another, and all against the Evil Thing only. Men's souls ought to be left to see clearly; not jaundiced, blinded, twisted all awry, by revenge, mutual abhorrence, and the like. An Insurrection that can announce the disease, and then retire with no such balance-account opened anywhere, has attained the highest success possible for it.

And this was what these poor Manchester operatives, with all the darkness that was in them and round them, did manage to perform. They put their huge inarticulate question, "What do you mean to do with us?" in a manner audible to every reflective soul in this kingdom.; exciting deep pity in all good men, deep anxiety in all men whatever;. and no conflagration or outburst of madness came to cloud that feeling anywhere, but everywhere it operates unclouded. All England heard the question: it is the first practical form of *our* Sphinx-riddle. England will answer it; or, on the whole, England will perish;—one does not yet expect the latter result!

For the rest, that the Manchester Insurrection could yet discern no radiance of Heaven on any side of its horizon; but feared that all lights, of the O'Connor or other sorts, hitherto kindled, were but deceptive fish-oil transparencies, or bog will-o'-wisp lights,

and no dayspring from on high: for this also we will honour the
poor Manchester Insurrection, and augur well of it. A deep unspoken sense lies in these strong men,—inconsiderable, almost
stupid, as all they can articulate of it is. Amid all violent stupidity of speech, a right noble instinct of what is doable and what
is not doable never forsakes them: the strong inarticulate men
and workers, whom *Fact* patronises; of whom, in all difficulty and
work whatsoever, there is good augury! This work too is to be
done: Governors and Governing Classes that *can* articulate and
utter, in any measure, what the law of Fact and Justice is, may
calculate that here is a Governed Class who will listen.

And truly this first practical form of the Sphinx-question, inarticulately and so audibly put there, is one of the most impressive ever asked in the world. " Behold us here, so many thousands, millions, and increasing at the rate of fifty every hour. We
are right willing and able to work; and on the Planet Earth is
plenty of work and wages for a million times as many. We ask, If
you mean to lead us towards work; to try to lead us,—by ways
new, never yet heard of till this new unheard-of Time? Or if you
declare that you cannot lead us? And expect that we are to
remain quietly unled, and in a composed manner perish of starvation? What is it you expect of us? What is it you mean to do
with us?" This question, I say, has been put in the hearing of all
Britain; and will be again put, and ever again, till some answer be
given it.

Unhappy Workers, unhappier Idlers, unhappy men and women
of this actual England. We are yet very far from an answer, and
there will be no existence for us without finding one. "A fair
day's-wages for a fair day's-work:" it is as just a demand as Governed men ever made of Governing. It is the everlasting right
of man. Indisputable as Gospels, as arithmetical multiplication-
tables: it must and will have itself fulfilled;—and yet, in these
times of ours, with what enormous difficulty, next-door to impossibility! For the times are really strange; of a complexity intricate with all the new width of the ever-widening world; times here
of half-frantic velocity of impetus, there of the deadest-looking
stillness and paralysis; times definable as showing two qualities,
Dilettantism and Mammonism;—most intricate obstructed times!
Nay, if there were not a Heaven's radiance of Justice, prophetic,
clearly of Heaven, discernible behind all these confused world-
wide entanglements, of Landlord interests, Manufacturing interests, Tory-Whig interests, and who knows what other interests,
expediencies, vested interests, established possessions, inveterate
Dilettantisms, Midas-eared Mammonisms,—it would seem to every

one a flat impossibility, which all wise men might as well at once abandon. If you do not know eternal Justice from momentary Expediency, and understand in your heart of hearts how Justice, radiant, beneficent, as the all-victorious Light-element, is also in essence, if need be, an all-victorious *Fire*-element, and melts all manner of vested interests, and the hardest iron cannon, as if they were soft wax, and does ever in the long-run rule and reign, and allows nothing else to rule and reign,—you also would talk of impossibility! But it is only difficult, it is not impossible. Possible? It is, with whatever difficulty, very clearly inevitable.

Fair day's-wages for fair day's-work! exclaims a sarcastic man: Alas, in what corner of this Planet, since Adam first awoke on it, was that ever realised? The day's-wages of John Milton's day's-work, named *Paradise Lost* and *Milton's Works*, were Ten Pounds paid by instalments, and a rather close escape from death on the gallows. Consider that: it is no rhetorical flourish; it is an authentic, altogether quiet fact,—emblematic, quietly documentary of a whole world of such, ever since human history began. Oliver Cromwell quitted his farming; undertook a Hercules' Labour and lifelong wrestle with that Lernean Hydra-coil, wide as England, hissing heaven-high through its thousand crowned, coroneted, shovel-hatted quackheads; and he did wrestle with it, the truest and terriblest wrestle I have heard of; and he wrestled it, and mowed and cut it down a good many stages, so that its hissing is ever since pitiful in comparison, and one can walk abroad in comparative peace from it;—and his wages, as I understand, were burial under the gallows-tree near Tyburn Turnpike, with his head on the gable of Westminster Hall, and two centuries now of mixed cursing and ridicule from all manner of men. His dust lies under the Edgeware Road, near Tyburn Turnpike, at this hour; and his memory is—Nay, what matters what his memory is? His memory, at bottom, is or yet shall be as that of a god: a terror and horror to all quacks and cowards and insincere persons; an everlasting encouragement, new memento, battleword, and pledge of victory to all the brave. It is the natural course and history of the Godlike, in every place, in every time. What god ever carried it with the Tenpound Franchisers; in Open Vestry, or with any Sanhedrim of considerable standing? When was a god found 'agreeable' to everybody? The regular way is to hang, kill, crucify your gods, and execrate and trample them under your stupid hoofs for a century or two; till you discover that they are gods,—and then take to braying over them, still in a very long-eared manner!—So speaks the sarcastic man; in his wild way, very mournful truths.

Day's-wages for day's-work? continues he: The Progress of Human Society consists even in this same, The better and better apportioning of wages to work. Give me this, you have given me all. Pay to every man accurately what he has worked for, what he has earned and done and deserved,—to this man broad lands and honours, to that man high gibbets and treadmills: what more have I to ask? Heaven's Kingdom, which we daily pray for, *has* come; God's will is done on Earth even as it is in Heaven! This *is* the radiance of celestial Justice; in the light or in the fire of which all impediments, vested interests, and iron cannon, are more and more melting like wax, and disappearing from the pathways of men. A thing ever struggling forward; irrepressible, advancing inevitable; perfecting itself, all days, more and more,—never to be *perfect* till that general Doomsday, the ultimate Consummation, and Last of earthly Days.

True, as to 'perfection' and so forth, answer we; true enough! And yet withal we have to remark, that imperfect Human Society holds itself together, and finds place under the Sun, in virtue simply of some *approximation* to perfection being actually made and put in practice. We remark farther, that there are supportable approximations, and then likewise insupportable. With some, almost with any, supportable approximation men are apt, perhaps too apt, to rest indolently patient, and say, It will do. Thus these poor Manchester manual workers mean only, by day's-wages for day's-work, certain coins of money adequate to keep them living; —in return for their work, such modicum of food, clothes and fuel as will enable them to continue their work itself! They as yet clamour for no more; the rest, still inarticulate, cannot yet shape itself into a demand at all, and only lies in them as a dumb wish; perhaps only, still more inarticulate, as a dumb, altogether unconscious want. *This* is the supportable approximation they would rest patient with, That by their work they might be kept alive to work more!—*This* once grown unattainable, I think your approximation may consider itself to have reached the *in*supportable stage; and may prepare, with whatever difficulty, reluctance and astonishment, for one of two things, for changing or perishing! With the millions no longer able to live, how can the units keep living? It is too clear the Nation itself is on the way to suicidal death.

Shall we say then, The world has retrograded in its talent of apportioning wages to work, in late days? The world had always a talent of that sort, better or worse. Time was when the mere *hand*worker needed not announce his claim to the world by Manchester Insurrections!—The world, with its Wealth of Nations, Supply-and-demand and such like, has of late days been terribly inattentive to that question of work and wages. We will not say, the poor world has retrograded even here: we will say rather, the world has been rushing on with such fiery animation to get work and ever more work done, it has had no time to think of dividing the wages; and has merely left them to be scrambled for by the Law of the Stronger, law of Supply-and-demand, law of Laissez-faire, and other idle Laws and Un-laws,—saying, in its dire haste to get the work done, That is well enough!

And now the world will have to pause a little, and take up that other side of the problem, and in right earnest strive for some solution of that. For it has become pressing. What is the use of your spun shirts? They hang there by the million unsaleable; and here, by the million, are diligent bare backs that can get no hold of them. Shirts are useful for covering human backs; useless otherwise, an unbearable mockery otherwise. You have fallen terribly behind with that side of the problem! Manchester Insurrections, French Revolutions, and thousandfold phenomena great and small, announce loudly that you must bring it forward a little again. Never till now, in the history of an Earth which to this hour nowhere refuses to grow corn if you will plough it, to yield shirts if you will spin and weave in it, did the mere manual two-handed worker (however it might fare with other workers) cry in vain for such 'wages' as *he* means by 'fair wages,' namely food and warmth! The Godlike could not and cannot be paid; but the Earthly always could. Gurth, a mere swineherd, born thrall of Cedric the Saxon, tended pigs in the wood, and did get some parings of the pork. Why, the four-footed worker has already *got* all that this two-handed one is clamouring for! How often must I remind you? There is not a horse in England, able and willing to work, but *has* due food and lodging; and goes about sleek-coated, satisfied in heart. And you say, It is impossible. Bro-thers, I answer, if for you it be impossible, what is to become of you? It is impossible for us to believe it to be impossible. The human brain, looking at these sleek English horses, refuses to believe in such impossibility for English men. Do you depart quickly; clear the ways soon, lest worse befal. We for our share do purpose, with full view of the enormous difficulty, with total disbelief in the impossibility, to endeavour while life is in us, and to die endeavouring, we and our sons, till we attain it or have all died and ended.

Such a Platitude of a World, in which all working horses could be well fed, and innumerable working men should die starved, were it not best to end it; to have done with it, and restore it once for all to the *Jötuns*, Mud-giants, Frost-giants, and Chaotic Brute-gods of the Beginning? For the old Anarchic Brute-gods it may be well enough; but it is a Platitude which Men should be above countenancing by their presence in it. We pray you, let the word *impossible* disappear from your vocabulary in this matter. It is of awful omen; to all of us, and to yourselves first of all.

CHAPTER IV.

MORRISON'S PILL.

WHAT is to be done, what would you have us do? asks many a one, with a tone of impatience, almost of reproach; and then, if you mention some one thing, some two things, twenty things that might be done, turns round with a satirical tehee, and " These are your remedies!" The state of mind indicated by such question, and such rejoinder, is worth reflecting on.

It seems to be taken for granted, by these interrogative philosophers, that there is some 'thing,' or handful of 'things,' which could be done; some Act of Parliament, 'remedial measure' or the like, which could be passed, whereby the social malady were fairly fronted, conquered, put an end to; so that, with your remedial measure in your pocket, you could then go on triumphant, and be troubled no farther. "You tell us the evil," cry such persons, as if justly aggrieved, "and do not tell us how it is to be cured!"

How it is to be cured? Brothers, I am sorry I have got no Morrison's Pill for curing the maladies of Society. It were infinitely handier if we had a Morrison's Pill, Act of Parliament, or remedial measure, which men could swallow, one good time, and then go on in their old courses, cleared from all miseries and mischiefs! Unluckily we have none such; unluckily the Heavens themselves, in their rich pharmacopœia, contain none such. There will no 'thing' be done that will cure you. There will a radical universal alteration of your regimen and way of life take place; there will a most agonising divorce between you and your chimeras, luxuries and falsities, take place; a most toilsome, all-but 'impossible' return to Nature, and her veracities and her integrities, take place: that so the inner fountains of life may again begin, like eternal Light-fountains, to irradiate and purify your bloated, swollen, foul existence, drawing nigh, as at present, to nameless death! Either death or else all this will take place. Judge if, with such diagnosis, any Morrison's Pill is like to be discoverable!

But the Life-fountain within you once again set flowing, what innumerable 'things,' whole sets and classes and continents of 'things,' year after year, and decade after decade, and century after century, will then be doable and done! Not Emigration, Education, Corn-Law Abrogation, Sanitary Regulation, Land Property-Tax; not these alone, nor a thousand times as much as these. Good Heavens, there will then be light in the inner heart of here and there a man, to discern what is just, what is commanded by the Most High God, what *must* be done, were it never so 'impossible.' Vain jargon in favour of the palpably unjust will then abridge itself within limits. Vain jargon, on Hustings, in Parliaments or wherever else, when here and there a man has vision for the essential God's-Truth of the things jargoned of, will become very vain indeed. The silence of here and there such a man, how eloquent in answer to such jargon! Such jargon, frightened at its own gaunt echo, will unspeakably abate; nay, for a while, may almost in a manner disappear,—the wise answering it in silence, and even the simple taking cue from them to hoot it down wherever heard. It will be a blessed time; and many 'things' will become doable,—and when the brains are out, an absurdity will die! Not easily again shall a Corn-Law argue ten years for itself; and still talk and argue, when impartial persons have to say with a sigh that, for so long back, they have heard no 'argument' advanced for it but such as might make the angels and almost the very jackasses weep!—

Wholly a blessed time: when jargon might abate, and here and there some genuine speech begin. When to the noble opened heart, as to such heart they alone do, all noble things began to grow visible; and the difference between just and unjust, between true and false, between work and sham-work, between speech and jargon, was once more, what to our happier Fathers it used to be, *infinite*,—as between a Heavenly thing and an Infernal: the one a thing which you were *not* to do, which you were wise not to attempt doing; which it were better for you to have a millstone tied round your neck, and be cast into the sea, than concern yourself with doing!—Brothers, it will not be a Morrison's Pill, or remedial measure, that will bring all this about for us.

And yet, very literally, till, in some shape or other, it be brought about, we remain cureless; till it begin to be brought about, the cure does not begin. For Nature and Fact, not Redtape and Semblance, are to this hour the basis of man's life; and on those, through never such strata of these, man and his life and all his interests do, sooner or later, infallibly come to rest,—and to be supported or be swallowed according as they agree with those. The question is asked of them, not, How do you agree with Downing Street and accredited Semblance? but, How do you agree with God's Universe and the actual Reality of things? This Universe *has* its Laws. If we walk according to the Law, the Law-Maker will befriend us; if not, not. Alas, by no Reform Bill, Ballot-box, Five-point Charter, by no boxes or bills or charters, can you perform this alchemy: 'Given a world of Knaves, to produce an Honesty from their united action!' It is a distillation, once for all, not possible. You pass it through alembic after alembic, it comes out still a Dishonesty, with a new dress on it, a new colour to it. 'While we ourselves continue valets, how *can* any hero come to govern us?' We are governed, very infallibly, by the 'sham-hero,' —whose name is Quack, whose work and governance is Plausibility, and also is Falsity and Fatuity; to which Nature says, and must say when it comes to *her* to speak, eternally No! Nations cease to be befriended of the Law-Maker, when they walk *not* according to the Law. The Sphinx-question remains unsolved by them, becomes ever more insoluble.

If thou ask again, therefore, on the Morrison's-Pill hypothesis, What is to be done? allow me to reply: By thee, for the present, almost nothing. Thou there, the thing for thee to do is, if possible, to cease to be a hollow sounding-shell of hearsays, egoisms, purblind dilettantisms; and become, were it on the infinitely small scale, a faithful discerning soul. Thou shalt descend into thy inner man, and see if there be any traces of a *soul* there; till then there can be nothing done! O brother, we must if possible resuscitate some soul and conscience in us, exchange our dilettantisms for sincerities, our dead hearts of stone for living hearts of flesh. Then shall we discern, not one thing, but, in clearer or dimmer sequence, a whole endless host of things that can be done. *Do* the first of these; do it; the second will already have become clearer, doabler; the second, third and three-thousandth will then have begun to be possible for us. Not any universal Morrison's Pill shall we then, either as swallowers or as venders, ask after at all; but a far different sort of remedies: Quacks shall no more have dominion over us, but true Heroes and Healers!

Will not that be a thing worthy of 'doing;' to deliver ourselves from quacks, sham-heroes; to deliver the whole world more and more from such? They are the one bane of the world. Once clear the world of them, it ceases to be a Devil's-world, in all fibres of it wretched, accursed; and begins to be a God's-world, blessed, and working hourly towards blessedness. Thou for one wilt not again vote for any quack, do honour to any edge-gilt vacuity in man's shape: cant shall be known to thee by the sound of it;—thou wilt fly from cant with a shudder never felt before; as from the opened litany of Sorcerers' Sabbaths, the true Devil-worship of this age, more horrible than any other blasphemy, profanity or genuine blackguardism elsewhere audible among men. It is alarming to witness,—in its present completed state! And Quack and Dupe, as we must ever keep in mind, are upper-side and under of the selfsame substance; convertible personages: turn up your dupe into the proper fostering element, and he himself can become a quack; there is in him the due prurient insincerity, open voracity for profit, and closed sense for truth, whereof quacks too, in all their kinds, are made.

Alas, it is not to the hero, it is to the sham-hero that, of right and necessity, the valet-world belongs. 'What is to be done?' The reader sees whether it is like to be the seeking and swallowing of some 'remedial measure!'

CHAPTER V.

ARISTOCRACY OF TALENT.

WHEN an individual is miserable, what does it most of all behove him to do? To complain of this man or of that, of this thing or of that? To fill the world and the street with lamentation, objurgation? Not so at all: the reverse of so. All moralists advise him not to complain of any person or of any thing, but of himself only. He is to know of a truth that being miserable he has been unwise, he. Had he faithfully followed Nature and her Laws, Nature, ever true to her Laws, would have yielded fruit and increase and felicity to him: but he has followed other than Nature's Laws; and now Nature, her patience with him being ended, leaves him desolate; answers with very emphatic significance to him: No. Not by this road, my son; by another road shalt thou attain well-being: this, thou perceivest is the road to ill-being; quit this!—So do all moralists advise: that the man penitently say to himself first of all, Behold I was not wise enough; I quitted the laws of Fact, which are also called the Laws of God, and mistook for them the Laws of Sham and Semblance, which are called the Devil's Laws; therefore am I here!

Neither with Nations that become miserable is it fundamentally otherwise. The ancient guides of Nations, Prophets, Priests, or whatever their name, were well aware of this; and, down to a late epoch, impressively taught and inculcated it. The modern guides of Nations, who also go under a great variety of names, Journalists, Political Economists, Politicians, Pamphleteers, have entirely forgotten this, and are ready to deny this. But it nevertheless remains eternally undeniable: nor is there any doubt but we shall all be taught it yet, and made again to confess it: we shall all be striped and scourged till we do learn it; and shall at last either get to know it, or be striped to death in the process. For it is undeniable! When a Nation is unhappy, the old Prophet was right and not wrong in saying to it: Ye have forgotten God, ye have quitted the ways of God, or ye would not have been unhappy. It is not according to the laws of Fact that ye have lived and guided yourselves, but according to the laws of Delusion, Imposture, and wilful and unwilful *Mistake* of Fact; behold therefore the Unveracity is worn out; Nature's long-suffering with you is exhausted; and ye are here!

Surely there is nothing very inconceivable in this, even to the Journalist, to the Political Economist, Modern Pamphleteer, or any two-legged animal without feathers! If a country finds itself wretched, sure enough that country has been *misguided*: it is with the wretched Twenty-seven Millions, fallen wretched, as with the Unit fallen wretched: they as he have quitted the course prescribed by Nature and the Supreme Powers, and so are fallen into scarcity, disaster, infelicity; and pausing to consider themselves, have to lament and say: Alas, we were not wise enough! We took transient superficial Semblance for everlasting central Substance; we have departed far away from the *Laws* of this Universe, and behold now lawless-Chaos and inane Chimera is ready to devour us!—'Nature in late centuries,' says Sauerteig, 'was universally ' supposed to be dead; an old eight-day clock, made many thousand ' years ago, and still ticking, but dead as brass,—which the Maker, ' at most, sat looking at, in a distant, singular, and indeed incre- ' dible manner: but now I am happy to observe, she is everywhere ' asserting herself to be not dead and brass at all, but alive and ' miraculous, celestial-infernal, with an emphasis that will again ' penetrate the thickest head of this Planet by and by!'— —

Indisputable enough to all mortals now, the guidance of this country has not been sufficiently wise: men too foolish have been set to the guiding and governing of it, and have guided it *hither;* we must find wiser,—wiser, or else we perish! To this length of insight all England has now advanced; but as yet no further. All

England stands wringing its hands, asking itself, nigh desperate, What farther? Reform Bill proves to be a failure; Benthamee Radicalism, the gospel of 'Enlightened Selfishness,' dies out, or dwindles into Five-point Chartism, amid the tears and hootings of men: what next are we to hope or try? Five-point Charter, Free-trade, Church-extension, Sliding-scale; what, in Heaven's name, are we next to attempt, that we sink not in inane Chimera, and be devoured of Chaos?—The case is pressing, and one of the most complicated in the world. A God's-message never came to thicker-skinned people; never had a God's-message to pierce through thicker integuments, into heavier ears. It is Fact, speaking once more, in miraculous thunder-voice, from out of the centre of the world;—how unknown its language to the deaf and foolish many; how distinct, undeniable, terrible and yet beneficent, to the hear-ing few: Behold, ye shall grow wisor, or ye shall die! Truer to Nature's Fact, or inane Chimera will swallow you; in whirlwinds of fire, you and your Mammonisms, Dilettantisms, your Midas-eared philosophies, double-barrelled Aristocracies, shall disappear!— Such is the God's-message to *us*, once more, in these modern days.

We must have more Wisdom to govern us, we must be governed by the Wisest, we must have an Aristocracy of Talent! cry many. True, most true; but how to get it? The following extract from our young friend of the *Houndsditch Indicator* is worth perusing: ' At this time,' says he, 'while there is a cry everywhere, articulate ' or inarticulate, for an "Aristocracy of Talent," a Governing Class ' namely which did govern, not merely which took the wages of ' governing, and could not with all our industry be kept from mis-' governing, corn-lawing, and playing the very deuce with us,—it ' may not be altogether useless to remind some of the greener-' headed sort what a dreadfully difficult affair the getting of such ' an Aristocracy is! Do you expect, my friends, that your indis-' pensable Aristocracy of Talent is to be enlisted straightway, by ' some sort of recruitment aforethought, out of the general popu-' lation; arranged in supreme regimental order; and set to rule ' over us? That it will be got sifted, like wheat out of chaff, from ' the Twenty-seven Million British subjects; that any Ballot-box, ' Reform Bill, or other Political Machine, with Force of Public ' Opinion never so active on it, is likely to perform said process of ' sifting? Would to Heaven that we had a sieve; that we could ' so much as fancy any kind of sieve, wind-fanners, or ne-plus-ultra ' of machinery, devisable by man, that would do it!

'Done nevertheless, sure enough, it must be; it shall and will

' be. We are rushing swiftly on the road to destruction; every hour
' bringing us nearer, until it be, in some measure, done. The doing
' of it is not doubtful; only the method and the costs! Nay I will
' even mention to you an infallible sifting-process whereby he that
' has ability will be sifted out to rule among us, and that same
' blessed Aristocracy of Talent be verily, in an approximate degree,
' vouchsafed us by and by: an infallible sifting-process; to which,
' however, no soul can help his neighbour, but each must, with
' devout prayer to Heaven, endeavour to help himself. It is, O
' friends, that all of us, that many of us, should acquire the true
' *eye* for talent, which is dreadfully wanting at present! The true
' eye for talent presupposes the true reverence for it,—O Heavens,
' presupposes so many things!

    ' For example, you Bobus Higgins, Sausage-maker on the great
' scale, who are raising such a clamour for this Aristocracy of Ta-
' lent, what is it that you do, in that big heart of yours, chiefly in
' very fact pay reverence to? Is it to talent, intrinsic manly worth
' of any kind, you unfortunate Bobus? The manliest man that
' you saw going in a ragged coat, did you ever reverence him; did
' you so much as know that he was a manly man at all, till his coat
' grew better? Talent! I understand you to be able to worship
' the fame of talent, the power, cash, celebrity or other success of
' talent; but the talent itself is a thing you never saw with eyes.
' Nay what is it in yourself that you are proudest of, that you take
' most pleasure in surveying meditatively in thoughtful moments?
' Speak now, is it the bare Bobus stript of his very name and shirt,
' and turned loose upon society, that you admire and thank Heaven
' for; or Bobus with his cash-accounts and larders dropping fat-
' ness, with his respectabilities, warm garnitures, and pony-chaise,
' admirable in some measure to certain of the flunkey species?
' Your own degree of worth and talent, is it of *infinite* value to you;
' or only of finite,—measurable by the degree of currency, and con-
' quest of praise or pudding, it has brought you to? Bobus, you
' are in a vicious circle, rounder than one of your own sausages;
' and will never vote for or promote any talent, except what talent
' or sham-talent has already *got* itself voted for!'—We here cut
short the *Indicator;* all readers perceiving whither he now tends.

    ' More Wisdom' indeed: but where to find more Wisdom? We
have already a Collective Wisdom, after its kind,—though ' class-
legislation,' and another thing or two, affect it somewhat! On the
whole, as they say, Like people like priest; so we may say, Like
people like king. The man gets himself appointed and elected
who is ablest—to be appointed and elected. What can the incor-

ruptiblest *Bobuses* elect, if it be not some *Bobissimus*, should they find such?

Or, again, perhaps there is not, in the whole Nation, Wisdom enough, 'collect' it as we may, to make an adequate Collective! That too is a case which may befal: a ruined man staggers down to ruin because there was not wisdom enough in him; so, clearly also, may Twenty-seven Million collective men!—But indeed one of the infalliblest fruits of Unwisdom in a Nation is that it cannot get the use of what Wisdom is actually in it: that it is not governed by the wisest it has, who alone have a divine right to govern in all Nations; but by the sham-wisest, or even by the openly not-so-wise if they are handiest otherwise! This is the infalliblest result of Unwisdom; and also the balefullest, immeasurablest,—not so much what we can call a poison-*fruit*, as a universal death-disease, and poisoning of the whole tree. For hereby are fostered, fed into gigantic bulk, all manner of Unwisdoms, poison-fruits; till, as we say, the life-tree everywhere is made a upas-tree, deadly Unwisdom overshadowing all things; and there is done what lies in human skill to stifle all Wisdom everywhere in the birth, to smite our poor world barren of Wisdom,—and make your utmost Collective Wisdom, were it collected and elected by Rhadamanthus, Æacus and Minos, not to speak of drunken Tenpound Franchisers with their ballot-boxes, an inadequate Collective! The Wisdom is not now there: how will you 'collect' it? As well wash Thames mud, by improved methods, to find more gold in it.

Truly, the first condition is indispensable, That Wisdom be there: but the second is like unto it, is properly one with it; these two conditions act and react through every fibre of them, and go inseparably together. If you have much Wisdom in your Nation, you will get it faithfully collected; for the wise love Wisdom, and will search for it as for life and salvation. If you have little Wisdom, you will get even that little ill-collected, trampled under foot, reduced as near as possible to annihilation; for fools do not love Wisdom; they are foolish, first of all, because they have never loved Wisdom,—but have loved their own appetites, ambitions, their coroneted coaches, tankards of heavy-wet. Thus is your candle lighted at both ends, and the progress towards consummation is swift. Thus is fulfilled that saying in the Gospel: To him that hath shall be given; and from him that hath not shall be taken away even that which he hath. Very literally, in a very fatal manner, that saying is here fulfilled.

Our 'Aristocracy of Talent' seems at a considerable distance yet; does it not, O Bobus?

CHAPTER VI.

HERO-WORSHIP.

To the present Editor, not less than to Bobus, a Government of the Wisest, what Bobus calls an Aristocracy of Talent, seems the one healing remedy: but he is not so sanguine as Bobus with respect to the means of realising it. He thinks that we have at once missed realising it, and come to need it so pressingly, by departing far from the inner eternal Laws, and taking up with the temporary outer semblances of Laws. He thinks that 'enlightened Egoism,' never so luminous, is not the rule by which man's life can be led. That 'Laissez-faire,' 'Supply-and-demand,' 'Cash-payment for the sole nexus,' and so forth, were not, are not, and will never be, a practicable Law of Union for a Society of Men. That Poor and Rich, that Governed and Governing, cannot long live together on any such Law of Union. Alas, he thinks that man has a soul in him, *different* from the stomach in any sense of this word; that if said soul be asphyxied, and lie quietly forgotten, the man and his affairs are in a bad way. He thinks that said soul will have to be resuscitated from its asphyxia; that if it prove irresuscitable, the man is not long for this world. In brief, that Midas-eared Mammonism, double-barrelled Dilettantism, and their thousand adjuncts and corollaries, are *not* the Law by which God Almighty has appointed this his Universe to go. That, once for all, these are not the Law: and then farther that we shall have to return to what *is* the Law,—not by smooth flowery paths, it is like, and with 'tremendous cheers' in our throat; but over steep untrodden places, through stormclad chasms, waste oceans, and the bosom of tornadoes; thank Heaven, if not through very Chaos and the Abyss! The resuscitating of a soul that has gone to asphyxia is no momentary or pleasant process, but a long and terrible one.

To the present Editor, 'Hero-worship,' as he has elsewhere named it, means much more than an elected Parliament, or stated Aristocracy, of the Wisest; for, in his dialect, it is the summary, ultimate essence, and supreme practical perfection of all manner of 'worship,' and true worthships and noblenesses whatsoever. Such blessed Parliament and, were it once in perfection, blessed Aristocracy of the Wisest, god-honoured and man-honoured, he does look for, more and more perfected,—as the topmost blessed practical apex of a whole world reformed from sham-worship, informed anew with worship, with truth and blessedness! He thinks that Hero-worship, done differently in every different epoch of the world, is the soul of all social business among men; that the doing of it well, or the doing of it ill, measures accurately what degree of well-being or of ill-being there is in the world's affairs. He thinks that we, on the whole, do our Hero-worship worse than any Nation in this world ever did it before: that the Burns an Exciseman, the Byron a Literary Lion, are intrinsically, all things considered, a baser and falser phenomenon than the Odin a God, the Mahomet a Prophet of God. It is this Editor's clear opinion, accordingly, that we must learn to do our Hero-worship better; that to do it better and better, means the awakening of the Nation's soul from its asphyxia, and the return of blessed life to us,—Heaven's blessed life, not Mammon's galvanic accursed one. To resuscitate the Asphyxied, apparently now moribund, and in the last agony if not resuscitated: such and no other seems the consummation.

' Hero-worship,' if you will,—yes, friends; but, first of all, by being ourselves of heroic mind. A whole world of Heroes; a world not of Flunkeys, where no Hero-King *can* reign: that is what we aim at! We, for our share, will put away all Flunkeyism, Baseness, Unveracity from us; we shall then hope to have Noblenesses and Veracities set over us; never till then. Let Bobus and Company sneer, "That is your Reform!" Yes, Bobus, that is our Reform; and except in that, and what will follow out of that, we have no hope at all. Reform, like Charity, O Bobus, must begin at home. Once well at home, how will it radiate outwards, irrepressible, into all that we touch and handle, speak and work; kindling ever new light, by incalculable contagion, spreading in geometric ratio, far and wide,—doing good only, wheresoever it spreads, and not evil.

By Reform Bills, Anti-Corn-Law Bills, and thousand other bills and methods, we will demand of our Governors, with emphasis, and for the first time not without effect, that they cease to be quacks, or else depart; that they set no quackeries and blockheadisms anywhere to rule over us, that they utter or act no cant to us, —it will be better if they do not. For we shall now know quacks when we see them; cant, when we hear it, shall be horrible to us! We will say, with the poor Frenchman at the Bar of the Convention, though in wiser style than he, and ' for the space' not ' of an hour' but of a lifetime: " *Je demande l'arrestation des coquins et des lâches.*" ' Arrestment of the knaves and dastards:' ah, we know what a work that is; how long it will be before *they* are all or mostly got ' arrested:'—but here is one; arrest him, in God's name; it is one fewer! We will, in all practicable ways, by word and silence, by act and refusal to act, energetically demand that arrestment,—"*je demande cette arrestation-là!*"—and by degrees infallibly attain it. Infallibly: for light spreads; all human souls, never so bedarkened. love light. light once kindled spreads, till all is luminous;—till the cry, "*Arrest* your knaves and dastards" rises imperative from millions of hearts, and rings and reigns from sea to sea. Nay, how many of them may we not 'arrest' with our own hands, even now; we! Do not countenance them, thou there: turn away from their lackered sumptuosities, their belauded sophistries, their serpent graciosities, their spoken and acted cant, with a sacred horror, with an *Apage Satanas.*—Bobus and Company, and all men will gradually join us. We demand arrestment of the knaves and dastards, and begin by arresting our own poor selves out of that fraternity. There is no other reform conceivable. Thou and I, my friend, can, in the most flunkey world, make. each of us, *one* non-flunkey, one hero, if we like: that will be two heroes to begin with:—Courage! even that is a whole world of heroes to end with, or what we poor Two can do in furtherance thereof!

Yes, friends: Hero-kings, and a whole world not unheroic,—there lies the port and happy haven, towards which, through all these stormtost seas, French Revolutions, Chartisms, Manchester Insurrections, that make the heart sick in these bad days, the Supreme Powers are driving us. On the whole, blessed be the Supreme Powers, stern as they are! Towards that haven will we, O friends; let all true men, with what of faculty is in them, bend valiantly, incessantly, with thousandfold endeavour, thither, thither! There, or else in the Ocean-abysses, it is very clear to me, we shall arrive.

Well; here truly is no answer to the Sphinx-question; not the answer a disconsolate public, inquiring at the College of Health, was in hopes of! A total change of regimen, change of constitution and existence from the very centre of it; a new body to be got, with resuscitated soul,—not without convulsive travail-throes: as all birth and new-birth presupposes travail! This is sad news to a disconsolate discerning Public, hoping to have got off by some Morrison's Pill, some Saint-John's corrosive mixture and perhaps a little blistery friction on the back!—We were prepared to part with our Corn-Law, with various Laws and Unlaws: but this, what is this?

Nor has the Editor forgotten how it fares with your ill-boding Cassandras in Sieges of Troy. Imminent perdition is not usually driven away by words of warning. Didactic Destiny has other methods in store; or these would fail always. Such words should, nevertheless, be uttered, when they dwell truly in the soul of any man. Words are hard, are importunate; but how much harder

the importunate events they foreshadow! Here and there a human soul may listen to the words,—who knows how many human
souls? whereby the importunate events, if not diverted and pre-
vented, will be rendered *less* hard.   The present Editor's purpose
is to himself full of hope.

For though fierce travails, though wide seas and roaring gulfs
lie before us, is it not something if a Loadstar, in the eternal sky,
do once more disclose itself; an everlasting light, shining through
all cloud-tempests and roaring billows, ever as we emerge from the
trough of the sea: the blessed beacon, far off on the edge of far
horizons, towards which we are to steer incessantly for life?   Is it
not something; O Heavens, is it not all?   There lies the Heroic
Promised Land; under that Heaven's-light, my brethren, bloom the
Happy Isles,—there, O there!   Thither will we;

> ' There dwells the great Achilles whom we knew.' [1]

There dwell all Heroes, and will dwell: thither, all ye heroic-
minded!—The Heaven's Loadstar once clearly in our eye, how will
each true man stand truly to *his* work in the ship; how, with un-
dying hope, will all things be fronted, all be conquered.   Nay, with
the ship's prow once turned in that direction, is not all, as it were,
already well?   Sick wasting misery has become noble manful effort
with a goal in our eye.   'The choking Nightmare chokes us no
longer; for we *stir* under it; the Nightmare has already fled.'—

Certainly, could the present Editor instruct men how to know
Wisdom, Heroism, when they see it, that they might do reverence
to *it* only, and loyally make it ruler over them,—yes, he were the
living epitome of all Editors, Teachers, Prophets, that now teach
and prophesy; he were an *Apollo*-Morrison, a Trismegistus and
effective Cassandra!   Let no Able Editor hope such things.   It is
to be expected the present laws of copyright, rate of reward per
sheet, and other considerations, will save him from that peril.   Let
no Editor hope such things: no;—and yet let all Editors aim towards such things, and even towards such alone!   One knows
not what the meaning of editing and writing is, if even this be
not it.

Enough, to the present Editor it has seemed possible some
glimmering of light, for here and there a human soul, might lie in
these confused Paper-Masses now intrusted to him; wherefore he
determines to edit the same.   Out of old Books, new Writings, and
much Meditation not of yesterday, he will endeavour to select a
thing or two; and from the Past, in a circuitous way, illustrate the
Present and the Future.   The Past is a dim indubitable fact: the

---

[1] Tennyson's Poems (*Ulysses*).

Future too is one, only dimmer; nay properly it is the *same* fact in new dress and development. For the Present holds in it both the whole Past and the whole Future;—as the LIFE-TREE IGDRASIL, wide-waving, many-toned, has its roots down deep in the Death-kingdoms, among the oldest dead dust of men, and with its boughs reaches always beyond the stars; and in all times and places is one and the same Life-tree!

BOOK II.—THE ANCIENT MONK.

CHAPTER I.

JOCELIN OF BRAKELOND.

WE will, in this Second Portion of our Work, strive to penetrate
a little, by means of certain confused Papers, printed and other,
into a somewhat remote Century; and to look face to face on it,
in hope of perhaps illustrating our own poor Century thereby.
It seems a circuitous way; but it may prove a way nevertheless.
For man has ever been a striving, struggling, and, in spite of wide-
spread calumnies to the contrary, a veracious creature: the Centuries too are all lineal children of one another; and often, in the
portrait of early grandfathers, this and the other enigmatic feature
of the newest grandson shall disclose itself, to mutual elucidation.
This Editor will venture on such a thing.

Besides, in Editors' Books, and indeed everywhere else in the
world of Today, a certain latitude of movement grows more and
more becoming for the practical man. Salvation lies not in tight
lacing, in these times;—how far from that, in any province whatsoever! Readers and men generally are getting into strange
habits of asking all persons and things, from poor Editors' Books
up to Church Bishops and State Potentates, not, By what designation art thou called; in what wig and black triangle dost thou
walk abroad? Heavens, I know thy designation and black triangle well enough! But, in God's name, what *art* thou? Not
Nothing, sayest thou! Then, How much and what? This is the
thing I would know; and even *must* soon know, such a pass am I
come to!— —What weather-symptoms,—not for the poor Editor
of Books alone! The Editor of Books may understand withal
that if, as is said, 'many kinds are permissible,' there is one kind
not permissible, 'the kind that has nothing in it, *le genre ennuyeux;*'
and go on his way accordingly.

A certain Jocelinus de Brakelonda, a natural-born Englishman, has left us an extremely foreign Book,[1] which the labours of the Camden Society have brought to light in these days. Jocelin's Book, the 'Chronicle,' or private Boswellean Notebook, of Jocelin, a certain old St. Edmundsbury Monk and Boswell, now seven centuries old, how remote is it from us; exotic, extraneous; in all ways, coming from far abroad! The language of it is not foreign only but dead: Monk-Latin lies across not the British Channel, but the ninefold Stygian Marshes, Stream of Lethe, and one knows not where! Roman Latin itself, still alive for us in the Elysian Fields of Memory, is domestic in comparison. And then the ideas, life-furniture, whole workings and ways of this worthy Jocelin; covered deeper than Pompeii with the lava-ashes and inarticulate wreck of seven hundred years!

Jocelin of Brakelond cannot be called a conspicuous literary character; indeed few mortals that have left so visible a work, or footmark, behind them can be more obscure. One other of those vanished Existences, whose work has not yet vanished;—almost a pathetic phenomenon, were not the whole world full of such! The builders of Stonehenge, for example:—or alas, what say we, Stonehenge and builders? The writers of the *Universal Review* and *Homer's Iliad;* the paviers of London streets;—sooner or later, the entire Posterity of Adam! It is a pathetic phenomenon; but an irremediable, nay, if well meditated, a consoling one.

By his dialect of Monk-Latin, and indeed by his name, this Jocelin seems to have been a Norman Englishman; the surname *de Brakelonda* indicates a native of St. Edmundsbury itself, *Brakelond* being the known old name of a street or quarter in that venerable Town. Then farther, sure enough, our Jocelin was a Monk of St. Edmundsbury Convent; held some 'obedientia,' subaltern officiality there, or rather, in succession several; was, for one thing, 'chaplain to my Lord Abbot, living beside him night and day for the space of six years;'—which last, indeed, is the grand fact of Jocelin's existence, and properly the origin of this present Book, and of the chief meaning it has for us now. He was, as we have hinted, a kind of born *Boswell*, though an infinitesimally small one; neither did he altogether want his *Johnson* even there and then. Johnsons are rare; yet, as has been asserted, Boswells perhaps still rarer,—the more is the pity on both sides! This Jocelin, as we can discern well, was an ingenious and ingenuous, a cheery-hearted, innocent, yet withal shrewd, noticing, quick-witted man; and from under his monk's cowl has looked

---

[1] *Chronica* JOCELINI DE BRAKELONDA, *de rebus gestis Samsonis Abbatis Monasterii Sancti Edmundi: nunc primum typis mandata, curante* JOHANNE GAGE ROKEWOOD. (Camden Society, London, 1840.)

out on that narrow section of the world in a really *human* manner; not in any *simial*, canine, ovine, or otherwise inhuman manner,— afflictive to all that have humanity! The man is of patient, peaceable, loving, clear-smiling nature; open for this and that. A wise simplicity is in him; much natural sense; a *veracity* that goes deeper than words. Veracity: it is the basis of all; and, some say, means genius itself; the prime essence of all genius whatsoever. Our Jocelin, for the rest, has read his classical manuscripts, his Virgilius, his Flaccus, Ovidius Naso; of course still more, his Homilies and Breviaries, and if not the Bible, considerable extracts of the Bible. Then also he has a pleasant wit; and loves a timely joke, though in mild subdued manner: very amiable to see. A learned grown man, yet with the heart as of a good child; whose whole life indeed has been that of a child,— St. Edmundsbury Monastery a larger kind of cradle for him, in which his whole prescribed duty was to *sleep* kindly, and love his mother well! This is the Biography of Jocelin; 'a man of excellent religion,' says one of his contemporary Brother Monks, '*eximiæ religionis, potens sermone et opere.*'

For one thing, he had learned to write a kind of Monk or Dog-Latin, still readable to mankind; and, by good luck for us, had bethought him of noting down thereby what things seemed notablest to him. Hence gradually resulted a *Chronica Jocelini;* new Manuscript in the *Liber Albus* of St. Edmundsbury. Which Chronicle, once written in its childlike transparency, in its innocent good-humour, not without touches of ready pleasant wit and many kinds of worth, other men liked naturally to read: whereby it failed not to be copied, to be multiplied, to be inserted in the *Liber Albus;* and so surviving Henry the Eighth, Putney Cromwell, the Dissolution of Monasteries, and all accidents of malice and neglect for six centuries or so, it got into the *Harleian Collection,*—and has now therefrom, by Mr. Rokewood of the Camden Society, been deciphered into clear print; and lies before us, a dainty thin quarto, to interest for a few minutes whomsoever it can.

Here too it will behove a just Historian gratefully to say that Mr. Rokewood, Jocelin's Editor, has done his editorial function well. Not only has he deciphered his crabbed Manuscript into clear print; but he has attended, what his fellow editors are not always in the habit of doing, to the important truth that the Manuscript so deciphered ought to have a meaning for the reader. Standing faithfully by his text, and printing its very errors in spelling, in grammar or otherwise, he has taken care by some note to indicate that they are errors, and what the correction of them ought to be. Jocelin's Monk-Latin is generally transparent, as shallow limpid water. But at any stop that may occur, of which there are a few, and only a very few, we have the comfortable assurance that a meaning does lie in the passage, and may by industry be got at; that a faithful editor's industry had already got at it before passing on. A compendious useful Glossary is given; nearly adequate to help the uninitiated through: sometimes one wishes it had been a trifle larger; but, with a Spelman and Ducange at your elbow, how easy to have made it far too large! Notes are added, generally brief; sufficiently explanatory of most points. Lastly, a copious correct Index; which no such Book should want, and which unluckily very few possess. And so, in a word, the *Chronicle of Jocelin* is, as it professes to be, unwrapped from its thick cerements, and fairly brought forth into the common daylight, so that he who runs, and has a smattering of grammar, may read.

We have heard so much of Monks; everywhere, in real and fictitious History, from Muratori Annals to Radcliffe Romances, these singular two-legged animals, with their rosaries and breviaries, with their shaven crowns, hair-cilices, and vows of poverty, masquerade so strangely through our fancy; and they are in fact so very strange an extinct species of the human family,—a veritable Monk of Bury St. Edmunds is worth attending to, if by chance made visible and audible. Here he is; and in his hand a magical speculum, much gone to rust indeed, yet in fragments still clear; wherein the marvellous image of his existence does still shadow itself, though fitfully, and as with an intermittent light! Will not the reader peep with us into this singular *camera lucida*, where an extinct species, though fitfully, can still be seen alive? Extinct species, we say; for the live specimens which still go about under that character are too evidently to be classed as spurious in Natural History: the Gospel of Richard Arkwright once promulgated, no Monk of the old sort is any longer possible in this world. But fancy a deep-buried Mastodon, some fossil Megatherion, Ichthyosaurus, were to begin to *speak* from amid its rock-swathings, never so indistinctly! The most extinct fossil species of Men or Monks can do, and does, this miracle,—thanks to the Letters of the Alphabet, good for so many things.

Jocelin, we said, was somewhat of a Boswell; but unfortunately, by Nature, he is none of the largest, and distance has now dwarfed him to an extreme degree. His light is most feeble, intermittent, and requires the intensest kindest inspection; otherwise it will disclose mere vacant haze. It must be owned, the good Jocelin, spite of his beautiful childlike character, is but an altogether imperfect 'mirror' of these old-world things! The good man, he looks on us so clear and cheery, and in his neighbourly soft-smiling eyes we see so well our *own* shadow,—we have a longing always to cross-question him, to force from him an explanation of much. But no; Jocelin, though he talks with such clear familiarity, like a next-door neighbour, will not answer any question: that is the peculiarity of him, dead these six hundred and fifty years, and quite deaf *to* us, though still so audible! The good man, he cannot help it, nor can we.

But truly it is a strange consideration this simple one, as we go on with him, or indeed with any lucid simple-hearted soul like him: Behold therefore, this England of the Year 1200 was no chimerical vacuity or dreamland, peopled with mere vaporous Fantasms, Rymer's Fœdera, and Doctrines of the Constitution; but a green solid place, that grew corn and several other things. The Sun shone on it; the vicissitude of seasons and human fortunes. Cloth was woven and worn; ditches were dug, furrow-fields ploughed, and houses built. Day by day all men and cattle rose to labour, and night by night returned home weary to their several lairs. In wondrous Dualism, then as now, lived nations of breathing men; alternating, in all ways, between Light and Dark; between joy and sorrow, between rest and toil,—between hope, hope reaching high as Heaven, and fear deep as very Hell. Not vapour Fantasms, Rymer's Fœdera at all! Cœur-de-Lion was not a theatrical popinjay with greaves and steel-cap on it, but a man living upon victuals,—*not* imported by Peel's Tariff. Cœur-de-Lion came palpably athwart this Jocelin at St. Edmundsbury; and had almost peeled the sacred gold '*Feretrum*,' or St. Edmund Shrine itself, to ransom him out of the Danube Jail.

These clear eyes of neighbour Jocelin looked on the bodily presence of King John; the very John *Sansterre*, or Lackland, who signed *Magna Charta* afterwards in Runnymead. Lackland, with a great retinue, boarded once, for the matter of a fortnight, in St. Edmundsbury Convent; daily in the very eyesight, palpable *to* the very fingers of our Jocelin: O Jocelin, what did he say, what did he do; how looked he, lived he;—at the very lowest, what coat or breeches had he on? Jocelin is obstinately silent. Jocelin marks down what interests *him;* entirely deaf to *us.* With Jocelin's eyes we discern almost nothing of John Lackland. As through a glass darkly, we with our own eyes and appliances, intensely looking, discern at most: A blustering, dissipated human figure, with a kind of blackguard quality air, in cramoisy velvet, or other uncertain texture, uncertain cut, with much plumage and fringing;

amid numerous other human figures of the like; riding abroad
with hawks; talking noisy nonsense;—tearing out the bowels of
St. Edmundsbury Convent (its larders namely and cellars) in the
most ruinous way, by living at rack and manger there.   Jocelin
notes only, with a slight subacidity of manner, that the King's
Majesty, *Dominus Rex*, did leave, as gift for our St. Edmund
Shrine, a handsome enough silk cloak,—or rather pretended to
leave, for one of his retinue borrowed it of us, and *we* never got
sight of it again; and, on the whole, that the *Dominus Rex*, at departing, gave us ' thirteen *sterlingii*,' one shilling and one penny, to
say a mass for him; and so departed,—like a shabby Lackland as
he was!   ' Thirteen pence sterling,' this was what the Convent
got from Lackland, for all the victuals he and his had made away
with.   We of course said our mass for him, having covenanted
to do it,—but let impartial posterity judge with what degree of
fervour!

And in this manner vanishes King Lackland; traverses swiftly
our strange intermittent magic-mirror, jingling the shabby thirteen pence merely; and rides with his hawks into Egyptian night
again.   It is Jocelin's manner with all things; and it is men's
manner and men's necessity.   How intermittent is our good Jocelin; marking down, without eye to *us*, what *he* finds interesting!
How much in Jocelin, as in all History, and indeed in all Nature,
is at once inscrutable and certain; so dim, yet so indubitable;
exciting us to endless considerations.   For King Lackland *was*
there, verily he; and did leave these *tredecim sterlingii*, if nothing
more, and did live and look in one way or the other, and a whole
world was living and looking along with him!   There, we say, is
the grand peculiarity; the immeasurable one; distinguishing, to a
really infinite degree, the poorest historical Fact from all Fiction
whatsoever.   Fiction, 'Imagination,' 'Imaginative Poetry,' &c. &c.,
except as the vehicle for truth, or *fact* of some sort,—which surely
a man should first try various other ways of vehiculating, and con-
veying safe,—what is it?   Let the Minerva and other Presses
respond!—

But it is time we were in St. Edmundsbury Monastery, and
Seven good Centuries off.   If indeed it be possible, by any aid of
Jocelin, by any human art, to get thither, with a reader or two
still following us?

———

CHAPTER II.

ST. EDMUNDSBURY.

THE *Burg*, Bury, or 'Berry' as they call it, of St. Edmund is still a prosperous brisk Town; beautifully diversifying, with its clear brick houses, ancient clean streets, and twenty or fifteen thousand busy souls, the general grassy face of Suffolk; looking out right pleasantly, from its hill-slope, towards the rising Sun: and on the eastern edge of it, still runs, long, black and massive, a range of monastic ruins; into the wide internal spaces of which the stranger is admitted on payment of one shilling. Internal spaces laid out, at present, as a botanic garden. Here stranger or townsman, sauntering at his leisure amid these vast grim venerable ruins, may persuade himself that an Abbey of St. Edmundsbury did once exist; nay there is no doubt of it: see here the ancient massive Gateway, of architecture interesting to the eye of Dilettantism; and farther on, that other ancient Gateway, now about to tumble, unless Dilettantism, in these very months, can subscribe money to cramp it and prop it!

Here, sure enough, is an Abbey; beautiful in the eye of Dilettantism. Giant Pedantry also will step in, with its huge *Dugdale* and other enormous *Monasticons* under its arm, and cheerfully apprise you, That this was a very great Abbey, owner and indeed creator of St. Edmund's Town itself, owner of wide lands and revenues; nay that its lands were once a county of themselves; that indeed King Canute or Knut was very kind to it, and gave St. Edmund his own gold crown off his head, on one occasion: for the rest, that the Monks were of such and such a genus, such and such a number; that they had so many carucates of land in this hundred, and so many in that; and then farther that the large Tower or Belfry was built by such a one, and the smaller Belfry was built by &c. &c.—Till human nature can stand no more of it; till human nature desperately take refuge in forgetfulness, almost in flat disbelief of the whole business, Monks, Monastery, Belfries, Carucates and all! Alas, what mountains of dead ashes, wreck and burnt bones, does assiduous Pedantry dig up from the Past Time, and name it History, and Philosophy of History; till, as we say, the human soul sinks wearied and bewildered; till the Past Time seems all one infinite incredible gray void, without sun, stars, hearth-fires, or candle-light; dim offensive dust-whirlwinds filling universal Nature; and over your Historical Library, it is as if all the Titans had written for themselves: DRY RUBBISH SHOT HERE!

And yet these grim old walls are not a dilettantism and dubiety; they are an earnest fact. It was a most real and serious purpose they were built for! Yes, another world it was, when these black ruins, white in their new mortar and fresh chiselling, first saw the sun as walls, long ago. Gauge not, with thy dilettante compasses, with that placid dilettante simper, the Heaven's-Watchtower of our Fathers, the fallen God's-Houses, the Golgotha of true Souls departed!

Their architecture, belfries, land-carucates? Yes,—and that is but a small item of the matter. Does it never give thee pause, this other strange item of it, that men then had a *soul*,—not by hearsay alone, and as a figure of speech; but as a truth that they *know*, and practically went upon! Verily it was another world then. Their Missals have become incredible, a sheer platitude, sayest thou? Yes, a most poor platitude; and even, if thou wilt, an idolatry and blasphemy, should any one persuade *thee* to believe them, to pretend praying by them. But yet it is pity we had lost tidings of our souls:—actually we shall have to go in quest of them again, or worse in all ways will befal! A certain degree of soul, as Ben Jonson reminds us, is indispensable to keep the very body from destruction of the frightfullest sort; to 'save us,' says he, 'the expense of *salt*.' Ben has known men who had soul enough to keep their body and five senses from becoming carrion, and save salt:—men, and also Nations. You may look in Manchester Hunger-mobs and Corn-law Commons Houses, and various other quarters, and say whether either soul or else salt is not somewhat wanted at present!—

Another world, truly: and this present poor distressed world might get some profit by looking wisely into it, instead of foolishly. But at lowest, O dilettante friend, let us know always that it *was* a world, and not a void infinite of gray haze with fantasms swimming in it. These old St. Edmundsbury walls, I say, were not peopled with fantasms; but with men of flesh and blood, made altogether as we are. Had thou and I then been, who knows but we ourselves had taken refuge from an evil Time, and fled to dwell here, and meditate on an Eternity, in such fashion as we could? Alas, how like an old osseous fragment, a broken blackened shin-bone of the old dead Ages, this black ruin looks out, not yet covered by the soil; still indicating what a once gigantic Life lies buried there! It is dead now, and dumb; but was alive once, and spake. For twenty generations, here was the earthly arena where painful living men worked out their life-wrestle,—looked at by Earth, by Heaven and Hell. Bells tolled to prayers; and men, of many humours, various thoughts, chanted vespers, matins;—and round the little islet of their life rolled forever (as round ours still rolls, though we are blind and deaf) the illimitable Ocean, tinting all things with *its* eternal hues and reflexes; making strange prophetic music! How silent now; all departed, clean gone. The World-Dramaturgist has written: *Exeunt.* The devouring Time-Demons have made away with it all: and in its stead, there is either nothing; or what is worse, offensive universal dust-clouds, and gray eclipse of Earth and Heaven, from ' dry rubbish shot here!'—

Truly it is no easy matter to get across the chasm of Seven Centuries, filled with such material. But here, of all helps, is not a Boswell the welcomest; even a small Boswell? Veracity, true simplicity of heart, how valuable are these always! He that speaks what *is* really in him, will find men to listen, though under never such impediments. Even gossip, springing free and cheery from a human heart, this too is a kind of veracity and *speech;*—much preferable to pedantry and inane gray haze! Jocelin is weak and garrulous, but he is human. Through the thin watery gossip of our Jocelin, we do get some glimpses of that deep-buried Time; discern veritably, though in a fitful intermittent manner, these antique figures and their life-method, face to face! Beautifully, in our earnest loving glance, the old centuries melt from opaque to partially translucent, transparent here and there; and the void black Night, one finds, is but the summing-up of innumerable peopled luminous *Days.* Not parchment Chartularies, Doctrines of the Constitution, O Dryasdust; not altogether, my erudite friend!—

Readers who please to go along with us into this poor *Jocelini Chronica* shall wander inconveniently enough, as in wintry twilight, through some poor stript hazel-grove, rustling with foolish noises, and perpetually hindering the eyesight; but across which, here and there, some real human figure is seen moving: very strange; whom we could hail if he would answer;—and we look into a pair of eyes deep as our own, *imaging* our own, but all unconscious of us; to whom we for the time are become as spirits and invisible!

CHAPTER III.

LANDLORD EDMUND.

SOME three centuries or so had elapsed since *Beodric's-worth*[1] became St. Edmund's *Stow*, St. Edmund's *Town* and Monastery, before Jocelin entered himself a Novice there. 'It was,' says he, 'the year after the Flemings were defeated at Fornham St. Genevieve.'

Much passes away into oblivion : this glorious victory over the Flemings at Fornham has, at the present date, greatly dimmed itself out of the minds of men. A victory and battle nevertheless it was, in its time : some thrice-renowned Earl of Leicester, not of the De Montfort breed (as may be read in Philosophical and other Histories, could any human memory retain such things), had quarrelled with his sovereign, Henry Second of the name ; had been worsted, it is like, and maltreated, and obliged to fly to foreign parts ; but had rallied there into new vigour ; and so, in the year 1173, returns across the German Sea with a vengeful army of Flemings. Returns, to the coast of Suffolk ; to Framlingham Castle, where he is welcomed ; westward towards St. Edmundsbury and Fornham Church, where he is met by the constituted authorities with *posse comitatus ;* and swiftly cut in pieces, he and his, or laid by the heels ; on the right bank of the obscure river Lark,—as traces still existing will verify.

For the river Lark, though not very discoverably, still runs or stagnates in that country ; and the battle-ground is there ; serving at present as a pleasure-ground to his Grace of Northumberland. Copper pennies of Henry II. are still found there ;—rotted out from the pouches of poor slain soldiers, who had not had *time* to buy liquor with them. In the river Lark itself was fished up, within man's memory, an antique gold ring ; which fond Dilettantism can almost believe may have been the very ring Countess

---

[1] Dryasdust puzzles and pokes for some biography of this Beodric ; and repugns to consider him a mere East-Anglian Person of Condition, not in need of a biography,—whose peopð, *weorth* or *worth*, that is to say, *Growth*, Increase, or as we should now name it, *Estate*, that same Hamlet and wood Mansion, now St. Edmund's Bury, originally was. For, adds our erudite Friend, the Saxon peopðan, equivalent to the German *werden*, means to *grow*, to *become ;* traces of which old vocable are still found in the North-country dialects, as, 'What is *word* of him ?' meaning 'What is *become* of him ?' and the like. Nay we in modern English still say, 'Woe *worth* the hour' (Woo *beful* the hour), and speak of the '*Weird* Sisters ;' not to mention the innumerable other names of places still ending in *weorth* or *worth*. And indeed, our common noun *worth*, in the sense of *value*, does not this mean simply, What a thing has *grown* to, What a man has *grown* to, How much he amounts to,—by the Threadneedle-street standard or another !

Leicester threw away, in her flight, into that same Lark river or ditch.[1] Nay, few years ago, in tearing out an enormous superannuated ash-tree, now grown quite corpulent, bursten, superfluous, but long a fixture in the soil, and not to be dislodged without revolution,—there was laid bare, under its roots, 'a circular mound of skeletons wonderfully complete,' all radiating from a centre, faces upwards, feet inwards; a 'radiation' not of Light, but of the Nether Darkness rather; and evidently the fruit of battle; for 'many of the heads were cleft, or had arrow-holes in them.' The Battle of Fornham, therefore, is a fact, though a forgotten one; no less obscure than undeniable,—like so many other facts.

Like the St. Edmund's Monastery itself! Who can doubt, after what we have said, that there was a Monastery here at one time? No doubt at all there was a Monastery here; no doubt, some three centuries prior to this Fornham Battle, there dwelt a man in these parts of the name of Edmund, King, Landlord, Duke or whatever his title was, of the Eastern Counties;—and a very singular man and landlord he must have been.

For his tenants, it would appear, did not in the least complain of him; his labourers did not think of burning his wheatstacks, breaking into his game-preserves; very far the reverse of all that. Clear evidence, satisfactory even to my friend Dryasdust, exists that, on the contrary, they honoured, loved, admired this ancient Landlord to a quite astonishing degree,—and indeed at last to an immeasurable and inexpressible degree; for, finding no limits or utterable words for their sense of his worth, they took to beatifying and adoring him! 'Infinite admiration,' we are taught, 'means worship.'

Very singular,—could we discover it! What Edmund's specific duties were; above all, what his method of discharging them with such results was, would surely be interesting to know; but are *not* very discoverable now. His Life has become a poetic, nay a religious *Mythus*; though, undeniably enough, it was once a prose Fact, as our poor lives are; and even a very rugged unmanageable one. This landlord Edmund did go about in leather shoes, with *femoralia* and bodycoat of some sort on him; and daily had his breakfast to procure; and daily had contradictory speeches, and most contradictory facts not a few, to reconcile with himself. No man becomes a Saint in his sleep. Edmund, for instance, instead of *reconciling* those same contradictory facts and speeches to himself,—which means *subduing*, and in a manlike and godlike manner conquering them to himself,—might have merely thrown new con-

[1] Lyttelton's History of Henry II. (2d Edition), v. 169, &c.

tention into them, new unwisdom into them, and so been conquered
by them; much the commoner case! In that way he had proved
no 'Saint,' or Divine-looking Man, but a mere Sinner, and unfortunate, blameable, more or less Diabolic-looking man! No landlord
Edmund becomes infinitely admirable in his sleep.

With what degree of wholesome rigour his rents were collected,
we hear not. Still less by what methods he preserved his game,
whether by 'bushing' or how,—and if the partridge-seasons were
'excellent,' or were indifferent. Neither do we ascertain what kind
of Corn-bill he passed, or wisely-adjusted Sliding-scale:—but indeed
there were few spinners in those days; and the nuisance of spinning, and other dusty labour, was not yet so glaring a one.

How then, it may be asked, did this Edmund rise into favour,
become to such astonishing extent a recognised Farmer's Friend?
Really, except it were by doing justly and loving mercy to an un-
precedented extent, one does not know. The man, it would seem,
'had walked,' as they say, 'humbly with God;' humbly and valiantly
with God; struggling to make the Earth heavenly as he could:
instead of walking sumptuously and pridefully with Mammon,
leaving the Earth to grow hellish as it liked. Not sumptuously
with Mammon? How then could he 'encourage trade,'—cause
Howel and James, and many wine-merchants, to bless him, and
the tailor's heart (though in a very short-sighted manner) to sing
for joy? Much in this Edmund's Life is mysterious.

That he could, on occasion, do what he liked with his own is,
meanwhile, evident enough. Certain Heathen Physical-Force Ultra-
Chartists, 'Danes' as they were then called, coming into his territory with their 'five points,' or rather with their five-and-twenty
thousand *points* and edges too, of pikes namely and battle-axes;
and proposing mere Heathenism, confiscation, spoliation, and fire
and sword,—Edmund answered that he would oppose to the utmost such savagery. They took him prisoner; again required his
sanction to said proposals. Edmund again refused. Cannot we
kill you? cried they.—Cannot I die? answered he. My life, I
think, is my own to do what I like with! And he died, under barbarous tortures, refusing to the last breath; and the Ultra-Chartist
Danes *lost* their propositions;—and went with their 'points' and
other apparatus, as is supposed, to the Devil, the Father of them.
Some say, indeed, these Danes were not Ultra-Chartists, but Ultra-
Tories, demanding to reap where they had not sown, and live in this
world without working, though all the world should starve for it;
which likewise seems a possible hypothesis. Be what they might,
they went, as we say, to the Devil; and Edmund doing what he
liked with his own, the Earth was got cleared of them.

Another version is, that Edmund on this and the like occasions stood by his order; the oldest, and indeed only true order of Nobility known under the stars, that of Just Men and Sons of God, in opposition to Unjust and Sons of Belial,—which latter indeed are *second*-oldest, but yet a very unvenerable order. This, truly, seems the likeliest hypothesis of all. Names and appearances alter so strangely, in some half-score centuries; and all fluctuates chameleon-like, taking now this hue, now that. Thus much is very plain, and does not change hue: Landlord Edmund was seen and felt by all men to have done verily a man's part in this life-pilgrimage of his; and benedictions, and outflowing love and admiration from the universal heart, were his meed. Well-done! Well-done! cried the hearts of all men. They raised his slain and martyred body; washed its wounds with fast-flowing universal tears; tears of endless pity, and yet of a sacred joy and triumph. The beautifullest kind of tears,—indeed perhaps the beautifullest kind of thing: like a sky all flashing diamonds and prismatic radiance; all weeping, yet shone on by the everlasting Sun :—and *this* is not a sky, it is a Soul and living Face! Nothing liker the *Temple of the Highest*, bright with some real effulgence of the Highest, is seen in this world.

Oh, if all Yankee-land follow a small good ' Schnüspel the distinguished Novelist' with blazing torches, dinner-invitations, universal hep-hep-hurrah, feeling that he, though small, *is* something; how might all Angle-land once follow a hero-martyr and great true Son of Heaven! It is the very joy of man's heart to admire, where he can; nothing so lifts him from all his mean imprisonments, were it but for moments, as true admiration. Thus it has been said, ' all men, especially all women, are born worshipers;' and will worship, if it be but possible. Possible to worship a Something, even a small one; not so possible a mere loud-blaring Nothing! What sight is more pathetic than that of poor multitudes of persons met to gaze at Kings' Progresses, Lord Mayors' Shows, and other gilt-gingerbread phenomena of the worshipful sort, in these times; each so eager to worship; each, with a dim fatal sense of disappointment, finding that he cannot rightly here! These be thy gods, O Israel? And thou art so *willing* to worship,—poor Israel!

In this manner, however, did the men of the Eastern Counties take up the slain body of their Edmund, where it lay cast forth in the village of Hoxne; seek out the severed head, and reverently reunite the same. They embalmed him with myrrh and sweet spices, with love, pity, and all high and awful thoughts; consecrating him with a very storm of melodious adoring admiration,

I

and sun-dyed showers of tears;—joyfully, yet with awe (as all deep joy has something of the awful in it), commemorating his noble deeds and godlike walk and conversation while on Earth. Till, at length, the very Pope and Cardinals at Rome were forced to hear of it; and they, summing up as correctly as they well could, with *Advocatus-Diaboli* pleadings and their other forms of process, the general verdict of mankind, declared: That he had, in very fact, led a hero's life in this world; and being now *gone*, was gone, as they conceived, to God above, and reaping his reward *there*. Such, they said, was the best judgment they could form of the case;— and truly not a bad judgment. Acquiesced in, zealously adopted, with full assent of ' private judgment,' by all mortals.

The rest of St. Edmund's history, for the reader sees he has now become a *Saint*, is easily conceivable. Pious munificence provided him a *loculus*, a *feretrum* or shrine; built for him a wooden chapel, a stone temple, ever widening and growing by new pious gifts;—such the overflowing heart feels it a blessedness to solace itself by giving. St. Edmund's Shrine glitters now with diamond flowerages, with a plating of wrought gold. The wooden chapel, as we say, has become a stone temple. Stately masonries, long-drawn arches, cloisters, sounding aisles buttress it, begirdle it far and wide. Regimented companies of men, of whom our Jocelin is one, devote themselves, in every generation, to meditate here on man's Nobleness and Awfulness, and celebrate and show forth the same, as they best can,—thinking they will do it better here, in presence of God the Maker, and of the so Awful and so Noble made by Him. In one word, St. Edmund's Body has raised a Monastery round it. To such length, in such manner, has the Spirit of the Time visibly taken body, and crystallised itself here. New gifts, houses, farms, *katalla*[1]— come ever in. King Knut, whom men call Canute, whom the Ocean-tide would not be forbidden to wet, —we heard already of this wise King, with his crown and gifts; but of many others, Kings, Queens, wise men and noble loyal women, let Dryasdust and divine Silence be the record! Beodric's-Worth has become St. Edmund's *Bury*;—and lasts visible to this hour. All this that thou now seest, and namest Bury Town, is properly the Funeral Monument of Saint or Landlord Edmund. The present respectable Mayor of Bury may be said, like a Fakeer (little as he thinks of it), to have his dwelling in the extensive, many-sculptured Tombstone of St. Edmund; in one of the brick niches thereof dwells the present respectable Mayor of Bury.

---

[1] Goods, properties; what we now call *chattels*, and still more singularly *cattle*, says my erudite friend!

Certain Times do crystallise themselves in a magnificent manner; and others, perhaps, are like to do it in rather a shabby one! —But Richard Arkwright too will have his Monument a thousand years hence: all Lancashire and Yorkshire, and how many other shires and countries, with their machineries and industries, for his monument! A true *pyramid* or '*flame*-mountain,' flaming with steam fires and useful labour over wide continents, usefully towards the Stars, to a certain height;—how much grander than your foolish Cheops Pyramids or Sakhara clay ones! Let us withal be hopeful, be content or patient.

CHAPTER IV.

ABBOT HUGO.

IT is true, all things have two faces, a light one and a dark. It is true, in three centuries much imperfection accumulates; many an Ideal, monastic or other, shooting forth into practice as it can, grows to a strange enough Reality; and we have to ask with amazement, Is this your Ideal! For, alas, the Ideal always has to grow in the Real, and to seek out its bed and board there, often in a very sorry way. No beautifullest Poet is a Bird-of-Paradise, living on perfumes; sleeping in the æther with outspread wings. The Heroic, *independent* of bed and board, is found in Drury-Lane Theatre only; to avoid disappointments, let us bear this in mind.

By the law of Nature, too, all manner of Ideals have their fatal limits and lot; their appointed periods, of youth, of maturity or perfection, of decline, degradation, and final death and disappearance. There is nothing born but has to die. Ideal monasteries, once grown real, do seek bed and board in this world; do find it more and more successfully; do get at length too intent on finding it, exclusively intent on that. They are then like diseased corpulent bodies fallen idiotic, which merely eat and sleep; *ready* for ' dissolution,' by a Henry the Eighth or some other. Jocelin's St. Edmundsbury is still far from this last dreadful state: but here too the reader will prepare himself to see an Ideal not sleeping in the æther like a bird-of-paradise, but roosting as the common woodfowl do, in an imperfect, uncomfortable, more or less contemptible manner!—

Abbot Hugo, as Jocelin, breaking at once into the heart of the business, apprises us, had in those days grown old, grown rather blind, and his eyes were somewhat darkened, *aliquantulum caliga-*

verunt oculi ejus. He dwelt apart very much, in his *Talamus* or peculiar Chamber; got into the hands of flatterers, a set of mealy-mouthed persons who strove to make the passing hour easy for him,—for him easy, and for themselves profitable; accumulating in the distance mere mountains of confusion. Old Dominus Hugo sat inaccessible in this way, far in the interior, wrapt in his warm flannels and delusions; inaccessible to all voice of Fact; and bad grew ever worse with us. Not that our worthy old *Dominus Abbas* was inattentive to the divine offices, or to the maintenance of a devout spirit in us or in himself; but the Account-Books of the Convent fell into the frightfullest state, and Hugo's annual Budget grew yearly emptier, or filled with futile expectations, fatal deficit, wind and debts!

His one worldly care was to raise ready money; sufficient for the day is the evil thereof. And how he raised it: From usurious insatiable Jews; every fresh Jew sticking on him like a fresh horse-leech, sucking his and our life out; crying continually, Give, give! Take one example instead of scores. Our *Camera* having fallen into ruin, William the Sacristan received charge to repair it; strict charge, but no money; Abbot Hugo would, and indeed could, give him no fraction of money. The *Camera* in ruins, and Hugo penni-less and inaccessible, Willelmus Sacrista borrowed Forty Marcs (some Seven-and-twenty Pounds) of Benedict the Jew, and patched up our Camera again. But the means of repaying him? There were no means. Hardly could *Sacrista, Cellerarius,* or any public officer, get ends to meet, on the indispensablest scale, with their shrunk allowances: ready money had vanished.

Benedict's Twenty-seven pounds grew rapidly at compound-interest; and at length, when it had amounted to a Hundred pounds, he, on a day of settlement, presents the account to Hugo himself. Hugo already owed him another Hundred of his own; and so here it has become Two Hundred! Hugo, in a fine frenzy, threatens to depose the Sacristan, to do this and do that; but, in the mean while, How to quiet your insatiable Jew? Hugo, for this couple of hundreds, grants the Jew his bond for Four hundred payable at the end of four years. At the end of four years there is, of course, still no money; and the Jew now gets a bond for Eight hundred and eighty pounds, to be paid by instalments, Fourscore pounds every year. Here was a way of doing business!

Neither yet is this insatiable Jew satisfied or settled with: he had papers against us of 'small debts fourteen years old;' his modest claim amounts finally to 'Twelve hundred pounds besides interest;'—and one hopes he never got satisfied in this world; one almost hopes he was one of those beleaguered Jews who hanged themselves in York Castle shortly afterwards, and had his usances and quittances and horseleech papers summarily set fire to! For approximate justice will strive to accomplish itself; if not in one way, then in another. Jews, and also Christians and Heathens, who accumulate in this manner, though furnished with never so many parchments, do, at times, 'get their grinder-teeth successively pulled out of their head, each day a new grinder,' till they consent to disgorge again. A sad fact,—worth reflecting on.

Jocelin, we see, is not without secularity: Our *Dominus Abbas* was intent enough on the divine offices; but then his Account-Books —?— One of the things that strike us most, throughout, in Jocelin's *Chronicle*, and indeed in Eadmer's *Anselm*, and other old monastic Books, written evidently by pious men, is this, That there is almost no mention whatever of 'personal religion' in them; that the whole gist of their thinking and speculation seems to be the 'privileges of our order,' 'strict exaction of our dues,' 'God's honour' (meaning the honour of our Saint), and so forth. Is not this singular? A body of men, set apart for perfecting and purifying their own souls, do not seem disturbed about that in any measure: the 'Ideal' says nothing about its idea; says much about finding bed and board for itself! How is this?

Why, for one thing, bed and board are a matter very apt to come to speech: it is much easier to *speak* of them than of ideas; and they are sometimes much more pressing with some! Nay, for another thing, may not this religious reticence, in these devout good souls, be perhaps a merit, and sign of health in them? Jocelin, Eadmer, and such religious men, have as yet nothing of 'Methodism;' no Doubt or even root of Doubt. Religion is not a diseased self-introspection, an agonising inquiry: their duties are clear to them, the way of supreme good plain, indisputable, and they are travelling on it. Religion lies over them like an all-embracing heavenly canopy, like an atmosphere and life-element, which is not spoken of, which in all things is presupposed without speech. Is not serene or complete Religion the highest aspect of human nature; as serene Cant, or complete No-religion, is the lowest and miserablest? Between which two, all manner of earnest Methodisms, introspections, agonising inquiries, never so morbid, shall play their respective parts, not without approbation.

But let any reader fancy himself one of the Brethren in St. Edmundsbury Monastery under such circumstances! How can a Lord Abbot, all stuck over with horseleeches of this nature, front the world? He is fast losing his life-blood, and the Convent will be

as one of Pharaoh's lean kine. Old monks of experience draw their
hoods deeper down; careful what they say: the monk's first duty
is obedience. Our Lord the King, hearing of such work, sends
down his Almoner to. make investigations: but what boots it?
Abbot Hugo assembles us in Chapter; asks, " If there is any complaint ?" Not a soul of us dare answer, "Yes, thousands !" but we
all stand silent, and the Prior even says that things are in a very
comfortable condition. Whereupon old Abbot Hugo, turning to the
royal messenger, says, "You see !"—and the business terminates
in that way. I, as a brisk-eyed, noticing youth and novice, could
not help asking of the elders, asking of Magister Samson in particular: Why he, well-instructed and a knowing man, had not
spoken out, and brought matters to a bearing? Magister Samson
was Teacher of the Novices, appointed to breed us up to the rules,
and I loved him well. "*Fili mi*," answered Samson, "the burnt
child shuns the fire. Dost thou not know, our Lord the Abbot
sent me once to Acre in Norfolk, to solitary confinement and
bread and water, already? The Hinghams, Hugo and Robert, have
just got home from banishment for speaking. This is the hour of
darkness: the hour when flatterers rule and are believed. *Videat
Dominus*, let the Lord see, and judge."

In very truth, what could poor old Abbot Hugo do? A frail
old man; and the Philistines were upon him,—that is to say, the
Hebrews. He had nothing for it but to shrink away from them;
get back into his warm flannels, into his warm delusions again.
Happily, before it was quite too late, he bethought him of pilgrim-
ing to St. Thomas of Canterbury. He set out, with a fit train, in
the autumn days of the year 1180; near Rochester City, his mule
threw him, dislocated his poor kneepan, raised incurable inflam-
matory fever; and the poor old man got his dismissal from the
whole coil at once. St. Thomas à Becket, though in a circuitous
way, had *brought* deliverance! Neither Jew usurers, nor grumbling
monks, nor other importunate despicability of men or mud-ele-
ments afflicted Abbot Hugo any more; but he dropt his rosaries,
closed his account-books, closed his old eyes, and lay down into
the long sleep. Heavy-laden hoary old Dominus Hugo, fare thee
well.

One thing we cannot mention without a due thrill of horror:
namely, that, in the empty exchequer of Dominus Hugo, there was
not found one penny to distribute to the Poor that they might pray
for his soul! By a kind of godsend, Fifty shillings did, in the very
nick of time, fall due, or seem to fall due, from one of his Farmers
(the *Firmarius* de Palegrava), and he paid it, and the Poor had it ;
though, alas, this too only *seemed* to fall due, and we had it to pay

again afterwards. Dominus Hugo's apartments were plundered
by his servants, to the last portable stool, in a few minutes after
the breath was out of his body. Forlorn old Hugo, fare thee well
forever.

CHAPTER V.

TWELFTH CENTURY.

OUR Abbot being dead, the *Dominus Rex*, Henry II., or Ranulf de
Glanvill *Justiciarius* of England for him, set Inspectors or Custodiars over us ;—not in any breathless haste to appoint a new Abbot,
our revenues coming into his own *Scaccarium*, or royal Exchequer,
in the mean while. They proceeded with some rigour, these Custodiars; took written inventories, clapt-on seals, exacted everywhere
strict tale and measure : but wherefore should a living monk complain? The living monk has to do his devotional drill-exercise ;
consume his allotted *pitantia*, what we call *pittance*, or ration of
victual ; and possess his soul in patience.

Dim, as through a long vista of Seven Centuries, dim and very
strange looks that monk-life to us; the ever-surprising circumstance this, That it is a *fact* and no dream, that we see it there,
and gaze into the very eyes of it! Smoke rises daily from those
culinary chimney-throats; there are living human beings there,
who chant, loud-braying, their matins, nones, vespers; awakening
echoes, not to the bodily ear alone. St. Edmund's Shrine, perpetually illuminated, glows ruddy through the Night, and through
the Night of Centuries withal; St. Edmundsbury Town paying
yearly Forty pounds for that express end. Bells clang out; on
great occasions, all the bells. We have Processions, Preachings,
Festivals, Christmas Plays, *Mysteries* shown in the Churchyard, at
which latter the Townsfolk sometimes quarrel. Time was, Time
is, as Friar Bacon's Brass Head remarked ; and withal Time will
be. There are three Tenses, *Tempora*, or Times ; and there is one
Eternity; and as for us,

'We are such stuff as Dreams are made of!'

Indisputable, though very dim to modern vision, rests on its
hill-slope that same *Bury*, *Stow*, or Town of St. Edmund; already
a considerable place, not without traffic, nay manufactures, would
Jocelin only tell us what. Jocelin is totally careless of telling:
but, through dim fitful apertures, we can see *Fullones*, 'Fullers,'
see cloth-making; looms dimly going, dye-vats, and old women
spinning yarn. We have Fairs too, *Nundinæ*, in due course; and

the Londoners give us much trouble, pretending that they, as a metropolitan people, are exempt from toll. Besides there is Field-husbandry, with perplexed settlement of Convent rents: corn-ricks pile themselves within burgh, in their season; and cattle depart and enter; and even the poor weaver has his cow,—'dungheaps' lying quiet at most doors (*ante foras*, says the incidental Jocelin), for the Town has yet no improved police. Watch and ward nevertheless we do keep, and have Gates,—as what Town must not; thieves so abounding; war, *werra*, such a frequent thing! Our thieves, at the Abbot's judgment-bar, deny; claim wager of battle; fight, are beaten, and *then* hanged. 'Ketel, the thief,' took this course; and it did nothing for him,—merely brought us, and indeed himself, new trouble!

Everyway a most foreign Time. What difficulty, for example, has our *Cellerarius* to collect the *repselver*, 'reaping silver,' or penny, which each householder is by law bound to pay for cutting down the Convent grain! Richer people pretend that it is commuted, that it is this and the other; that, in short, they will not pay it. Our *Cellerarius* gives up calling on the rich. In the houses of the poor, our *Cellerarius* finding, in like manner, neither penny nor good promise, snatches, without ceremony, what *vadium* (pledge, *wad*) he can come at: a joint-stool, kettle, nay the very house-door, '*hostium*;' and old women, thus exposed to the unfeeling gaze of the public, rush out after him with their distaffs and the angriest shrieks: '*vetulæ exibant cum colis suis*,' says Jocelin, '*minantes et exprobrantes.*'

What a historical picture, glowing visible, as St. Edmund's Shrine by night, after Seven long Centuries or so! *Vetulæ cum colis*: My venerable ancient spinning grandmothers,—ah, and ye too have to shriek, and rush out with your distaffs; and become Female Chartists, and scold all evening with void doorway;—and in old Saxon, as we in modern, would fain demand some Five-point Charter, could it be fallen in with, the Earth being too tyrannous! —Wise Lord Abbots, hearing of such phenomena, did in time abolish or commute the reap-penny, and one nuisance was abated. But the image of these justly offended old women, in their old wool costumes, with their angry features, and spindles brandished, lives forever in the historical memory. Thanks to thee, Jocelin Boswell. Jerusalem was taken by the Crusaders, and again lost by them; and Richard Cœur-de-Lion 'veiled his face' as he passed in sight of it: but how many other things went on, the while!

Thus, too, our trouble with the Lakenheath eels is very great. King Knut namely, or rather his Queen who also did herself honour by honouring St. Edmund, decreed by authentic deed yet extant on parchment, that the Holders of the Town Fields, once Beodric's, should, for one thing, go yearly and catch us four thousand eels in the marsh-pools of Lakenheath. Well, they went, they continued to go; but, in later times, got into the way of returning with a most short account of eels. Not the due six-score apiece; no, Here are two-score, Here are twenty, ten,—sometimes, Here are none at all; Heaven help us, we *could* catch no more, they were not there! What is a distressed *Cellrarius* to do? We agree that each Holder of so many acres shall pay one penny yearly, and let go the eels as too slippery. But alas, neither is this quite effectual: the Fields, in my time, have got divided among so many hands, there is no catching of *them* either; I have known our Cellarer get seven-and-twenty pence formerly, and now it is much if he get ten pence farthing (*vix decem denarios et obolum*). And·then their sheep, which they are bound to fold nightly in our pens, for the manure's sake; and, I fear, do not always fold: and their *averpennies*, and their *avragiums*, and their *fodercorns*, and mill-and-market dues! Thus, in its undeniable but dim manner, does old St. Edmundsbury spin and till, and laboriously keep its pot boiling, and St. Edmund's Shrine lighted, under such conditions and averages as it can.

How much is still alive in England; how much has not yet come into life! A Feudal Aristocracy is still alive, in the prime of life; superintending the cultivation of the land, and less consciously the distribution of the produce of the land, the adjustment of the quarrels of the land; judging, soldiering, adjusting; everywhere governing the people,—so that even a Gurth born thrall of Cedric lacks not his due parings of the pigs he tends. Governing; —and, alas, also game-preserving, so that a Robert Hood, a William Scarlet and others have, in these days, put on Lincoln coats, and taken to living, in some universal-suffrage manner, under the greenwood-tree!

How silent, on the other hand, lie all Cotton-trades and such like; not a steeple-chimney yet got on end from sea to sea! North of the Humber, a stern Willelmus Conquestor burnt the Country, finding it unruly, into very stern repose. Wild fowl scream in those ancient silences, wild cattle roam in those ancient solitudes; the scanty sulky Norse-bred population all coerced into silence,—feeling that, under these new Norman Governors, their history has probably as good as *ended*. Men and Northumbrian Norse populations know little what has ended, what is but beginning! The Ribble and the Aire roll down, as yet unpolluted by dyers' chemistry; tenanted by merry trouts and piscatory otters;

the sunbeam and the vacant wind's-blast alone traversing those moors. Side by side sleep the coal-strata and the iron-strata for so many ages; no Steam-Demon has yet risen smoking into being. Saint Mungo rules in Glasgow; James Watt still slumbering in the deep of Time. *Mancunium*, Manceaster, what we now call Manchester, spins no cotton,—if it be not *wool* 'cottons,' clipped from the backs of mountain sheep. The Creek of the Mersey gurgles, twice in the four-and-twenty hours, with eddying brine, clangorous with sea-fowl; and is a *Lither*-Pool, a *lazy* or sullen Pool, no monstrous pitchy City, and Seahaven of the world! The Centuries are big; and the birth-hour is coming, not yet come. *Tempus ferax, tempus edax rerum.*

CHAPTER VI.

MONK SAMSON.

WITHIN doors, down at the hill-foot, in our Convent here, we are a peculiar people,—hardly conceivable in the Arkwright Corn-Law ages, of mere Spinning-Mills and Joe-Mantons! There is yet no Methodism among us, and we speak much of Secularities: no Methodism; our Religion is not yet a horrible restless Doubt, still less a far horribler composed Cant; but a great heaven-high Unquestionability, encompassing, interpenetrating the whole of Life. Imperfect as we may be, we are here, with our litanies, shaven crowns, vows of poverty, to testify incessantly and indisputably to every heart, That this Earthly Life and *its* riches and possessions, and good and evil hap, are not intrinsically a reality at all, but *are* a shadow of realities eternal, infinite; that this Time-world, as an air-image, fearfully *emblematic*, plays and flickers in the grand still mirror of Eternity; and man's little Life has Duties that are great, that are alone great, and go up to Heaven and down to Hell. This, with our poor litanies, we testify and struggle to testify.

Which, testified or not, remembered by all men, or forgotten by all men, does verily remain the fact, even in Arkwright Joe-Manton ages! But it is incalculable, when litanies have grown obsolete; when *fodercorns*, *avragiums*, and all human dues and reciprocities have been fully changed into one great due of *cash payment*; and man's duty to man reduces itself to handing him certain metal coins, or covenanted money-wages, and then shoving him out of doors; and man's duty to God becomes a cant, a doubt, a dim inanity, a 'pleasure of virtue' or such like; and the thing a man does infinitely fear (the real *Hell* of a man) is, 'that he do not make money and advance himself,'—I say, it is incalculable what a change has introduced itself everywhere into human affairs! How human affairs shall now circulate everywhere not healthy life-blood in them, but, as it were, a detestable copperas banker's ink; and all is grown acrid, divisive, threatening dissolution; and the huge tumultuous Life of Society is galvanic, devil-ridden, too truly possessed by a devil! For, in short, Mammon *is* not a god at all; but a devil, and even a very despicable devil. Follow the Devil faithfully, you are sure enough to *go* to the Devil: whither else can you go?—In such situations, men look back with a kind of mournful recognition even on poor limited Monk-figures, with their poor litanies; and reflect, with Ben Jonson, that soul is indispensable, some degree of soul, even to save you the expense of salt!—

For the rest, it must be owned, we Monks of St. Edmundsbury are but a limited class of creatures, and seem to have a somewhat dull life of it. Much given to idle gossip; having indeed no other work, when our chanting is over. Listless gossip, for most part, and a mitigated slander; the fruit of idleness, not of spleen. We are dull, insipid men, many of us; easy-minded; whom prayer and digestion of food will avail for a life. We have to receive all strangers in our Convent, and lodge them gratis; such and such sorts go by rule to the Lord Abbot and his special revenues; such and such to us and our poor Cellarer, however straitened. Jews themselves send their wives and little ones hither in war-time, into our *Pitanceria;* where they abide safe, with due *pittances,*— for a consideration. We have the fairest chances for collecting news. Some of us have a turn for reading Books; for meditation, silence; at times we even write Books. Some of us can preach, in English-Saxon, in Norman-French, and even in Monk-Latin; others cannot in any language or jargon, being stupid.

Failing all else, what gossip about one another! This is a perennial resource. How one hooded head applies itself to the ear of another, and whispers—*tacenda.* Willelmus Sacrista, for instance, what does he nightly, over in that Sacristy of his? Frequent bibations, '*frequentes bibationes et quædam tacenda,*'—eheu! We have '*tempora minutionis,*' stated seasons of blood-letting, when we are all let blood together; and then there is a general free-conference, a sanhedrim of clatter. Notwithstanding our vow of poverty, we can by rule amass to the extent of 'two shillings;' but it is to be given to our necessitous kindred, or in charity. Poor Monks! Thus too a certain Canterbury Monk was in the habit of 'slipping, *clanculo* from his sleeve,' five shillings into the hand of his mother, when she came to see him, at the divine offices, every two months. Once, slipping the money clandestinely, just in the act of taking leave, he slipt it not into her hand but on the floor, and another had it; whereupon the poor Monk, coming to know it, looked mere despair for some days; till Lanfranc the noble Archbishop, questioning his secret from him, nobly made the sum *seven* shillings,[1] and said, Never mind!

One Monk of a taciturn nature distinguishes himself among these babbling ones: the name of him Samson; he that answered Jocelin, "*Fili mi*, a burnt child shuns the fire." They call him 'Norfolk *Barrator*,' or litigious person; for indeed, being of grave taciturn ways, he is not universally a favourite; he has been in trouble more than once. The reader is desired to mark this Monk. A personable man of seven-and-forty; stout-made, stands erect as a pillar; with bushy eyebrows, the eyes of him beaming into you in a really strange way; the face massive, grave, with 'a very eminent nose;' his head almost bald, its auburn remnants of hair, and the copious ruddy beard, getting slightly streaked with gray. This is Brother Samson; a man worth looking at.

He is from Norfolk, as the nickname indicates; from Tottington in Norfolk, as we guess; the son of poor parents there. He has told me, Jocelin, for I loved him much, That once in his ninth year he had an alarming dream;—as indeed we are all somewhat given to dreaming here. Little Samson, lying uneasily in his crib at Tottington, dreamed that he saw the Arch Enemy in person, just alighted in front of some grand building, with outspread bat-wings, and stretching forth detestable clawed hands to grip him, little Samson, and fly off with him: whereupon the little dreamer shrieked desperate to St. Edmund for help, shrieked and again shrieked; and St. Edmund, a reverend heavenly figure, did come,—and indeed poor little Samson's mother, awakened by his shrieking, did come; and the Devil and the Dream both fled away fruitless. On the morrow, his mother, pondering such an awful dream, thought it were good to take him over to St. Edmund's own Shrine, and pray with him there. See, said, little Samson at sight of the Abbey-Gate; see, mother, this is the building I dreamed of! His poor mother dedicated him to St. Edmund,—left him there with prayers and tears: what better could she do? The exposition of the dream, Brother Samson used to say, was this: *Diabolus* with outspread bat-wings shadowed forth the pleasures of this world, *voluptates hujus sæculi*, which were about to snatch and fly away with me, had not St. Edmund flung his arms round me, that is to say, made me a monk of his. A

[1] Eadmeri Hist. p. 8.

monk, accordingly, Brother Samson is; and here to this day where his mother left him. A learned man, of devout grave nature; has studied at Paris, has taught in the Town Schools here, and done much else; can preach in three languages, and, like Dr. Caius, 'has had losses' in his time. A thoughtful, firm-standing man; much loved by some, not loved by all; his clear eyes flashing into you, in an almost inconvenient way!

Abbot Hugo, as we said, had his own difficulties with him; Abbot Hugo had him in prison once, to teach him what authority was, and how to dread the fire in future. For Brother Samson, in the time of the Antipopes, had been sent to Rome on business; and, returning successful, was too late,—the business had all misgone in the interim! As tours to Rome are still frequent with us English, perhaps the reader will not grudge to look at the method of travelling thither in those remote ages. We happily have, in small compass, a personal narrative of it. Through the clear eyes and memory of Brother Samson, one peeps direct into the very bosom of that Twelfth Century, and finds it rather curious. The actual *Papa*, Father, or universal President of Christendom, as yet not grown chimerical, sat there; think of that only! Brother Samson went to Rome as to the real Light-fountain of this lower world; we now —!— But let us hear Brother Samson, as to his mode of travelling:

'You know what trouble I had for that Church of Woolpit;
'how I was despatched to Rome in the time of the Schism be-
'tween Pope Alexander and Octavian; and passed through Italy
'at that season, when all clergy carrying letters for our Lord
'Pope Alexander were laid hold of, and some were clapt in prison,
'some hanged; and some, with nose and lips cut off, were sent
'forward to our Lord the Pope, for the disgrace and confusion of
'him (*in dedecus et confusionem ejus*). I, however, pretended to be
'Scotch, and putting on the garb of a Scotchman, and taking the
'gesture of one, walked along; and when anybody mocked at me,
'I would brandish my staff in the manner of that weapon they
'call *gaveloc*,[1] uttering comminatory words after the way of the
'Scotch. To those that met and questioned me who I was, I
'made no answer but: *Ride, ride Rome; turne Cantwereberei.*[2] Thus
'did I, to conceal myself and my errand, and get safer to Rome
'under the guise of a Scotchman.

'Having at last obtained a Letter from our Lord the Pope

[1] Javelin, missile pike. *Gaveloc* is still the Scotch name for *crowbar*.
[2] Does this mean, "Rome forever; Canterbury *not*" (which claims an unjust Supremacy over us)! Mr. Rokewood is silent. Dryasdust would perhaps explain it,—in the course of a week or two of talking; did one dare to question him!

' according to my wishes, I turned homewards again. I had to
' pass through a certain strong town on my road; and lo, the
' soldiers thereof surrounded me, seizing me, and saying: " This
' vagabond (*iste solivagus*), who pretends to be Scotch, is either a
' spy, or has Letters from the false Pope Alexander." And whilst
' they examined every stitch and rag of me, my leggings (*caligas*),
' breeches, and even the old shoes that I carried over my shoulder
' in the way of the Scotch,—I put my hand into the leather scrip
' I wore, wherein our Lord the Pope's Letter lay, close by a little
' jug (*ciffus*) I had for drinking out of; and the Lord God so
' pleasing, and St. Edmund, I got out both the Letter and the jug
' together; in such a way that, extending my arm aloft, I held
' the Letter hidden between jug and hand: they saw the jug, but
' the Letter they saw not. And thus I escaped out of their hands
' in the name of the Lord. Whatever money I had, they took from
' me; wherefore I had to beg from door to door, without any pay-
' ment (*sine omni expensa*) till I came to England again. But hear-
' ing that the Woolpit Church was already given to Geoffry Ridell,
' my soul was struck with sorrow because I had laboured in vain.
' Coming home, therefore, I sat me down secretly under the
' Shrine of St. Edmund, fearing lest our Lord Abbot should seize
' and imprison me, though I had done no mischief; nor was there
' a monk who durst speak to me, nor a laic who durst bring me
' food except by stealth.'[1]

Such resting and welcoming found Brother Samson, with his
worn soles, and strong heart! He sits silent, revolving many
thoughts, at the foot of St. Edmund's Shrine. In the wide Earth,
if it be not Saint Edmund, what friend or refuge has he? Our
Lord Abbot, hearing of him, sent the proper officer to lead him
down to prison, and clap ' foot-gyves on him' there. Another poor
official furtively brought him a cup of wine; bade him "be comforted in the Lord." Samson utters no complaint; obeys in silence. ' Our Lord Abbot, taking counsel of it, banished me to
Acre, and there I had to stay long.'

Our Lord Abbot next tried Samson with promotions; made
him Subsacristan, made him Librarian, which he liked best of all,
being passionately fond of Books: Samson, with many thoughts
in him, again obeyed in silence; discharged his offices to perfection, but never thanked our Lord Abbot,—seemed rather as if
looking into him, with those clear eyes of his. Whereupon Abbot
Hugo said, *Se nunquam vidisse*, He had never seen such a man;
whom no severity would break to complain, and no kindness soften
into smiles or thanks:—a questionable kind of man!

[1] Jocelini Chronica, p. 36.

In this way, not without troubles, but still in an erect clear-standing manner, has Brother Samson reached his forty-seventh year; and his ruddy beard is getting slightly grizzled. He is endeavouring, in these days, to have various broken things thatched in; nay perhaps to have the Choir itself completed, for he can bear nothing ruinous. He has gathered ' heaps of lime and sand;' has masons, slaters working, he and *Warinus monachus noster*, who are joint keepers of the Shrine; paying out the money duly,—furnished by charitable burghers of St. Edmundsbury, they say. Charitable burghers of St. Edmundsbury? To me Jocelin it seems rather, Samson, and Warinus whom he leads, have privily hoarded the oblations at the Shrine itself, in these late years of indolent dilapidation, while Abbot Hugo sat wrapt inaccessible; and are struggling, in this prudent way, to have the rain kept out![1]—Under what conditions, sometimes, has Wisdom to struggle with Folly; get Folly persuaded to so much as thatch out the rain from itself! For, indeed, if the Infant govern the Nurse, what dextrous practice on the Nurse's part will not be necessary!

It is a new regret to us that, in these circumstances, our Lord the King's Custodiars, interfering, prohibited all building or thatching from whatever source; and no Choir shall be completed, and Rain and Time, for the present, shall have their way. Willelmus Sacrista, he of ' the frequent bibations and some things not to be spoken of;' he, with his red nose, I am of opinion, had made complaint to the Custodiars; wishing to do Samson an ill turn:— Samson his *Sub*-sacristan, with those clear eyes, could not be a prime favourite of his! Samson again obeys in silence.

CHAPTER VII.

THE CANVASSING.

Now, however, come great news to St. Edmundsbury: That there is to be an Abbot elected; that our interlunar obscuration is to cease; St. Edmund's Convent no more to be a doleful widow, but joyous and once again a bride! Often in our widowed state had we prayed to the Lord and St. Edmund, singing weekly a matter of ' one-and-twenty penitential Psalms, on our knees in the Choir,' that a fit Pastor might be vouchsafed us. And, says Jocelin, had some known what Abbot we were to get, they had not been so devout, I believe!—Bozzy Jocelin opens to mankind the floodgates

[1] Jocelini Chronica, p. 7.

of authentic Convent gossip; we listen, as in a Dionysius' Ear,
to the inanest hubbub, like the voices at Virgil's Horn-Gate of
Dreams. Even gossip, seven centuries off, has significance. List,
list, how like men are to one another in all centuries:

' *Dixit quidam de quodam*, A certain person said of a certain
' person, " He, that *Frater*, is a good monk, *probabilis persona;*
' knows much of the order and customs of the church; and though
' not so perfect a philosopher as some others, would make a very
' good Abbot. Old Abbot Ording, still famed among us, knew
' little of letters. Besides, as we read in Fables, it is better to
' choose a log for king, than a serpent never so wise, that will
' venomously hiss and bite his subjects."—"Impossible!" an-
' swered the other: " How can such a man make a sermon in the
' Chapter, or to the people on festival days, when he is without
' letters? How can he have the skill to bind and to loose, he who
' does not understand the Scriptures? How—?"'

And then ' another said of another, *alius de alio*, " That *Frater*
' is a *homo literatus*, eloquent, sagacious; vigorous in discipline;
' loves the Convent much, has suffered much for its sake." To
' which a third party answers, "From all your great clerks good
' Lord deliver us! From Norfolk barrators, and surly persons,
' That it would please thee to preserve us, We beseech thee to
' hear us, good Lord!"' Then another *quidam* said of another
' *quodam*, " That *Frater* is a good manager (*husebondus*);" but was
' swiftly answered, "God forbid that a man who can neither read
' nor chant, nor celebrate the divine offices, an unjust person
' withal, and grinder of the faces of the poor, should ever be Ab-
' bot!"' One man, it appears, is nice in his victuals. Another is
indeed wise; but apt to slight inferiors; hardly at the pains to
answer, if they argue with him too foolishly. And so each *aliquis*
concerning his *aliquo*,—through whole pages of electioneering babble. ' For,' says Jocelin, ' So many men, as many minds.' Our
Monks ' at time of blood-letting, *tempore minutionis*,' holding their
sanhedrim of babble, would talk in this manner: Brother Samson,
I remarked, never said anything; sat silent, sometimes smiling;
but he took good note of what others said, and would bring it up,
on occasion, twenty years after. As for me Jocelin, I was of opinion that ' some skill in Dialectics, to distinguish true from false,'
would be good in an Abbot. I spake, as a rash Novice in those
days, some conscientious words of a certain benefactor of mine;
' and behold, one of those sons of Belial' ran and reported them to
him, so that he never after looked at me with the same face again!
Poor Bozzy!—

Such is the buzz and frothy simmering ferment of the general mind and no-mind; struggling to 'make itself up,' as the phrase is, or ascertain what *it* does really want: no easy matter, in most cases. St. Edmundsbury, in that Candlemas season of the year 1182, is a busily fermenting place. The very clothmakers sit meditative at their looms; asking, Who shall be Abbot? The *sochemanni* speak of it, driving their ox-teams afield; the old women with their spindles: and none yet knows what the days will bring forth.

The Prior, however, as our interim chief, must proceed to work; get ready 'Twelve Monks,' and set off with them to his Majesty at Waltham, there shall the election be made. An election, whether managed directly by ballot-box on public hustings, or indirectly by force of public opinion, or were it even by open alehouses, landlords' coercion, popular club-law, or whatever electoral methods, is always an interesting phenomenon. A mountain tumbling in great travail, throwing up dustclouds and absurd noises, is visibly there; uncertain yet what mouse or monster it will give birth to.

Besides, it is a most important social act; nay, at bottom, the one important social act. Given the men a People choose, the People itself, in its exact worth and worthlessness, is given. A heroic people chooses heroes, and is happy; a valet or flunkey people chooses sham-heroes, what are called quacks, thinking them heroes, and is not happy. The grand summary of a man's spiritual condition, what brings out all his herohood and insight, or all his flunkeyhood and horn-eyed dimness, is this question put to him, What man dost thou honour? Which is thy ideal of a man; or nearest that? So too of a People: for a People too, every People, *speaks* its choice,—were it only by silently obeying, and not revolting,—in the course of a century or so. Nor are electoral methods, Reform Bills and such like, unimportant. A People's electoral methods are, in the long-run, the express image of its electoral *talent;* tending and gravitating perpetually, irresistibly, to a conformity with that: and are, at all stages, very significant of the People. Judicious readers, of these times, are not disinclined to see how Monks elect their Abbot in the Twelfth Century: how the St. Edmundsbury mountain manages its midwifery; and what mouse or man the outcome is.

x

CHAPTER VIII.

THE ELECTION.

ACCORDINGLY our Prior assembles us in Chapter; and, we adjuring him before God to do justly, nominates, not by our selection, yet with our assent, Twelve Monks, moderately satisfactory. Of whom are Hugo Third-Prior, Brother Dennis a venerable man, Walter the *Medicus*, Samson *Subsacrista*, and other esteemed characters,— though Willelmus *Sacrista*, of the red nose, too is one. These shall proceed straightway to Waltham; and there elect the Abbot as they may and can. Monks are sworn to obedience; must not speak too loud, under penalty of foot-gyves, limbo, and bread and water: yet monks too would know what it is they are obeying. The St. Edmundsbury Community has no hustings, ballot-box, indeed no open voting: yet by various vague manipulations, pulse-feelings, we struggle to ascertain what its virtual aim is, and succeed better or worse.

This question, however, rises; alas, a quite preliminary question: Will the *Dominus Rex* allow us to choose freely? It is to be hoped! Well, if so, we agree to choose one of our own Convent. If not, if the *Dominus Rex* will force a stranger on us, we decide on demurring, the Prior and his Twelve shall demur: we can appeal, plead, remonstrate; appeal even to the Pope, but trust it will not be necessary. Then there is this other question, raised by Brother Samson: What if the Thirteen should not themselves be able to agree? Brother Samson *Subsacrista*, one remarks, is ready oftenest with some question, some suggestion, that has wisdom in it. Though a servant of servants, and saying little, his words all tell, having sense in them; it seems by his light mainly that we steer ourselves in this great dimness.

What if the Thirteen should not themselves be able to agree? Speak, Samson, and advise.—Could not, hints Samson, Six of our venerablest elders be chosen by us, a kind of electoral committee, here and now: of these, 'with their hand on the Gospels, with their eye on the *Sacrosancta*,' we take oath that they will do faithfully; let these, in secret and as before God, agree on Three whom they reckon fittest; write their names in a Paper, and deliver the same sealed, forthwith, to the Thirteen: one of those Three the Thirteen shall fix on, if permitted. If not permitted, that is to say, if the *Dominus Rex* force us to demur,—the Paper shall be brought back unopened, and publicly burned, that no man's secret bring him into trouble.

So Samson advises, so we act; wisely, in this and in other crises of the business. Our electoral committee, its eye on the *Sacrosancta*, is soon named, soon sworn; and we striking up the Fifth Psalm, ' *Verba mea*,

> ' Give ear unto my words, O Lord,
> My meditation weigh,'

march out chanting, and leave the Six to their work in the Chapter here. Their work, before long, they announce as finished : they, with their eye on the Sacrosancta, imprecating the Lord to weigh and witness their meditation, have fixed on Three Names, and written them in this Sealed Paper. Let Samson Subsacrista, general servant of the party, take charge of it. On the morrow morning, our Prior and his Twelve will be ready to get under way.

This then is the ballot-box and electoral winnowing-machine they have at St. Edmundsbury : a mind fixed on the Thrice Holy, an appeal to God on high to witness their meditation : by far the best, and indeed the only good electoral winnowing-machine,—if men have souls in them. Totally worthless, it is true, and even hideous and poisonous, if men have no souls. But without soul, alas what winnowing-machine in human elections, can be of avail? We cannot get along without soul; we stick fast, the mournfullest spectacle; and salt itself will not save us !

On the morrow morning, accordingly, our Thirteen set forth; or rather our Prior and Eleven ; for Samson, as general servant of the party, has to linger, settling many things. At length he too gets upon the road; and, 'carrying the sealed Paper in a leather pouch hung round his neck ; and *froccum bajulans in ulnis*' (thanks to thee Bozzy Jocelin), ' his frock-skirts looped over his elbow,' showing substantial stern-works, tramps stoutly along. Away across the Heath, not yet of Newmarket and horse-jockeying; across your Fleam-dike and Devil's-dike, no longer useful as a Mercian East-Anglian boundary or bulwark: continually towards Waltham, and the Bishop of Winchester's House there, for his Majesty is in that. Brother Samson, as purse-bearer, has the reckoning always, when there is one, to pay; ' delays are numerous,' progress none of the swiftest.

But, in the solitude of the Convent, Destiny thus big and in her birthtime, what gossiping, what babbling, what dreaming of dreams ! The secret of the Three our electoral elders alone know : some Abbot we shall have to govern us; but which Abbot, O which! One Monk discerns in a vision of the night-watches, that we shall get an Abbot of our own body, without needing to demur : a prophet appeared to him clad all in white, and said, " Ye shall have one of

yours, and he will rage among you like a wolf, *sæviet ut lupus*."
Verily!—then which of ours? Another Monk now dreams: he has
seen clearly which; a certain Figure taller by head and shoulders
than the other two, dressed in alb and *pallium*, and with the attitude of one about to fight;—which tall Figure a wise Editor would
rather not name at this stage of the business! Enough that the
vision is true: that Saint Edmund himself, pale and awful, seemed
to rise from his Shrine, with naked feet, and say audibly, "He,
ille, shall veil my feet;" which part of the vision also proves true.
Such guessing, visioning, dim perscrutation of the momentous
future: the very clothmakers, old women, all townsfolk speak
of it, 'and more than once it is reported in St. Edmundsbury,
This one is elected; and then, This one and That other.' Who
knows?

But now, sure enough, at Waltham 'on the Second Sunday of
Quadragesima,' which Dryasdust declares to mean the 22d day of
February, year 1182, Thirteen St. Edmundsbury Monks are, at last,
seen processioning towards the Winchester Manorhouse; and in
some high Presence-chamber, and Hall of State, get access to
Henry II. in all his glory. What a Hall,—not imaginary in the
least, but entirely real and indisputable, though so extremely dim
to us; sunk in the deep distances of Night! The Winchester
Manorhouse has fled bodily, like a Dream of the old Night; not
Dryasdust himself can show a wreck of it. House and people,
royal and episcopal, lords and varlets, where are they? Why *there*,
I say, Seven Centuries off; sunk *so* far in the Night, there they
are; peep through the blankets of the old Night, and thou wilt
see! King Henry himself is visibly there, a vivid, noble-looking
man, with grizzled beard, in glittering uncertain costume; with
earls round him, and bishops and dignitaries, in the like. The
Hall is large, and has for one thing an altar near it,—chapel and
altar adjoining it; but what gilt seats, carved tables, carpeting of
rush-cloth, what arras-hangings, and huge fire of logs:—alas, it has
Human Life in it; and is not that the grand miracle, in what hang-
ings or costume soever?—

The *Dominus Rex*, benignantly receiving our Thirteen with their
obeisance, and graciously declaring that he will strive to act for
God's honour, and the Church's good, commands, 'by the Bishop
of Winchester and Geoffrey the Chancellor,'—*Galfridus Cancellarius*,
Henry's and the Fair Rosamond's authentic Son present here!—
commands, "That they, the said Thirteen, do now withdraw, and
fix upon Three from their own Monastery." A work soon done; the
Three hanging ready round Samson's neck, in that leather pouch

of his. Breaking the seal, we find the names,—what think *ye* of it, ye higher dignitaries, thou indolent Prior, thou Willelmus *Sacrista* with the red bottle-nose?—the names, in this order: of Samson *Subsacrista*, of Roger the distressed Cellarer, of Hugo *Tertius-Prior.*

The higher dignitaries, all omitted here, 'flush suddenly red in the face;' but have nothing to say. One curious fact and question certainly is, How Hugo Third-Prior, who was of the electoral committee, came to nominate *himself* as one of the Three? A curious fact, which Hugo Third-Prior has never yet entirely explained, that I know of!—However, we return, and report to the King our Three names; merely altering the order; putting Samson last, as lowest of all. The King, at recitation of our Three, asks us: "Who are they? Were they born in my domain? Totally unknown to me! You must nominate three others." Whereupon Willelmus Sacrista says, "Our Prior must be named, *quia caput nostrum est*, being already our head." And the Prior responds, Willelmus Sacrista is a fit man, *bonus vir est*,"—for all his red nose. Tickle me, Toby, and I'll tickle thee! Venerable Dennis too is named; none in his conscience can say nay. There are now Six on our List. "Well," said the King, "they have done it swiftly, they! *Deus est cum eis.*" The Monks withdraw again; and Majesty revolves, for a little, with his *Pares* and *Episcopi*, Lords or '*Law-wards*' and Soul-Overseers, the thoughts of the royal breast. The Monks wait silent in an outer room.

In short while, they are next ordered, To add yet another three; but not from their own Convent; from other Convents, "for the honour of my kingdom." Here,—what is to be done here? We will demur, if need be! We do name three, however, for the nonce: the Prior of St. Faith's, a good Monk of St. Neot's, a good Monk of St. Alban's; good men all; all made abbots and dignitaries since, at this hour. There are now Nine upon our List. What the thoughts of the Dominus Rex may be farther? The Dominus Rex, thanking graciously, sends out word that we shall now strike off three. The three strangers are instantly struck off. Willelmus Sacrista adds, that he will of his own accord decline,— a touch of grace and respect for the *Sacrosancta*, even in Willelmus! The King then orders us to strike off a couple more; then yet one more: Hugo Third-Prior goes, and Roger *Cellerarius*, and venerable Monk Dennis;—and now there remain on our List two only, Samson Subsacrista and the Prior.

Which of these two? It were hard to say,—by Monks who may get themselves foot-gyved and thrown into limbo, for speaking! We humbly request that the Bishop of Winchester and Geoffrey the Chancellor may again enter, and help us to decide. "Which do you want?" asks the Bishop. Venerable Dennis made a speech, ' commending the persons of the Prior and Samson; but always ' in the corner of his discourse, *in angulo sui sermonis*, brought Sam-' son in.' "I see!" said the Bishop: "We are to understand that your Prior is somewhat remiss; that you want to have him you call Samson for Abbot." "Either of them is good," said venerable Dennis, almost trembling; "but we would have the better, if it pleased God." "Which of the two *do* you want?" inquires the Bishop pointedly. "Samson!" answered Dennis; "Samson!" echoed all of the rest that durst speak or echo anything: and Samson is reported to the King accordingly. His Majesty, advising of it for a moment, orders that Samson be brought in with the other Twelve.

The King's Majesty, looking at us somewhat sternly, then says: "You present to me Samson; I do not know him: had it been your Prior, whom I do know, I should have accepted him: however, I will now do as you wish. But have a care of yourselves. By the true eyes of God, *per veros oculos Dei*, if you manage badly, I will be upon you!" Samson, therefore, steps forward, kisses the King's feet; but swiftly rises erect again, swiftly turns towards the altar, uplifting with the other Twelve, in clear tenor-note, the Fifty-first Psalm, ' *Miserere mei Deus,*

> ' After thy loving-kindness, Lord,
> Have mercy upon *me*,'

with firm voice, firm step and head, no change in his countenance whatever. "By God's eyes," said the King, "that one, I think, will govern the Abbey well." By the same oath (charged to your Majesty's account), I too am precisely of that opinion! It is some while since I fell in with a likelier man anywhere than this new Abbot Samson. Long life to him, and may the Lord *have* mercy on him as Abbot!

Thus, then, have the St. Edmundsbury Monks, without express ballot-box or other good winnowing-machine, contrived to accomplish the most important social feat a body of men can do, to winnow out the man that is to govern them: and truly one sees not that, by any winnowing-machine whatever, they could have done it better. O ye kind Heavens, there is in every Nation and Community *a fittest*, a wisest, bravest, best; whom could we find and make King over us, all were in very truth well;—the best that God and Nature had permitted *us* to make it! By what art discover him? Will the Heavens in their pity teach us no art; for our need of him is great!

Ballot-boxes, Reform Bills, winnowing-machines: all these are good, or are not so good;—alas, brethren, how *can* these, I say, be other than inadequate, be other than failures, melancholy to behold? Dim all souls of men to the divine, the high and awful meaning of Human Worth and Truth, we shall never, by all the machinery in Birmingham, discover the True and Worthy. It is written, ' if we are ourselves valets, there shall exist no hero for us; we shall not know the hero when we see him;'—we shall take the quack for a hero; and cry, audibly through all ballot-boxes and machinery whatsoever, Thou art he; be thou King over us!

What boots it? Seek only deceitful Speciosity, money with gilt carriages, ' fame' with newspaper-paragraphs, whatever name it bear, you will find only deceitful Speciosity; godlike Reality will be forever far from you. The Quack shall be legitimate inevitable King of you; no earthly machinery able to exclude the Quack. Ye shall be born thralls of the Quack, and suffer under him, till your hearts are near broken, and no French Revolution or Manchester Insurrection, or partial or universal volcanic combustions and explosions, never so many, can do more than ' change the *figure* of your Quack;' the essence of him remaining, for a time and times.—" How long, O Prophet?" say some, with a rather melancholy sneer. Alas, ye *un*prophetic, ever till this come about: Till deep misery, if nothing softer will, have driven you out of your Speciosities *into* your Sincerities; and you find that there either is a Godlike in the world, or else ye are an unintelligible madness; that there is a God, as well as a Mammon and a Devil, and a Genius of Luxuries and canting Dilettantisms and Vain Shows! How long that will be, compute for yourselves. My unhappy brothers!—

———

CHAPTER IX.

ABBOT SAMSON.

So then the bells of St. Edmundsbury clang out one and all, and in church and chapel the organs go: Convent and Town, and all the west side of Suffolk, are in gala; knights, viscounts, weavers, spinners, the entire population, male and female, young and old, the very sockmen with their chubby infants,—out to have a holiday, and see the Lord Abbot arrive! And there is ' stripping barefoot' of the Lord Abbot at the Gate, and solemn leading of him in to the High Altar and Shrine: with sudden ' silence of all the bells and organs,' as we kneel in deep prayer there; and again

with outburst of all the bells and organs, and loud *Te Deum* from
the general human windpipe; and speeches by the leading viscount, and giving of the kiss of brotherhood; the whole wound up
with popular games, and dinner within doors of more than a thousand strong, *plus quam mille comedentibus in gaudio magno.*

In such manner is the selfsame Samson once again returning
to us, welcomed on *this* occasion. He that went away with his
frock-skirts looped over his arm, comes back riding high; suddenly made one of the dignitaries of this world. Reflective readers
will admit that here was a trial for a man. Yesterday a poor mendicant, allowed to possess not above two shillings of money, and
without authority to bid a dog run for him, this man today finds
himself a *Dominus Abbas*, mitred Peer of Parliament, Lord of
manorhouses, farms, manors, and wide lands; a man with 'Fifty
Knights under him,' and dependent, swiftly obedient multitudes
of men. It is a change greater than Napoleon's; so sudden withal.
As if one of the Chandos day-drudges had, on awakening some
morning, found that *he* overnight was become Duke! Let Samson
with his clear-beaming eyes see into that, and discern it if he can.
We shall now get the measure of him by a new scale of inches,
considerably more rigorous than the former was. For if a noble
soul is rendered tenfold beautifuller by victory and prosperity,
springing now radiant as into his own due element and sun-throne;
an ignoble one is rendered tenfold and hundredfold uglier, piti-
fuller. Whatsoever vices, whatsoever weaknesses were in the man,
the parvenu will show us them enlarged, as in the solar micro-
scope, into frightful distortion. Nay, how many mere seminal principles of vice, hitherto all wholesomely kept latent, may we now
see unfolded, as in the solar hothouse, into growth, into huge uni-
versally-conspicuous luxuriance and development!

But is not this, at any rate, a singular aspect of what political
and social capabilities, nay let us say what depth and opulence of
true social vitality, lay in those old barbarous ages, That the fit
Governor could be met with under such disguises, could be recognised and laid hold of under such? Here he is discovered with a
maximum of two shillings in his pocket, and a leather scrip round
his neck; trudging along the highway, his frock-skirts looped over
his arm. They think this is he nevertheless, the true Governor;
and he proves to be so. Brethren, have we no need of discovering
true Governors, but will sham ones forever do for us? These
were absurd superstitious blockheads of Monks; and we are enlightened Tenpound Franchisers, without taxes on knowledge!
Where, I say, are our superior, are our similar or at all comparable

discoveries? We also have eyes, or ought to have; we have hustings, telescopes; we have lights, link-lights and rush-lights of an enlightened free Press, burning and dancing everywhere, as in a universal torch-dance; singeing your whiskers as you traverse the public thoroughfares in town and country. Great souls, true Governors, go about under all manner of disguises now as then. Such telescopes, such enlightenment,—and such discovery! How comes it, I say; how comes it? Is it not lamentable; is it not even, in some sense, amazing?

Alas, the defect, as we must often urge and again urge, is less a defect of telescopes than of some eyesight. Those superstitious blockheads of the Twelfth Century had no telescopes, but they had still an eye; not ballot-boxes; only reverence for Worth, abhorrence of Unworth. It is the way with all barbarians. Thus Mr. Sale informs me, the old Arab Tribes would gather in liveliest *gaudeamus*, and sing, and kindle bonfires, and wreathe crowns of honour, and solemnly thank the gods that, in their Tribe too, a Poet had shown himself. As indeed they well might; for what usefuller, I say not nobler and heavenlier thing could the gods, doing their very kindest, send to any Tribe or Nation, in any time or circumstances? I declare to thee, my afflicted quack-ridden brother, in spite of thy astonishment, it is very lamentable! We English find a Poet, as brave a man as has been made for a hundred years or so anywhere under the Sun; and do we kindle bonfires, or thank the gods? Not at all. We, taking due counsel of it, set the man to gauge ale-barrels in the Burgh of Dumfries; and pique ourselves on our ' patronage of genius.'

Genius, Poet: do we know what these words mean? An inspired Soul once more vouchsafed us, direct from Nature's own great fire-heart, to see the Truth, and speak it, and do it; Nature's own sacred voice heard once more athwart the dreary boundless element of hearsaying and canting, of twaddle and poltroonery, in which the bewildered Earth, nigh perishing, has *lost its way*. Hear once more, ye bewildered benighted mortals; listen once again to a voice from the inner Light-sea and Flame-sea, Nature's and Truth's own heart; know the Fact of your Existence what it is, put away the Cant of it which it is *not;* and knowing, do, and let it be well with you!—

George the Third is Defender of something we call ' the Faith' in those years; George the Third is head charioteer of the Destinies of England, to guide them through the gulf of French Revolutions, American Independences; and Robert Burns is Gauger of ale in Dumfries. It is an Iliad in a nutshell. The physiognomy of a world now verging towards dissolution, reduced now to spasms and death-throes, lies pictured in that one fact,—which astonishes nobody, except at me for being astonished at it. The fruit of long ages of confirmed Valethood, entirely confirmed as into a Law of Nature; cloth-worship and quack-worship: entirely *confirmed* Valethood,—which will have to *unconfirm* itself again; God knows, with difficulty enough!—

Abbot Samson had found a Convent all in dilapidation; rain beating through it, material rain and metaphorical, from all quarters of the compass. Willelmus Sacrista sits drinking nightly, and doing mere *tacenda*. Our larders are reduced to leanness, Jew harpies and unclean creatures our purveyors; in our basket is no bread. Old women with their distaffs rush out on a distressed Cellarer in shrill Chartism. 'You cannot stir abroad but Jews and Christians pounce upon you with unsettled bonds;' debts boundless seemingly as the National Debt of England. For four years our new Lord Abbot never went abroad but Jew creditors and Christian, and all manner of creditors, were about him; driving him to very despair. Our Prior is remiss; our Cellarers, officials are remiss, our monks are remiss: what man is not remiss? Front this, Samson, thou alone art there to front it; it is thy task to front and fight this, and to die or kill it. May the Lord have mercy on thee!

To our antiquarian interest in poor Jocelin and his Convent, where the whole aspect of existence, the whole dialect, of thought, of speech, of activity, is so obsolete, strange, long-vanished, there now superadds itself a mild glow of human interest for Abbot Samson; a real pleasure, as at sight of man's work, especially of governing, which is man's highest work, done *well*. Abbot Samson had no experience in governing; had served no apprenticeship to the trade of governing,—alas, only the hardest apprenticeship to that of obeying. He had never in any court given *vadium* or *plegium*, says Jocelin; hardly ever seen a court, when he was set to preside in one. But it is astonishing, continues Jocelin, how soon he learned the ways of business; and, in all sort of affairs, became expert beyond others. Of the many persons offering him their service, 'he retained one Knight skilled in taking *vadia* and *plegia*;' and within the year was himself well skilled. Nay, by and by, the Pope appoints him Justiciary in certain causes; the King one of his new Circuit Judges: official Osbert is heard saying, "That Abbot is one of your shrewd ones, *disputator est;* if he go on as he begins, he will cut out every lawyer of us!"[1]

---

[1] Jocelini Chronica, p. 25.

Why not? What is to hinder this Samson from governing? There is in him what far transcends all apprenticeships; in the man himself there exists a model of governing, something to govern by! There exists in him a heart-abhorrence of whatever is incoherent, pusillanimous, unveracious,—that is to say, chaotic, *ungoverned;* of the Devil, not of God. A man of this kind cannot help governing! He has the living ideal of a governor in him; and the incessant necessity of struggling to unfold the same out of him. Not the Devil or Chaos, for any wages, will he serve: no, this man is the born servant of Another than them. Alas, how little avail all apprenticeships, when there is in your governor himself what we may well call *nothing* to govern by: nothing;— a general gray twilight, looming with shapes of expediencies, parliamentary traditions, division-lists, election-funds, leading-articles; this, with what of vulpine alertness and adroitness soever, is not much!

But indeed what say we, apprenticeship? Had not this Samson served, in his way, a right good apprenticeship to governing; namely, the harshest slave-apprenticeship to obeying! Walk this world with no friend in it but God and St. Edmund, you will either fall into the ditch, or learn a good many things. To learn obeying is the fundamental art of governing. How much would many a Serene Highness have learned, had he travelled through the world with water-jug and empty wallet, *sine omni expensa;* and, at his victorious return, sat down not to newspaper-paragraphs and city-illuminations, but at the foot of St. Edmund's Shrine to shackles and bread and water! He that cannot be servant of many, will never be master, true guide and deliverer of many;— that is the meaning of true mastership. Had not the Monk-life extraordinary 'political capabilities' in it; if not imitable by us, yet enviable? Heavens, had a Duke of Logwood, now rolling sumptuously to his place in the Collective Wisdom, but himself happened to plough daily, at one time, on seven-and-sixpence a week, with no out-door relief,—what a light, unquenchable by logic and statistic and arithmetic. would it have thrown on several things for him!

In all cases, therefore, we will agree with the judicious Mrs. Glass: 'First catch your hare!' First get your man; all is got: he can learn to do all things, from making boots, to decreeing judgments, governing communities; and will do them like a man. Catch your no-man,—alas, have you not caught the terriblest Tartar in the world! Perhaps all the terribler, the quieter and gentler he looks. For the mischief that one blockhead, that every blockhead does, in a world so feracious, teeming with endless results as ours, no ciphering will sum up. The quack bootmaker is considerable; as corn-cutters can testify, and desperate men reduced to buckskin and list-shoes. But the quack priest, quack high-priest, the quack king! Why do not all just citizens rush, half-frantic, to stop him, as they would a conflagration? Surely a just citizen *is* admonished by God and his own Soul, by all silent and articulate voices of this Universe, to do what in *him* lies towards relief of this poor blockhead-quack, and of a world that groans under him. Run swiftly; relieve him,—were it even by extinguishing him! For all things have grown so old, tinder-dry, combustible; and he is more ruinous than conflagration. Sweep him *down*, at least; keep him strictly within the hearth: he will then cease to be conflagration; he will then become useful, more or less, as culinary fire. Fire is the best of servants; but what a master! This poor blockhead too is born for uses: why, elevating him to mastership, will you make a conflagration, a parish-curse or world-curse of him?

————

CHAPTER X.

GOVERNMENT.

How Abbot Samson, giving his new subjects seriatim the kiss of fatherhood in the St. Edmundsbury chapterhouse, proceeded with cautious energy to set about reforming their disjointed distracted way of life; how he managed with his Fifty rough *Milites* (Feudal Knights), with his lazy Farmers, remiss refractory Monks, with Pope's Legates, Viscounts, Bishops, Kings; how on all sides he laid about him like a man, and putting consequence on premiss, and everywhere the saddle on the right horse, struggled incessantly to educe organic method out of lazily fermenting wreck,— the careful reader will discern, not without true interest, in these pages of Jocelin Boswell. In most antiquarian quaint costume, not of garments alone, but of thought, word, action, outlook and position, the substantial figure of a man with eminent nose, bushy brows and clear-flashing eyes, his russet beard growing daily grayer, is visible, engaged in true governing of men. It is beautiful how the chrysalis governing-soul, shaking off its dusty slough and prison, starts forth winged, a true royal soul! Our new Abbot has a right honest unconscious feeling, without insolence as without fear or flutter, of what he is and what others are. A courage to quell the proudest, an honest pity to encourage the humblest. Withal there is a noble reticence in this Lord Abbot:

much vain unreason he hears ; lays up without response. He is not there to expect reason and nobleness of others ; he is there to give them of his own reason and nobleness. Is he not their servant, as we said, who can suffer from them, and for them ; bear the burden their poor spindle-limbs totter and stagger under ; and in virtue *thereof* govern them, lead them out of weakness into strength, out of defeat into victory !

One of the first Herculean Labours Abbot Samson undertook, or the very first, was to institute a strenuous review and radical reform of his economics. It is the first labour of every governing man, from *Paterfamilias* to *Dominus Rex*. To get the rain thatched out from you is the preliminary of whatever farther, in the way of speculation or of action, you may mean to do. Old Abbot Hugo's budget, as we saw, had become empty, filled with deficit and wind. To see his account-books clear, be delivered from those ravening flights of Jew and Christian creditors, pouncing on him like obscene harpies wherever he showed face, was a necessity for Abbot Samson.

On the morrow after his instalment, he brings in a load of money - bonds, all duly stamped, sealed with this or the other Convent Seal : frightful, unmanageable, a bottomless confusion of Convent finance. There they are ;—but there at least they all are ; all that shall be of them. Our Lord Abbot demands that all the official seals in use among us be now produced and delivered to him. Three-and-thirty seals turn up ; are straightway broken, and shall seal no more : the Abbot only, and those duly authorised by him shall seal any bond. There are but two ways of paying debt : increase of industry in raising income, increase of thrift in laying it out. With iron energy, in slow but steady undeviating perseverance, Abbot Samson sets to work in both directions. His troubles are manifold : cunning *milites*, unjust bailiffs, lazy sockmen, he an inexperienced Abbot ; relaxed lazy monks, not disinclined to mutiny in mass : but continued vigilance, rigorous method, what we call ' the eye of the master,' work wonders. The clear-beaming eyesight of Abbot Samson, steadfast, severe, all-penetrating,—it is like *Fiat lux* in that inorganic waste whirlpool ; penetrates gradually to all nooks, and of the chaos makes a *kosmos* or ordered world !

He arranges everywhere, struggles unweariedly to arrange, and place on some intelligible footing, the ' affairs and dues, *res ac redditus*,' of his dominion. The Lakenheath eels cease to breed squabbles between human beings ; the penny of *reap-silver* to explode into the streets the Female Chartism of St. Edmundsbury.

These and innumerable greater things. Wheresoever Disorder may stand or lie, let it have a care; here is the man that has declared war with it, that never will make peace with it. Man is the Missionary of Order; he is the servant not of the Devil and Chaos, but of God and the Universe! Let all sluggards and cowards, remiss, false-spoken, unjust, and otherwise diabolic persons have a care: this is a dangerous man for them. He has a mild grave face; a thoughtful sternness, a sorrowful pity: but there is a terrible flash of anger in him too; lazy monks often have to murmur, "*Sævit ut lupus*, He rages like a wolf; was not our Dream true!" 'To repress and hold-in such sudden anger he was continually careful,' and succeeded well :—right, Samson; that it may become in thee as noble central heat, fruitful, strong, beneficent; not blaze out, or the seldomest possible blaze out, as wasteful volcanoism to scorch and consume!

"We must first creep, and gradually learn to walk," had Abbot Samson said of himself, at starting. In four years he has become a great walker; striding prosperously along; driving much before him. In less than four years, says Jocelin, the Convent Debts were all liquidated: the harpy Jews not only settled with, but banished, bag and baggage, out of the *Bannaleuca* (Liberties, *Banlieue*) of St. Edmundsbury,—so has the King's Majesty been persuaded to permit. Farewell to *you*, at any rate; let us, in no extremity, apply again to you! Armed men march them over the borders, dismiss them under stern penalties,—sentence of excommunication on all that shall again harbour them here: there were many dry eyes at their departure.

New life enters everywhere, springs up beneficent, the Incubus of Debt once rolled away. Samson hastes not; but neither does he pause to rest. This of the Finance is a life-long business with him;—Jocelin's anecdotes are filled to weariness with it. As indeed to Jocelin it was of very primary interest.

But we have to record also, with a lively satisfaction, that spiritual rubbish is as little tolerated in Samson's Monastery as material. With due rigour, Willelmus Sacrista, and his bibations and *tacenda* are, at the earliest opportunity, softly, yet irrevocably put an end to. The bibations, namely, had to end; even the building where they used to be carried on was razed from the soil of St. Edmundsbury, and 'on its place grow rows of beans :' Willelmus himself, deposed from the Sacristy and all offices, retires into obscurity, into absolute taciturnity unbroken thenceforth to this hour. Whether the poor Willelmus did not still, by secret channels, occasionally get some slight wetting of vinous or alcoholic liquor,—now grown, in a manner, indispensable to the poor man? Jocelin hints not; one knows not how to hope, what to hope! But if he did, it was in silence and darkness; with an ever-present feeling that teetotalism was his only true course. Drunken dissolute Monks are a class of persons who had better keep out of Abbot Samson's way. *Sævit ut lupus;* was not the Dream true! murmured many a Monk. Nay Ranulf de Glanville, Justiciary in Chief, took umbrage at him, seeing these strict ways; and watched farther with suspicion : but discerned gradually that there was nothing wrong, that there was much the opposite of wrong.

CHAPTER XI.

THE ABBOT'S WAYS.

ABBOT SAMSON showed no extraordinary favour to the Monks who had been his familiars of old; did not promote them to offices,— *nisi essent idonei,* unless they chanced to be fit men! Whence great discontent among certain of these, who had contributed to make him Abbot : reproaches, open and secret, of his being ' ungrateful, hard-tempered, unsocial, a Norfolk *barrator* and *palterorius.*'

Indeed, except it were for *idonei,* 'fit men,' in all kinds, it was hard to say for whom Abbot Samson had much favour. He loved his kindred well, and tenderly enough acknowledged the poor part of them ; with the rich part, who in old days had never acknowledged him, he totally refused to have any business. But even the former he did not promote into offices; finding none of them *idonei.* ' Some whom he thought suitable he put into ' situations in his own household, or made keepers of his country ' places : if they behaved ill, he dismissed them without hope of ' return.' In his promotions, nay almost in his benefits, you would have said there was a certain impartiality. ' The official ' person who had, by Abbot Hugo's order, put the fetters on him ' at his return from Italy, was now supported with food and clothes ' to the end of his days at Abbot Samson's expense.'

Yet he did not forget benefits; far the reverse, when an opportunity occurred of paying them at his own cost. How pay them at the public cost ;—how, above all, by *setting fire* to the public, as we said ; clapping ' conflagrations' on the public, which the services of blockheads, *non-idonei,* intrinsically are! He was right willing to remember friends, when it could be done. Take these instances : ' A certain chaplain who had maintained him at the

' Schools of Paris by the sale of holy water, *quæstu aquæ benedictæ;*
' —to this good chaplain he did give a vicarage, adequate to the
' comfortable sustenance of him.'   ' The Son of Elias too, that is,
' of old Abbot Hugo's Cupbearer, coming to do homage for his
' Father's land, our Lord Abbot said to him in full court: "I have,
' for these seven years, put off taking thy homage for the land
' which Abbot Hugo gave thy Father, because that gift was to the
' damage of Elmswell, and a questionable one: but now I must
' profess myself overcome; mindful of the kindness thy Father did
' me when I was in bonds; because he sent me a cup of the very
' wine his master had been drinking, and bade me be comforted
' in God."'

' To Magister Walter, son of Magister William de Dice, who
' wanted the vicarage of Chevington, he answered: "Thy Father
' was Master of the Schools; and when I was an indigent *clericus*,
' he granted me freely and in charity an entrance to his School,
' and opportunity of learning; wherefore I now, for the sake of
' God, grant to thee what thou askest."'   Or lastly, take this good
instance,—and a glimpse, along with it, into long-obsolete times:
' Two *Milites* of Risby, Willelm and Norman, being adjudged in
' Court to come under his mercy, *in misericordia ejus*,' for a certain
very considerable fine of twenty shillings, ' he thus addressed
' them publicly on the spot: "When I was a Cloister-monk, I was
' once sent to Durham on business of our Church; and coming
' home again, the dark night caught me at Risby, and I had to beg
' a lodging there. I went to Dominus Norman's, and he gave me
' a flat refusal. Going then to Dominus Willelm's, and begging
' hospitality, I was by him honourably received. The twenty shil-
' lings therefore of *mercy*, I, without mercy, will exact from Domi-
' nus Norman; to Dominus Willelm, on the other hand, I, with
' thanks, will wholly remit the said sum."'   Men know not always
to whom they refuse lodgings; men have lodged Angels un-
awares!—

It is clear Abbot Samson had a talent; he had learned to judge
better than Lawyers, to manage better than bred Bailiffs:—a talent
shining out indisputable, on whatever side you took him. 'An
' eloquent man he was,' says Jocelin, 'both in French and Latin;
' but intent more on the substance and method of what was to be
' said, than on the ornamental way of saying it. He could read
' English Manuscripts very elegantly, *elegantissime:* he was wont to
' preach to the people in the English tongue, though according to
' the dialect of Norfolk, where he had been brought up; wherefore
' indeed he had caused a Pulpit to be erected in our Church both

'for ornament of the same, and for the use of his audiences.'
There preached he, according to the dialect of Norfolk: a man
worth going to hear.

That he was a just clear-hearted man, this, as the basis of all
true talent, is presupposed. How can a man, without clear vision
in his heart first of all, have any clear vision in the head? It is
impossible! Abbot Samson was one of the justest of judges; insisted on understanding the case to the bottom, and then swiftly
decided without feud or favour. For which reason, indeed, the
Dominus Rex, searching for such men, as for hidden treasure and
healing to his distressed realm, had made him one of the new Itin-
erant Judges,—such as continue to this day. "My curse on that
Abbot's court," a suitor was heard imprecating, "*Maledicta sit curia
istius Abbatis*, where neither gold nor silver can help me to con-
found my enemy!" And old friendships and all connexions forgotten, when you go to seek an office from him! "A kinless loon,"
as the Scotch said of Cromwell's new judges,—intent on mere indifferent fair-play!

Eloquence in three languages is good; but it is not the best.
To us, as already hinted, the Lord Abbot's eloquence is less admirable than his *in*eloquence, his great invaluable 'talent of silence!'
' "*Deus, Deus*," said the Lord Abbot to me once, when he heard
' the Convent were murmuring at some act of his, "I have much
' need to remember that Dream they had of me, that I was to
' rage among them like a wolf. Above all earthly things I dread
' their driving me to do it. How much do I hold in, and wink at;
' raging and shuddering in my own secret mind, and not outwardly
' at all!" He would boast to me at other times: "This and that I
' have seen, this and that I have heard; yet patiently stood it."
' He had this way, too, which I have never seen in any other man,
' that he affectionately loved many persons to whom he never or
' hardly ever showed a countenance of love. Once on my venturing
' to expostulate with him on the subject, he reminded me of Solo-
' mon: "Many sons I have; it is not fit that I should smile on
' them." He would suffer faults, damage from his servants, and
' know what he suffered, and not speak of it; but I think the rea-
' son was, he waited a good time for speaking of it, and in a wise
' way amending it. He intimated, openly in chapter to us all, that
' he would have no eavesdropping: "Let none," said he, "come to
' me secretly accusing another, unless he will publicly stand to the
' same; if he come otherwise, I will openly proclaim the name of
' him. I wish, too, that every Monk of you have free access to me,
' to speak of your needs or grievances when you will." '

The kinds of people Abbot Samson liked worst were these three:

L

' *Mendaces, ebriosi, verbosi*, Liars, drunkards, and wordy or windy
' persons;'—not good kinds, any of them! He also much condemned ' persons given to murmur at their meat or drink, especially
' Monks of that disposition.' We remark, from the very first, his
strict anxious order to his servants to provide handsomely for
hospitality, to guard ' above all things that there be no shabbiness
' in the matter of meat and drink; no look of mean parsimony, *in*
' *novitate mea*, at the beginning of my Abbotship;' and to the last
he maintains a due opulence of table and equipment for others:
but he is himself in the highest degree indifferent to all such
things.

' Sweet milk, honey, and other naturally sweet kinds of food,
' were what he preferred to eat: but he had this virtue,' says Jocelin, ' he never changed the dish (*ferculum*) you set before him, be
' what it might. Once when I, still a novice, happened to be
' waiting table in the refectory, it came into my head' (rogue that
I was!) ' to try if this were true; and I thought I would place
' before him a *ferculum* that would have displeased any other per-
' son, the very platter being black and broken. But he, seeing it,
' was as one that saw it not: and now some little delay taking
' place, my heart smote me that I had done this; and so, snatch-
' ing up the platter (*discus*), I changed both it and its contents for
' a better, and put down that instead; which emendation he was
' angry at, and rebuked me for,'—the stoical monastic man! ' For
' the first seven years he had commonly four sorts of dishes on his
' table; afterwards only three, except it might be presents, or veni-
' son from his own parks, or fishes from his ponds. And if, at any
' time, he had guests living in his house at the request of some
' great person, or of some friend, or had public messengers, or
' had harpers (*citharœdos*), or any one of that sort, he took the first
' opportunity of shifting to another of his Manor-houses, and so
' got rid of such superfluous individuals,'[1]—very prudently, I
think.

As to his parks, of these, in the general repair of buildings,
general improvement and adornment of the St. Edmund Domains,
' he had laid out several, and stocked them with animals, retaining
' a proper huntsman with hounds: and, if any guest of great quality
' were there, our Lord Abbot with his Monks would sit in some
' opening of the woods, and see the dogs run; but he himself never
' meddled with hunting, that I saw.'[2]

' In an opening of the woods;'—for the country was still dark
with wood in those days; and Scotland itself still rustled shaggy

<hr/>

[1] Jocelini Chronica,' p. 31.   [2] Ibid. p. 21.

and leafy, like a damp black American Forest, with cleared spots and spaces here and there. Dryasdust advances several absurd hypotheses as to the insensible but almost total disappearance of these woods; the thick wreck of which now lies as *peat*, sometimes with huge heart-of-oak timber logs imbedded in it, on many a height and hollow. The simplest reason doubtless is, that by increase of husbandry, there was increase of cattle; increase of hunger for green spring food; and so, more and more, the new seedlings got yearly eaten out in April; and the old trees, having only a certain length of life in them, died gradually, no man heeding it, and disappeared into *peat*.

A sorrowful waste of noble wood and umbrage! Yes,—but a very common one; the course of most things in this world. Monachism itself, so rich and fruitful once, is now all rotted into *peat;* lies sleek and buried,—and a most feeble bog-grass of Dilettantism all the crop we reap from it! That also was frightful waste; perhaps among the saddest our England ever saw. Why will men destroy noble Forests, even when in part a nuisance, in such reckless manner; turning loose four-footed cattle and Henry-the-Eighths into them! The fifth part of our English soil, Dryasdust computes, lay consecrated to 'spiritual uses,' better or worse; solemnly set apart to foster spiritual growth and culture of the soul, by the methods then known: and now—it too, like the four-fifths, fosters what? Gentle shepherd, tell me what!

CHAPTER XII.

THE ABBOT'S TROUBLES.

THE troubles of Abbot Samson, as he went along in this abstemious, reticent, rigorous way, were more than tongue can tell. The Abbot's mitre once set on his head, he knew rest no more. Double, double toil and trouble; that is the life of all governors that really govern: not the spoil of victory, only the glorious toil of battle can be theirs. Abbot Samson found all men more or less headstrong, irrational, prone to disorder; continually threatening to prove *un*governable.

His lazy Monks gave him most trouble. 'My heart is tortured,' said he, 'till we get out of debt, *cor meum cruciatum est.*' Your heart, indeed;—but not altogether ours! By no devisable method, or none of three or four that he devised, could Abbot Samson get these Monks of his to keep their accounts straight; but always, do as he might, the Cellerarius at the end of the term is in a coil, in a flat deficit,—verging again towards debt and Jews. The Lord Abbot at last declares sternly he will keep our accounts too himself; will appoint an officer of his own to see our Cellerarius keep them. Murmurs thereupon among us: Was the like ever heard? Our Cellerarius a cipher; the very Townsfolk know it: *subsannatio et derisio sumus,* we have become a laughingstock to mankind. The Norfolk barrator and paltener!

And consider, if the Abbot found such difficulty in the mere economic department, how much in more complex ones, in spiritual ones perhaps! He wears a stern calm face; raging and gnashing teeth, *fremens* and *frendens,* many times, in the secret of his mind. Withal, however, there is a noble slow perseverance in him; a strength of 'subdued rage' calculated to subdue most things: always, in the long-run, he contrives to gain his point.

Murmurs from the Monks, meanwhile, cannot fail; ever deeper murmurs, new grudges accumulating. At one time, on slight cause, some drop making the cup run over, they burst into open mutiny: the Cellarer will not obey, prefers arrest on bread and water to obeying; the Monks thereupon strike work; refuse to do the regular chanting of the day, at least the younger part of them with loud clamour and uproar refuse:—Abbot Samson has withdrawn to another residence, acting only by messengers: the awful report circulates through St. Edmundsbury that the Abbot is in danger of being murdered by the Monks with their knives! How wilt thou appease this, Abbot Samson! Return; for the Monastery seems near catching fire!

Abbot Samson returns; sits in his *Thalamus* or inner room, hurls out a bolt or two of excommunication: lo, one disobedient Monk sits in limbo, excommunicated, with foot-shackles on him, all day; and three more our Abbot has gyved 'with the lesser sentence, to strike fear into the others!' Let the others think with whom they have to do. The others think; and fear enters into them. 'On the morrow morning we decide on humbling ourselves 'before the Abbot, by word and gesture, in order to mitigate his 'mind. And so accordingly was done. He, on the other side, 'replying with much humility, yet always alleging his own justice 'and turning the blame on us, when he saw that we were con-'quered, became himself conquered. And bursting into tears, *per-*'*fusus lachrymis,* he swore that he had never grieved so much for 'anything in the world as for this, first on his own account, and 'then secondly and chiefly for the public scandal which had gone 'abroad, that St. Edmund's Monks were going to kill their Abbot. 'And when he had narrated how he went away on purpose till

' his anger should cool, repeating this word of the philosopher, " I
' would have taken vengeance on thee, had not I been angry," he
' arose weeping, and embraced each and all of us with the kiss of
' peace. He wept; we all wept:'[1]—what a picture! Behave better, ye remiss Monks, and thank Heaven for such an Abbot; or
know at least that ye must and shall obey him.

Worn down in this manner, with incessant toil and tribulation,
Abbot Samson had a sore time of it; his grizzled hair and beard
grew daily grayer. Those Jews, in the first four years, had ' visibly emaciated him:' Time, Jews, and the task of Governing, will
make a man's beard very gray! ' In twelve years,' says Jocelin,
' our Lord Abbot had grown wholly white as snow, *totus efficitur*
' *albus sicut nix*.' White atop, like the granite mountains:—but his
clear-beaming eyes still look out, in their stern clearness, in their
sorrow and pity; the heart within him remains unconquered.

Nay sometimes there are gleams of hilarity too; little snatches
of encouragement granted even to a Governor. ' Once my Lord
' Abbot and I, coming down from London through the Forest, I
' inquired of an old woman whom we came up to, Whose wood this
' was, and of what manor; who the master, who the keeper?'—All
this I knew very well beforehand, and my Lord Abbot too, Bozzy
that I was! But 'the old woman answered, The wood belonged
' to the new Abbot of St. Edmund's, was of the manor of Harlow,
' and the keeper of it was one Arnald. How did he behave to the
' people of the manor? I asked farther. She answered that he
' used to be a devil incarnate, *dæmon vivus*, an enemy of God, and
' flayer of the peasants' skins,'—skinning them like live eels, as
the manner of some is: ' but that now he dreads the new Abbot,
' knowing him to be a wise and sharp man, and so treats the people
' reasonably, *tractat homines pacifice*.' Whereat the Lord Abbot *fac-
tus est hilaris*,—could not but take a triumphant laugh for himself;
and determines to leave that Harlow manor yet unmeddled with,
for a while.[2]

A brave man, strenuously fighting, fails not of a little triumph,
now and then, to keep him in heart. Everywhere we try at least
to give the adversary as good as he brings; and, with swift force
or slow watchful manœuvre, extinguish this and the other solecism, leave one solecism less in God's Creation; and so *proceed*
with our battle, not slacken or surrender in it! The Fifty feudal
Knights, for example, were of unjust greedy temper, and cheated
us, in the Installation-day, of ten knights'-fees ;—but they know now
whether that has profited them aught, and I Jocelin know. Our

<hr>

[1] Jocelini Chronica, p. 85.   [2] Ibid. p. 24.

Lord Abbot for the moment had to endure it, and say nothing; but he watched his time.

Look also how my Lord of Clare, coming to claim his *undue* 'debt' in the Court at Witham, with barons and apparatus, gets a Rowland for his Oliver! Jocelin shall report: 'The Earl, crowded 'round (*constipatus*) with many barons and men-at-arms, Earl Al-'beric and others standing by him, said, "That his bailiffs had 'given him to understand they were wont annually to receive for 'his behoof, from the Hundred of Risebridge and the bailiffs 'thereof, a sum of five shillings, which sum was now unjustly held 'back;" and he alleged farther that his predecessors had been in-'feft, at the Conquest, in the lands of Alfric son of Wisgar, who 'was Lord of that Hundred, as may be read in Domesday Book 'by all persons.—The Abbot, reflecting for a moment, without stir-'ring from his place, made answer: "A wonderful deficit, my Lord 'Earl, this that thou mentionest! King Edward gave to St. Ed-'mund that entire Hundred, and confirmed the same with his 'Charter; nor is there any mention there of those five shillings. 'It will behove thee to say, for what service, or on what ground, 'thou exactest those five shillings." Whereupon the Earl, con-'sulting with his followers, replied, That he had to carry the Ban-'ner of St. Edmund in war-time, and for this duty the five shillings 'were his. To which the Abbot: "Certainly, it seems inglorious, 'if so great a man, Earl of Clare no less, receive so small a gift for 'such a service. To the Abbot of St. Edmund's it is no unbearable 'burden to give five shillings. But Roger Earl Bigot holds himself 'duly seised, and asserts that he by such seisin has the office of 'carrying St. Edmund's Banner; and he did carry it when the Earl 'of Leicester and his Flemings were beaten at Fornham. Then 'again Thomas de Mendham says that the right is his. When you 'have made out with one another, that this right is thine, come 'then and claim the five shillings, and I will promptly pay them!" 'Whereupon the Earl said, He would speak with Earl Roger his 'relative; and so the matter *cepit dilationem*,' and lies undecided to the end of the world. Abbot Samson answers by word or act, in this or the like pregnant manner, having justice on his side, in-numerable persons: Pope's Legates, King's Viscounts, Canterbury Archbishops, Cellarers, *Sochemanni ;*—and leaves many a solecism extinguished.

On the whole, however, it is and remains sore work. 'One 'time, during my chaplaincy, I ventured to say to him: "*Domine*, I 'heard thee, this night after matins, wakeful, and sighing deeply, '*valde suspirantem*, contrary to thy usual wont." He answered: '"No wonder. Thou, son Jocelin, sharest in my good things, in

' food and drink, in riding and such like; but thou little thinkest
' concerning the management of House and Family, the various
' and arduous businesses of the Pastoral Care, which harass me,
' and make my soul to sigh and be anxious." Whereto I, lifting
' up my hands to Heaven: ."From such anxiety, Omnipotent Mer-
' ciful Lord deliver me!"—I have heard the Abbot say, If he had
' been as he was before he became a Monk, and could have any-
' where got five or six marcs of income,' some three pound ten of
yearly revenue, 'whereby to support himself in the schools, he
' would never have been Monk nor Abbot. Another time he said
' with an oath, If he had known what a business it was to govern
' the Abbey, he would rather have been Almoner, how much rather
' Keeper of the Books, than Abbot and Lord. That latter office he
' said he had always longed for, beyond any other. *Quis talia cre-*
' *deret*,' concludes Jocelin, ' Who can believe such things ?'

Three pound ten, and a life of Literature, especially of quiet
Literature, without copyright, or world-celebrity of literary-ga-
zettes,—yes, thou brave Abbot Samson, for thyself it had been
better, easier, perhaps also nobler! But then, for thy disobedient
Monks, unjust Viscounts; for a Domain of St. Edmund overgrown
with Solecisms, human and other, it had not been so well. Nay
neither could *thy* Literature, never so quiet, have been easy. Literature, when noble, is not easy; but only when ignoble. Literature too is a quarrel, and internecine duel, with the whole World
of Darkness that lies without one and within one;—rather a hard
fight at times, even with the three pound ten secure. Thou, there
where thou art, wrestle and duel along, cheerfully to the end; and
make no remarks !

CHAPTER XIII.

IN PARLIAMENT.

Of Abbot Samson's public business we say little, though that also
was great. He had to judge the people as Justice Errant, to
decide in weighty arbitrations and public controversies; to equip
his *milites*, send them duly in war-time to the King;—strive every
way that the Commonweal, in his quarter of it, take no damage.

Once, in the confused days of Lackland's usurpation, while
Cœur-de-Lion was away, our brave Abbot took helmet himself,
having first excommunicated all that should favour Lackland ; and
led his men in person to the siege of *Windleshora*, what we now
call Windsor ; where Lackland had entrenched himself, the centre

of infinite confusions; some Reform Bill, then as now, being greatly needed. There did Abbot Samson ' fight the battle of reform,'—with other ammunition, one hopes, than ' tremendous cheering' and such like! For these things he was called ' the magnanimous Abbot.'

He also attended duly in his place in Parliament *de arduis regni;* attended especially, as in *arduissimo,* when ' the news reached London that King Richard was a captive in Germany.' Here ' while all the barons sat to consult,' and many of them looked blank enough, ' the Abbot started forth, *prosiliit coram omnibus,* in ' his place in Parliament, and said, That *he* was ready to go and ' seek his Lord the King, either clandestinely by subterfuge (*in* ' *tapinagio*), or by any other method; and search till he found him, ' and got certain notice of him; he for one! By which word,' says Jocelin, ' he acquired great praise for himself,'—unfeigned commendation from the Able Editors of that age.

By which word;—and also by which *deed:* for the Abbot actually went ' with rich gifts to the King in Germany;'[1] Usurper Lackland being first rooted out from Windsor, and the King's peace somewhat settled.

As to these ' rich gifts,' however, we have to note one thing: In all England, as appeared to the Collective Wisdom, there was not like to be treasure enough for ransoming King Richard; in which extremity certain Lords of the Treasury, *Justiciarii ad Scaccarium,* suggested that St. Edmund's Shrine, covered with thick gold, was still untouched. Could not it, in this extremity, be peeled off, at least in part; under condition, of course, of its being replaced, when times mended? The Abbot, starting plumb up, *se erigens,* answered: "Know ye for certain, that I will in nowise do this thing; nor is there any man who could force me to consent thereto. But I will open the doors of the Church: Let him that likes enter; let him that dares come forward!" Emphatic words, which created a sensation round the woolsack. For the Justiciaries of the *Scaccarium* answered, ' with oaths, each for him- ' self: "I won't come forward, for my share; nor will I, nor I! ' The distant and absent who offended him, Saint Edmund has ' been known to punish fearfully; much more will he those close ' by, who lay violent hands on his coat, and would strip it off!" ' These things being said, the Shrine was not meddled with, nor ' any ransom levied for it.'[2]

For Lords of the Treasury have in all times their impassable limits, be it by ' force of public opinion' or otherwise; and in those

[1] Jocelini Chronica, pp. 39, 40.   [2] Ibid. p. 71.

days a Heavenly Awe overshadowed and encompassed, as it still ought and must, all earthly Business whatsoever.

CHAPTER XIV.

HENRY OF ESSEX.

Of St. Edmund's fearful avengements have they not the remarkablest instance still before their eyes? He that will go to Reading Monastery may find there, now tonsured into a mournful penitent Monk, the once proud Henry Earl of Essex; and discern how St. Edmund punishes terribly, yet with mercy! This Narrative is too significant to be omitted as a document of the Time. Our Lord Abbot, once on a visit at Reading, heard the particulars from Henry's own mouth; and thereupon charged one of his monks to write it down;—as accordingly the Monk has done, in ambitious rhetorical Latin; inserting the same, as episode, among Jocelin's garrulous leaves. Read it here; with ancient yet with modern eyes.

Henry Earl of Essex, standard-bearer of England, had high places and emoluments; had a haughty high soul, yet with various flaws, or rather with one many-branched flaw and crack, running through the texture of it. For example, did he not treat Gilbert de Cereville in the most shocking manner? He cast Gilbert into prison; and, with chains and slow torments, wore the life out of him there. And Gilbert's crime was understood to be only that of innocent Joseph: the Lady Essex was a Potiphar's Wife, and had accused poor Gilbert! Other cracks, and branches of that widespread flaw in the Standard-bearer's soul we could point out: but indeed the main stem and trunk of all is too visible in this, That he had no right reverence for the Heavenly in Man,—that far from showing due reverence to St. Edmund, he did not even show him common justice. While others in the Eastern Counties were adorning and enlarging with rich gifts St. Edmund's resting-place, which had become a city of refuge for many things, this Earl of Essex flatly defrauded him, by violence or quirk of law, of five shillings yearly, and converted said sum to his own poor uses! Nay, in another case of litigation, the unjust Standard-bearer, for his own profit, asserting that the cause belonged not to St. Edmund's Court, but to *his* in Lailand Hundred, 'involved ' us in travellings and innumerable expenses, vexing the servants ' of St. Edmund for a long tract of time.' In short, he is without

reverence for the Heavenly, this Standard-bearer; reveres only the
Earthly, Gold-coined; and has a most morbid lamentable flaw in
the texture of him. It cannot come to good.

Accordingly, the same flaw, or St.-Vitus' *tic*, manifests itself
ere long in another way. In the year 1157, he went with his
Standard to attend King Henry, our blessed Sovereign (whom *we*
saw afterwards at Waltham), in his War with the Welsh. A somewhat disastrous War; in which while King Henry and his force
were struggling to retreat Parthian-like, endless clouds of exasperated Welshmen hemming them in, and now we had come to
the 'difficult pass of Coleshill,' and as it were to the nick of destruction,—Henry Earl of Essex shrieks out on a sudden (blinded
doubtless by his inner flaw, or 'evil genius' as some name it),
That King Henry is killed, That all is lost,—and flings down his
Standard to shift for itself there! And, certainly enough, all *had*
been lost, had all men been as he;—had not brave men, without
such miserable jerking *tic-douloureux* in the souls of them, come
dashing up, with blazing swords and looks, and asserted That nothing was lost yet, that all must be regained yet. In this manner
King Henry and his force got safely retreated, Parthian-like, from
the pass of Coleshill and the Welsh War.[1] But, once home again,
Earl Robert de Montfort, a kinsman of this Standard-bearer's,
rises up in the King's Assembly to declare openly that such a
man is unfit for bearing English Standards, being in fact either
a special traitor, or something almost worse, a coward namely, or
universal traitor. Wager of Battle in consequence; solemn Duel,
by the King's appointment, 'in a certain Island of the Thames-
'stream at Reading, *apud Radingas*, short way from the Abbey
'there.' King, Peers, and an immense multitude of people, on
such scaffoldings and heights as they can come at, are gathered
round, to see what issue the business will take. The business
takes this bad issue, in our Monk's own words faithfully rendered:

'And it came to pass, while Robert de Montfort thundered on
'him manfully (*viriliter intonúisset*) with hard and frequent strokes,
'and a valiant beginning promised the fruit of victory, Henry of
'Essex, rather giving way, glanced round on all sides; and lo, at
'the rim of the horizon, on the confines of the River and land,
'he discerned the glorious King and Martyr Edmund, in shining
'armour, and as if hovering in the air; looking towards him with
'severe countenance, nodding his head with a mien and motion
'of austere anger. At St. Edmund's hand there stood also an-
'other Knight, Gilbert de Cereville, whose armour was not so

[1] See Lyttelton's Henry II., ii. 384.

' splendid, whose stature was less gigantic; casting vengeful looks
' at him. This he seeing with his eyes, remembered that old
' crime brings new shame. And now wholly desperate, and chang-
' ing reason into violence, he took the part of one blindly attack-
' ing, not skilfully defending. Who while he struck fiercely was
' more fiercely struck; and so, in short, fell down vanquished,
' and it was thought, slain. As he lay there for dead, his kins-
' men, Magnates of England, besought the King, that the Monks
' of Reading might have leave to bury him. However, he proved
' not to be dead, but got well again among them; and now, with
' recovered health, assuming the Regular Habit, he strove to wipe
' out the stain of his former life, to cleanse the long week of his
' dissolute history by at least a purifying sabbath, and cultivate
' the studies of Virtue into fruits of eternal Felicity.'[1]

Thus does the Conscience of man project itself athwart whatsoever of knowledge or surmise, of imagination, understanding,
faculty, acquirement, or natural disposition he has in him; and,
like light through coloured glass, paint strange pictures ' on the
rim of the horizon' and elsewhere! Truly, this same 'sense of
the Infinite nature of Duty' is the central part of all with us; a
ray as of Eternity and Immortality, immured in dusky many-co-
loured Time, and its deaths and births. Your ' coloured glass'
varies so much from century to century;—and, in certain money-
making, game-preserving centuries, it gets so terribly opaque!
Not a Heaven with cherubim surrounds you then, but a kind of
vacant leaden-coloured Hell. One day it will again cease to be
opaque, this ' coloured glass.' Nay, may it not become at once
translucent and *un*coloured? Painting no Pictures more for us,
but only the everlasting Azure itself? That will be a right glorious consummation!—

Saint Edmund from the horizon's edge, in shining armour,
threatening the misdoer in his hour of extreme need : it is beautiful, it is great and true. So old, yet so modern, actual; true yet
for every one of us, as for Henry the Earl and Monk! A glimpse
as of the Deepest in Man's Destiny, which is the same for all
times and ages. Yes, Henry my brother, there in thy extreme
need, thy soul is *lamed;* and behold thou canst not so much as
fight! For Justice and Reverence *are* the everlasting central Law
of this Universe; and to forget them, and have all the Universe
against one, God and one's own Self for enemies, and only the
Devil and the Dragons for friends, is not that a ' lameness' like
few? That some shining armed St. Edmund hang minatory on

[1] Jocelini Chronica, p. 52.

thy horizon, that infinite sulphur-lakes hang minatory, or do not now hang,—this alters no whit the eternal fact of the thing. I say, thy soul is lamed, and the God and all Godlike in it marred: lamed, paralytic, tending towards baleful eternal death, whether thou know it or not;—nay hadst thou never known it, that surely had been worst of all!—

Thus, at any rate, by the heavenly Awe that overshadows earthly Business, does Samson, readily in those days, save St. Edmund's Shrine, and innumerable still more precious things.

CHAPTER XV.

PRACTICAL-DEVOTIONAL.

HERE indeed, perhaps, by rule of antagonisms, may be the place to mention that, after King Richard's return, there was a liberty of tourneying given to the fighting-men of England: that a Tournament was proclaimed in the Abbot's domain, 'between Thetford and St. Edmundsbury,'—perhaps in the Euston region, on Fakenham Heights, midway between these two localities: that it was publicly prohibited by our Lord Abbot; and nevertheless was held in spite of him,—and by the parties, as would seem, considered ' a gentle and free passage of arms.'

Nay, next year, there came to the same spot four-and-twenty young men, sons of Nobles, for another passage of arms; who, having completed the same, all rode into St. Edmundsbury to lodge for the night. Here is modesty! Our Lord Abbot, being instructed of it, ordered the Gates to be closed; the whole party shut in. The morrow was the Vigil of the Apostles Peter and Paul; no outgate on the morrow. Giving their promise not to depart without permission, those four-and-twenty young bloods dieted all that day (*manducaverunt*) with the Lord Abbot, waiting for trial on the morrow. ' But after dinner,'—mark it, posterity!—
' the Lord Abbot retiring into his *Thalamus*, they all started up,
' and began carolling and singing (*carolare et cantare*); sending into
' the Town for wine; drinking, and afterwards howling (*ululantes*);
' —totally depriving the Abbot and Convent of their afternoon's
' nap; doing all this in derision of the Lord Abbot, and spending
' in such fashion the whole day till evening, nor would they desist
' at the Lord Abbot's order! Night coming on, they broke the bolts
' of the Town-Gates, and went off by violence!'[1] Was the like ever heard of? The roysterous young dogs; carolling, howling, break-

[1] Jocelini Chronica, p. 40.

ing the Lord Abbot's sleep,—after that sinful chivalry cockfight of theirs! They too are a feature of distant centuries, as of near ones. St. Edmund on the edge of your horizon, or whatever else there, young scamps, in the dandy state, whether cased in iron or in whalebone, begin to caper and carol on the green Earth! Our Lord Abbot excommunicated most of them; and they gradually came in for repentance.

Excommunication is a great recipe with our Lord Abbot; the prevailing purifier in those ages. Thus when the Townsfolk and Monks-menials quarrelled once at the Christmas Mysteries in St. Edmund's Churchyard, and 'from words it came to cuffs, and from cuffs to cuttings and the effusion of blood,'—our Lord Abbot excommunicates sixty of the rioters, with bell, book and caudle (*accensis candelis*), at one stroke.[1] Whereupon they all come suppliant, indeed nearly naked, 'nothing on but their breeches, *omnino* 'nudi præter femoralia*, and prostrate themselves at the Church-'door.' Figure that!

In fact, by excommunication or persuasion, by impetuosity of driving or adroitness in leading, this Abbot, it is now becoming plain everywhere, is a man that generally remains master at last. He tempers his medicine to the malady, now hot, now cool; prudent though fiery, an eminently practical man. Nay sometimes in his adroit practice there are swift turns almost of a surprising nature! Once, for example, it chanced that Geoffrey Riddell Bishop of Ely, a Prelate rather troublesome to our Abbot, made a request of him for timber from his woods towards certain edifices going on at Glemsford. The Abbot, a great builder himself, disliked the request; could not however give it a negative. While he lay, therefore, at his Manorhouse of Melford not long after, there comes to him one of the Lord Bishop's men or monks, with a message from his Lordship, "That he now begged permission to cut down the requisite trees in Elmswell Wood,"—so said the monk: Elms*well*, where there are no trees but scrubs and shrubs, instead of Elm*set*, our true *nemus*, and high-towering oak-wood, here on Melford Manor! Elmswell? The Lord Abbot, in surprise, inquires privily of Richard his Forester; Richard answers that my Lord of Ely has already had his *carpentarii* in Elm*set*, and marked out for his own use all the best trees in the compass of it. Abbot Samson thereupon answers the monk: "Elmswell? Yes surely, be it as my Lord Bishop wishes." The successful monk, on the morrow morning, hastens home to Ely; but, on the morrow morning, 'directly after mass,' Abbot Samson too was busy! The successful monk, arriving at Ely, is rated for a goose and an owl; is

[1] Jocelini Chronica, p. 68.

ordered back to say that Elmset was the place meant. Alas, on arriving at Elmset, he finds the Bishop's trees, they 'and a hundred
more,' all felled and piled, and the stamp of St. Edmund's Monastery burnt into them,—for roofing of the great tower we are building
there! Your importunate Bishop must seek wood for Glemsford
edifices in some other *nemus* than this. A practical Abbot!

We said withal there was a terrible flash of anger in him: witness his address to old Herbert the Dean, who in a too thrifty
manner has erected a windmill for himself on his glebe-lands at
Haberdon. On the morrow, after mass, our Lord Abbot orders the
Cellerarius to send off his carpenters to demolish the said structure *brevi manu*, and lay up the wood in safe keeping. Old Dean
Herbert, hearing what was toward, comes tottering along hither,
to plead humbly for himself and his mill. The Abbot answers: " I
am obliged to thee as if thou hadst cut off both my feet! By God's
face, *per os Dei*, I will not eat bread till that fabric be torn in
pieces. Thou art an old man, and shouldst have known that neither the King nor his Justiciary dare change aught within the
Liberties without consent of Abbot and Convent: and thou hast
presumed on such a thing? I tell thee, it will *not* be without damage to my mills; for the Townsfolk will go to thy mill, and grind
their corn (*bladum suum*) at their own good pleasure; nor can I
hinder them, since they are free men. I will allow no new mills
on such principle. Away, away; before thou gettest home again,
thou shalt see what thy mill has grown to!"[1]—The very reverend
the old Dean totters home again, in all haste; tears the mill in
pieces by his own *carpentarii*, to save at least the timber; and
Abbot Samson's workmen, coming up, find the ground already
clear of it.

Easy to bully-down poor old rural Deans, and blow their wind-
mills away: but who is the man that dare abide King Richard's
anger; cross the Lion in his path, and take him by the whiskers!
Abbot Samson too; he is that man, with justice on his side. The
case was this. Adam de Cokefield, one of the chief feudatories of
St. Edmund, and a principal man in the Eastern Counties, died,
leaving large possessions, and for heiress a daughter of three
months; who by clear law, as all men know, became thus Abbot
Samson's ward; whom accordingly he proceeded to dispose of to
such person as seemed fittest. But now King Richard has another
person in view, to whom the little ward and her great possessions
were a suitable thing. He, by letter, requests that Abbot Samson
will have the goodness to give her to this person. Abbot Samson,

[1] Jocelini Chronica, p. 43.

with deep humility, replies that she is already given. New letters from Richard, of severer tenor; answered with new deep humilities, with gifts and entreaties, with no promise of obedience. King Richard's ire is kindled; messengers arrive at St. Edmundsbury, with emphatic message to obey or tremble! Abbot Samson, wisely silent as to the King's threats, makes answer: "The King can send if he will, and seize the ward: force and power he has to do his pleasure, and abolish the whole Abbey. But I, for my part, never can be bent to wish this that he seeks, nor shall it by me be ever done. For there is danger lest such things be made a precedent of, to the prejudice of my successors. *Videat Altissimus*, Let the Most High look on it. Whatsoever thing shall befall I will patiently endure."

Such was Abbot Samson's deliberate decision. Why not? Cœur-de-Lion is very dreadful, but not the dreadfullest. *Videat Altissimus.* I reverence Cœur-de-Lion to the marrow of my bones, and will in all right things be *homo suus;* but it is not, properly speaking, with terror, with any fear at all. On the whole, have I not looked on the face of ' Satan with outspread wings;' steadily into Hellfire these seven-and-forty years;—and was not melted into terror even at that, such the Lord's goodness to me? Cœur-de-Lion!

Richard swore tornado oaths, worse than our armies in Flanders, To be revenged on that proud Priest. But in the end he discovered that the Priest was right; and forgave him, and even loved him. ' King Richard wrote, soon after, to Abbot Samson, ' That he wanted one or two of the St. Edmundsbury dogs, which ' he heard were good.' Abbot Samson sent him dogs of the best; Richard replied by the present of a ring, which Pope Innocent the Third had given him. Thou brave Richard, thou brave Samson! Richard too, I suppose, ' loved a man,' and knew one when he saw him.

No one will accuse our Lord Abbot of wanting worldly wisdom, due interest in worldly things. A skilful man; full of cunning insight, lively interests; always discerning the road to his object, be it circuit, be it short-cut, and victoriously travelling forward thereon. Nay rather it might seem, from Jocelin's Narrative, as if he had his eye all but exclusively directed on terrestrial matters, and was much too secular for a devout man. But this too, if we examine it, was right. For it is *in* the world that a man, devout or other, has his life to lead, his work waiting to be done. The basis of Abbot Samson's, we shall discover, was truly religion, after all. Returning from his dusty pilgrimage, with such welcome as we saw, ' he sat down at the foot of St. Edmund's Shrine.' Not a

talking theory that; no, a silent practice: Thou, St. Edmund, with
what lies in thee, thou now must help me, or none will!

This also is a significant fact: the zealous interest our Abbot
took in the Crusades. To all noble Christian hearts of that era,
what earthly enterprise so noble? 'When Henry II., having taken
' the cross, came to St. Edmund's, to pay his devotions before set-
' ting out, the Abbot secretly made for himself a cross of linen
' cloth: and, holding this in one hand and a threaded needle in
' the other, asked leave of the King to assume it.' The King could
not spare Samson out of England;—the King himself indeed never
went. But the Abbot's eye was set on the Holy Sepulchre, as on
the spot of this Earth where the true cause of Heaven was decid-
ing itself. 'At the retaking of Jerusalem by the Pagans, Abbot
' Samson put on a cilice and hair-shirt, and wore under-garments
' of hair-cloth ever after; he abstained also from flesh and flesh-
' meats (*carne et carneis*) thenceforth to the end of his life.' Like a
dark cloud eclipsing the hopes of Christendom, those tidings cast
their shadow over St. Edmundsbury too: Shall Samson Abbas take
pleasure while Christ's Tomb is in the hands of the Infidel? Samson, in pain of body, shall daily be reminded of it, daily be admonished to grieve for it.

The great antique heart: how like a child's in its simplicity,
like a man's in its earnest solemnity and depth! Heaven lies
over him wheresoever he goes or stands on the Earth; making all
the Earth a mystic Temple to him, the Earth's business all a kind
of worship. Glimpses of bright creatures flash in the common
sunlight; angels yet hover doing God's messages among men:
that rainbow was set in the clouds by the hand of God! Wonder,
miracle encompass the man; he lives in an element of miracle;
Heaven's splendour over his head, Hell's darkness under his feet.
A great Law of Duty, high as these two Infinitudes, dwarfing all
else, annihilating all else,—making royal Richard as small as peasant Samson, smaller if need be!—The ' imaginative faculties?'
' Rude poetic ages?' The ' primeval poetic element?' O for God's
sake, good reader, talk no more of all that! It was not a Dilettantism this of Abbot Samson. It was a Reality, and it is one.
The garment only of it is dead; the essence of it lives through
all Time and all Eternity!—

And truly, as we said above, is not this comparative silence of
Abbot Samson as to his religion, precisely the healthiest sign of
him and of it? 'The Unconscious is the alone Complete.' Abbot
Samson all along a busy working man, as all men are bound to
be, his religion, his worship was like his daily bread to him;—

which he did not take the trouble to talk much about; which he merely ate at stated intervals, and lived and did his work upon! This is Abbot Samson's Catholicism of the Twelfth Century;—something like the *Ism* of all true men in all true centuries, I fancy! Alas, compared with any of the *Isms* current in these poor days, what a thing! Compared with the respectablest, morbid, struggling Methodism, never so earnest; with the respectablest, ghastly, dead or galvanised Dilettantism, never so spasmodic!

Methodism with its eye forever turned on its own navel; asking itself with torturing anxiety of Hope and Fear, " Am I right, am I wrong? Shall I be saved, shall I not be damned?"—what is this, at bottom, but a new phasis of *Egoism*, stretched out into the Infinite; not always the heavenlier for its infinitude! Brother, so soon as possible, endeavour to rise above all that. "Thou *art* wrong; thou art like to be damned:" consider that as the fact, reconcile thyself even to that, if thou be a man ;—then first is the devouring Universe subdued under thee, and from the black murk of midnight and noise of greedy Acheron, dawn as of an everlasting morning, how far above all Hope and all Fear, springs for thee, enlightening thy steep path, awakening in thy heart celestial Memnon's music!

But of our Dilettantisms, and galvanised Dilettantisms; of Puseyism—O Heavens, what shall we say of Puseyism, in comparison to Twelfth-Century Catholicism? Little or nothing; for indeed it is a matter to strike one dumb.

> The Builder of this Universe was wise,
> He plann'd all souls, all systems, planets, particles:
> The Plan He shap'd all Worlds and Æons by,
> Was — — Heavens !—Was thy small Nine-and-thirty Articles ?

That certain human souls, living on this practical Earth, should think to save themselves and a ruined world by noisy theoretic demonstrations and laudations of *the* Church, instead of some unnoisy, unconscious, but *practical*, total, heart-and-soul demonstration of *a* Church: this, in the circle of revolving ages, this also was a thing we were to see. A kind of penultimate thing, precursor of very strange consummations; last thing but one? If there is no atmosphere, what will it serve a man to demonstrate the excellence of lungs? How much profitabler when you can, like Abbot Samson, breathe; and go along your way!

———

CHAPTER XVI.

ST. EDMUND.

ABBOT SAMSON built many useful, many pious edifices; human dwellings, churches, church-steeples, barns;—all fallen now and vanished, but useful while they stood. He built and endowed 'the Hospital of Babwell;' built 'fit houses for the St. Edmundsbury Schools.' Many are the roofs once 'thatched with reeds' which he 'caused to be covered with tiles;' or if they were churches, probably 'with lead.' For all ruinous incomplete things, buildings or other, were an eye-sorrow to the man. We saw his 'great tower of St. Edmund's;' or at least the roof-timbers of it, lying cut and stamped in Elmset Wood. To change combustible decaying reed-thatch into tile or lead; and material, still more, moral wreck into rain-tight order, what a comfort to Samson!

One of the things he could not in any wise but rebuild was the great Altar, aloft on which stood the Shrine itself; the great Altar, which had been damaged by fire, by the careless rubbish and careless candle of two somnolent Monks, one night,—the Shrine escaping almost as if by miracle! Abbot Samson read his Monks a severe lecture: "A Dream one of us had, that he saw St. Edmund naked and in lamentable plight. Know ye the interpretation of that Dream? St. Edmund proclaims himself naked, because ye defraud the naked Poor of your old clothes, and give with reluctance what ye are bound to give them of meat and drink: the idleness moreover and negligence of the Sacristan and his people is too evident from the late misfortune by fire. Well might our Holy Martyr seem to lie cast out from his Shrine, and say with groans that he was stript of his garments, and wasted with hunger and thirst!"

This is Abbot Samson's interpretation of the Dream;—diametrically the reverse of that given by the Monks themselves, who scruple not to say privily, "It is *we* that are the naked and famished limbs of the Martyr; we whom the Abbot curtails of all our privileges, setting his own official to control our very Cellarer!" Abbot Samson adds, that this judgment by fire has fallen upon them for murmuring about their meat and drink.

Clearly enough, meanwhile, the Altar, whatever the burning of it mean or foreshadow, must needs be reëdified. Abbot Samson reëdifies it, all of polished marble; with the highest stretch of art and sumptuosity, reëmbellishes the Shrine for which it is to serve as pediment. Nay farther, as had ever been among his prayers, he enjoys, he sinner, a glimpse of the glorious Martyr's very Body in the process; having solemnly opened the *Loculus*, Chest or sacred Coffin, for that purpose. It is the culminating moment of Abbot Samson's life. Bozzy Jocelin himself rises into a kind of Psalmist solemnity on this occasion; the laziest monk 'weeps' warm tears, as *Te Deum* is sung.

Very strange;—how far vanished from us in these unworshiping ages of ours! The Patriot Hampden, best beatified man we have, had lain in like manner some two centuries in his narrow home, when certain dignitaries of us, 'and twelve grave-diggers with pulleys,' raised him also up, under cloud of night, cut off his arm with penknives, pulled the scalp off his head,—and otherwise worshiped our Hero Saint in the most amazing manner![1] Let the modern eye look earnestly on that old midnight hour in St. Edmundsbury Church, shining yet on us, ruddy-bright, through the depths of seven hundred years; and consider mournfully what our Hero-worship once was, and what it now is! We translate with all the fidelity we can:

'The Festival of St. Edmund now approaching, the marble
' blocks are polished, and all things are in readiness for lifting of
' the Shrine to its new place. A fast of three days was held by all
' the people, the cause and meaning thereof being publicly set
' forth to them. The Abbot announces to the Convent that all
' must prepare themselves for transferring of the Shrine, and
' appoints time and way for the work. Coming therefore that
' night to matins, we found the great Shrine (*feretrum magnum*)
' raised upon the Altar, but empty; covered all over with white
' doeskin leather, fixed to the wood with silver nails; but one
' pannel of the Shrine was left down below, and resting thereon,
' beside its old column of the Church, the Loculus with the Sa-
' cred Body yet lay where it was wont. Praises being sung, we
' all proceeded to commence our disciplines (*ad disciplinas susci-*
' *piendas*). These finished, the Abbot and certain with him are
' clothed in their albs; and, approaching reverently, set about
' uncovering the Loculus. There was an outer cloth of linen, en-
' wrapping the Loculus and all; this we found tied on the upper
' side with strings of its own: within this was a cloth of silk, and
' then another linen cloth, and then a third; and so at last the
' Loculus was uncovered, and seen resting on a little tray of wood,
' that the bottom of it might not be injured by the stone. Over
' the breast of the Martyr, there lay, fixed to the surface of the

[1] Annual Register (year 1828, Chronicle, p. 93), Gentleman's Magazine, &c. &c.

' Loculus, a Golden Angel about the length of a human foot;
' holding in one hand a golden sword, and in the other a banner :
' under this there was a hole in the lid of the Loculus, on which
· the ancient servants of the Martyr had been wont to lay their
' hands for touching the Sacred Body. And over the figure of
' the Angel was this verse inscribed :

' Martiris ecce zoma servat Michaelis agalma.[1]

' At the head and foot of the Loculus were iron rings whereby it
' could be lifted.

 ' Lifting the Loculus and Body, therefore, they carried it to
' the Altar ; and I put-to my sinful hand to help in carrying,
' though the Abbot had commanded that none should approach
' except called. And the Loculus was placed in the Shrine ; and
' the pannel it had stood on was put in its place, and the Shrine
' for the present closed. We all thought that the Abbot would
' show the Loculus to the people ; and bring out the Sacred Body
' again, at a certain period of the Festival. But in this we were
' wofully mistaken, as the sequel shows.

 ' For in the fourth holiday of the Festival, while the Convent
' were all singing <i>Completorium</i>, our Lord Abbot spoke privily with
' the Sacristan and Walter the Medicus ; and order was taken
' that twelve of the Brethren should be appointed against mid-
· night, who were strong for carrying the pannel-planks of the
· Shrine, and skilful in unfixing them, and putting them together
' again. The Abbot then said that it was among his prayers to
· look once upon the Body of his Patron ; and that he wished the
· Sacristan and Walter the Medicus to be with him. The Twelve
' appointed Brethren were these : The Abbot's two Chaplains, the
' two Keepers of the Shrine, the two Masters of the Vestry ; and
· six more, namely, the Sacristan Hugo, Walter the Medicus, Au-
' gustin, William of Dice, Robert, and Richard. I, alas, was not
' of the number.

 ' The Convent therefore being all asleep, these Twelve, clothed
' in their albs, with the Abbot, assembled at the Altar ; and open-
· ing a pannel of the Shrine, they took out the Loculus ; laid it on
' a table, near where the Shrine used to be ; and made ready for
' unfastening the lid, which was joined and fixed to the Loculus
· with sixteen very long nails. Which when, with difficulty, they
' had done, all except the two forenamed associates are ordered to
' draw back. The Abbot and they two were alone privileged to
' look in. The Loculus was so filled with the Sacred Body that
' you could scarcely put a needle between the head and the wood,

---

[1] This is the Martyr's Garment, which Michael's Image guards.

' or between the feet and the wood : the head lay united to the
' body, a little raised with a small pillow. But the Abbot, looking
' close, found now a silk cloth veiling the whole Body, and then
' a linen cloth of wondrous whiteness; and upon the head was
' spread a small linen cloth, and then another small and most fine
' silk cloth, as if it were the veil of a nun. These coverings being
' lifted off, they found now the Sacred Body all wrapt in linen ;
' and so at length the lineaments of the same appeared. But here
' the Abbot stopped ; saying he durst not proceed farther, or look
' at the sacred flesh naked. Taking the head between his hands.
' he thus spake groaning: " Glorious Martyr, holy Edmund, blessed
' be the hour when thou wert born. Glorious Martyr, turn it not
' to my perdition that I have so dared to touch thee, I miserable
' and sinful ; thou knowest my devout love, and the intention of
' my mind." And proceeding, he touched the eyes ; and the nose,
' which was very massive and prominent (*valde grossum et valde
' eminentem*) ; and then he touched the breast and arms ; and rais-
' ing the left arm he touched the fingers, and placed his own fingers
' between the sacred fingers. And proceeding he found the feet
' standing stiff up, like the feet of a man dead yesterday ; and he
' touched the toes, and counted them (*tangendo numeravit*).

  ' And now it was agreed that the other Brethren should be
' called forward to see the miracles; and accordingly those ten
' now advanced, and along with them six others who had stolen
' in without the Abbot's assent, namely, Walter of St. Alban's,
' Hugh the Infirmirarius, Gilbert brother of the Prior, Richard
' of Henham, Jocellus our Cellarer, and Turstan the Little; and
' all these saw the Sacred Body, but Turstan alone of them put
' forth his hand, and touched the Saint's knees and feet. And
' that there might be abundance of witnesses, one of our Breth-
' ren, John of Dice, sitting on the roof of the Church, with the
' servants of the Vestry, and looking through, clearly saw all these
' things.'

  What a scene; shining luminous effulgent, as the lamps of St.
Edmund do, through the dark Night; John of Dice, with vestry
men, clambering on the roof to look through; the Convent all
asleep, and the Earth all asleep,—and since then, Seven Centuries
of Time mostly gone to sleep ! Yes, there, sure enough, is the
martyred Body of Edmund landlord of the Eastern Counties, who,
nobly doing what he liked with his own, was slain three hundred
years ago : and a noble awe surrounds the memory of him, symbol
and promoter of many other right noble things.

  But have not we now advanced to strange new stages of Hero-worship, now in the little Church of Hampden, with our penknives out, and twelve grave-diggers with pulleys?   The manner of men's Hero-worship, verily it is the innermost fact of their existence, and determines all the rest,—at public hustings, in private drawing-rooms, in church, in market, and wherever else.   Have true rever-ence, and what indeed is inseparable therefrom, reverence the right man, all is well; have sham-reverence, and what also follows, greet with it the wrong man, then all is ill, and there is nothing well.   Alas, if Hero-worship become Dilettantism, and all except Mammonism be a vain grimace, how much, in this most earnest Earth, has gone and is evermore going to fatal destruction, and lies wasting in quiet lazy ruin, no man regarding it!   Till at length no heavenly *Ism* any longer coming down upon us, *Isms* from the other quarter have to mount up.   For the Earth, I say, is an earnest place; Life is no grimace, but a most serious fact.   And so, under universal Dilettantism much having been stript bare, not the souls of men only, but their very bodies and bread-cupboards having been stript bare, and life now no longer possible,—all is reduced to desperation, to the iron law of Necessity and very Fact again; and to temper Dilettantism, and astonish it, and burn it up with in-fernal fire, arises Chartism, *Bare-back-ism*, Sansculottism so-called! May the gods, and what of unworshiped heroes still remain among us, avert the omen.—

But however this may be, St. Edmund's Loculus, we find, has the veils of silk and linen reverently replaced, the lid fastened down again with its sixteen ancient nails; is wrapt in a new costly covering of silk, the gift of Hubert Archbishop of Canterbury: and through the sky-window John of Dice sees it lifted to its place in the Shrine, the pannels of this latter duly refixed, fit parchment documents being introduced withal;—and now John and his ves-trymen can slide down from the roof, for all is over, and the Con-vent wholly awakens to matins.   'When we assembled to sing ' matins,' says Jocelin, ' and understood what had been done, grief ' took hold of all that had not seen these things, each saying to ' himself, "Alas, I was deceived."   Matins over, the Abbot called ' the Convent to the great Altar; and briefly recounting the matter, ' alleged that it had not been in his power, nor was it permissible ' or fit, to invite us all to the sight of such things.   At hearing of ' which, we all wept, and with tears sang *Te Deum laudamus;* and ' hastened to toll the bells in the Choir.'
Stupid blockheads, to reverence their St. Edmund's dead Body in this manner?   Yes, brother;—and yet, on the whole, who knows how to reverence the Body of a Man?   It is the most reverend

phenomenon under this Sun. For the Highest God dwells visible
in that mystic unfathomable Visibility, which calls itself "I" on
the Earth. 'Bending before men,' says Novalis, 'is a reverence
' done to this Revelation in the Flesh. We touch Heaven when
' we lay our hand on a human Body.' And the Body of one Dead;
—a temple where the Hero-soul once was and now is not: Oh,
all mystery, all pity, all mute *awe* and wonder; *Super*naturalism
brought home to the very dullest; Eternity laid open, and the
nether Darkness and the upper Light-Kingdoms, —do conjoin
there, or exist nowhere! Sauerteig used to say to me, in his peculiar way: "A Chancery Lawsuit; justice, nay justice in mere
money, denied a man, for all his pleading, till twenty, till forty
years of his Life are gone seeking it: and a Cockney Funeral,
Death reverenced by hatchments, horsehair, brass-lacker, and un-
concerned bipeds carrying long poles and bags of black silk :—
are not these two reverences, this reverence for Death and that
reverence for Life, a notable pair of reverences among you English?"

Abbot Samson, at this culminating point of his existence, may,
and indeed must, be left to vanish with his Life-scenery from the
eyes of modern men. He had to run into France, to settle with
King Richard for the military service there of his St. Edmundsbury Knights; and with great labour got it done. He had to
decide on the dilapidated Coventry Monks; and with great labour,
and much pleading and journeying, got them reinstated; dined
with them all, and with the 'Masters of the Schools of Oxneford,'
—the veritable Oxford *Caput* sitting there at dinner, in a dim but
undeniable manner, in the City of Peeping Tom! He had, not
without labour, to controvert the intrusive Bishop of Ely, the intrusive Abbot of Cluny. Magnanimous Samson, his life is but a
labour and a journey; a bustling and a justling, till the still Night
come. He is sent for again, over sea, to advise King Richard
touching certain Peers of England, who had taken the Cross, but
never followed it to Palestine; whom the Pope is inquiring after.
The magnanimous Abbot makes preparation for departure; de-
parts, and——And Jocelin's Boswellean Narrative, suddenly shorn
through by the scissors of Destiny, *ends*. There are no words
more; but a black line, and leaves of blank paper. Irremediable:
the miraculous hand that held all this theatric-machinery suddenly
quits hold; impenetrable Time-Curtains rush down; in the mind's
eye all is again dark, void; with loud dinning in the mind's ear, our
real-phantasmagory of St. Edmundsbury plunges into the bosom
of the Twelfth Century again, and all is over. Monks, Abbot,

Hero-worship, Government, Obedience, Cœur-de-Lion and St. Edmund's Shrine, vanish like Mirza's Vision; and there is nothing left but a mutilated black Ruin amid green botanic expanses, and oxen, sheep and dilettanti pasturing in their places.

———

CHAPTER XVII.

THE BEGINNINGS.

WHAT a singular shape of a Man, shape of a Time, have we in this Abbot Samson and his history; how strangely do modes, creeds, formularies, and the date and place of a man's birth, modify the figure of the man!

Formulas too, as we call them, have a *reality* in Human Life. They are real as the very *skin* and *muscular tissue* of a Man's Life; and a most blessed indispensable thing, so long as they have *vitality* withal, and are a *living* skin and tissue to him! No man, or man's life, can go abroad and do business in the world without skin and tissues. No; first of all, these have to fashion themselves,—as indeed they spontaneously and inevitably do. Foam itself, and this is worth thinking of, can harden into oyster-shell; all living objects do by necessity form to themselves a skin.

And yet, again, when a man's Formulas become *dead;* as all Formulas, in the progress of living growth, are very sure to do! When the poor man's integuments, no longer nourished from within, become dead skin, mere adscititious leather and callosity, wearing thicker and thicker, uglier and uglier; till no *heart* any longer can be felt beating through them, so thick, callous, calcified are they; and all over it has now grown mere calcified oyster-shell, or were it polished mother-of-pearl, inwards almost to the very heart of the poor man:—yes then, you may say, his usefulness once more is quite obstructed; once more, he cannot go abroad and do business in the world; it is time that *he* take to bed, and prepare for departure, which cannot now be distant!

Ubi homines sunt modi sunt. Habit is the deepest law of human nature. It is our supreme strength; if also, in certain circumstances, our miserablest weakness.—From Stoke to Stowe is as yet a field, all pathless, untrodden: from Stoke where I live, to Stowe where I have to make my merchandises, perform my businesses, consult my heavenly oracles, there is as yet no path or human footprint; and I, impelled by such necessities, must nevertheless undertake the journey. Let me go once, scanning my way with any earnestness of outlook, and successfully arriving, my footprints are an invitation to me a second time to go by the same way. It is easier than any other way: the industry of 'scanning' lies already invested in it for me; I can go this time with less of scanning, or without scanning at all. Nay the very sight of my footprints, what a comfort for me; and in a degree, for all my brethren of mankind! The footprints are trodden and retrodden; the path wears ever broader, smoother, into a broad highway, where even wheels can run; and many travel it;—till—till the Town of Stowe disappear from that locality (as towns have been known to do), or no merchandising, heavenly oracle, or real business any longer exist for one there: then why should anybody travel the way?—Habit is our primal, fundamental law; Habit and Imitation, there is nothing more perennial in us than these two. They are the source of all Working and all Apprenticeship, of all Practice and all Learning, in this world.

Yes, the wise man too speaks, and acts, in Formulas; all men do so. And in general, the more completely cased with Formulas a man may be, the safer, happier is it for him. Thou who, in an All of rotten Formulas, seemest to stand nigh bare, having indignantly shaken off the superannuated rags and unsound callosities of Formulas,—consider how thou too art still clothed! This English Nationality, whatsoever from uncounted ages is genuine and a fact among thy native People, in their words and ways: all this, has it not made for thee a skin or second-skin, adhesive actually as thy natural skin? This thou hast not stript off, this thou wilt never strip off: the humour that thy mother gave thee has to show itself through this. A common, or it may be an uncommon Englishman thou art: but good Heavens, what sort of Arab, Chinaman, Jew-Clothesman, Turk, Hindoo, African Mandingo, wouldst thou have been, *thou* with those mother-qualities of thine!

It strikes me dumb to look over the long series of faces, such as any full Church, Courthouse, London-Tavern Meeting, or miscellany of men will show them. Some score or two of years ago, all these were little red-coloured pulpy infants; each of them capable of being kneaded, baked into any social form you chose: yet see now how they are fixed and hardened,—into artisans, artists, clergy, gentry, learned sergeants, unlearned dandies, and can and shall now be nothing else henceforth!

Mark on that nose the colour left by too copious port and viands; to which the profuse cravat with exorbitant breast-pin, and the fixed, forward, and as it were menacing glance of the eyes correspond. That is a 'Man of Business;' prosperous manufacturer, house-contractor, engineer, law-manager; his eye, nose,

cravat have, in such work and fortune, got such a character: deny
him not thy praise, thy pity. Pity him too, the Hard-handed, with
bony brow, rudely combed hair, eyes looking out as in labour, in
difficulty and uncertainty; rude mouth, the lips coarse, loose, as
in hard toil and lifelong fatigue they have got the habit of hanging:—hast thou seen aught more touching than the rude intelligence, so cramped, yet energetic, unsubduable, true, which looks
out of that marred visage? Alas, and his poor wife, with her own
hands, washed that cotton neckcloth for him, buttoned that coarse
shirt, sent him forth creditably trimmed as she could. In such
imprisonment lives he, for his part; man cannot now deliver him:
the red pulpy infant has been baked and fashioned *so*.

Or what kind of baking was it that this other brother-mortal
got, which has baked him into the genus Dandy? Elegant Vacuum; serenely looking down upon all Plenums and Entities, as
low and poor to his serene Chimeraship and *Non*entity laboriously
attained! Heroic Vacuum; inexpugnable, while purse and present
condition of society hold out; curable by no hellebore. The doom
of Fate was, Be thou a Dandy! Have thy eye-glasses, opera-
glasses, thy Long-Acre cabs with white-breeched tiger, thy yawning
impassivities, pococurantisms; *fix* thyself in Dandyhood, undeliverable; it is thy doom.

And all these, we say, were red-coloured infants; of the same
pulp and stuff, few years ago; now irretrievably shaped and kneaded
as we see! Formulas? There is no mortal extant, out of the depths
of Bedlam, but lives all skinned, thatched, covered over with Formulas; and is, as it were, held in from delirium and the Inane
by his Formulas! They are withal the most beneficent, indispensable of human equipments: blessed he who has a skin and
tissues, so it be a living one, and the heart-pulse everywhere discernible through it. Monachism, Feudalism, with a real King
Plantagenet, with real Abbots Samson, and their other living realities, how blessed!—

Not without a mournful interest have we surveyed that authentic image of a Time new wholly swallowed. Mournful reflections
crowd on us;—and yet consolatory. How many brave men have
lived before Agamemnon! Here is a brave governor Samson, a
man fearing God, and fearing nothing else; of whom as First Lord
of the Treasury, as King, Chief Editor, High Priest, we could be
so glad and proud; of whom nevertheless Fame has altogether forgotten to make mention! The faint image of him, revived in this
hour, is found in the gossip of one poor Monk, and in Nature nowhere else. Oblivion had so nigh swallowed him altogether, even

to the echo of his ever having existed. What regiments and hosts and generations of such has Oblivion already swallowed! Their crumbled dust makes up the soil our life-fruit grows on. Said I not, as my old Norse Fathers taught me, The Life-tree Igdrasil, which waves round thee in this hour, whereof thou in this hour art portion, has its roots down deep in the oldest Death-Kingdoms; and grows; the Three Nornas, or *Times*, Past, Present, Future, watering it from the Sacred Well!

For example, who taught thee to *speak?* From the day when two hairy-naked or fig-leaved Human Figures began, as uncomfortable dummies, anxious no longer to be dumb, but to impart themselves to one another; and endeavoured, with gaspings, gesturings. with unsyllabled cries, with painful pantomime and interjections, in a very unsuccessful manner,—up to the writing of this present copyright Book, which also is not very successful! Between that day and this, I say, there has been a pretty space of time; a pretty spell of work, which *somebody* has done! Thinkest thou there were no poets till Dan Chaucer? No heart burning with a thought, which it could not hold, and had no word for; and needed to shape and coin a word for,—what thou callest a metaphor, trope, or the like? For every word we have, there was such a man and poet. The coldest word was once a glowing new metaphor, and bold questionable originality. ' Thy very ATTENTION, does it not mean an *attentio*, a STRETCHING-TO?' Fancy that act of the mind, which all were conscious of, which none had yet named,—when this new ' poet' first felt bound and driven to name it! His questionable originality, and new glowing metaphor, was found adoptable, intelligible; and remains our name for it to this day.

Literature:—and look at Paul's Cathedral, and the Masonries and Worships and Quasi-Worships that are there; not to speak of Westminster Hall and its wigs! Men had not a hammer to begin with, not a syllabled articulation: they had it all to make;—and they have made it. What thousand thousand articulate, semi-articulate, earnest-stammering *Prayers* ascending up to Heaven, from hut and cell, in many lands, in many centuries, from the fervent kindled souls of innumerable men, each struggling to pour itself forth incompletely as it might, before the incompletest *Liturgy* could be compiled! The Liturgy, or adoptable and generally adopted Set of Prayers and Prayer-Method, was what we can call the Select Adoptabilities, ' Select Beauties' well-edited (by Œcumenic Councils and other Useful-Knowledge Societies) from that wide waste imbroglio of Prayers already extant and accumulated, good and bad. The good were found adoptable by men; were gradually got together, well-edited, accredited: the bad, found inappropriate, unadoptable, were gradually forgotten, disused and burnt. It is the way with human things. The first man who, looking with opened soul on this august Heaven and Earth, this Beautiful and Awful, which we name Nature, Universe and such like, the essence of which remains forever UNNAMEABLE; he who first, gazing into this, fell on his knees awestruck, in silence as is likeliest,—he, driven by inner necessity, the 'audacious original' that he was, had done a thing, too, which all thoughtful hearts saw straightway to be an expressive, altogether adoptable thing! To bow the knee was ever since the attitude of supplication. Earlier than any spoken Prayers, *Litanias*, or *Leitourgias;* the beginning of all Worship,—which needed but a beginning, so rational was it. What a poet he! Yes, this bold original was a successful one withal. The wellhead this one, hidden in the primeval dusks and distances, from whom as from a Nile-source all *Forms of Worship* flow:—such a Nile-river (somewhat muddy and malarious now!) of Forms of Worship sprang there, and flowed, and flows, down to Puseyism, Rotatory Calabash, Archbishop Laud at St. Catherine Creed's, and perhaps lower!

Things rise, I say, in that way. The *Iliad* Poem, and indeed most other poetic, especially epic things, have risen as the Liturgy did. The great *Iliad* in Greece, and the small *Robin Hood's Garland* in England, are each, as I understand, the well-edited 'Select Beauties' of an immeasurable waste imbroglio of Heroic Ballads in their respective centuries and countries. Think what strumming of the seven-stringed heroic lyre, torturing of the less heroic fiddle-catgut, in Hellenic Kings' Courts, and English wayside Public Houses; and beating of the studious Poetic brain, and gasping here too in the semi-articulate windpipe of Poetic men, before the Wrath of a Divine Achilles, the Prowess of a Will Scarlet or Wakefield Pindar, could be adequately sung! Honour to you, ye nameless great and greatest ones, ye long-forgotten brave!

Nor was the Statute *De Tallagio non concedendo*, nor any Statute, Law-method, Lawyer's-wig, much less were the Statute-Book and Four Courts, with Coke upon Lyttelton and Three Estates of Parliament in the rear of them, got together without human labour, —mostly forgotten now! From the time of Cain's slaying Abel by swift head-breakage, to this time of killing your man in Chancery by inches, and slow heart-break for forty years,—there too is an interval! Venerable Justice herself began by Wild-Justice; all Law is as a tamed furrowfield, slowly worked out, and rendered arable, from the waste jungle of Club-Law. Valiant Wisdom tilling and draining; escorted by owl-eyed Pedantry, by owlish and vulturish and many other forms of Folly;—the valiant husbandman assiduously tilling; the blind greedy enemy *too* assiduously sowing tares! It is because there is yet in venerable wigged Justice some wisdom, amid such mountains of wiggeries and folly, that men have not cast her into the River; that she still sits there, like Dryden's Head in the *Battle of the Books*,—a huge helmet, a huge mountain of greased parchment, of unclean horsehair, first striking the eye; and then in the innermost corner, visible at last, in size as a hazelnut, a real fraction of God's Justice, perhaps not yet unattainable to some, surely still indispensable to all;—and men know not what to do with her! Lawyers were not all pedants, voluminous voracious persons; Lawyers too were poets, were heroes,—or their Law had been past the Nore long before this time. Their Owlisms, Vulturisms, to an incredible extent, will disappear by and by, their Heroisms only remaining, and the helmet be reduced to something like the size of the head, we hope!—

It is all work and forgotten work, this peopled, clothed, articulate-speaking, high-towered, wide-acred World. The hands of forgotten brave men have made it a World for us; they,—honour to them; they, in *spite* of the idle and the dastard. This English Land, here and now, is the summary of what was found of wise, and noble, and accordant with God's Truth, in all the generations of English Men. Our English Speech is speakable because there were Hero-Poets of our blood and lineage; speakable in proportion to the number of these. This Land of England has its conquerors, possessors, which change from epoch to epoch, from day to day; but its real conquerors, creators, and eternal proprietors are these following, and their representatives if you can find them: All the Heroic Souls that ever were in England, each in their degree; all the men that ever cut a thistle, drained a puddle out of England, contrived a wise scheme in England, did or said a true and valiant thing in England. I tell thee, they had not a hammer to begin with; and yet Wren built St. Paul's: not an articulated syllable; and yet there have come English Literatures, Elizabethan Literatures, Satanic-School, Cockney-School and other Literatures;—once more, as in the old time of the *Leitourgia*, a most waste imbroglio, and world-wide jungle and jumble; waiting terribly to be 'well-edited' and 'well-burnt!' Arachne started with forefinger and thumb, and had not even a distaff; yet thou seest Manchester, and Cotton Cloth, which will shelter naked backs, at twopence an ell.

Work? The quantity of done and forgotten work that lies silent under my feet in this world, and escorts and attends me, and supports and keeps me alive, wheresoever I walk or stand, whatsoever I think or do, gives rise to reflections! Is it not

enough, at any rate, to strike the thing called 'Fame' into total
silence for a wise man? For fools and unreflective persons, she
is and will be very noisy, this 'Fame,' and talks of her 'immortals'
and so forth: but if you will consider it, what is she? Abbot
Samson was not nothing because nobody *said* anything of him.
Or thinkest thou, the Right Honourable Sir Jabesh Windbag can
be made something by Parliamentary Majorities and Leading Articles? Her 'immortals!' Scarcely two hundred years back can
Fame recollect articulately at all; and there she but maunders and
mumbles. She manages to recollect a Shakspeare or so; and
prates, considerably like a goose, about him;—and in the rear of
that, onwards to the birth of Theuth, to Hengst's Invasion, and
the bosom of Eternity, it was all blank; and the respectable Teutonic Languages, Teutonic Practices, Existences, all came of their
own accord, as the grass springs, as the trees grow; no Poet, no
work from the inspired heart of a Man needed there; and Fame
has not an articulate word to say about it! Or ask her, What,
with all conceivable appliances and mnemonics, including apo-
theosis and human sacrifices among the number, she carries in
her head with regard to a Wodan, even a Moses, or other such?
She begins to be uncertain as to what they were, whether spirits or
men of mould,—gods, charlatans; begins sometimes to have a
misgiving that they were mere symbols, ideas of the mind; perhaps nonentities, and Letters of the Alphabet! She is the noisiest,
inarticulately babbling, hissing, screaming, foolishest, unmusical-
lest of fowls that fly; and needs no 'trumpet,' I think, but her own
enormous goose-throat,—measuring several degrees of celestial
latitude, so to speak. Her 'wings,' in these days, have grown far
swifter than ever; but her goose-throat hitherto seems only larger,
louder and foolisher than ever. *She* is transitory, futile, a goose-
goddess:—if she were not transitory, what would become of us!
It is a chief comfort that she forgets us all; all, even to the very
Wodans; and grows to consider us, at last, as probably nonentities
and Letters of the Alphabet.

Yes, a noble Abbot Samson resigns himself to Oblivion too;
feels *it* no hardship, but a comfort; counts it as a still resting-
place, from much sick fret and fever and stupidity, which in the
night-watches often made his strong heart sigh. Your most sweet
voices, making one enormous goose-voice, O Bobus and Company,
how can they be a guidance for any Son of Adam? In *silence* of
you and the like of you, the 'small still voices' will speak to him
better; in which does lie guidance.

My friend, all speech and rumour is short-lived, foolish, untrue.
Genuine Work alone, what thou workest faithfully, that is eternal,

as the Almighty Founder and World-Builder himself. Stand thou by that; and let ' Fame' and the rest of it go prating.

> ' Heard are the Voices,
> Heard are the Sages,
> The Worlds and the Ages :
> " Choose well, your choice is
> Brief and yet endless.
>
> Here eyes do regard you,
> In Eternity's stillness;
> Here is all fulness,
> Ye brave, to reward you;
> Work, and despair not.' '[1]

[1] Goethe.

BOOK III.—THE MODERN WORKER.

CHAPTER I.

PHENOMENA.

But, it is said, our religion is gone: we no longer believe in St. Edmund, no longer see the figure of him ' on the rim of the sky,' minatory or confirmatory! God's absolute Laws, sanctioned by an eternal Heaven and an eternal Hell, have become Moral Philosophies, sanctioned by able computations of Profit and Loss, by weak considerations of Pleasures of Virtue and the Moral Sublime.

It is even so. To speak in the ancient dialect, we ' have forgotten God;'—in the most modern dialect and very truth of the matter, we have taken up the Fact of this Universe as it *is not*. We have quietly closed our eyes to the eternal Substance of things, and opened them only to the Shows and Shams of things. We quietly believe this Universe to be intrinsically a great unintelligible PERHAPS; extrinsically, clear enough, it is a great, most extensive Cattlefold and Workhouse, with most extensive Kitchenranges, Dining-tables,—whereat he is wise who can find a place! All the Truth of this Universe is uncertain; only the profit and loss of it, the pudding and praise of it, are and remain very visible to the practical man.

There is no longer any God for us! God's Laws are become a Greatest-Happiness Principle, a Parliamentary Expediency: the Heavens overarch us only as an Astronomical Time-keeper; a butt for Herschel-telescopes to shoot science at, to shoot sentimentalities at:—in our and old Jonson's dialect, man has lost the *soul* out of him; and now, after the due period,—begins to find the want of it! This is verily the plague-spot; centre of the universal Social Gangrene, threatening all modern things with frightful death. To him that will consider it, here is the stem, with its roots and taproot, with its world-wide upas-boughs and accursed poison-exudations, under which the world lies writhing in

N

atrophy and agony. You touch the focal-centre of all our disease,
of our frightful nosology of diseases, when you lay your hand on
this. There is no religion; there is no God; man has lost his
soul, and vainly seeks antiseptic salt. Vainly: in killing Kings,
in passing Reform Bills, in French Revolutions, Manchester Insurrections, is found no remedy. The foul elephantine leprosy,
alleviated for an hour, reappears in new force and desperateness
next hour.

For actually this is *not* the real fact of the world; the world is
not made so, but otherwise!—Truly, any Society setting out from
this No-God hypothesis will arrive at a result or two. The *Un*-
veracities, escorted, each Unveracity of them by its corresponding
Misery and Penalty; the Phantasms, and Fatuities, and ten-years
Corn-Law Debatings, that shall walk the Earth at noonday,—
must needs be numerous! The Universe *being* intrinsically a
Perhaps, being too probably an 'infinite Humbug,' why should
any minor Humbug astonish us? It is all according to the order
of Nature; and Phantasms riding with huge clatter along the
streets, from end to end of our existence, astonish nobody. Enchanted St. Ives' Workhouses and Joe-Manton Aristocracies; giant
Working Mammonism near strangled in the partridge-nets of
giant-looking Idle Dilettantism,—this, in all its branches, in its
thousand thousand modes and figures, is a sight familiar to us.

The Popish Religion, we are told, flourishes extremely in these
years; and is the most vivacious looking religion to be met with
at present. "*Elle a trois cents ans dans le ventre,*" counts M. Jouf-
froy; "*c'est pourquoi je la respecte!*"—The old Pope of Rome, finding it laborious to kneel so long while they cart him through the
streets to bless the people on *Corpus-Christi* Day, complains of
rheumatism; whereupon his Cardinals consult;—construct him,
after some study, a stuffed cloaked figure, of iron and wood, with
wool or baked hair; and place it in a kneeling posture. Stuffed
figure, or rump of a figure; to this stuffed rump he, sitting at his
ease on a lower level, joins, by the aid of cloaks and drapery, his
living head and outspread hands: the rump with its cloaks kneels,
the Pope looks, and holds his hands spread; and so the two in
concert bless the Roman population on *Corpus-Christi* Day, as well
as they can.

I have considered this amphibious Pope, with the wool-and-
iron back, with the flesh head and hands; and endeavoured to
calculate his horoscope. I reckon him the remarkablest Pontiff
that has darkened God's daylight, or painted himself in the human retina, for these several thousand years. Nay, since Chaos

first shivered, and ' sneezed,' as the Arabs say, with the first shaft
of sunlight shot through it, what stranger product was there of
Nature and Art working together? Here is a Supreme Priest
who believes God to be—What, in the name of God, *does* he believe God to be?—and discerns that all worship of God is a scenic
phantasmagory of wax-candles, organ-blasts, Gregorian Chants,
mass-brayings, purple monsignori, wool-and-iron rumps, artisti-
cally spread out,—to save the ignorant from worse.

O reader, I say not who are Belial's elect. This poor amphibious Pope too gives loaves to the Poor; has in him more good
latent than he is himself aware of. His poor Jesuits, in the late
Italian Cholera, were, with a few German Doctors, the only creatures whom dastard terror had not driven mad: they descended
fearless into all gulfs and bedlams; watched over the pillow of
the dying, with help, with counsel and hope; shone as luminous
fixed stars, when all else had gone out in chaotic night: honour
to them! This poor Pope,—who knows what good is in him? In
a Time otherwise too prone to forget, he keeps up the mournfullest ghastly memorial of the Highest, Blessedest, which once was;
which, in new fit forms, will again partly have to be. Is he not
as a perpetual death's-head and cross-bones, with their *Resurgam*,
on the grave of a Universal Heroism,—grave of a Christianity?
Such Noblenesses, purchased by the world's best heart's-blood,
must not be lost; we cannot afford to lose them, in what confusions soever. To all of us the day will come, to a few of us it has
already come, when no mortal, with his heart yearning for a ' Divine Humility,' or other ' Highest form of Valour,' will need to
look for it in death's-heads, but will see it round him in here and
there a beautiful living head.

Besides, there is in this poor Pope, and his practice of the
Scenic Theory of Worship, a frankness which I rather honour.
Not half and half, but with undivided heart does *he* set about
worshiping by stage-machinery; as if there were now, and could
again be, in Nature no other. He will ask you, What other?
Under this my Gregorian Chant, and beautiful wax-light Phantasmagory, kindly hidden from you is an Abyss, of Black Doubt,
Scepticism, nay Sansculottic Jacobinism; an Orcus that has no
bottom. Think of that. ' Groby Pool *is* thatched with pancakes,'
—as Jeannie Deans's Innkeeper defied it to be! The Bottomless
of Scepticism, Atheism, Jacobinism, behold, it is thatched over,
hidden from your despair, by stage-properties judiciously arranged.
This stuffed rump of mine saves not me only from rheumatism,
but you also from what other *isms!* In this your Life-pilgrimage Nowhither, a fine Squallacci marching-music, and Gregorian

Chant, accompanies you, and the hollow Night of Orcus is well hid!

Yes truly, few men that worship by the rotatory Calabash of the Calmucks do it in half so great, frank or effectual a way. Drury-Lane, it is said, and that is saying much, might learn from him in the dressing of parts, in the arrangement of lights and shadows. He is the greatest Play-actor that at present draws salary in this world. Poor Pope; and I am told he is fast growing bankrupt too; and will, in a measurable term of years (a great way *within* the 'three hundred'), not have a penny to make his pot boil! His old rheumatic back will then get to rest; and himself and his stage-properties sleep well in Chaos forevermore.

Or, alas, why go to Rome for Phantasms walking the streets? Phantasms, ghosts, in this midnight hour, hold jubilee, and screech and jabber; and the question rather were, What high Reality anywhere is yet awake? Aristocracy has become Phantasm-Aristocracy, no longer able to *do* its work, not in the least conscious that it has any work longer to do. Unable, totally careless to *do* its work; careful only to clamour for the *wages* of doing its work,—nay for higher, and *palpably* undue wages, and Corn-Laws and *increase* of rents; the old rate of wages not being adequate now! In hydra-wrestle, giant '*Millo*cracy' so-called, a real giant, though as yet a blind one and but half-awake, wrestles and wrings in choking nightmare, 'like to be strangled in the partridge-nets of Phantasm-Aristocracy,' as we said, which fancies itself still to be a giant. Wrestles, as under nightmare, till it do awaken; and gasps and struggles thousandfold, we may say, in a truly painful manner, through all fibres of our English Existence, in these hours and years! Is our poor English Existence wholly becoming a Nightmare; full of mere Phantasms?—

The Champion of England, cased in iron or tin, rides into Westminster Hall, 'being lifted into his saddle with little assistance,' and there asks, If in the four quarters of the world, under the cope of Heaven, is any man or demon that dare question the right of this King? Under the cope of Heaven no man makes intelligible answer,—as several men ought already to have done. Does not this Champion too know the world; that it is a huge Imposture, and bottomless Inanity, thatched over with bright cloth and other ingenious tissues? Him let us leave there, questioning all men and demons.

Him we have left to his destiny; but whom else have we found? From this the highest apex of things, downwards through all strata and breadths, how many fully awakened Realities have we fallen in with:—alas, on the contrary, what troops and populations of Phantasms, not God-Veracities but Devil-Falsities, down to the very lowest stratum,—which now, by such superincumbent weight of Unveracities, lies enchanted in St. Ives' Workhouses, broad enough, helpless enough! You will walk in no public thoroughfare or remotest byway of English Existence but you will meet a man, an interest of men, that has given up hope in the Everlasting, True, and placed its hope in the Temporary, half or wholly False. The Honourable Member complains unmusically that there is 'devil's-dust' in Yorkshire cloth. Yorkshire cloth,—why, the very Paper I now write on is made, it seems, partly of plaster-lime well-smoothed, and obstructs my writing! You are lucky if you can find now any good Paper,—any work really *done;* search where you will, from highest Phantasm apex to lowest Enchanted basis.

Consider, for example, that great Hat seven-feet high, which now perambulates London Streets; which my Friend Sauerteig regarded justly as one of our English notabilities; "the topmost point as yet," said he, "would it were your culminating and returning point, to which English Puffery has been observed to reach!" —The Hatter in the Strand of London, instead of making better felt-hats than another, mounts a huge lath-and-plaster Hat, seven-feet high, upon wheels; sends a man to drive it through the streets; hoping to be saved *thereby.* He has not attempted to *make* better hats, as he was appointed by the Universe to do, and as with this ingenuity of his he could very probably have done; but his whole industry is turned to *persuade* us that he has made such! He too knows that the Quack has become God. Laugh not at him, O reader; or do not laugh only. He has ceased to be comic; he is fast becoming tragic. To me this all-deafening blast of Puffery, of poor Falsehood grown necessitous, of poor Heart-Atheism fallen now into Enchanted Workhouses, sounds too surely like a Doom's-blast! I have to say to myself in old dialect: "God's blessing is not written on all this; His curse is written on all this!" Unless perhaps the Universe *be* a chimera;—some old totally deranged eightday clock, dead as brass; which the Maker, if there ever was any Maker, has long ceased to meddle with?—To my Friend Sauerteig this poor seven-feet Hat-manufacturer, as the topstone of English Puffery, was very notable.

Alas, that we natives note him little, that we view him as a thing of course, is the very burden of the misery. We take it for granted, the most rigorous of us, that all men who have made anything are expected and entitled to make the loudest possible proclamation of it, and call on a discerning public to reward them for it. Every man his own trumpeter; that is, to a really alarming extent, the accepted rule. Make loudest possible proclamation of your Hat: true proclamation if that will do; if that will not do, then false proclamation,—to such extent of falsity as will serve your purpose; as will not seem too false to be credible!—I answer, once for all, that the fact is not so. Nature requires no man to make proclamation of his doings and hat-makings; Nature forbids all men to make such. There is not a man or hat-maker born into the world but feels, or has felt, that he is degrading himself if he speak of his excellencies and prowesses, and supremacy in his craft: his inmost heart says to him, " Leave thy friends to speak of these; if possible, thy enemies to speak of these; but at all events, thy friends!" He feels that he is already a poor braggart; fast hastening to be a falsity and speaker of the Untruth.

Nature's Laws, I must repeat, are eternal: her small still voice, speaking from the inmost heart of us, shall not, under terrible penalties, be disregarded. No one man can depart from the truth without damage to himself; no one million of men; no Twenty-seven Millions of men. Show me a Nation fallen everywhere into this course, so that each expects it, permits it to others and himself, I will show you a Nation travelling with one assent on the broad way. The broad way, however many Banks of England, Cotton-Mills and Duke's Palaces it may have. Not at happy Elysian fields, and everlasting crowns of victory, earned by silent Valour, will this Nation arrive; but at precipices, devouring gulfs, if it pause not. Nature has appointed happy fields, victorious laurel-crowns; but only to the brave and true: *Un*nature, what we call Chaos, holds nothing in it but vacuities, devouring gulfs. What are Twenty-seven Millions, and their unanimity? Believe them not: the Worlds and the Ages, God and Nature and All Men say otherwise.

' Rhetoric all this?" No, my brother, very singular to say, it is Fact all this. Cocker's Arithmetic is not truer. Forgotten in these days, it is old as the foundations of the Universe, and will endure till the Universe cease. It is forgotten now; and the first mention of it puckers thy sweet countenance into a sneer: but it will be brought to mind again,—unless indeed the Law of Gravitation chance to cease, and men find that they *can* walk on vacancy. Unanimity of the Twenty-seven Millions will do nothing; walk not thou with them; fly from them as for thy life. Twenty-seven Millions travelling on such courses, with gold jingling in every pocket, with vivats heaven-high, are incessantly advancing, let me again remind thee, towards the *firm-land's end*,—towards the end and extinction of what Faithfulness, Veracity, real Worth, was in their way of life. Their noble ancestors have fashioned for them a 'life-road;'—in how many thousand senses, this! There is not an old wise Proverb on their tongue, an honest Principle articulated in their hearts into utterance, a wise true method of doing and despatching any work or commerce of men, but helps yet to carry them forward. Life is still possible to them, because all is not yet Puffery, Falsity, Mammon-worship and Unnature; because somewhat is yet Faithfulness, Veracity and Valour. With a certain very considerable finite quantity of Unveracity and Phantasm, social life is still possible; not with an infinite quantity! Exceed your certain quantity, the seven-feet Hat, and all things upwards to the very Champion cased in tin, begin to reel and flounder,—in Manchester Insurrections, Chartisms, Sliding-scales; the Law of Gravitation not forgetting to act. You advance incessantly towards the land's end; you are, literally enough, 'consuming the way.' Step after step, Twenty-seven Million unconscious men;—till you are *at* the land's end; till there is not Faithfulness enough among you any more: and the next step now is lifted *not* over land, but into air, over ocean-deeps and roaring abysses:—unless perhaps the Law of Gravitation have forgotten to act?

O, it is frightful when a whole Nation, as our Fathers used to say, has 'forgotten God;' has remembered only Mammon, and what Mammon leads to! When your self-trumpeting Hatmaker is the emblem of almost all makers, and workers, and men, that make anything,—from soul-overseerships, body-overseerships, epic poems, acts of parliament, to hats and shoe-blacking! Not one false man but does uncountable mischief: how much, in a generation or two, will Twenty-seven Millions, mostly false, manage to accumulate? The sum of it, visible in every street, market-place, senate-house, circulating-library, cathedral, cotton-mill, and union-workhouse, fills one *not* with a comic feeling!

CHAPTER II.

GOSPEL OF MAMMONISM.

READER, even Christian Reader as thy title goes, hast thou any notion of Heaven and Hell? I rather apprehend, not. Often as the words are on our tongue, they have got a fabulous or semifabulous character for most of us, and pass on like a kind of transient similitude, like a sound signifying little.

Yet it is well worth while for us to know, once and always, that they are not a similitude, nor a fable nor semi-fable; that they are an everlasting highest fact! "No Lake of Sicilian or other sul-

phur burns now anywhere in these ages," sayest thou? Well, and
if there did not! Believe that there does not; believe it if thou
wilt, nay hold by it as a real increase, a rise to higher stages, to
wider horizons and empires. All this has vanished, or has not
vanished; believe as thou wilt as to all this. But that an Infinite
of Practical Importance, speaking with strict arithmetical exact-
ness, an *Infinite*, has vanished or can vanish from the Life of any
Man: this thou shalt not believe! O brother, the Infinite of Terror, of Hope, of Pity, did it not at any moment disclose itself to
thee, indubitable, unnameable? Came it never, like the gleam of
*preter*natural eternal Oceans, like the voice of old Eternities, far-
sounding through thy heart of hearts? Never? Alas, it was not
thy Liberalism then; it was thy Animalism! The Infinite is more
sure than any other fact. But only men can discern it; mere
building beavers, spinning arachnes, much more the predatory
vulturous and vulpine species, do not discern it well!—

'The word Hell,' says Sauerteig, 'is still frequently in use
'among the English People: but I could not without difficulty
'ascertain what they meant by it. Hell generally signifies the
'Infinite Terror, the thing a man *is* infinitely afraid of, and shud-
'ders and shrinks from, struggling with his whole soul to escape
'from it. There is a Hell therefore, if you will consider, which
'accompanies man, in all stages of his history, and religious or
'other development: but the Hells of men and Peoples differ not-
'ably. With Christians it is the infinite terror of being found
'guilty before the Just Judge. With old Romans, I conjecture,
'it was the terror not of Pluto, for whom probably they cared
'little, but of doing unworthily, doing unvirtuously, which was
'their word for un*man*fully. And now what is it, if you pierce
'through his Cants, his oft-repeated Hearsays, what he calls his
'Worships and so forth,—what is it that the modern English soul
'does, in very truth, dread infinitely, and contemplate with entire
'despair? What *is* his Hell, after all these reputable, oft-re-
'peated Hearsays, what is it? With hesitation, with astonish-
'ment, I pronounce it to be: The terror of "Not succeeding;"
'of not making money, fame, or some other figure in the world,
'—chiefly of not making money! Is not that a somewhat sin-
'gular Hell?'

Yes, O Sauerteig, it is very singular. If we do not 'succeed,'
where is the use of us? We had better never have been born.
"Tremble intensely," as our friend the Emperor of China says:
there is the black Bottomless of Terror; what Sauerteig calls the
'Hell of the English!'—But indeed this Hell belongs naturally to
the Gospel of Mammonism, which also has its corresponding Hea-

ven. For there *is* one Reality among so many Phantasms; about one thing we are entirely in earnest: The making of money. Working Mammonism does divide the world with idle game-preserving Dilettantism:—thank Heaven that there is even a Mammonism, *anything* we are in earnest about! Idleness is worst, Idleness alone is without hope: work earnestly at anything, you will by degrees learn to work at almost all things. There is endless hope in work, were it even work at making money.

True, it must be owned, we for the present, with our Mammon-Gospel, have come to strange conclusions. We call it a Society; and go about professing openly the totallest separation, isolation. Our life is not a mutual helpfulness; but rather, cloaked under due laws-of-war, named 'fair competition' and so forth, it is a mutual hostility. We have profoundly forgotten everywhere that *Cash-payment* is not the sole relation of human beings; we think, nothing doubting, that *it* absolves and liquidates all engagements of man. "My starving workers?" answers the rich Millowner: "Did not I hire them fairly in the market? Did I not pay them, to the last sixpence, the sum covenanted for? What have I to do with them more?"—Verily Mammon-worship is a melancholy creed. When Cain, for his own behoof, had killed Abel, and was questioned, "Where is thy brother?" he too made answer, "Am I my brother's keeper?" Did I not pay my brother *his* wages, the thing he had merited from me?

O sumptuous Merchant-Prince, illustrious game-preserving Duke, is there no way of 'killing' thy brother but Cain's rude way! 'A good man by the very look of him, by his very presence 'with us as a fellow wayfarer in this Life-pilgrimage, *promises* so 'much:' woe to him if he forget all such promises, if he never know that they were given! To a deadened soul, seared with the brute Idolatry of Sense, to whom going to Hell is equivalent to not making money, all 'promises,' and moral duties, that cannot be pleaded for in Courts of Requests, address themselves in vain. Money he can be ordered to pay, but nothing more. I have not heard in all Past History, and expect not to hear in all Future History, of any Society anywhere under God's Heaven supporting itself on such Philosophy. The Universe is not made so; it is made otherwise than so. The man or nation of men that thinks it is made so, marches forward nothing doubting, step after step; but marches—whither we know! In these last two centuries of Atheistic Government (near two centuries now, since the blessed restoration of his Sacred Majesty, and Defender of the Faith, Charles Second), I reckon that we have pretty well exhausted what of 'firm earth' there was for us to march on;—and are now, very ominously, shuddering, reeling, and let us hope trying to recoil, on the cliff's edge !—

For out of this that we call Atheism come so many other *isms* and falsities, each falsity with its misery at its heels !—A SOUL is not like wind (*spiritus*, or breath) contained within a capsule; the ALMIGHTY MAKER is not like a Clockmaker that once, in old immemorial ages, having *made* his Horologe of a Universe, sits ever since and sees it go! Not at all. Hence comes Atheism; come, as we say, many other *isms*; and as the sum of all, comes Valetism, the *reverse* of Heroism; sad root of all woes whatsoever. For indeed, as no man ever saw the above-said wind-element enclosed within its capsule, and finds it at bottom more deniable than conceivable; so too he finds, in spite of Bridgewater Bequests, your Clockmaker Almighty an entirely questionable affair, a deniable affair;—and accordingly denies it, and along with it so much else. Alas, one knows not what and how much else! For the faith in an Invisible, Unnameable, Godlike, present everywhere in all that we see and work and suffer, is the essence of all faith whatsoever; and that once denied, or still worse, asserted with lips only, and out of bound prayerbooks only, what other thing remains believable? That Cant well-ordered is marketable Cant; that Heroism means gas-lighted Histrionism; that seen with ' clear eyes' (as they call Valet-eyes), no man is a Hero, or ever was a Hero, but all men are Valets and Varlets. The accursed practical quintessence of all sorts of Unbelief! For if there be now no Hero, and the Histrio himself begin to be seen into, what hope is there for the seed of Adam here below? We are the doomed everlasting prey of the Quack; who, now in this guise, now in that, is to filch us, to pluck and eat us, by such modes as are convenient for him. For the modes and guises I care little. The Quack once inevitable, let him come swiftly, let him pluck and eat me;—swiftly, that I may at least have done with him; for in his Quack-world I can have no wish to linger. Though he slay me, yet will I *not* trust in him. Though he conquer nations, and have all the Flunkeys of the Universe shouting at his heels, yet will I know well that *he* is an Inanity; that for him and his there is no continuance appointed, save only in Gehenna and the Pool. Alas, the Atheist world, from its utmost summits of Heaven and Westminster Hall, downwards through poor seven-feet Hats and ' Unveracities fallen hungry,' down to the lowest cellars and neglected hunger-dens of it, is very wretched.

One of Dr. Alison's Scotch facts struck us much.[1]   A poor

---

[1] Observations on the Management of the Poor in Scotland: By William Pulteney Alison, M.D. (Edinburgh, 1840.)

Irish Widow, her husband having died in one of the Lanes of Edinburgh, went forth with her three children, bare of all resource, to solicit help from the Charitable Establishments of that City. At this Charitable Establishment and then at that she was refused; referred from one to the other, helped by none;—till she had exhausted them all; till her strength and heart failed her: she sank down in typhus-fever; died, and infected her Lane with 'fever, so that ' seventeen other persons' died of fever there in consequence. The humane Physician asks thereupon, as with a heart too full for speaking, Would it not have been *economy* to help this poor Widow? She took typhus-fever, and killed seventeen of you!—Very curious. The forlorn Irish Widow applies to her fellow-creatures, as if saying. " Behold I am sinking, bare of help: ye must help me! I am your sister, bone of your bone; one God made us: ye must help me!" They answer, " No; impossible; thou art no sister of ours." But she proves her sisterhood; her typhus-fever kills *them:* they actually were her brothers, though denying it! Had human creature ever to go lower for a proof?

For, as indeed was very natural in such case, all government of the Poor by the Rich has long ago been given over to Supply-and-demand, Laissez-faire and such like, and universally declared to be ' impossible.' " You are no sister of ours; what shadow of proof is there? Here are our parchments, our padlocks, proving indisputably our money-safes to be *ours*, and you to have no business with them. Depart! It is impossible !"—Nay, what wouldst thou thyself have us do? cry indignant readers. Nothing, my friends,—till you have got a soul for yourselves again. Till then all things are ' impossible.' Till then I cannot even bid you buy, as the old Spartans would have done, two-pence worth of powder and lead, and compendiously shoot to death this poor Irish Widow: even that is ' impossible' for you. Nothing is left but that she prove her sisterhood by dying, and infecting you with typhus. Seventeen of you lying dead will not deny such proof that she *was* flesh of your flesh; and perhaps some of the living may lay it to heart.

' Impossible :' of a certain two-legged animal with feathers it is said, if you draw a distinct chalk-circle round him, he sits imprisoned, as if girt with the iron ring of Fate; and will die there, though within sight of victuals,—or sit in sick misery there, and be fatted to death. The name of this poor two-legged animal is —Goose; and they make of him, when well fattened, *Pâté de foie gras*, much prized by some!

CHAPTER III.

GOSPEL OF DILETTANTISM.

BUT after all, the Gospel of Dilettantism, producing a Governing Class who do not govern, nor understand in the least that they are bound or expected to govern, is still mournfuller than that of Mammonism. Mammonism, as we said, at least works; this goes idle. Mammonism has seized some portion of the message of Nature to man; and seizing that, and following it, will seize and appropriate more and more of Nature's message: but Dilettantism has missed it wholly. 'Make money:' that will mean withal, 'Do work in order to make money.' But, 'Go gracefully idle in May-fair,' what does or can that mean? An idle, game-preserving and even corn-lawing Aristocracy, in such an England as ours: has the world, if we take thought of it, ever seen such a phenomenon till very lately? Can it long continue to see such?

Accordingly the impotent, insolent Donothingism in Practice, and Saynothingism in Speech, which we have to witness on that side of our affairs, is altogether amazing. A Corn-Law demonstrating itself openly, for ten years or more, with 'arguments' to make the angels, and some other classes of creatures, weep! For men are not ashamed to rise in Parliament and elsewhere, and speak the things they do *not* think. 'Expediency,' 'Necessities of Party,' &c. &c.! It is not known that the Tongue of Man is a sacred organ; that Man himself is definable in Philosophy as an 'Incarnate *Word*;' the Word not there, you have no Man there either, but a Phantasm instead! In this way it is that Absurdities may live long enough,—still walking, and talking for themselves, years and decades after the brains are quite out! How are 'the knaves and dastards' ever to be got 'arrested' at that rate?—

"No man in this fashionable London of yours," friend Sauerteig would say, "speaks a plain word to me. Every man feels bound to be something more than plain; to be pungent withal, witty, ornamental. His poor fraction of sense has to be perked into some epigrammatic shape, that it may prick into me;—perhaps (this is the commonest) to be topsyturvied, left standing on its head, that I may remember it the better! Such grinning inanity is very sad to the soul of man. Human faces should not grin on one like masks; they should look on one like faces! I love honest laughter, as I do sunlight; but not dishonest: most kinds of dancing too; but the St.-Vitus kind not at all! A fashionable wit, *ach Himmel*, if you ask, Which, he or a Death's-head, will be the cheerier company for me? pray send *not* him!"

Insincere Speech, truly, is the prime material of insincere Action. Action hangs, as it were, *dissolved* in Speech, in Thought whereof Speech is the shadow; and precipitates itself therefrom. The kind of Speech in a man betokens the kind of Action you will get from him. Our Speech, in these modern days, has become amazing. Johnson complained, "Nobody speaks in earnest, Sir; there is no serious conversation." To us all serious speech of men, as that of Seventeenth-Century Puritans, Twelfth-Century Catholics, German Poets of this Century, has become jargon, more or less insane. Cromwell was mad and a quack; Anselm, Becket, Goethe, *ditto ditto*.

Perhaps few narratives in History or Mythology are more significant than that Moslem one, of Moses and the Dwellers by the Dead Sea. A tribe of men dwelt on the shores of that same Asphaltic Lake; and having forgotten, as we are all too prone to do, the inner facts of Nature, and taken up with the falsities and outer semblances of it, were fallen into sad conditions,—verging indeed towards a certain far deeper Lake. Whereupon it pleased kind Heaven to send them the Prophet Moses, with an instructive word of warning, out of which might have sprung 'remedial measures' not a few. But no: the men of the Dead Sea discovered, as the valet-species always does in heroes or prophets, no comeliness in Moses; listened with real tedium to Moses, with light grinning, or with splenetic sniffs and sneers, affecting even to yawn; and signified, in short, that they found him a humbug, and even a bore. Such was the candid theory these men of the Asphalt Lake formed to themselves of Moses, That probably he was a humbug, that certainly he was a bore.

Moses withdrew; but Nature and her rigorous veracities did not withdraw. The men of the Dead Sea, when we next went to visit them, were all 'changed into Apes;'[1] sitting on the trees there, grinning now in the most *unaffected* manner; gibbering and chattering very genuine nonsense; finding the whole Universe now a most indisputable Humbug! The Universe has *become* a Humbug to these Apes who thought it one. There they sit and chatter, to this hour: only, I believe, every Sabbath there returns to them a bewildered half-consciousness, half-reminiscence; and they sit, with their wizzened smoke-dried visages, and such an air of supreme tragicality as Apes may; looking out through those blinking smoke-bleared eyes of theirs, into the

[1] Sale's Koran (*Introduction*).

wonderfullest universal smoky Twilight and undecipherable disordered Dusk of Things; wholly an Uncertainty, Unintelligibility, they and it; and for commentary thereon, here and there an unmusical chatter or mew:—truest, tragicallest Humbug conceivable by the mind of man or ape! They made no use of their souls; and so have lost them. Their worship on the Sabbath now is to roost there, with unmusical screeches, and half-remember that they had souls.

Didst thou never, O Traveller, fall in with parties of this tribe? Meseems they are grown somewhat numerous in our day.

CHAPTER IV.

HAPPY.

ALL work, even cotton-spinning, is noble; work is alone noble: be that here said and asserted once more. And in like manner, too, all dignity is painful; a life of ease is not for any man, nor for any god. The life of all gods figures itself to us as a Sublime Sadness,—earnestness of Infinite Battle against Infinite Labour. Our highest religion is named the 'Worship of Sorrow.' For the son of man there is no noble crown, well worn, or even ill worn, but is a crown of thorns!—These things, in spoken words, or still better, in felt instincts alive in every heart, were once well known.

Does not the whole wretchedness, the whole *Atheism* as I call it, of man's ways, in these generations, shadow itself for us in that unspeakable Life-philosophy of his: The pretension to be what he calls 'happy?' Every pitifullest whipster that walks within a skin has his head filled with the notion that he is, shall be, or by all human and divine laws ought to be, 'happy.' His wishes, the pitifullest whipster's, are to be fulfilled for him; his days, the pitifullest whipster's, are to flow on in ever-gentle current of enjoyment, impossible even for the gods. The prophets preach to us, Thou shalt be happy; thou shalt love pleasant things, and find them. The people clamour, Why have we not found pleasant things?

We construct our theory of Human Duties, not on any Greatest-Nobleness Principle, never so mistaken; no, but on a Greatest-Happiness Principle. 'The word *Soul* with us, as in some Slavonic dialects, seems to be synonymous with *Stomach*.' We plead and speak, in our Parliaments and elsewhere, not as from the Soul, but from the Stomach;—wherefore, indeed, our pleadings are so slow to profit. We plead not for God's Justice; we are not ashamed to stand clamouring and pleading for our own ' interests,' our own rents and trade-profits; we say, They are the ' interests' of so many; there is such an intense desire in us for them! We demand Free-Trade, with much just vociferation and benevolence, That the poorer classes, who are terribly ill-off at present, may have cheaper New-Orleans bacon. Men ask on Free-trade platforms, How can the indomitable spirit of Englishmen be kept up without plenty of bacon? We shall become a ruined Nation!— Surely, my friends, plenty of bacon is good and indispensable: but, I doubt, you will never get even bacon by aiming only at that. You are men, not animals of prey, well-used or ill-used! Your Greatest-Happiness Principle seems to me fast becoming a rather unhappy one.—What if we should cease babbling about ' happiness,' and leave *it* resting on its own basis, as it used to do!

A gifted Byron rises in his wrath ; and feeling too surely that he for his part is not ' happy,' declares the same in very violent language, as a piece of news that may be interesting. It evidently has surprised him much. One dislikes to see a man and poet reduced to proclaim on the streets such tidings : but on the whole, as matters go, that is not the most dislikable. Byron speaks the *truth* in this matter. Byron's large audience indicates how true it is felt to be.

' Happy,' my brother? First of all, what difference is it whether thou art happy or not! Today becomes Yesterday so fast, all Tomorrows become Yesterdays; and then there is no question whatever of the ' happiness,' but quite another question. Nay, thou hast such a sacred pity left at least for thyself, thy very pains, once gone over into Yesterday, become joys to thee. Besides, thou knowest not what heavenly blessedness and indispensable sanative virtue was in them; thou shalt only know it after many days, when thou art wiser!—A benevolent old Surgeon sat once in our company, with a Patient fallen sick by gourmandising, whom he had just, too briefly in the Patient's judgment, been examining. The foolish Patient still at intervals continued to break in on our discourse, which rather promised to take a philosophic turn : " But I have lost my appetite," said he, objurgatively, with a tone of irritated pathos; " I have no appetite; I can't eat!"— " My dear fellow," answered the Doctor in mildest tone, " it isn't of the slightest consequence;"—and continued his philosophical discoursings with us!

Or does the reader not know the history of that Scottish iron Misanthrope? The inmates of some town-mansion, in those Northern parts, were thrown into the fearfullest alarm by indubitable symptoms of a ghost inhabiting the next house, or perhaps even the partition-wall! Ever at a certain hour, with preternatural gnarring, growling and screeching, which attended as running bass, there began, in a horrid, semi-articulate, unearthly voice, this song: " Once I was hap-hap-happy, but now I'm *mees*-erable! Clack-clack-clack, gnarr-r-r, whuz-z: Once I was hap-hap-happy, but now I'm *mees*-erable!"—Rest, rest, perturbed spirit;—or indeed, as the good old Doctor said: My dear fellow, it isn't of the slightest consequence! But no; the perturbed spirit could not rest; and to the neighbours, fretted, affrighted, or at least insufferably bored by him, it *was* of such consequence that they had to go and examine in his haunted chamber. In his haunted chamber, they find that the perturbed spirit is an unfortunate—Imitator of Byron? No, is an unfortunate rusty Meat-jack, gnarring and creaking with rust and work; and this, in Scottish dialect, is *its* Byronian musical Life-philosophy, sung according to ability!

Truly, I think the man who goes about pothering and uproaring for his 'happiness,'—pothering, and were it ballot-boxing, poem-making, or in what way soever fussing and exerting himself, —he is not the man that will help us to ' get our knaves and dastards arrested!' No; he rather is on the way to increase the number,—by at least one unit and his tail! Observe, too, that this is all a modern affair; belongs not to the old heroic times, but to these dastard new times. ' Happiness our being's end and aim,' all that very paltry speculation, is at bottom, if we will count well, not yet two centuries old in the world.

The only happiness a brave man ever troubled himself with asking much about was, happiness enough to get his work done. Not "I can't eat!" but "I can't work!" that was the burden of all wise complaining among men. It is, after all, the one unhappiness of a man. That he cannot work; that he cannot get his destiny as a man fulfilled. Behold, the day is passing swiftly over, our life is passing swiftly over; and the night cometh, wherein no man can work. The night once come, our happiness, our unhappiness, —it is all abolished; vanished, clean gone; a thing that has been: ' not of the slightest consequence' whether we were happy as eupeptic Curtis, as the fattest pig of Epicurus, or unhappy as Job with potsherds, as musical Byron with Giaours and sensibilities of the heart; as the unmusical Meat-jack with hard labour and rust! But our work,—behold that is not abolished, that has not vanished: our work, behold, it remains, or the want of it remains; —for endless Times and Eternities, remains; and that is now the sole question with us forevermore! Brief brawling Day, with its noisy phantasms, its poor paper-crowns tinsel-gilt, is gone; and divine everlasting Night, with her star-diadems, with her silences and her veracities, is come! What hast thou done, and how? Happiness, unhappiness: all that was but the *wages* thou hadst; thou hast spent all that, in sustaining thyself hitherward; not a coin of it remains with thee, it is all spent, eaten: and now thy work, where is thy work? Swift, out with it, let us see thy work!

Of a truth, if man were not a poor hungry dastard, and even much of a blockhead withal, he would cease criticising his victuals to such extent; and criticise himself rather, what he does with his victuals!

CHAPTER V.

THE ENGLISH.

AND yet, with all thy theoretic platitudes, what a depth of practical sense in thee, great England! A depth of sense, of justice, and courage; in which, under all emergencies and world-bewilderments, and under this most complex of emergencies we now live in, there is still hope, there is still assurance!

The English are a dumb people. They can do great acts, but not describe them. Like the old Romans, and some few others, *their* Epic Poem is written on the Earth's surface: England her Mark! It is complained that they have no artists: one Shakspeare indeed; but for Raphael only a Reynolds; for Mozart nothing but a Mr. Bishop: not a picture, not a song. And yet they did produce one Shakspeare: consider how the element of Shakspearean melody does lie imprisoned in their nature; reduced to unfold itself in mere Cotton-mills, Constitutional Governments, and such like;—all the more interesting when it does become visible, as even in such unexpected shapes it succeeds in doing! Goethe spoke of the Horse, how impressive, almost affecting it was that an animal of such qualities should stand obstructed so; its speech nothing but an inarticulate neighing, its handiness mere *hoof*iness, the fingers all constricted, tied together, the finger-nails coagulated into a mere hoof, shod with iron. The more significant, thinks he, are those eye-flashings of the generous noble quadruped; those prancings, curvings of the neck clothed with thunder.

A Dog of Knowledge has free utterance; but the Warhorse is almost mute, very far from free! It is even so. Truly, your freest utterances are not by any means always the best: they are the

worst rather; the feeblest, triviallest; their meaning prompt, but
small, ephemeral.   Commend me to the silent English, to the
silent Romans.   Nay, the silent Russians too I believe to be worth
something: are they not even now drilling, under much obloquy,
an immense semi-barbarous half-world from Finland to Kam-
tschatka, into rule, subordination, civilisation,—really in an old
Roman fashion; speaking no word about it; quietly hearing all
manner of vituperative Able Editors speak!   While your ever-talk-
ing, ever-gesticulating French, for example, what are they at this
moment drilling?—Nay, of all animals, the freest of utterance, I
should judge, is the genus *Simia:* go into the Indian woods, say
all Travellers, and look what a brisk, adroit, unresting Ape-popu-
lation it is!

The spoken Word, the written Poem, is said to be an epitome of
the man; how much more the done Work.   Whatsoever of morality
and of intelligence; what of patience, perseverance, faithfulness,
of method, insight, ingenuity, energy; in a word, whatsoever of
Strength the man had in him will lie written in the Work he does.
To work: why, it is to try himself against Nature, and her everlasting unerring Laws; these will tell a true verdict as to the man.   So
much of virtue and of faculty did *we* find in him; so much and no
more!   He had such capacity of harmonising himself with *me* and
my unalterable ever-veracious Laws; of coöperating and working
as *I* bade him;—and has prospered, and has not prospered, as you
see!—Working as great Nature bade him: does not that mean
virtue of a kind; nay, of all kinds?   Cotton can be spun and sold,
Lancashire operatives can be got to spin it, and at length one has
the woven webs and sells them, by following Nature's regulations
in that matter: by not following Nature's regulations, you have
them not.   You have them not;—there is no Cotton-web to sell:
Nature finds a bill against you; your 'Strength' is not Strength,
but Futility!   Let faculty be honoured, so far as it is faculty.   A
man that can succeed in working is to me always a man.

How one loves to see the burly figure of him, this thick-skinned,
seemingly opaque, perhaps sulky, almost stupid Man of Practice,
pitted against some light adroit Man of Theory, all equipt with
clear logic, and able anywhere to give you Why for Wherefore!
The adroit Man of Theory, so light of movement, clear of utterance, with his bow full-bent and quiver full of arrow-arguments,—
surely he will strike down the game, transfix everywhere the heart
of the matter; triumph everywhere, as he proves that he shall and
must do?   To your astonishment, it turns out oftenest No.   The
cloudy-browed, thick-soled, opaque Practicality, with no logic utter-

ance, in silence mainly, with here and there a low grunt or growl, has in him what transcends all logic-utterance: a Congruity with the Unuttered. The Speakable, which lies atop, as a superficial film, or outer skin, is his or is not his: but the Doable, which reaches down to the World's centre, you find him there!

The rugged Brindley has little to say for himself; the rugged Brindley, when difficulties accumulate on him, retires silent, 'generally to his bed;' retires 'sometimes for three days together to his bed, that he may be in perfect privacy there,' and ascertain in his rough head how the difficulties can be overcome. The ineloquent Brindley, behold he *has* chained seas together; his ships do visibly float over valleys, invisibly through the hearts of mountains; the Mersey and the Thames, the Humber and the Severn have shaken hands: Nature most audibly answers, Yea! The man of Theory twangs his full-bent bow: Nature's Fact ought to fall stricken, but does not: his logic-arrow glances from it as from a scaly dragon, and the obstinate Fact keeps walking its way. How singular! At bottom, you will have to grapple closer with the dragon; take it home to you, by real faculty, not by seeming faculty; try whether you are stronger or it is stronger. Close with it, wrestle it: sheer obstinate toughness of muscle; but much more, what we call toughness of heart, which will mean persistence hopeful and even desperate, unsubduable patience, composed candid openness, clearness of mind: all this shall be 'strength' in wrestling your dragon; the whole man's real strength is in this work, we shall get the measure of him here.

Of all the Nations in the world at present the English are the stupidest in speech, the wisest in action. As good as a 'dumb' Nation, I say, who cannot speak, and have never yet spoken,—spite of the Shakspeares and Miltons who show us what possibilities there are!—O Mr. Bull, I look in that surly face of thine with a mixture of pity and laughter, yet also with wonder and veneration. Thou complainest not, my illustrious friend; and yet I believe the heart of thee is full of sorrow, of unspoken sadness, seriousness,—profound melancholy (as some have said) the basis of thy being. Unconsciously, for thou speakest of nothing, this great Universe is great to thee. Not by levity of floating, but by stubborn force of swimming, shalt thou make thy way. The Fates sing of thee that thou shalt many times be thought an ass and a dull ox, and shalt with a godlike indifference believe it. My friend, —and it is all untrue, nothing ever falser in point of fact! Thou art of those great ones whose greatness the small passer-by does not discern. Thy very stupidity is wiser than their wisdom. A grand *vis inertiæ* is in thee; how many grand qualities unknown

to small men! Nature alone knows thee, acknowledges the bulk
and strength of thee: thy Epic, unsung in words, is written in
huge characters on the face of this Planet,—sea-moles, cotton-
trades, railways, fleets and cities, Indian Empires, Americas, New-
Hollands; legible throughout the Solar System!

But the dumb Russians too, as I said, they, drilling all wild
Asia and wild Europe into military rank and file, a terrible yet
hitherto a prospering enterprise, are still dumber. The old Romans also could not *speak*, for many centuries:—not till the world
was theirs; and so many speaking Greekdoms, their logic-arrows
all spent, had been absorbed and abolished. The logic-arrows, how
they glanced futile from obdurate thick-skinned Facts; Facts to
be wrestled down only by the real vigour of Roman thews!—As
for me, I honour, in these loud-babbling days, all the Silent rather.
A grand Silence that of Romans;—nay the grandest of all, is it not
that of the gods! Even Triviality, Imbecility, that can sit silent,
how respectable is it in comparison! The 'talent of silence' is our
fundamental one. Great honour to him whose Epic is a melodious
hexameter Iliad; not a jingling Sham-Iliad, nothing true in it but
the hexameters and forms merely. But still greater honour, if his
Epic be a mighty Empire slowly built together, a mighty Series of
Heroic Deeds,—a mighty Conquest over Chaos; *which* Epic the
' Eternal Melodies' have, and must have, informed and dwelt in,
as *it* sung itself! There is no mistaking that latter Epic. Deeds
are greater than Words. Deeds have such a life, mute but undeniable, and grow as living trees and fruit-trees do; they people
the vacuity of Time, and make it green and worthy. Why should
the oak prove logically that it ought to grow, and will grow? Plant
it, try it; what gifts of diligent judicious assimilation and secretion
it has, of progress and resistance, of *force* to grow, will then declare themselves. My much-honoured, illustrious, extremely inarticulate Mr. Bull!—

Ask Bull his spoken opinion of any matter,—oftentimes the
force of dullness can no farther go. You stand silent, incredu-
lous, as over a platitude that borders on the Infinite. The man's
Churchisms, Dissenterisms, Puseyisms, Benthamisms, College
Philosophies, Fashionable Literatures, are unexampled in this
world. Fate's prophecy is fulfilled; you call the man an ox and
an ass. But set him once to work,—respectable man! His spoken
sense is next to nothing, nine-tenths of it palpable *non*sense: but
his unspoken sense, his inner silent feeling of what is true, what
does agree with fact, what is doable and what is not doable,—this
seeks its fellow in the world. A terrible worker; irresistible against
marshes, mountains, impediments, disorder, incivilisation; every-

where vanquishing disorder, leaving it behind him as method and order. He ' retires to his bed three days,' and considers!

Nay withal, stupid as he is, our dear John,—ever, after infinite tumblings, and spoken platitudes innumerable from barrel-heads and parliament-benches, he does settle down somewhere about the just conclusion; you are certain that his jumblings and tumblings will end, after years or centuries, in the stable equilibrium. Stable equilibrium, I say; centre-of-gravity lowest;—not the unstable, with centre-of-gravity highest, as I have known it done by quicker people! For indeed, do but jumble and tumble sufficiently, you avoid that worst fault, of settling with your centre-of-gravity highest; your centre-of-gravity is certain to come lowest, and to stay there. If slowness, what we in our impatience call 'stupidity,' be the price of stable equilibrium over unstable, shall we grudge a little slowness? Not the least admirable quality of Bull is, after all, that of remaining insensible to logic; holding out for considerable periods, ten years or more, as in this of the Corn-Laws, after all arguments and shadow of arguments have faded away from him, till the very urchins on the street titter at the arguments he brings. Logic,—Λογική, the 'Art of Speech,'—does indeed speak so and so; clear enough: nevertheless Bull still shakes his head; will see whether nothing else *illogical*, not yet 'spoken,' not yet able to be 'spoken,' do not lie in the business, as there so often does!—My firm belief is, that, finding himself now enchanted, hand-shackled, foot-shackled, in Poor-Law Bastilles and elsewhere, he will retire three days to his bed, and *arrive* at a conclusion or two! His three-years 'total stagnation of trade,' alas, is not that a painful enough 'lying in bed to consider himself?' Poor Bull!

Bull is a born Conservative; for this too I inexpressibly honour him. All great Peoples are conservative; slow to believe in novelties; patient of much error in actualities; deeply and forever certain of the greatness that is in LAW, in Custom once solemnly established, and now long recognised as just and final.—True, O Radical Reformer, there is no Custom that can, properly speaking, be final; none. And yet thou seest *Customs* which, in all civilised countries, are accounted final; nay, under the Old-Roman name of *Mores*, are accounted *Morality*, Virtue, Laws of God Himself. Such, I assure thee, not a few of them are; such almost all of them once were. And greatly do I respect the solid character,—a blockhead, thou wilt say; yes, but a well-conditioned blockhead, and the best-conditioned,—who esteems all 'Customs once solemnly acknowledged' to be ultimate, divine, and the rule for a man to walk by, nothing doubting, not inquiring farther. What a time of it had we, were all men's life and trade still, in all parts of it, a problem, a hypothetic seeking, to be settled by painful Logics and Baconian Inductions! The Clerk in Eastcheap cannot spend the day in verifying his Ready-Reckoner; he must take it as verified, true and indisputable; or his Book-keeping by Double Entry will stand still. " Where is your Posted Ledger?" asks the Master at night.— " Sir," answers the other, " I was verifying my Ready-Reckoner, and find some errors. The Ledger is—!"—Fancy such a thing!

True, all turns on your Ready-Reckoner being moderately correct,—being *not* insupportably incorrect! A Ready-Reckoner which has led to distinct entries in your Ledger such as these: ' *Creditor* ' an English People by fifteen hundred years of good Labour; and ' *Debtor* to lodging in enchanted Poor-Law Bastilles: *Creditor* by ' conquering the largest Empire the Sun ever saw; and *Debtor* to ' Donothingism and "Impossible" written on all departments of ' the government thereof: *Creditor* by mountains of gold ingots ' earned; and *Debtor* to No Bread purchasable by them :'—*such* Ready-Reckoner, methinks, is beginning to be suspect; nay is ceasing, and has ceased, to be suspect! Such Ready-Reckoner is a Solecism in Eastcheap; and must, whatever be the press of business, and will and shall be rectified a little. Business can go on no longer with *it*. The most Conservative English People, thickest-skinned, most patient of Peoples, is driven alike by its Logic and its Unlogic, by things ' spoken,' and by things not yet spoken or very speakable, but only felt and very unendurable, to be wholly a Reforming People. Their Life as it is has ceased to be longer possible for them.

Urge not this noble silent People: rouse not the Berserkir-rage that lies in them! Do you know their Cromwells, Hampdens, their Pyms and Bradshaws? Men very peaceable, but men that can be made very terrible! Men who, like their old Teutsch Fathers in Agrippa's days, ' have a soul that despises death;' to whom ' death,' compared with falsehoods and injustices, is light;—' in whom there is a rage unconquerable by the immortal gods!' Before this, the English People have taken very preternatural-looking Spectres by the beard; saying virtually: " And if thou *wert* ' preternatural?' Thou with thy ' divine-rights' grown diabolic wrongs? Thou,—not even ' natural;' decapitable; totally extinguishable!"——Yes, just so godlike as this People's patience was, even so godlike will and must its impatience be. Away, ye scandalous Practical Solecisms, children actually of the Prince of Darkness; ye have near broken our hearts; we can and will endure you no longer. Begone, we say; depart, while the play is good! By the Most High God, whose sons and born missionaries true men are, ye shall not continue here! You and we have become incompatible; can inhabit one house no longer. Either you must go, or we. Are ye ambitious to try *which* it shall be?

O my Conservative friends, who still specially name and struggle to approve yourselves ' Conservative,' would to Heaven I could persuade you of this world-old fact, than which Fate is not surer, That Truth and Justice alone are *capable* of being ' conserved' and preserved ! The thing which is unjust, which is *not* according to God's Law, will you, in a God's Universe, try to conserve that? It is so old, say you? Yes, and the hotter haste ought *you*, of all others, to be in to let it grow no older! If but the faintest whisper in your hearts intimate to you that it is not fair,—hasten, for the sake of Conservatism itself, to probe it rigorously, to cast it forth at once and forever if guilty. How will or can you preserve *it*, the thing that is not fair? ' Impossibility' a thousandfold is marked on that. And ye call yourselves Conservatives, Aristocracies:— ought not honour and nobleness of mind, if they had departed from all the Earth elsewhere, to find their last refuge with you? Ye unfortunate !

The bough that is dead shall be cut away, for the sake of the tree itself. Old? Yes, it is too old. Many a weary winter has it swung and creaked there, and gnawed and fretted, with its dead wood, the organic substance and still living fibre of this good tree; many a long summer has its ugly naked brown defaced the fair green umbrage; every day it has done mischief, and that only: off with it, for the tree's sake, if for nothing more; let the Conservatism that would preserve cut *it* away. Did no wood-forester apprise you that a dead bough with its dead root left sticking there is extraneous, poisonous; is as a dead iron spike, some horrid rusty ploughshare driven into the living substance;—nay is far worse; for in every windstorm (' commercial crisis' or the like), it frets and creaks, jolts itself to and fro, and cannot lie quiet as your dead iron spike would.

If I were the Conservative Party of England (which is another bold figure of speech), I would not for a hundred thousand pounds an hour allow those Corn-Laws to continue ! Potosi and Golconda put together would not purchase my assent to them. Do you count what treasuries of bitter indignation they are laying up for you in every just English heart? Do you know what questions, not as to Corn-prices and Sliding-scales alone, they are *forcing* every reflective Englishman to ask himself? Questions insoluble, or hitherto unsolved; deeper than any of our Logic-plummets hitherto will sound: questions deep enough,—which it were better that we did not name even in thought! You are forcing us to think of them, to begin uttering them. The utterance of them is begun; and where will it be ended, think you? When two millions of one's brother-men sit in Workhouses, and five millions, as is insolently said, 'rejoice in potatoes,' there are various things that must be begun, let them end where they can.

———

CHAPTER VI.

TWO CENTURIES.

THE Settlement effected by our 'Healing Parliament' in the Year of Grace 1660, though accomplished under universal acclamations from the four corners of the British Dominions, turns out to have been one of the mournfullest that ever took place in this land of ours. It called and thought itself a Settlement of brightest hope and fulfilment, bright as the blaze of universal tar-barrels and bonfires could make it: and we find it now, on looking back on it with the insight which trial has yielded, a Settlement as of despair. Considered well, it was a settlement to govern henceforth without God, with only some decent Pretence of God.

Governing by the Christian Law of God had been found a thing of battle, convulsion, confusion, an infinitely difficult thing: wherefore let us now abandon it, and govern only by so much of God's Christian Law as—as may prove quiet and convenient for us. What is the end of Government? To guide men in the way wherein they should go; towards their true good in this life, the portal of infinite good in a life to come? To guide men in such way, and ourselves in such way, as the Maker of men, whose eye is upon us, will sanction at the Great Day?—Or alas, perhaps at bottom *is* there no Great Day, no sure outlook of any life to come; but only this poor life, and what of taxes, felicities, Nell-Gwyns and entertainments we can manage to muster here? In that case, the end of Government will be, To suppress all noise and disturbance, whether of Puritan preaching, Cameronian psalm-singing, thieves'-riot, murder, arson, or what noise soever, and—be careful that supplies do not fail! A very notable conclusion, if we will think of it, and not without an abundance of fruits for us. Oliver Cromwell's body hung on the Tyburn-gallows, as the type of Puritanism found futile, inexecutable, execrable,—yes, that gallows-tree has been a fingerpost into very strange country indeed. Let earnest Puritanism die; let decent Formalism, whatsoever cant it be or grow to, live! We have had a pleasant journey in that direction; and are—arriving at our inn?

To support the Four Pleas of the Crown, and keep Taxes

coming in : in very sad seriousness, has not this been, ever since, even in the best times, almost the one admitted end and aim of Government? Religion, Christian Church, Moral Duty; the fact that man had a soul at all; that in man's life there was any eternal truth or justice at all,—has been as good as left quietly out of sight. Church indeed,—alas, the endless talk and struggle we have had of High-Church, Low-Church, Church-Extension, Church-in-Danger: we invite the Christian reader to think whether it has not been a too miserable screech-owl phantasm of talk and struggle, as for a ' Church,'—which one had rather not define at present!

But now in these godless two centuries, looking at England and her efforts and doings, if we ask, What of England's doings the Law of Nature had accepted, Nature's King had actually furthered and pronounced to have truth in them,—where is our answer? Neither the ' Church' of Hurd and Warburton, nor the Anti-church of Hume and Paine; not in any shape the Spiritualism of England : all this is already seen, or beginning to be seen, for what it is; a thing that Nature does *not* own. On the one side is dreary Cant, with a *reminiscence* of things noble and divine; on the other is but acrid Candour, with a *prophecy* of things brutal, infernal. Hurd and Warburton are sunk into the sere and yellow leaf; no considerable body of true-seeing men looks thitherward for healing : the Paine-and-Hume Atheistic theory, of ' things well let alone,' with Liberty, Equality and the like, is also in these days declaring itself naught, unable to keep the world from taking fire.

The theories and speculations of both these parties, and, we may say, of all intermediate parties and persons, prove to be things which the Eternal Veracity did not accept; things superficial, ephemeral, which already a near Posterity, finding them already dead and brown-leafed, is about to suppress and forget. The Spiritualism of England, for those godless years, is, as it were, all forgettable. Much has been written : but the perennial Scriptures of Mankind have had small accession : from all English Books, in rhyme or prose, in leather binding or in paper wrappage, how many verses have been added to these? Our most melodious Singers have sung as from the throat outwards : from the inner Heart of Man, from the great Heart of Nature, through no Pope or Philips, has there come any tone. The Oracles have been dumb. In brief, the Spoken Word of England has not been true. The Spoken Word of England turns out to have been trivial; of short endurance; not valuable, not available as a Word, except for the passing day. It has been accordant with transitory Sem-

blance; discordant with eternal Fact. It has been unfortunately
not a Word, but a Cant; a helpless involuntary Cant, nay too often
a cunning voluntary one: either way, a very mournful Cant; the
Voice not of Nature and Fact, but of something other than these.

With all its miserable shortcomings, with its wars, controversies, with its trades-unions, famine-insurrections,—it is her Practical Material Work alone that England has to show for herself!
This, and hitherto almost nothing more; yet actually this. The
grim inarticulate veracity of the English People, unable to speak
its meaning in words, has turned itself silently on things; and
the dark powers of Material Nature have answered, "Yes, this at
least is true, this is not false!" So answers Nature. "Waste
desert-shrubs of the Tropical swamps have become Cotton-trees;
and here, under my furtherance, are verily woven shirts,—hanging
unsold, undistributed, but capable to be distributed, capable to
cover the bare backs of my children of men. Mountains, old as
the Creation, I have permitted to be bored through; bituminous
fuel-stores, the wreck of forests that were green a million years
ago,—I have opened them from my secret rock-chambers, and
they are yours, ye English. Your huge fleets, steamships, do sail
the sea; huge Indias do obey you; from huge *New* Englands and
Antipodal Australias comes profit and traffic to this Old England
of mine!" So answers Nature. The Practical Labour of England
is *not* a chimerical Triviality: it is a Fact, acknowledged by all
the Worlds; which no man and no demon will contradict. It is,
very audibly, though very inarticulately as yet, the one God's
Voice we have heard in these two atheistic centuries.

And now to observe with what bewildering obscurations and
impediments all this as yet stands entangled, and is yet intelligible to no man! How, with our gross Atheism, we hear it not
to be the Voice of God to us, but regard it merely as a Voice of
earthly Profit-and-Loss. And have a Hell in England,—the Hell
of not making money. And coldly see the all-conquering valiant
Sons of Toil sit enchanted, by the million, in their Poor-Law Bastille, as if this were Nature's Law;—mumbling to ourselves some
vague janglement of Laissez-faire, Supply-and-demand, Cash-payment the one nexus of man to man: Free-trade, Competition, and
Devil take the hindmost, our latest Gospel yet preached!

As if, in truth, there were no God of Labour; as if godlike Labour and brutal Mammonism were convertible terms. A serious,
most earnest Mammonism grown Midas-eared; an unserious Dilettantism, earnest about nothing, grinning with inarticulate incredu-
lous incredible jargon about all things, as the *enchanted* Dilettanti

do by the Dead Sea! It is mournful enough, for the present hour; were there not an endless hope in it withal. Giant LABOUR, truest emblem there is of God the World-Worker, Demiurgus, and Eternal Maker; noble LABOUR, which is yet to be the King of this Earth, and sit on the highest throne,—staggering hitherto like a blind irrational giant, hardly allowed to have his common place on the street-pavements; idle Dilettantism, Dead-Sea Apism crying out, " Down with him, he is dangerous!"

Labour must become a seeing rational giant, with a *soul* in the body of him, and take his place on the throne of things,— leaving his Mammonism, and several other adjuncts, on the lower steps of said throne.

CHAPTER VII.

OVER-PRODUCTION.

BUT what will reflective readers say of a Governing Class, such as ours, addressing its Workers with an indictment of ' Over-production !' Over-production : runs it not so? " Ye miscellaneous, ignoble manufacturing individuals, ye have produced too much! We accuse you of making above two-hundred thousand shirts for the bare backs of mankind. Your trousers too, which you have made, of fustian, of cassimere, of Scotch-plaid, of jane, nankeen and woollen broadcloth, are they not manifold? Of hats for the human head, of shoes for the human foot, of stools to sit on, spoons to eat with—Nay, what say we hats or shoes? You produce gold-watches, jewelleries, silver-forks and epergnes, commodes, chiffoniers, stuffed sofas—Heavens, the Commercial Bazaar and multitudinous Howel-and-Jameses cannot contain you. You have produced, produced ;—he that seeks your indictment, let him look around. Millions of shirts, and empty pairs of breeches, hang there in judgment against you. We accuse you of over-producing: you are criminally guilty of producing shirts, breeches, hats, shoes and commodities, in a frightful over-abundance. And now there is a glut, and your operatives cannot be fed!"

Never surely, against an earnest Working Mammonism was there brought, by Game-preserving aristocratic Dilettantism, a stranger accusation, since this world began. My lords and gentlemen,—why, it was *you* that were appointed, by the fact and by the theory of your position on the Earth, to ' make and administer Laws,'—that is to say, in a world such as ours, to guard against ' gluts ;' against honest operatives, who had done their work, remaining unfed! I say, *you* were appointed to preside over the

Distribution and Apportionment of the Wages of Work done; and to see well that there went no labourer without his hire, were it of money-coins, were it of hemp gallows-ropes: that function was yours, and from immemorial time has been; yours, and as yet no other's. These poor shirt-spinners have forgotten much, which by the virtual unwritten law of their position they should have remembered: but by any written recognised law of their position, what have they forgotten? They were set to make shirts. The Community with all its voices commanded them, saying, "Make shirts;"—and there the shirts are! Too many shirts? Well, that is a novelty, in this intemperate Earth, with its nine-hundred millions of bare backs! But the Community commanded you, saying, "See that the shirts are well apportioned, that our Human Laws be emblem of God's Laws;"—and where is the apportionment? Two million shirtless or ill-shirted workers sit enchanted in Workhouse Bastilles, five million more (according to some) in Ugolino Hunger-cellars; and for remedy, you say,—what say you?—"Raise *our* rents!" I have not in my time heard any stranger speech, not even on the Shores of the Dead Sea. You continue addressing those poor shirt-spinners and over-producers, in really a *too* triumphant manner:

"Will you bandy accusations, will you accuse *us* of over-production? We take the Heavens and the Earth to witness that we have produced nothing at all. Not from us proceeds this frightful overplus of shirts. In the wide domains of created Nature circulates no shirt or thing of our producing. Certain fox-brushes nailed upon our stable-door, the fruit of fair audacity at Melton Mowbray; these we have produced, and they are openly nailed up there. He that accuses us of producing, let him show himself, let him name what and when. We are innocent of producing;—ye ungrateful, what mountains of things have we not, on the contrary, had to ' consume,' and make away with! Mountains of those your heaped manufactures, wheresoever edible or wearable, have they not disappeared before us, as if we had the talent of ostriches, of cormorants, and a kind of divine faculty to eat? Ye ungrateful!—and did you not grow under the shadow of our wings? Are not your filthy mills built on these fields of ours; on this soil of England, which belongs to—whom think you? And we shall not offer you our own wheat at the price that pleases us, but that partly pleases you? A precious notion! What would become of you, if we chose, at any time, to decide on growing no wheat more?"

Yes, truly, *here* is the ultimate rock-basis of all Corn-Laws; whereon, at the bottom of much arguing, they rest, as securely as they can : What would become of you, if we decided, some day, on growing no more wheat at all? If we chose to grow only partridges henceforth, and a modicum of wheat for our own uses? Cannot we do what we like with our own?—Yes, indeed! For my share, if I could melt Gneiss Rock, and create Law of Gravitation; if I could stride out to the Doggerbank, some morning, and striking down my trident there into the mud-waves, say, "Be land, be fields, meadows, mountains and fresh-rolling streams!" by Heaven, I should incline to have the letting of *that* land in perpetuity, and sell the wheat of it, or burn the wheat of it, according to my own good judgment! My Corn-Lawing friends, you affright me.

To the 'Millo-cracy' so-called, to the Working Aristocracy, steeped too deep in mere ignoble Mammonism, and as yet all unconscious of its noble destinies, as yet but an irrational or semi-rational giant, struggling to awake some soul in itself,—the world will have much to say, reproachfully, reprovingly, admonishingly. But to the Idle Aristocracy, what will the world have to say? Things painful and not pleasant!

To the man who *works*, who attempts, in never so ungracious barbarous a way, to get forward with some work, you will hasten out with furtherances, with encouragements, corrections; you will say to him: "Welcome; thou art ours; our care shall be of thee." To the Idler, again, never so gracefully going idle, coming forward with never so many parchments, you will not hasten out; you will sit still, and be disinclined to rise. You will say to him: "Not welcome, O complex Anomaly; would thou hadst stayed out of doors: for who of mortals knows what to do with thee? Thy parchments: yes, they are old, of venerable yellowness; and we too honour parchment, old-established settlements, and venerable use and wont. Old parchments in very truth:—yet on the whole, if thou wilt remark, they are young to the Granite Rocks, to the Groundplan of God's Universe! We advise thee to put up thy parchments; to go home to thy place, and make no needless noise whatever. Our heart's wish is to save thee: yet there as thou art, hapless Anomaly, with nothing but thy yellow parchments, noisy futilities, and shotbelts and fox-brushes, who of gods or men can avert dark Fate? Be counselled, ascertain if no work exist for thee on God's Earth; if thou find no commanded-duty there but that of going gracefully idle? Ask, inquire earnestly, with a half-frantic earnestness; for the answer means Existence or Annihilation to thee. We apprise thee of the world-old fact, becoming sternly disclosed again in these days, That he who cannot work in this Universe cannot get existed in it: had he parchments to thatch the face of the world, these, combustible fallible sheepskin, cannot avail him. Home, thou unfortunate; and let us have at least no noise from thee !"

Suppose the unfortunate Idle Aristocracy, as the unfortunate Working one has done, were to 'retire three days to *its* bed,' and consider itself there, what o'clock it had become ?—

How have we to regret not only that men have ' no religion,' but that they have next to no reflection ; and go about with heads full of mere extraneous noises, with eyes wide-open but visionless, —for most part, in the somnambulist state !

CHAPTER VIII.

UNWORKING ARISTOCRACY.

It is well said, 'Land is the right basis of an Aristocracy;' whoever possesses the Land, he, more emphatically than any other, is the Governor, Viceking of the people on the Land. It is in these days as it was in those of Henry Plantagenet and Abbot Samson ; as it will in all days be. The Land is *Mother* of us all ; nourishes, shelters, gladdens, lovingly enriches us all ; in how many ways, from our first wakening to our last sleep on her blessed mother-bosom, does she, as with blessed mother-arms, enfold us all !

The Hill I first saw the Sun rise over, when the Sun and I and all things were yet in their auroral hour, who can divorce me from it ? Mystic, deep as the world's centre, are the roots I have struck into my Native Soil ; no *tree* that grows is rooted so. From noblest Patriotism to humblest industrial Mechanism ; from highest dying for your country, to lowest quarrying and coal-boring for it, a Nation's Life depends upon its Land. Again and again we have to say, there can be no true Aristocracy but must possess the Land.

Men talk of ' selling' Land. Land, it is true, like Epic Poems and even higher things, in such a trading world, has to be presented in the market for what it will bring, and as we say be ' sold :' but the notion of ' selling,' for certain bits of metal, the *Iliad* of Homer, how much more the *Land* of the World-Creator, is a ridiculous impossibility ! We buy what is saleable of it ; nothing more was ever buyable. Who can, or could, sell it to us ? Properly speaking, the Land belongs to these two: To the Almighty God; and to all His Children of Men that have ever worked well on it, or that shall ever work well on it. No generation of men can or could, with never such solemnity and effort, sell Land on any other principle: it is not the property of any generation, we say, but that of all the past generations that have worked on it, and of all the future ones that shall work on it.

Again, we hear it said, The soil of England, or of any country, is properly worth nothing, except 'the labour bestowed on it.' This, speaking even in the language of Eastcheap, is not correct. The rudest space of country equal in extent to England, could a whole English Nation, with all their habitudes, arrangements, skills, with whatsoever they do carry within the skins of them and cannot be stript of, suddenly take wing and alight on it,— would be worth a very considerable thing! Swiftly, within year and day, this English Nation, with its multiplex talents of ploughing, spinning, hammering, mining, road-making and trafficking, would bring a handsome value out of such a space of country. On the other hand, fancy what an English Nation, once 'on the wing,' could have done with itself, had there been simply no soil, not even an inarable one, to alight on? Vain all its talents for ploughing, hammering, and whatever else; there is no Earth-room for this Nation with its talents: this Nation will have to *keep* hovering on the wing, dolefully shrieking to and fro; and perish piecemeal; burying itself, down to the last soul of it, in the waste unfirmamented seas. Ah yes, soil, with or without ploughing, is the gift of God. The soil of all countries belongs evermore, in a very considerable degree, to the Almighty Maker! The last stroke of labour bestowed on it is not the making of its value, but only the increasing thereof.

It is very strange, the degree to which these truisms are forgotten in our days; how, in the ever-whirling chaos of Formulas, we have quietly lost sight of Fact,—which it is so perilous not to keep forever in sight. Fact, if we do not see it, will make us *feel* it by and by!—From much loud controversy, and Corn-Law debating there rises, loud though inarticulate, once more in these years, this very question among others, Who made the Land of England? Who made it, this respectable English Land, wheat-growing, metalliferous, carboniferous, which will let readily hand over head for seventy millions or upwards, as it here lies: who did make it?—"We!" answer the much-*consuming* Aristocracy; "We!" as they ride in, moist with the sweat of Melton Mowbray: "It is we that made it; or are the heirs, assigns and representatives of those who did!"—My brothers, You? Everlasting honour to you, then; and Corn-Laws as many as you will, till your own deep stomachs cry Enough, or some voice of Human pity for our famine bids you Hold! Ye are as gods, that can create soil. Soil-creating gods there is no withstanding. They have the might to sell wheat at what price they list; and the right, to all lengths, and famine-lengths,—if they be pitiless infernal gods! Celestial gods, I think, would stop short of the famine-price; but no infernal nor any kind of god can be bidden stop!——Infatuated mortals, into what questions are you driving every thinking man in England?

I say, you did *not* make the Land of England; and, by the possession of it, you *are* bound to furnish guidance and governance to England! That is the law of your position on this God's-Earth; an everlasting act of Heaven's Parliament, not repealable in St. Stephen's or elsewhere! True government and guidance; not no-government and Laissez-faire; how much less, *mis*-government and Corn-Law! There is not an imprisoned Worker looking out from these Bastilles but appeals, very audibly in Heaven's High Courts, against you, and me, and every one who is not imprisoned, "Why am I here?" His appeal is audible in Heaven; and will become audible enough on Earth too, if it remain unheeded here. His appeal is against you, foremost of all; you stand in the front-rank of the accused; you, by the very place you hold, have first of all to answer him and Heaven!

What looks maddest, miserablest in these mad and miserable Corn-Laws is independent altogether of their 'effect on wages,' their effect on 'increase of trade,' or any other such effect: it is the continual maddening proof they protrude into the faces of all men, that our Governing Class, called by God and Nature and the inflexible law of Fact, either to do something towards governing, or to die and be abolished,—have not yet learned even to sit still and do no mischief! For no Anti-Corn-Law League yet asks more of them than this;—Nature and Fact, very imperatively, asking so much more of them. Anti-Corn-Law League asks not, Do something; but, Cease your destructive misdoing, Do ye nothing!

Nature's message will have itself obeyed: messages of mere Free-Trade, Anti-Corn-Law League and Laissez-faire, will then need small obeying!—Ye fools, in name of Heaven, work, work, at the Ark of Deliverance for yourselves and us, while hours are still granted you! No: instead of working at the Ark, they say, "We cannot get our hands kept rightly warm;" and *sit obstinately burning the planks*. No madder spectacle at present exhibits itself under this Sun.

The Working Aristocracy; Mill-owners, Manufacturers, Commanders of Working Men : alas, against them also much shall be brought in accusation; much,—and the freest Trade in Corn, total abolition of Tariffs, and uttermost 'Increase of Manufactures' and 'Prosperity of Commerce,' will permanently mend no jot of it. The Working Aristocracy must strike into a new path; must understand that money alone is *not* the representative either of man's success in the world, or of man's duties to man; and reform their own selves from top to bottom, if they wish England reformed. England will not be habitable long, unreformed.

The Working Aristocracy—Yes, but on the threshold of all this, it is again and again to be asked, What of the Idle Aristocracy? Again and again, What shall we say of the Idle Aristocracy, the Owners of the Soil of England ; whose recognised function is that of handsomely consuming the rents of England, shooting the partridges of England, and as an agreeable amusement (if the purchase-money and other conveniences serve), dilettante-ing in Parliament and Quarter-Sessions for England? We will say mournfully, in the presence of Heaven and Earth,—that we stand speechless, stupent, and know not what to say! That a class of men entitled to live sumptuously on the marrow of the earth; permitted simply, nay entreated, and as yet entreated in vain, to do nothing at all in return, was never heretofore seen on the face of this Planet. That such a class is transitory, exceptional, and, unless Nature's Laws fall dead, cannot continue. That it has continued now a moderate while; has, for the last fifty years, been rapidly attaining its state of perfection. That it will have to find its duties and do them; or else that it must and will cease to be seen on the face of this Planet, which is a Working one, not an Idle one.

Alas, alas, the Working Aristocracy, admonished by Trades-unions, Chartist conflagrations, above all by their own shrewd sense kept in perpetual communion with the fact of things, will assuredly reform themselves, and a working world will still be possible:—but the fate of the Idle Aristocracy, as one reads its horoscope hitherto in Corn-Laws and such like, is an abyss that fills one with despair. Yes, my rosy fox-hunting brothers, a terrible *Hippocratic look* reveals itself (God knows, not to my joy) through those fresh buxom countenances of yours. Through your Corn-Law Majorities, Sliding-Scales, Protecting-Duties, Bribery-Elections, and triumphant Kentish-fire, a thinking eye discerns ghastly images of ruin, too ghastly for words ; a handwriting as of MENE, MENE. Men and brothers, on your Sliding-scale you seem sliding, and to have slid,—you little know whither! Good God! did not a French Donothing Aristocracy, hardly above half a cen-

P

tury ago, declare in like manner, and in its featherhead believe in
like manner, "We cannot exist, and continue to dress and parade
ourselves, on the just rent of the soil of France; but we must have
farther payment than rent of the soil, we must be exempted from
taxes too,"—we must have a Corn-Law to extend our rent? This
was in 1789: in four years more—Did you look into the Tanneries
of Meudon, and the long-naked making for themselves breeches of
human skins! May the merciful Heavens avert the omen; may
we be wiser, that so we be less wretched.

A High Class without duties to do is like a tree planted on
precipices; from the roots of which all the earth has been crumb-
ling. Nature owns no man who is not a Martyr withal. Is there
a man who pretends to live luxuriously housed up; screened from
all work, from want, danger, hardship, the victory over which is
what we name work;—he himself to sit serene, amid down-bolsters
and appliances, and have all his work and battling done by other
men? And such man calls himself a *noble*-man? His fathers
worked for him, he says; or successfully gambled for him: here *he*
sits; professes, not in sorrow but in pride, that he and his have
done no work, time out of mind. It is the law of the land, and
is thought to be the law of the Universe, that he, alone of recorded
men, shall have no task laid on him, except that of eating his
cooked victuals, and not flinging himself out of window. Once
more I will say, there was no stranger spectacle ever shown under
this Sun. A veritable fact in our England of the Nineteenth Century. His victuals he does eat: but as for keeping in the inside of
the window,—have not his friends, like me, enough to do? Truly,
looking at his Corn-Laws, Game-Laws, Chandos-Clauses, Bribery-
Elections and much else, you do shudder over the tumbling and
plunging he makes, held back by the lappels and coatskirts; only
a thin fence of window-glass before him,—and in the street mere
horrid iron spikes! My sick brother, as in hospital-maladies men
do, thou dreamest of Paradises and Eldorados, which are far from
thee. 'Cannot I do what I like with my own?' Gracious Heaven,
my brother, this that thou seest with those sick eyes is no firm
Eldorado, and Corn-Law Paradise of Donothings, but a dream
of thy own fevered brain. It is a glass-window, I tell thee, so
many stories from the street; where are iron spikes and the law
of gravitation!

What is the meaning of nobleness, if this be 'noble?' In a
valiant suffering for others, not in a slothful making others suffer
for us, did nobleness ever lie. The chief of men is he who stands
in the van of men; fronting the peril which frightens back all

others; which, if it be not vanquished, will devour the others. Every noble crown is, and on Earth will forever be, a crown of thorns. The Pagan Hercules, why was he accounted a hero? Because he had slain Nemean Lions, cleansed Augean Stables, undergone Twelve Labours only not too heavy for a god. In modern, as in ancient and all societies, the Aristocracy, they that assume the functions of an Aristocracy, doing them or not, have taken the post of honour; which is the post of difficulty, the post of danger,—of death, if the difficulty be not overcome. *Il faut payer de sa vie.* Why was our life given us, if not that we should manfully give it? Descend, O Donothing Pomp; quit thy down-cushions; expose thyself to learn what wretches feel, and how to cure it! The Czar of Russia became a dusty toiling shipwright; worked with his axe in the Docks of Saardam; and his aim was small to thine. Descend thou: undertake this horrid 'living chaos of Ignorance and Hunger' weltering round thy feet; say, " I will heal it, or behold I will die foremost in it." Such is verily the law. Everywhere and everywhen a man has to '*pay* with his life;' to do his work, as a soldier does, at the expense of life. In no Piepowder earthly Court can you sue an Aristocracy to do its work, at this moment: but in the Higher Court, which even *it* calls ' Court of Honour,' and which is the Court of Necessity withal, and the eternal Court of the Universe, in which all Fact comes to plead, and every Human Soul is an apparitor,—the Aristocracy is answerable, and even now answering, *there.*

Parchments? Parchments are venerable: but they ought at all times to represent, as near as they by possibility can, the writing of the Adamant Tablets; otherwise they are not so venerable! Benedict the Jew in vain pleaded parchments; his usuries were too many. The King said, " Go to, for all thy parchments, thou shalt pay just debt; down with thy dust, or observe this tooth-forceps!" Nature, a far juster Sovereign, has far terribler forceps. Aristocracies, actual and imaginary, reach a time when parchment pleading does not avail them. " Go to, for all thy parchments, thou shalt pay due debt!" shouts the Universe to them, in an emphatic manner. They refuse to pay, confidently pleading parchment: their best grinder-tooth, with horrible agony, goes out of their jaw. Wilt thou pay now? A second grinder, again in horrible agony, goes: a second, and a third, and if need be, all the teeth and grinders, and the life itself with them ;—and *then* there is free payment, and an anatomist-subject into the bargain!

Reform Bills, Corn-Law Abrogation Bills, and then Land-Tax Bill, Property-Tax Bill, and still dimmer list of *etceteras;* grinder

after grinder:—my lords and gentlemen, it were better for you
to arise, and begin doing your work, than sit there and plead
parchments!

We write no Chapter on the Corn-Laws, in this place; the
Corn-Laws are too mad to have a Chapter. There is a certain
immorality, when there is not a necessity, in speaking about
things finished; in chopping into small pieces the already slashed
and slain. When the brains are out, why does not a Solecism die!
It is at its own peril if it refuse to die; it ought to make all conceivable haste to die, and get itself buried! The trade of Anti-
Corn-Law Lecturer in these days, still an indispensable, is a highly
tragic one.

The Corn-Laws will go, and even soon go: would we were all
as sure of the Millennium as they are of going! They go swiftly in
these present months; with an increase of velocity, an ever-deepening, ever-widening sweep of momentum, truly notable. It is at
the Aristocracy's own damage and peril, still more than at any
other's whatsoever, that the Aristocracy maintains them;—at a
damage, say only, as above computed, of a 'hundred thousand
pounds an hour!' The Corn-Laws keep all the air hot: fostered
by their fever-warmth, much that is evil, but much also, how
much that is good and indispensable, is rapidly coming to life
among us!

CHAPTER IX.

WORKING ARISTOCRACY.

A POOR Working Mammonism getting itself 'strangled in the
partridge-nets of an Unworking Dilettantism,' and bellowing
dreadfully, and already black in the face, is surely a disastrous
spectacle! But of a Midas-eared Mammonism, which indeed
at bottom all pure Mammonisms are, what better can you expect?
No better;—if not this, then something other equally disastrous,
if not still more disastrous. Mammonisms, grown asinine, have
to become human again, and rational; they have, on the whole,
to cease to be Mammonisms, were it even on compulsion, and
pressure of the hemp round their neck!—My friends of the Working Aristocracy, there are now a great many things which you also,
in your extreme need, will have to consider.

The Continental people, it would seem, are 'exporting our

'machinery, beginning to spin cotton and manufacture for them-
'selves, to cut us out of this market and then out of that !' Sad
news indeed; but irremediable;—by no means the saddest news.
The saddest news is, that we should find our National Existence,
as I sometimes hear it said, depend on selling manufactured cotton at a farthing an ell cheaper than any other People. A most
narrow stand for a great Nation to base itself on ! A stand which,
with all the Corn-Law Abrogations conceivable, I do not think will
be capable of enduring.

My friends, suppose we quitted that stand; suppose we came
honestly down from it, and said: "This is our minimum of cotton-
prices. We care not, for the present, to make cotton any cheaper.
Do you, if it seem so blessed to you, make cotton cheaper. Fill
your lungs with cotton-fuz, your hearts with copperas-fumes, with
rage and mutiny; become ye the general gnomes of Europe, slaves
of the lamp !"—I admire a Nation which fancies it will die if it do
not undersell all other Nations, to the end of the world. Brothers,
we will cease to *under*sell them; we will be content to *equal*-sell
them; to be happy selling equally with them ! I do not see the
use of underselling them. Cotton-cloth is already two-pence a
yard or lower; and yet bare backs were never more numerous
among us. Let inventive men cease to spend their existence incessantly contriving how cotton can be made cheaper; and try to
invent, a little, how cotton at its present cheapness could be somewhat justlier divided among us. Let inventive men consider, Whether the Secret of this Universe, and of Man's Life there, does,
after all, as we rashly fancy it, consist in making money? There
is One God, just, supreme, almighty: but is Mammon the name
of him?—With a Hell which means 'Failing to make money,' I
do not think there is any Heaven possible that would suit one
well; nor so much as an Earth that can be habitable long! In
brief, all this Mammon-Gospel, of Supply-and-demand, Competition, Laissez-faire, and Devil take the hindmost, begins to be
one of the shabbiest Gospels ever preached; or altogether the
shabbiest. Even with Dilettante partridge-nets, and at a horrible
expenditure of pain, who shall regret to see the entirely transient,
and at best somewhat despicable life strangled out of *it?* At the
best, as we say, a somewhat despicable, unvenerable thing, this
same 'Laissez-faire;' and now, at the *worst*, fast growing an altogether detestable one !

"But what is to be done with our manufacturing population,
with our agricultural, with our ever-increasing population?" cry
many.—Aye, what? Many things can be done with them, a hundred things, and a thousand things,—had we once got a soul, and

begun to try. This one thing, of doing for them by 'underselling
all people,' and filling our own bursten pockets and appetites by
the road; and turning over all care for any · population,' or human
or divine consideration except cash only, to the winds, with a
"Laissez-faire" and the rest of it: this is evidently not the thing.
Farthing cheaper per yard? No great Nation can stand on the
apex of such a pyramid; screwing itself higher and higher; balanc-
ing itself on its great-toe! Can England not subsist without being
above all people in working? England never deliberately purposed
such a thing. If England work better than all people, it shall be
well. England, like an honest worker, will work as well as she
can; and hope the gods may allow her to live on that basis. Laissez-faire and much else being once well dead, how many 'impossibles' will become possible! They are impossible, as cotton-cloth
at two-pence an ell was—till men set about making it. The inventive genius of great England will not forever sit patient with
mere wheels and pinions, bobbins, straps and billy-rollers whirring
in the head of it. The inventive genius of England is not a Beaver's, or a Spinner's or Spider's genius: it is a *Man's* genius, I hope,
with a God over him!

Laissez-faire, Supply-and-demand,—one begins to be weary of
all that. Leave all to egoism, to ravenous greed of money, of
pleasure, of applause:—it is the Gospel of Despair! Man *is* a
Patent-Digester, then: only give him Free Trade, Free digesting-
room; and each of us digest what he can come at, leaving the rest
to Fate! My unhappy brethren of the Working Mammonism, my
unhappier brethren of the Idle Dilettantism, no world was ever
held together in that way for long. A world of mere Patent-Di-
gesters will soon have nothing to digest: such world ends, and by
Law of Nature must end, in 'over-population;' in howling universal famine, 'impossibility,' and suicidal madness, as of endless dog-
kennels run rabid. Supply-and-demand shall do its full part, and
Free Trade shall be free as air;—thou of the shotbelts, see thou
forbid it not, with those paltry, *worse* than Mammonish swindleries and Sliding-scales of thine, which are seen to be swindleries
for all thy canting, which in times like ours are very scandalous
to see! And Trade never so well freed, and all Tariffs settled or
abolished, and Supply-and-demand in full operation,—let us all
know that we have yet done nothing; that we have merely cleared
the ground for doing.

Yes, were the Corn-Laws ended tomorrow, there is nothing yet
ended; there is only room made for all manner of things beginning. The Corn-Laws gone, and Trade made free, it is as good as
certain this paralysis of industry will pass away. We shall have

another period of commercial enterprise, of victory and prosperity; during which, it is likely, much money will again be made, and all the people may, by the extant methods, still for a space of years, be kept alive and physically fed. The strangling band of Famine will be loosened from our necks; we shall have room again to breathe; time to bethink ourselves, to repent and consider! A precious and thrice-precious space of years; wherein to struggle as for life in reforming our foul ways; in alleviating, instructing, regulating our people; seeking, as for life, that something like spiritual food be imparted them, some real governance and guidance be provided them! It will be a priceless time. For our new period or paroxysm of commercial prosperity will and can, on the old methods of 'Competition and Devil take the hindmost,' prove but a paroxysm: a new paroxysm,—likely enough, if we do not use it better, to be our *last*. In this, of itself, is no salvation. If our Trade in twenty years, 'flourishing' as never Trade flourished, could double itself; yet then also, by the old Laissez-faire method, our Population is doubled: we shall then be as we are, only twice as many of us, twice and ten times as unmanageable!

All this dire misery, therefore; all this of our poor Workhouse Workmen, of our Chartisms, Trades-strikes, Corn-Laws, Toryisms, and the general downbreak of Laissez-faire in these days,—may we not regard it as a voice from the dumb bosom of Nature, saying to us: "Behold! Supply-and-demand is not the one Law of Nature; Cash-payment is not the sole nexus of man with man,—how far from it! Deep, far deeper than Supply-and-demand, are Laws, Obligations sacred as Man's Life itself: these also, if you will continue to do work, you shall now learn and obey. He that will learn them, behold Nature is on his side, he shall yet work and prosper with noble rewards. He that will not learn them, Nature is against him, he shall not be able to do work in Nature's empire,—not in hers. Perpetual mutiny, contention, hatred, isolation, execration shall wait on his footsteps, till all men discern that the thing which he attains, however golden it look or be, is not success, but the want of success."

Supply-and-demand,—alas! For what noble work was there ever yet any audible 'demand' in that poor sense? The man of Macedonia, speaking in vision to an Apostle Paul, "Come over and help us," did not specify what rate of wages he would give! Or was the Christian Religion itself accomplished by Prize-Essays, Bridgewater Bequests, and a 'minimum of Four thousand five hundred a year?' No demand that I heard of was made then, audible in any Labour-market, Manchester Chamber of Commerce, or other the like emporium and hiring establishment; silent were all these from any whisper of such demand;—powerless were all these to 'supply' it, had the demand been in thunder and earthquake, with gold Eldorados and Mahometan Paradises for the reward. Ah me, into what waste latitudes, in this Time-Voyage, have we wandered; like adventurous Sindbads;—where the men go about as if by galvanism, with meaningless glaring eyes, and have no soul, but only a beaver-faculty and stomach! The haggard despair of Cotton-factory, Coal-mine operatives, Chandos Farm-labourers, in these days, is painful to behold; but not so painful, hideous to the inner sense, as that brutish godforgetting Profit-and-Loss Philosophy and Life-theory, which we hear jangled on all hands of us, in senate-houses, spouting-clubs, leading-articles, pulpits and platforms, everywhere as the Ultimate Gospel and candid Plain-English of Man's Life, from the throats and pens and thoughts of all-but all men!—

Enlightened Philosophies, like Molière Doctors, will tell you: "Enthusiasms, Self-sacrifice, Heaven, Hell and such like: yes, all that was true enough for old stupid times; all that used to be true: but we have changed all that, *nous avons changé tout cela!*" Well; if the heart be got round now into the right side, and the liver to the left; if man have no heroism in him deeper than the wish to eat, and in his soul there dwell now no Infinite of Hope and Awe, and no divine Silence can become imperative because it is not Sinai Thunder, and no tie will bind if it be not that of Tyburn gallows-ropes,—then verily you have changed all that; and for it, and for you, and for me, behold the Abyss and nameless Annihilation is ready. So scandalous a beggarly Universe deserves indeed nothing else; I cannot say I would save it from Annihilation. Vacuum, and the serene Blue, will be much handsomer; easier too for all of us. I, for one, decline living as a Patent-Digester. Patent-Digester, Spinning-Mule, Mayfair Clothes-Horse: many thanks, but your Chaosships will have the goodness to excuse me!

CHAPTER X.

PLUGSON OF UNDERSHOT.

ONE thing I do know: Never, on this Earth, was the relation of man to man long carried on by Cash-payment alone. If, at any time, a philosophy of Laissez-faire, Competition and Supply-and-demand, start up as the exponent of human relations, expect that it will soon end.

Such philosophies will arise: for man's philosophies are usually the 'supplement of his practice;' some ornamental Logic-varnish, some outer skin of Articulate Intelligence, with which he strives to render his dumb Instinctive Doings presentable when they are done. Such philosophies will arise; be preached as Mammon-Gospels, the ultimate Evangel of the World; be believed, with what is called belief, with much superficial bluster, and a kind of shallow satisfaction real in its way:—but they are ominous gospels! They are the sure, and even swift, forerunner of great changes. Expect that the old System of Society is done, is dying and fallen into dotage, when it begins to rave in that fashion. Most Systems that I have watched the death of, for the last three thousand years, have gone just so. The Ideal, the True and Noble that was in them having faded out, and nothing now remaining but naked Egoism, vulturous Greediness, they cannot live; they are bound and inexorably ordained by the oldest Destinies, Mothers of the Universe, to die. Curious enough: they thereupon, as I have pretty generally noticed, devise some light comfortable kind of 'wine-and-walnuts philosophy' for themselves, this of Supply-and-demand or another; and keep saying, during hours of mastication and rumination, which they call hours of meditation: " Soul, take thy ease, it is all *well* that thou art a vulture-soul;"— and pangs of dissolution come upon them, oftenest before they are aware!

Cash-payment never was, or could except for a few years be, the union-bond of man to man. Cash never yet paid one man fully his deserts to another; nor could it, nor can it, now or henceforth to the end of the world. I invite his Grace of Castle-Rackrent to reflect on this;—does he think that a Land Aristocracy when it becomes a Land Auctioneership can have long to live? Or that Sliding-scales will increase the vital stamina of it? The indomitable Plugson too, of the respected Firm of Plugson, Hunks and Company, in St. Dolly Undershot, is invited to reflect on this; for to him also it will be new, perhaps even newer. Book-keeping by double entry is admirable, and records several things in an exact manner. But the Mother-Destinies also keep their Tablets; in Heaven's Chancery also there goes on a recording; and things, as my Moslem friends say, are 'written on the iron leaf.'

Your Grace and Plugson, it is like, go to Church occasionally: did you never in vacant moments, with perhaps a dull parson droning to you, glance into your New Testament, and the cash-account stated four times over, by a kind of quadruple entry,—in the Four Gospels there? I consider that a cash-account, and

balance-statement of work done and wages paid, worth attending
to. Precisely *such*, though on a smaller scale, go on at all moments under this Sun; and the statement and balance of them in
the Plugson Ledgers and on the Tablets of Heaven's Chancery are
discrepant exceedingly;—which ought really to teach, and to have
long since taught, an indomitable common-sense Plugson of Undershot, much more an unattackable *un*common-sense Grace of
Rackrent, a thing or two!—In brief, we shall have to dismiss the
Cash-Gospel rigorously into its own place : we shall have to know,
on the threshold, that either there is some infinitely deeper Gospel, subsidiary, explanatory and daily and hourly corrective, to the
Cash one; or else that the Cash one itself and all others are fast
travelling !

For all human things do require to have an Ideal in them; to
have some Soul in them, as we said, were it only to keep the Body
unputrefied. And wonderful it is to see how the Ideal or Soul,
place it in what ugliest Body you may, will irradiate said Body
with its own nobleness ; will gradually, incessantly, mould, modify,
new-form or reform said ugliest Body, and make it at last beautiful, and to a certain degree divine!—O, if you could dethrone that
Brute-god Mammon, and put a Spirit-god in his place ! One way
or other, he must and will have to be dethroned.

Fighting, for example, as I often say to myself, Fighting with
steel murder-tools is surely a much uglier operation than Working, take it how you will. Yet even of Fighting, in religious Abbot
Samson's days, see what a Feudalism there had grown,—a ' glorious Chivalry,' much besung down to the present day. Was not
that one of the 'impossiblest' things? Under the sky is no uglier
spectacle than two men with clenched teeth, and hellfire eyes,
hacking one another's flesh; converting precious living bodies,
and priceless living souls, into nameless masses of putrescence,
useful only for turnip-manure. How did a Chivalry ever come out
of that; how anything that was not hideous, scandalous, infernal?
It will be a question worth considering by and by.

I remark, for the present, only two things : first, that the Fighting itself was not, as we rashly suppose it, a Fighting without
cause, but more or less with cause. Man is created to fight; he
is perhaps best of all definable as a born soldier; his life 'a battle
and a march,' under the right General. It is forever indispensable for a man to fight: now with Necessity, with Barrenness,
Scarcity, with Puddles, Bogs, tangled Forests, unkempt Cotton;
—now also with the hallucinations of his poor fellow Men. Hal-
lucinatory visions rise in the head of my poor fellow man; make

him claim over me rights which are not his. All Fighting, as we noticed long ago, is the dusty conflict of strengths, each thinking itself the strongest, or, in other words, the justest;—of Mights which do in the long-run, and forever will in this just Universe in the long-run, mean Rights. In conflict the perishable part of them, beaten sufficiently, flies off into dust: this process ended, appears the imperishable, the true and exact.

And now let us remark a second thing: how, in these baleful operations, a noble devout-hearted Chevalier will comfort himself, and an ignoble godless Bucanier and Chactaw Indian. Victory is the aim of each. But deep in the heart of the noble man it lies forever legible, that, as an Invisible Just God made him, so will and must God's Justice and this only, were it never so invisible, ultimately prosper in all controversies and enterprises and battles whatsoever. What an Influence; ever-present,—like a Soul in the rudest Caliban of a body; like a ray of Heaven, and illuminative creative *Fiat-Lux*, in the wastest terrestrial Chaos! Blessed divine Influence, traceable even in the horror of Battlefields and garments rolled in blood: how it ennobles even the Battlefield; and, in place of a Chactaw Massacre, makes it a Field of Honour! A Battlefield too is great. Considered well, it is a kind of Quintessence of Labour; Labour distilled into its utmost concentration; the significance of years of it compressed into an hour. Here too thou shalt be strong, and not in muscle only, if thou wouldst prevail. Here too thou shalt be strong of heart, noble of soul; thou shalt dread no pain or death, thou shalt not love ease or life; in rage, thou shalt remember mercy, justice;—thou shalt be a Knight and not a Chactaw, if thou wouldst prevail! It is the rule of all battles, against hallucinating fellow Men, against unkempt Cotton, or whatsoever battles they may be, which a man in this world has to fight.

Howel Davies dyes the West-Indian Seas with blood, piles his decks with plunder; approves himself the expertest Seaman, the daringest Seafighter: but he gains no lasting victory, lasting victory is not possible for him. Not, had he fleets larger than the combined British Navy all united with him in bucaniering. He, once for all, cannot prosper in his duel. He strikes down his man: yes; but his man, or his man's representative, has no notion to lie struck down; neither, though slain ten times, will he keep so lying;—nor has the Universe any notion to keep him so lying! On the contrary, the Universe and he have, at all moments, all manner of motives to start up again, and desperately fight again. Your Napoleon is flung out, at last, to St. Helena; the latter end of him sternly compensating the beginning. The Bucanier strikes

down a man, a hundred or a million men: but what profits it?
He has one enemy never to be struck down; nay two enemies:
Mankind and the Maker of Men. On the great scale or on the
small, in fighting of men or fighting of difficulties, I will not
embark my venture with Howel Davies: it is not the Bucanier,
it is the Hero only that can gain victory, that can do more than
seem to succeed. These things will deserve meditating; for they
apply to all battle and soldiership, all struggle and effort whatsoever in this Fight of Life. It is a poor Gospel, Cash-Gospel or
whatever name it have, that does not, with clear tone, uncontra-
dictable, carrying conviction to all hearts, forever keep men in
mind of these things.

Unhappily, my indomitable friend Plugson of Undershot has,
in a great degree, forgotten them;—as, alas, all the world has; as,
alas, our very Dukes and Soul-Overseers have, whose special trade
it was to remember them! Hence these tears.—Plugson, who has
indomitably spun Cotton merely to gain thousands of pounds, I
have to call as yet a Bucanier and Chactaw; till there come something better, still more indomitable from him. His hundred
Thousand-pound Notes, if there be nothing other, are to me but
as the hundred Scalps in a Chactaw wigwam. The blind Plugson:
he was a Captain of Industry, born member of the Ultimate
genuine Aristocracy of this Universe, could he have known it!
These thousand men that span and toiled round him, they were
a regiment whom he had enlisted, man by man; to make war on
a very genuine enemy: Bareness of back, and disobedient Cotton-
fibre, which will not, unless forced to it, consent to cover bare
backs. Here is a most genuine enemy; over whom all creatures
will wish him victory. He enlisted his thousand men; said to
them, " Come, brothers, let us have a dash at Cotton!" They follow with cheerful shout; they gain such a victory over Cotton as
the Earth has to admire and clap hands at: but, alas, it is yet only
of the Bucanier or Chactaw sort,—as good as no victory! Foolish
Plugson of St. Dolly Undershot: does he hope to become illustrious by hanging up the scalps in his wigwam, the hundred thousands at his banker's, and saying, Behold my scalps? Why, Plugson, even thy own host is all in mutiny: Cotton is conquered; but
the ' bare backs'—are worse covered than ever! Indomitable
Plugson, thou must cease to be a Chactaw; thou and others; thou
thyself, if no other!

Did William the Norman Bastard, or any of his Taillefers, *Iron-
cutters*, manage so? Ironcutter, at the end of the campaign, did
not turn off his thousand fighters, but said to them: " Noble
fighters, this is the land we have gained; be I Lord in it,—what

we will call *Law-ward*, maintainer and *keeper* of Heaven's *Laws:* be I *Law-ward*, or in brief orthoepy *Lord* in it, and be ye Loyal Men around me in it; and we will stand by one another, as soldiers round a captain, for again we shall have need of one another!" Plugson, bucanier-like, says to them : " Noble spinners, this is the Hundred Thousand we have gained, wherein I mean to dwell and plant vineyards; the hundred thousand is mine, the three and sixpence daily was yours: adieu, noble spinners; drink my health with this groat each, which I give you over and above!" The entirely unjust Captain of Industry, say I; not Chevalier, but Bucanier! ' Commercial Law' does indeed acquit him; asks, with wide eyes, What else? So too Howel Davies asks, Was it not according to the strictest Bucanier Custom? Did I depart in any jot or tittle from the Laws of the Bucaniers?

After all, money, as they say, is miraculous. Plugson wanted victory; as Chevaliers and Bucaniers, and all men alike do. He found money recognised, by the whole world with one assent, as the true symbol, exact equivalent and synonym of victory;—and here we have him, a grimbrowed, indomitable Bucanier, coming home to us with a ' victory,' which the whole world is *ceasing* to clap hands at! The whole world, taught somewhat impressively, is beginning to recognise that such victory is but half a victory; and that now, if it please the Powers, we must—have the other half!

Money is miraculous. What miraculous facilities has it yielded, will it yield us; but also what never-imagined confusions, obscurations has it brought in; down almost to total extinction of the moral-sense in large masses of mankind! ' Protection of property,' of what is ' *mine*,' means with most men protection of money,—the thing which, had I a thousand padlocks over it, is least of all *mine*; is, in a manner, scarcely worth calling mine! The symbol shall be held sacred, defended everywhere with tipstaves, ropes and gibbets; the thing signified shall be composedly cast to the dogs. A human being who has worked with human beings clears all scores with them, cuts himself with triumphant completeness forever loose from them, by paying down certain shillings and pounds. Was it not the wages I promised you? There they are, to the last sixpence,—according to the Laws of the Bucaniers! —Yes, indeed;—and, at such times, it becomes imperatively necessary to ask all persons, bucaniers and others, Whether these same respectable Laws of the Bucaniers are written on God's eternal Heavens at all, on the inner Heart of Man at all; or on the respectable Bucanier Logbook merely, for the convenience of bucaniering merely? What a question;—whereat Westminster Hall shudders

to its driest parchment; and on the dead wigs each particular
horsehair stands on end!

The Laws of Laissez-faire, O Westminster, the laws of industrial
Captain and industrial Soldier, how much more of idle Captain
and industrial Soldier, will need to be remodelled, and modified,
and rectified in a hundred and a hundred ways,—and *not* in the
Sliding-scale direction, but in the totally opposite one! With two
million industrial Soldiers already sitting in Bastilles, and five
million pining on potatoes, methinks Westminster cannot begin
too soon!—A man has other obligations laid on him, in God's Universe, than the payment of cash: these also Westminster, if it will
continue to exist and have board-wages, must contrive to take
some charge of:—by Westminster or by another, they must and
will be taken charge of; be, with whatever difficulty, got articulated, got enforced, and to a certain approximate extent put in
practice. And, as I say, it cannot be too soon! For Mammonism,
left to itself, has become Midas-eared; and with all its gold mountains, sits starving for want of bread: and Dilettantism with its
partridge-nets, in this extremely earnest Universe of ours, is playing somewhat too high a game. 'A man by the very look of him
promises so much:' yes; and by the rent-roll of him does he promise nothing?—

Alas, what a business will this be, which our Continental
friends, groping this long while somewhat absurdly about it and
about it, call ' Organisation of Labour;'—which must be taken out
of the hands of absurd windy persons, and put into the hands of
wise, laborious, modest and valiant men, to begin with it straightway: to proceed with it, and succeed in it more and more, if Europe, at any rate if England, is to continue habitable much longer
Looking at the kind of most noble Corn-Law Dukes or Practical
Duces we have, and also of right reverend Soul-Overseers, Christian
Spiritual *Duces* ' on a minimum of four thousand five hundred,'
one's hopes are a little chilled. Courage, nevertheless; there are
many brave men in England! My indomitable Plugson,—nay is
there not even in thee some hope? Thou art hitherto a Bucanier,
as it was written and prescribed for thee by an evil world: but in
that grim brow, in that indomitable heart which *can* conquer Cotton, do there not perhaps lie other ten-times nobler conquests?

CHAPTER XI.

LABOUR.

FOR there is a perennial nobleness, and even sacredness, in Work. Were he never so benighted, forgetful of his high calling, there is always hope in a man that actually and earnestly works: in Idleness alone is there perpetual despair. Work, never so Mammonish, mean, *is* in communication with Nature; the real desire to get Work done will itself lead one more and more to truth, to Nature's appointments and regulations, which are truth.

The latest Gospel in this world is, Know thy work and do it. 'Know thyself:' long enough has that poor 'self' of thine tormented thee; thou wilt never get to 'know' it, I believe! Think it not thy business, this of knowing thyself; thou art an unknowable individual: know what thou canst work at; and work at it, like a Hercules! That will be thy better plan.

It has been written, 'an endless significance lies in Work;' a man perfects himself by working. Foul jungles are cleared away, fair seedfields rise instead, and stately cities; and withal the man himself first ceases to be a jungle and foul unwholesome desert thereby. Consider how, even in the meanest sorts of Labour, the whole soul of a man is composed into a kind of real harmony, the instant he sets himself to work! Doubt, Desire, Sorrow, Remorse, Indignation, Despair itself, all these like helldogs lie beleaguering the soul of the poor dayworker, as of every man: but he bends himself with free valour against his task, and all these are stilled, all these shrink murmuring far off into their caves. The man is now a man. The blessed glow of Labour in him, is it not as purifying fire, wherein all poison is burnt up, and of sour smoke itself there is made bright blessed flame!

Destiny, on the whole, has no other way of cultivating us. A formless Chaos, once set it *revolving*, grows round and ever rounder; ranges itself, by mere force of gravity, into strata, spherical courses; is no longer a Chaos, but a round compacted World. What would become of the Earth, did she cease to revolve? In the poor old Earth, so long as she revolves, all inequalities, irregularities disperse themselves; all irregularities are incessantly becoming regular. Hast thou looked on the Potter's wheel,—one of the venerablest objects; old as the Prophet Ezechiel and far older? Rude lumps of clay, how they spin themselves up, by mere quick whirling, into beautiful circular dishes. And fancy the most assiduous Potter, but without his wheel; reduced to

make dishes, or rather amorphous botches, by mere kneading and
baking! Even such a Potter were Destiny, with a human soul
that would rest and lie at ease, that would not work and spin!
Of an idle unrevolving man the kindest Destiny, like the most
assiduous Potter without wheel, can bake and knead nothing other
than a botch; let her spend on him what expensive colouring,
what gilding and enamelling she will, he is but a botch. Not a
dish; no, a bulging, kneaded, crooked, shambling, squint-cornered,
amorphous botch,—a mere enamelled vessel of dishonour! Let
the idle think of this.

Blessed is he who has found his work; let him ask no other
blessedness. He has a work, a life-purpose; he has found it, and
will follow it! How, as a free-flowing channel, dug and torn by
noble force through the sour mud-swamp of one's existence, like
an ever-deepening river there, it runs and flows;—draining off the
sour festering water, gradually from the root of the remotest grass-
blade; making, instead of pestilential swamp, a green fruitful
meadow with its clear-flowing stream. How blessed for the meadow itself, let the stream and *its* value be great or small! Labour
is Life: from the inmost heart of the Worker rises his god-given
Force, the sacred celestial Life-essence breathed into him by Almighty God; from his inmost heart awakens him to all nobleness,
—to all knowledge, 'self-knowledge' and much else, so soon as
Work fitly begins. Knowledge? The knowledge that will hold
good in working, cleave thou to that; for Nature herself accredits
that, says Yea to that. Properly thou hast no other knowledge
but what thou hast got by working: the rest is yet all a hypothesis of knowledge; a thing to be argued of in schools, a thing floating in the clouds, in endless logic-vortices, till we try it and fix it.
'Doubt, of whatever kind, can be ended by Action alone.'

And again, hast thou valued Patience, Courage, Perseverance,
Openness to light; readiness to own thyself mistaken, to do better next time? All these, all virtues, in wrestling with the dim
brute Powers of Fact, in ordering of thy fellows in such wrestle,
there and elsewhere not at all, thou wilt continually learn. Set
down a brave Sir Christopher in the middle of black ruined Stone-
heaps, of foolish unarchitectural Bishops, redtape Officials, idle
Nell-Gwyn Defenders of the Faith; and see whether he will ever
raise a Paul's Cathedral out of all that, yea or no! Rough, rude,
contradictory are all things and persons, from the mutinous masons and Irish hodmen, up to the idle Nell-Gwyn Defenders, to
blustering redtape Officials, foolish unarchitectural Bishops. All
these things and persons are there not for Christopher's sake and

his Cathedral's; they are there for their own sake mainly! Christopher will have to conquer and constrain all these,—if he be able. All these are against him. Equitable Nature herself, who carries her mathematics and architectonics not on the face of her, but deep in the hidden heart of her,—Nature herself is but partially for him; will be wholly against him, if he constrain her not! His very money, where is it to come from? The pious munificence of England lies far-scattered, distant, unable to speak, and say, "I am here;"—must be spoken to before it can speak. Pious munificence, and all help, is so silent, invisible like the gods; impediment, contradictions manifold are so loud and near! O brave Sir Christopher, trust thou in those, notwithstanding, and front all these; understand all these; by valiant patience, noble effort, insight, by man's-strength, vanquish and compel all these,—and, on the whole, strike down victoriously the last topstone of that Paul's Edifice; thy monument for certain centuries, the stamp 'Great Man' impressed very legibly on Portland-stone there!—

Yes, all manner of help, and pious response from Men or Nature, is always what we call silent; cannot speak or come to light, till it be seen, till it be spoken to. Every noble work is at first 'impossible.' In very truth, for every noble work the possibilities will lie diffused through Immensity; inarticulate, undiscoverable except to faith. Like Gideon thou shalt spread out thy fleece at the door of thy tent; see whether under the wide arch of Heaven there be any bounteous moisture, or none. Thy heart and life-purpose shall be as a miraculous Gideon's fleece, spread out in silent appeal to Heaven; and from the kind Immensities, what from the poor unkind Localities and town and country Parishes there never could, blessed dew-moisture to suffice thee shall have fallen!

Work is of a religious nature:—work is of a *brave* nature; which it is the aim of all religion to be. All work of man is as the swimmer's: a waste ocean threatens to devour him; if he front it not bravely, it will keep its word. By incessant wise defiance of it, lusty rebuke and buffet of it, behold how it loyally supports him, bears him as its conqueror along. 'It is so,' says Goethe, 'with all things that man undertakes in this world.'

Brave Sea-captain, Norse Sea-king,—Columbus, my hero, royallest Sea-king of all! it is no friendly environment this of thine, in the waste deep waters; around thee mutinous discouraged souls, behind thee disgrace and ruin, before thee the unpenetrated veil of Night. Brother, these wild water-mountains, bounding from their deep bases (ten miles deep, I am told), are not entirely there on thy behalf! Meseems *they* have other work than floating

Q

thee forward:—and the huge Winds, that sweep from Ursa Major
to the Tropics and Equators, dancing their giant-waltz through
the kingdoms of Chaos and Immensity, they care little about filling rightly or filling wrongly the small shoulder-of-mutton sails in
this cockle-skiff of thine! Thou art not among articulate-speaking
friends, my brother; thou art among immeasurable dumb mon-
sters, tumbling, howling wide as the world here. Secret, far off,
invisible to all hearts but thine, there lies a help in them: see
how thou wilt get at that. Patiently thou wilt wait till the mad
South-wester spend itself, saving thyself by dextrous science of
defence, the while: valiantly, with swift decision, wilt thou strike
in, when the favouring East, the Possible, springs up. Mutiny of
men thou wilt sternly repress; weakness, despondency, thou wilt
cheerily encourage: thou wilt swallow down complaint, unreason,
weariness, weakness of others and thyself;—how much wilt thou
swallow down! There shall be a depth of Silence in thee, deeper
than this Sea, which is but ten miles deep: a Silence unsoundable; known to God only. Thou shalt be a Great Man. Yes, my
World-Soldier, thou of the World Marine-service,—thou wilt have
to be *greater* than this tumultuous unmeasured World here round
thee is: thou, in thy strong soul, as with wrestler's arms, shalt
embrace it, harness it down; and make it bear thee on,—to new
Americas, or whither God wills!

———

CHAPTER XII.

REWARD.

'RELIGION,' I said; for, properly speaking, all true Work is Religion: and whatsoever Religion is not Work may go and dwell
among the Brahmins, Antinomians, Spinning Dervishes, or where
it will; with me it shall have no harbour. Admirable was that of
the old Monks, '*Laborare est Orare*, Work is Worship.'

Older than all preached Gospels was this unpreached, inarticulate, but ineradicable, forever-enduring Gospel: Work, and
therein have wellbeing. Man, Son of Earth and of Heaven, lies
there not, in the innermost heart of thee, a Spirit of active Method, a Force for Work;—and burns like a painfully smouldering
fire, giving thee no rest till thou unfold it, till thou write it down
in beneficent Facts around thee! What is immethodic, waste, thou
shalt make methodic, regulated, arable; obedient and productive
to thee. Wheresoever thou findest Disorder, there is thy eternal
enemy; attack him swiftly, subdue him; make Order of him, the

subject not of Chaos, but of Intelligence, Divinity and Thee! The thistle that grows in thy path, dig it out, that a blade of useful grass, a drop of nourishing milk, may grow there instead. The waste cotton-shrub, gather its waste white down, spin it, weave it; that, in place of idle litter, there may be folded webs, and the naked skin of man be covered.

But above all, where thou findest Ignorance, Stupidity, Brute-mindedness,—yes, there, with or without Church-tithes and Shovel-hat, with or without Talfourd-Mahon Copyrights, or were it with mere dungeons and gibbets and crosses, attack it, I say; smite it wisely, unweariedly, and rest not while thou livest and it lives; but smite, smite, in the name of God! The Highest God, as I understand it, does audibly so command thee; still audibly. if thou have ears to hear. He, even He, with his *unspoken* voice, awfuller than any Sinai thunders or syllabled speech of Whirlwinds; for the Silence of deep Eternities, of Worlds from beyond the morning-stars, does it not speak to thee? The unborn Ages; the old Graves, with their long-mouldering dust, the very tears that wetted it now all dry,—do not these speak to thee, what ear hath not heard? The deep Death-kingdoms, the Stars in their never-resting courses, all Space and all Time, proclaim it to thee in continual silent admonition. Thou too, if ever man should, shalt work while it is called Today. For the Night cometh, wherein no man can work.

All true Work is sacred; in all true Work, were it but true hand-labour, there is something of divineness. Labour, wide as the Earth, has its summit in Heaven. Sweat of the brow; and up from that to sweat of the brain, sweat of the heart; which includes all Kepler calculations, Newton meditations, all Sciences, all spoken Epics, all acted Heroisms, Martyrdoms,—up to that ' Agony of bloody sweat,' which all men have called divine! O brother, if this is not ' worship,' then I say, the more pity for worship; for this is the noblest thing yet discovered under God's sky. Who art thou that complainest of thy life of toil? Complain not. Look up, my wearied brother; see thy fellow Workmen there, in God's Eternity; surviving there, they alone surviving: sacred Band of the Immortals, celestial Bodyguard of the Empire of Mankind. Even in the weak Human Memory they survive so long, as saints, as heroes, as gods; they alone surviving; peopling, they alone, the unmeasured solitudes of Time! To thee Heaven, though severe, is *not* unkind; Heaven is kind,—as a noble Mother; as that Spartan Mother, saying while she gave her son his shield, "With it, my son, or upon it!" Thou too shalt return *home* in honour; to thy far-distant Home, in honour; doubt it not,—if in

the battle thou keep thy shield! Thou, in the Eternities and
deepest Death-kingdoms, art not an alien; thou everywhere art a
denizen! Complain not; the very Spartans did not *complain.*

And who art thou that braggest of thy life of Idleness; com-
placently showest thy bright gilt equipages; sumptuous cushions;
appliances for folding of the hands to mere sleep? Looking up,
looking down, around, behind or before, discernest thou, if it be
not in Mayfair alone, any *idle* hero, saint, god, or even devil? Not
a vestige of one. In the Heavens, in the Earth, in the Waters
under the Earth, is none like unto thee. Thou art an original
figure in this Creation; a denizen in Mayfair alone, in this extraordinary Century or Half-Century alone! One monster there is
in the world: the idle man. What is his 'Religion?' That Nature is a Phantasm, where cunning beggary or thievery may sometimes find good victual. That God is a lie; and that Man and his
Life are a lie.—Alas, alas, who of us *is* there that can say, I have
worked? The faithfullest of us are unprofitable servants; the
faithfullest of us know that best. The faithfullest of us may say,
with sad and true old Samuel, "Much of my life has been trifled
away!" But he that has, and except 'on public occasions' professes to have, no function but that of going idle in a graceful or
graceless manner; and of begetting sons to go idle; and to address Chief Spinners and Diggers, who at least *are* spinning and
digging, "Ye scandalous persons who produce too much"—My
Corn-Law friends, on what imaginary still richer Eldorados, and
true iron-spikes with law of gravitation, are ye rushing!

As to the Wages of Work there might innumerable things be
said; there will and must yet innumerable things be said and
spoken, in St. Stephen's and out of St. Stephen's; and gradually
not a few things be ascertained and written, on Law-parchment,
concerning this very matter:—'Fair day's-wages for a fair day's-
work' is the most unrefusable demand! Money-wages 'to the
extent of keeping your worker alive that he may work more;' these,
unless you mean to dismiss him straightway out of this world, are
indispensable alike to the noblest Worker and to the least noble!

One thing only I will say here, in special reference to the former class, the noble and noblest; but throwing light on all the
other classes and their arrangements of this difficult matter: The
'wages' of every noble Work do yet lie in Heaven or else Nowhere.
Not in Bank-of-England bills, in Owen's Labour-bank, or any the
most improved establishment of banking and money-changing,
needest thou, heroic soul, present thy account of earnings. Human banks and labour-banks know thee not; or know thee after

generations and centuries have passed away, and thou art clean gone from 'rewarding,'—all manner of bank-drafts, shop-tills, and Downing-street Exchequers lying very invisible, so far from thee! Nay, at bottom, dost thou need any reward? Was it thy aim and life-purpose to be filled with good things for thy heroism; to have a life of pomp and ease, and be what men call 'happy,' in this world, or in any other world? I answer for thee deliberately, No. The whole spiritual secret of the new epoch lies in this, that thou canst answer for thyself, with thy whole clearness of head and heart, deliberately, No!

My brother, the brave man has to give his Life away. Give it, I advise thee;—thou dost not expect to *sell* thy Life in an adequate manner? What price, for example, would content thee? The just price of thy LIFE to thee,—why, God's entire Creation to thyself, the whole Universe of Space, the whole Eternity of Time, and what they hold: that is the price which would content thee; that, and if thou wilt be candid, nothing short of that! It is thy all; and for it thou wouldst have all. Thou art an unreasonable mortal;—or rather thou art a poor *infinite* mortal, who, in thy narrow clay-prison here, *seemest* so unreasonable! Thou wilt never sell thy Life, or any part of thy Life, in a satisfactory manner. Give it, like a royal heart; let the price be Nothing: thou *hast* then, in a certain sense, got All for it! The heroic man,—and is not every man, God be thanked, a potential hero?—has to do so, in all times and circumstances. In the most heroic age, as in the most un-heroic, he will have to say, as Burns said proudly and humbly of his little Scottish Songs, little dewdrops of Celestial Melody in an age when so much was unmelodious: "By Heaven, they shall either be invaluable or of no value; I do not need your guineas for them!" It is an element which should, and must, enter deeply into all settlements of wages here below. They never will be 'satisfactory' otherwise; they cannot, O Mammon Gospel, they never can! Money for my little piece of work ' to the extent that will allow me to keep working;' yes, this,—unless you mean that I shall go my ways *before* the work is all taken out of me: but as to 'wages'—!—

On the whole, we do entirely agree with those old Monks, *Laborare est Orare*. In a thousand senses, from one end of it to the other, true Work *is* Worship. He that works, whatsoever be his work, he bodies forth the form of Things Unseen; a small Poet every Worker is. The idea, were it but of his poor Delf Platter, how much more of his Epic Poem, is as yet 'seen,' half-seen, only by himself; to all others it is a thing unseen, impossible; to Na-ture herself it is a thing unseen, a thing which never hitherto was;

—very 'impossible,' for it is as yet a No-thing! The Unseen Powers had need to watch over such a man; he works in and for the Unseen. Alas, if he look to the Seen Powers only, he may as well quit the business; his No-thing will never rightly issue as a Thing, but as a Deceptivity, a Sham-thing,—which it had better not do!

Thy No-thing of an Intended Poem, O Poet who hast looked merely to reviewers, copyrights, booksellers, popularities, behold it has not yet become a Thing; for the truth is not in it! Though printed, hotpressed, reviewed, celebrated, sold to the twentieth edition: what is all that? The Thing, in philosophical uncommercial language, is still a No-thing, mostly semblance, and deception of the sight;—benign Oblivion incessantly gnawing at it, impatient till Chaos, to which it belongs, do reabsorb it!—

He who takes not counsel of the Unseen and Silent, from him will never come real visibility and speech. Thou must descend to the *Mothers*, to the *Manes*, and Hercules-like long suffer and labour there, wouldst thou emerge with victory into the sunlight. As in battle and the shock of war,—for is not this a battle?—thou too shalt fear no pain or death, shalt love no ease or life; the voice of festive Lubberlands, the noise of greedy Acheron shall alike lie silent under thy victorious feet. Thy work, like Dante's, shall 'make thee lean for many years.' The world and its wages, its criticisms, counsels, helps, impediments, shall be as a waste ocean-flood; the chaos through which thou art to swim and sail. Not the waste waves and their weedy gulf-streams, shalt thou take for guidance: thy star alone,—' *Se tu segui tua stella!*' Thy star alone, now clear-beaming over Chaos, nay now by fits gone out, disastrously eclipsed: this only shalt thou strive to follow. O, it is a business, as I fancy, that of weltering your way through Chaos and the murk of Hell! Green-eyed dragons watching you, three-headed Cerberuses,—not without sympathy of *their* sort! "*Eccovi l' uom ch' è stato all' Inferno*." For in fine, as Poet Dryden says, you do walk hand in hand with sheer Madness, all the way, —who is by no means pleasant company! You look fixedly into Madness, and *her* undiscovered, boundless, bottomless Night-empire; that you may extort new Wisdom out of it, as an Eurydice from Tartarus. The higher the Wisdom, the closer was its neighbourhood and kindred with mere Insanity; literally so;—and thou wilt, with a speechless feeling, observe how highest Wisdom, struggling up into this world, has oftentimes carried such tinctures and adhesions of Insanity still cleaving to it hither!

All Works, each in their degree, are a making of Madness sane; —truly enough a religious operation; which cannot be carried on without religion. You have not work otherwise; you have eye-service, greedy grasping of wages, swift and ever swifter manu-facture of semblances to get hold of wages. Instead of better felt-hats to cover your head, you have bigger lath-and-plaster hats set travelling the streets on wheels. Instead of heavenly and earthly Guidance for the souls of men, you have ' Black or White Surplice' Controversies, stuffed hair-and-leather Popes;—terrestrial *Law-wards*, Lords and Law-bringers, ' organising Labour' in these years, by passing Corn-Laws. With all which, alas, this distracted Earth is now full, nigh to bursting. Semblances most smooth to the touch and eye; most accursed nevertheless to body and soul. Semblances, be they of Sham-woven Cloth or of Dilettante Legis-lation, which are *not* real wool or substance, but Devil's-dust, accursed of God and man! No man has worked, or can work, except religiously; not even the poor day-labourer, the weaver of your coat, the sewer of your shoes. All men, if they work not as in a Great Taskmaster's eye, will work wrong, work unhappily for themselves and you.

Industrial work, still under bondage to Mammon, the rational soul of it not yet awakened, is a tragic spectacle. Men in the rapidest motion and self-motion; restless, with convulsive energy, as if driven by Galvanism, as if possessed by a Devil; tearing asunder mountains,—to no purpose, for Mammonism is always Midas-eared! This is sad, on the face of it. Yet courage: the bene-ficent Destinies, kind in their sternness, are apprising us that this cannot continue. Labour is not a devil, even while encased in Mammonism; Labour is ever an imprisoned god, writhing uncon-sciously or consciously to escape out of Mammonism! Plugson of Undershot, like Taillefer of Normandy, wants victory; how much happier will even Plugson be to have a Chivalrous victory than a Chactaw one. The unredeemed ugliness is that of a slothful People. Show me a People energetically busy; heaving, struggling, all shoul-ders at the wheel; their heart pulsing, every muscle swelling, with man's energy and will;—I show you a People of whom great good is already predicable; to whom all manner of good is yet certain, if their energy endure. By very working, they will learn; they have, Antæus-like, their foot on Mother Fact: how can they but learn?

The vulgarest Plugson of a Master-Worker, who can command Workers, and get work out of them, is already a considerable man. Blessed and thrice-blessed symptoms I discern of Master-Workers who are not vulgar men; who are Nobles, and begin to feel that they must act as such: all speed to these, they are England's hope at present! But in this Plugson himself, conscious of almost no nobleness whatever, how much is there! Not without man's faculty, insight, courage, hard energy, is this rugged figure. His words none of the wisest; but his actings cannot be altogether foolish. Think, how were it, stoodst thou suddenly in his shoes! He has to command a thousand men. And not imaginary commanding; no, it is real, incessantly practical. The evil passions of so many men (with the Devil in them, as in all of us) he has to vanquish; by manifold force of speech and of silence, to repress or evade. What a force of silence, to say nothing of the others, is in Plugson! For these his thousand men he has to provide raw-material, machinery, arrangement, houseroom; and ever at the week's end, wages by due sale. No Civil-List, or Goulburn-Baring Budget has he to fall back upon, for paying of his regiment; he has to pick his supplies from this confused face of the whole Earth and Contemporaneous History, by his dexterity alone. There will be dry eyes if he fail to do it!—He exclaims, at present, 'black in the face,' near strangled with Dilettante Legislation: "Let me have elbow-room, throat-room, and I will not fail! No, I will spin yet, and conquer like a giant: what 'sinews of war' lie in me, untold resources towards the Conquest of this Planet, if instead of hanging me, you husband them, and help me!"—My indomitable friend, it is *true;* and thou shalt and must be helped.

This is not a man I would kill and strangle by Corn-Laws, even if I could! No, I would fling my Corn-Laws and Shotbelts to the Devil; and try to help this man. I would teach him, by noble precept and law-precept, by noble example most of all, that Mammonism was not the essence of his or of my station in God's Universe; but the adscititious excrescence of it; the gross, terrene, godless embodiment of it; which would have to become, more or less, a godlike one. By noble *real* legislation, by true *noble's*-work, by unwearied, valiant, and were it wageless effort, in my Parliament and in my Parish, I would aid, constrain, encourage him to effect more or less this blessed change. I should know that it would have to be effected; that unless it were in some measure effected, he and I and all of us, I first and soonest of all, were doomed to perdition!—Effected it will be; unless it were a Demon that made this Universe; which I, for my own part, do at no moment, under no form, in the least believe.

May it please your Serene Highnesses, your Majesties, Lord-ships and Law-wardships, the proper Epic of this world is not now 'Arms and the Man;' how much less, 'Shirt-frills and the Man:' no, it is now 'Tools and the Man:' that, henceforth to all time is now our Epic;—and you, first of all others, I think, were wise to take note of that!

CHAPTER XIII.

DEMOCRACY.

If the Serene Highnesses and Majesties do not take note of that, then, as I perceive, *that* will take note of itself! The time for levity, insincerity, and idle babble and play-acting, in all kinds, is gone by; it is a serious, grave time. Old long-vexed questions, not yet solved in logical words or parliamentary laws, are fast solving themselves in facts, somewhat unblessed to behold! This largest of questions, this question of Work and Wages, which ought, had we heeded Heaven's voice, to have begun two generations ago or more, cannot be delayed longer without hearing Earth's voice. 'Labour' will verily need to be somewhat 'organised,' as they say,—God knows with what difficulty. Man will actually need to have his debts and earnings a little better paid by man; which, let Parliaments speak of them or be silent of them, are eternally his due from man, and cannot, without penalty and at length not without death-penalty, be withheld. How much ought to cease among us straightway; how much ought to begin straightway, while the hours yet are!

Truly they are strange results to which this of leaving all to 'Cash;' of quietly shutting up the God's Temple, and gradually opening wide-open the Mammon's Temple, with 'Laissez-faire, and Every man for himself,'—have led us in these days! We have Upper, speaking Classes, who indeed do 'speak' as never man spake before; the withered flimsiness, the godless baseness and barrenness of whose Speech might of itself indicate what kind of Doing and practical Governing went on under it! For Speech is the gaseous element out of which most kinds of Practice and Performance, especially all kinds of moral Performance, condense themselves, and take shape; as the one is, so will the other be. Descending, accordingly, into the Dumb Class in its Stockport Cellars and Poor-Law Bastilles, have we not to announce that they also are hitherto unexampled in the History of Adam's Posterity?

Life was never a May-game for men: in all times the lot of the dumb millions born to toil was defaced with manifold sufferings, injustices, heavy burdens, avoidable and unavoidable; not play at all, but hard work that made the sinews sore and the heart sore. As bond-slaves, *villani, bordarii, sochemanni*, nay indeed as dukes, earls and kings, men were oftentimes made weary of their life; and had to say, in the sweat of their brow and of their soul, Behold it is not sport, it is grim earnest, and our back can bear no more! Who knows not what massacrings and harryings there have been; grinding, long-continuing, unbearable injustices,—till the heart had to rise in madness, and some " *Eu Sachsen, nimith euer sachses,* You Saxons, out with your gully-knives then!" You Saxons, some 'arrestment,' partial 'arrestment of the Knaves and Dastards' has become indispensable!—The page of Dryasdust is heavy with such details.

And yet I will venture to believe that in no time, since the beginnings of Society, was the lot of those same dumb millions of toilers so entirely unbearable as it is even in the days now passing over us. It is not to die, or even to die of hunger, that makes a man wretched; many men have died; all men must die,—the last exit of us all is in a Fire-Chariot of Pain. But it is to live miserable we know not why; to work sore and yet gain nothing; to be heart-worn, weary, yet isolated, unrelated, girt-in with a cold universal Laissez-faire: it is to die slowly all our life long, imprisoned in a deaf, dead, Infinite Injustice, as in the accursed iron belly of a Phalaris' Bull! This is and remains forever intolerable to all men whom God has made. Do we wonder at French Revolutions, Chartisms, Revolts of Three Days? The times, if we will consider them, are really unexampled.

Never before did I hear of an Irish Widow reduced to 'prove ' her sisterhood by dying of typhus-fever and infecting seventeen ' persons,'—saying in such undeniable way, "You *see,* I was your sister!" Sisterhood, brotherhood, was often forgotten; but not till the rise of these ultimate Mammon and Shotbelt Gospels did I ever see it so expressly denied. If no pious Lord or *Law-ward* would remember it, always some pious Lady (' *Hlaf dig,*' Benefactress, ' *Loaf-giveress,*' they say she is,—blessings on her beautiful heart!) was there, with mild mother-voice and hand, to remember it; some pious thoughtful *Elder,* what we now call ' Prester,' *Presbyter* or ' Priest,' was there to put all men in mind of it, in the name of the God who had made all.

Not even in Black Dahomey was it ever, I think, forgotten to the typhus-fever length. Mungo Park, resourceless, had sunk down to die under the Negro Village-Tree, a horrible White object in the eyes of all. But in the poor Black Woman, and her daughter who stood aghast at him, whose earthly wealth and funded capital consisted of one small calabash of rice, there lived a heart richer than ' *Laissez-faire :*' they, with a royal munificence, boiled their rice for him; they sang all night to him, spinning assiduous on their cotton distaffs, as he lay to sleep: " Let us pity the poor white man; no mother has he to fetch him milk, no sister to grind him corn !"

Thou poor black Noble One,—thou *Lady* too : did not a God make thee too ; was there not in thee too something of a God!—

Gurth born thrall of Cedric the Saxon has been greatly pitied by Dryasdust and others. Gurth with the brass collar round his neck, tending Cedric's pigs in the glades of the wood, is not what I call an exemplar of human felicity : but Gurth, with the sky above him, with the free air and tinted boscage and umbrage round him, and in him at least the certainty of supper and social lodging when he came home; Gurth to me seems happy, in comparison with many a Lancashire and Buckinghamshire man, of these days, not born thrall of anybody ! Gurth's brass collar did not gall him : Cedric *deserved* to be his Master. The pigs were Cedric's, but Gurth too would get his pairings of them. Gurth had the inexpressible satisfaction of feeling himself related indissolubly, though in a rude brass-collar way, to his fellow-mortals in this Earth. He had superiors, inferiors, equals.—Gurth is now 'emancipated' long since ; has what we call 'Liberty.' Liberty, I am told, is a Divine thing. Liberty when it becomes the 'Liberty to die by starvation' is not so divine !

Liberty ? The true liberty of a man, you would say, consisted in his finding out, or being forced to find out the right path, and to walk thereon. To learn, or to be taught, what work he actually was able for ; and then by permission, persuasion, and even compulsion, to set about doing of the same ! That is his true blessedness, honour, 'liberty' and maximum of wellbeing : if liberty be not that, I for one have small care about liberty. You do not allow a palpable madman to leap over precipices ; you violate his liberty, you that are wise ; and keep him, were it in strait-waistcoats, away from the precipices ! Every stupid, every cowardly and foolish man is but a less palpable madman : his true liberty were that a wiser man, that any and every wiser man, could, by brass collars, or in whatever milder or sharper way, lay hold of him when he was going wrong, and order and compel him to go a little righter. O, if thou really art my *Senior*, Seigneur, my *Elder*, Presbyter or Priest,—if thou art in very deed my *Wiser*, may a beneficent instinct lead and impel thee to 'conquer' me, to command me ! If thou do know better than I what is good and right, I conjure thee in the name of God, force me to do it ; were it by never such brass collars, whips and handcuffs, leave me not to walk over precipices ! That I have been called, by all the Newspapers, a 'free man' will avail me little, if my pilgrimage have ended in death and wreck. O that the Newspapers had called me slave, coward, fool, or what it pleased their sweet voices to name me, and I had attained not death, but life!—Liberty requires new definitions.

A conscious abhorrence and intolerance of Folly, of Baseness, Stupidity, Poltroonery and all that brood of things, dwells deep in some men: still deeper in others an *unconscious* abhorrence and intolerance, clothed moreover by the beneficent Supreme Powers in what stout appetites, energies, egoisms so-called, are suitable to it;—these latter are your Conquerors, Romans, Normans, Russians, Indo-English; Founders of what we call Aristocracies. Which indeed have they not the most ‘ divine right’ to found;—being themselves very truly Ἄριστοι, BRAVEST, BEST; and conquering generally a confused rabble of WORST, or at lowest, clearly enough, of WORSE? I think their divine right, tried, with affirmatory verdict, in the greatest Law-Court known to me, was good! A class of men who are dreadfully exclaimed against by Dryasdust; of whom nevertheless beneficent Nature has oftentimes had need; and may, alas, again have need.

When, across the hundredfold poor scepticisms, trivialisms, and constitutional cobwebberies of Dryasdust, you catch any glimpse of a William the Conqueror, a Tancred of Hauteville or such like, —do you not discern veritably some rude outline of a true God-made King; whom not the Champion of England cased in tin, but all Nature and the Universe were calling to the throne? It is absolutely necessary that he get thither. Nature does not mean her poor Saxon children to perish, of obesity, stupor or other malady, as yet: a stern Ruler and Line of Rulers therefore is called in, —a stern but most beneficent *perpetual House-Surgeon* is by Nature herself called in, and even the appropriate *fees* are provided for him! Dryasdust talks lamentably about Hereward and the Fen Counties; fate of Earl Waltheof; Yorkshire and the North reduced to ashes; all which is undoubtedly lamentable. But even Dryasdust apprises me of one fact: ‘ A child, in this William's ‘ reign, might have carried a purse of gold from end to end of Eng- ‘ land.’ My erudite friend, it is a fact which outweighs a thousand! Sweep away thy constitutional, sentimental, and other cobwebberies; look eye to eye, if thou still have any eye, in the face of this big burly William Bastard: thou wilt see a fellow of most flashing discernment, of most strong lion-heart;—in whom, as it were, within a frame of oak and iron, the gods have planted the soul of ‘ a man of genius!’ Dost thou call that nothing? I call it an immense thing!—Rage enough was in this Willelmus Conquestor, rage enough for his occasions;—and yet the essential element of him, as of all such men, is not scorching *fire*, but shining illuminative *light*. Fire and light are strangely interchangeable;

nay, at bottom, I have found them different forms of the same most godlike 'elementary substance' in our world: a thing worth stating in these days. The essential element of this Conquestor is, first of all, the most sun-eyed perception of what *is* really what on this God's-Earth;—which, thou wilt find, does mean at bottom 'Justice,' and 'Virtues' not a few: *Conformity* to what the Maker has seen good to make; that, I suppose, will mean Justice and a Virtue or two?—

Dost thou think Willelmus Conquestor would have tolerated ten years' jargon, one hour's jargon, on the propriety of killing Cotton-manufactures by partridge Corn-Laws? I fancy, this was not the man to knock out of his night's-rest with nothing but a noisy bedlamism in your mouth! "Assist us still better to bush the partridges; strangle Plugson who spins the shirts?"—"*Par la Splendeur de Dieu!*"——Dost thou think Willelmus Conquestor, in this new time, with Steamengine Captains of Industry on one hand of him, and Joe-Manton Captains of Idleness on the other, would have doubted which *was* really the BEST; which did deserve strangling, and which not?

I have a certain indestructible regard for Willelmus Conquestor. A resident House-Surgeon, provided by Nature for her beloved English People, and even furnished with the requisite fees, as I said; for he by no means felt himself doing Nature's work, this Willelmus, but his own work exclusively! And his own work withal it was; informed '*par la Splendeur de Dieu.*'— I say, it is necessary to get the work out of such a man, however harsh that be! When a world, not yet doomed for death, is rushing down to ever-deeper Baseness and Confusion, it is a dire necessity of Nature's to bring in her ARISTOCRACIES, her BEST, even by forcible methods. When their descendants or representatives cease entirely to *be* the Best, Nature's poor world will very soon rush down again to Baseness; and it becomes a dire necessity of Nature's to cast them out. Hence French Revolutions, Five-point Charters, Democracies, and a mournful list of *Etceteras*, in these our afflicted times.

To what extent Democracy has now reached, how it advances irresistible with ominous, ever-increasing speed, he that will open his eyes on any province of human affairs may discern. Democracy is everywhere the inexorable demand of these ages, swiftly fulfilling itself. From the thunder of Napoleon battles, to the jabbering of Open-vestry in St. Mary Axe, all things announce Democracy. A distinguished man, whom some of my readers will hear again with pleasure, thus writes to me what in these days he notes from the Wahngasse of Weissnichtwo, where our London

fashions seem to be in full vogue. Let us hear the Herr Teufels-
dröckh again, were it but the smallest word!

   ' Democracy, which means despair of finding any Heroes to
' govern you, and contented putting up with the want of them,—
' alas, thou too, *mein Lieber*, seest well how close it is of kin to
' *Atheism*, and other sad *Isms :* he who discovers no God whatever,
' how shall he discover Heroes, the visible Temples of God?—
' Strange enough meanwhile it is, to observe with what thought-
' lessness, here in our rigidly Conservative Country, men rush
' into Democracy with full cry. Beyond doubt, his Excellenz the
' Titular-Herr Ritter Kauderwälsch von Pferdefuss-Quacksalber, he
' our distinguished Conservative Premier himself, and all but the
' thicker-headed of his Party, discern Democracy to be inevitable
' as death, and are even desperate of delaying it much!

   ' You cannot walk the streets without beholding Democracy
' announce itself: the very Tailor has become, if not properly
' Sansculottic, which to him would be ruinous, yet a Tailor un-
' consciously symbolising, and prophesying with his scissors, the
' reign of Equality. What now is our fashionable coat? A thing
' of superfinest texture, of deeply meditated cut; with Malines-
' lace cuffs; quilted with gold; so that a man can carry, without
' difficulty, an estate of land on his back? *Keineswegs*, By no man-
' ner of means! The Sumptuary Laws have fallen into such a
' state of desuetude as was never before seen. Our fashionable
' coat is an amphibium between barn-sack and drayman's doublet.
' The cloth of it is studiously coarse; the colour a speckled soot-
' black or rust-brown gray;—the nearest approach to a Peasant's.
' And for shape,—thou shouldst see it! The last consummation
' of the year now passing over us is definable as Three Bags; a
' big bag for the body, two small bags for the arms, and by way of
' collar a hem! The first Antique Cheruscan who, of felt-cloth or
' bear's-hide, with bone or metal needle, set about making himself
' a coat, before Tailors had yet awakened out of Nothing,—did not
' he make it even so? A loose wide poke for body, with two holes
' to let out the arms; this was his original coat: to which holes it
' was soon visible that two small loose pokes, or sleeves, easily ap-
' pended, would be an improvement.

   ' Thus has the Tailor-art, so to speak, overset itself, like most
' other things; changed its centre-of-gravity; whirled suddenly
' over from zenith to nadir. Your Stulz, with huge somerset,
' vaults from his high shopboard down to the depths of primal
' savagery,—carrying much along with him! For I will invite thee
' to reflect that the Tailor, as topmost ultimate froth of Human
' Society, is indeed swift-passing, evanescent, slippery to decipher;

' yet significant of much, nay of all. Topmost evanescent froth,
' he is churned up from the very lees, and from all intermediate
' regions of the liquor. The general outcome he, visible to the eye,
' of what men aimed to do, and were obliged and enabled to do, in
' this one public department of symbolising themselves to each
' other by covering of their skins. A smack of all Human Life
' lies in the Tailor: its wild struggles towards beauty, dignity,
' freedom, victory; and how, hemmed in by Sedan and Hudders-
' field, by Nescience, Dulness, Prurience, and other sad necessities
' and laws of Nature, it has attained just to this: Gray savagery of
' Three Sacks with a hem!

' When the very Tailor verges towards Sansculottism, is it not
' ominous? The last Divinity of poor mankind dethroning him-
' self; sinking *his* taper too, flame downmost, like the Genius of
' Sleep or of Death; admonitory that Tailor-time shall be no more!
' —For, little as one could advise Sumptuary Laws at the present
' epoch, yet nothing is clearer than that where ranks do actually
' exist, strict division of costumes will also be enforced; that if we
' ever have a new Hierarchy and Aristocracy, acknowledged verit-
' ably as such, for which I daily pray Heaven, the Tailor will re-
' awaken; and be, by volunteering and appointment, consciously
' and unconsciously, a safeguard of that same.'—Certain farther
observations, from the same invaluable pen, on our never-ending
changes of mode, our ' perpetual nomadic and even ape-like appe-
' tite for change and mere change' in all the equipments of our
existence, and the ' fatal revolutionary character' thereby mani-
fested, we suppress for the present. It may be admitted that
Democracy, in all meanings of the word, is in full career; irresistible by any Ritter Kauderwälsch or other Son of Adam, as times
go. ' Liberty' is a thing men are determined to have.

But truly, as I had to remark in the mean while, ' the liberty of
not being oppressed by your fellow man' is an indispensable, yet
one of the most insignificant fractional parts of Human Liberty.
No man oppresses thee, can bid thee fetch or carry, come or go,
without reason shown. True; from all men thou art emancipated:
but from Thyself and from the Devil—? No man, wiser, unwiser,
can make thee come or go: but thy own futilities, bewilderments,
thy false appetites for Money, Windsor Georges and such like?
No man oppresses thee, O free and independent Franchiser: but
does not this stupid Porter-pot oppress thee? No Son of Adam
can bid thee come or go; but this absurd Pot of Heavy-wet,
this can and does! Thou art the thrall not of Cedric the
Saxon, but of thy own brutal appetites, and this scoured dish

of liquor. And thou pratest of thy 'liberty?' Thou entire block-head!

Heavy-wet and gin: alas, these are not the only kinds of thral-dom. Thou who walkest in a vain show, looking out with orna-mental dilettante sniff, and serene supremacy, at all Life and all Death; and amblest jauntily; perking up thy poor talk into crot-chets, thy poor conduct into fatuous somnambulisms;—and *art* as an 'enchanted Ape' under God's sky, where thou mightest have been a man, had proper Schoolmasters and Conquerors, and Con-stables with cat-o'-nine tails, been vouchsafed thee: dost thou call that 'liberty?' Or your unreposing Mammon-worshiper, again, driven, as if by Galvanisms, by Devils and Fixed-Ideas, who rises early and sits late, chasing the impossible; straining every faculty to 'fill himself with the east wind,'—how merciful were it, could you, by mild persuasion or by the severest tyranny so-called, check him in his mad path, and turn him into a wiser one! All painful tyranny, in that case again, were but mild 'surgery;' the pain of it cheap, as health and life, instead of galvanism and fixed-idea, are cheap at any price.

Sure enough, of all paths a man could strike into, there *is*, at any given moment, a *best path* for every man; a thing which, here and now, it were of all things *wisest* for him to do;—which could he be but led or driven to do, he were then doing 'like a man,' as we phrase it; all men and gods agreeing with him, the whole Uni-verse virtually exclaiming Well-done to him! His success, in such case, were complete; his felicity a maximum. This path, to find this path and walk in it, is the one thing needful for him. What-soever forwards him in that, let it come to him even in the shape of blows and spurnings, is liberty: whatsoever hinders him, were it wardmotes, open-vestries, pollbooths, tremendous cheers, rivers of heavy-wet, is slavery.

The notion that a man's liberty consists in giving his vote at election-hustings, and saying, "Behold now I too have my twenty-thousandth part of a Talker in our National Palaver; will not all the gods be good to me?"—is one of the pleasantest! Nature nevertheless is kind at present; and puts it into the heads of many, almost of all. The liberty especially which has to purchase itself by social isolation, and each man standing separate from the other, having 'no business with him' but a cash-account: this is such a liberty as the Earth seldom saw;—as the Earth will not long put up with, recommend it how you may. This liberty turns out, before it have long continued in action, with all men flinging up their caps round it, to be, for the Working Millions a liberty to die by want of food; for the Idle Thousands and Units, alas, a still more fatal liberty to live in want of work; to have no earnest duty to do in this God's-World any more. What becomes of a man in such predicament? Earth's Laws are silent; and Heaven's speak in a voice which is not heard. No work, and the ineradicable need of work, give rise to new very wondrous life-philosophies, new very wondrous life-practices! Dilettantism, Pococurantism, Beau-Brummelism, with perhaps an occasional, half-mad, protesting burst of Byronism, establish themselves: at the end of a certain period,—if you go back to 'the Dead Sea,' there is, say our Moslem friends, a very strange 'Sabbath-day' transacting itself there!—Brethren, we know but imperfectly yet, after ages of Constitutional Government, what Liberty and Slavery are.

Democracy, the chase of Liberty in that direction, shall go its full course; unrestrainable by him of Pferdefuss-Quacksalber, or any of *his* household. The Toiling Millions of Mankind, in most vital need and passionate instinctive desire of Guidance, shall cast away False-Guidance; and hope, for an hour, that No-Guidance will suffice them: but it can be for an hour only. The smallest item of human Slavery is the oppression of man by his Mock-Superiors; the palpablest, but I say at bottom the smallest. Let him shake off such oppression, trample it indignantly under his feet; I blame him not, I pity and commend him. But oppression by your Mock-Superiors well shaken off, the grand problem yet remains to solve: That of finding government by your Real-Superiors! Alas, how shall we ever learn the solution of that, benighted, bewildered, sniffing, sneering, godforgetting unfortunates as we are? It is a work for centuries; to be taught us by tribulations, confusions, insurrections, obstructions; who knows if not by conflagration and despair! It is a lesson inclusive of all other lessons; the hardest of all lessons to learn.

One thing I do know: Those Apes, chattering on the branches by the Dead Sea, never got it learned; but chatter there to this day. To them no Moses need come a second time; a thousand Moseses would be but so many painted Phantasms, interesting Fellow-Apes of new strange aspect,—whom they would 'invite to dinner,' be glad to meet with in lion-soirées. To them the voice of Prophecy, of heavenly monition, is quite ended. They chatter there, all Heaven shut to them, to the end of the world. The unfortunates! Oh, what is dying of hunger, with honest tools in your hand, with a manful purpose in your heart, and much real labour lying round you done, in comparison? You honestly quit your tools; quit a most muddy confused coil of sore work, short rations, of sorrows, dispiritments and contradictions, having now honestly done with it all;—and await, not entirely in a distracted

R

manner, what the Supreme Powers, and the Silences and the Eternities may have to say to you.

A second thing I know: This lesson will have to be learned,—under penalties! England will either learn it, or England also will cease to exist among Nations. England will either learn to reverence its Heroes, and discriminate them from its Sham-Heroes and Valets and gaslighted Histrios; and to prize them as the audible God's-voice, amid all inane jargons and temporary market-cries, and say to them with heart-loyalty, "Be ye King and Priest, and Gospel and Guidance for us:" or else England will continue to worship new and ever-new forms of Quackhood,—and so, with what resiliences and reboundings matters little, go down to the Father of Quacks! Can I dread such things of England? Wretched, thick-eyed, gross-hearted mortals, why will ye worship lies, and ' Stuffed Clothes-suits, created by the ninth-parts of men!' It is not your purses that suffer; your farm-rents, your commerces, your mill-revenues, loud as ye lament over these; no, it is not these alone, but a far deeper than these: it is your souls that lie dead, crushed down under despicable Nightmares, Atheisms, Brain-fumes; and are not souls at all, but mere succedanea for *salt* to keep your bodies and their appetites from putrefying! Your cotton-spinning and thrice-miraculous mechanism, what is this too, by itself, but a larger kind of Animalism? Spiders can spin, Beavers can build and show contrivance; the Ant lays up accumulation of capital, and has, for aught I know, a Bank of Ant-land. If there is no soul in man higher than all that, did it reach to sailing on the cloud-rack and spinning sea-sand; then I say, man is but an animal, a more cunning kind of brute: he has no soul, but only a succedaneum for salt. Whereupon, seeing himself to be truly of the beasts that perish, he ought to admit it, I think;—and also straightway universally to kill himself; and so, in a manlike manner, at least, *end*, and wave these brute-worlds *his* dignified farewell!—

————

CHAPTER XIV.

SIR JABESH WINDBAG.

OLIVER CROMWELL, whose body they hung on their Tyburn Gallows because he had found the Christian Religion inexecutable in this country, remains to me by far the remarkablest Governor we have had here for the last five centuries or so. For the last five centuries, there has been no Governor among us with anything like similar talent; and for the last two centuries, no Governor, we may say, with the possibility of similar talent,—with an idea in the heart of him capable of inspiring similar talent, capable of co-existing therewith. When you consider that Oliver believed in a God, the difference between Oliver's position and that of any subsequent Governor of this Country becomes, the more you reflect on it, the more immeasurable!

Oliver, no volunteer in Public Life, but plainly a balloted soldier strictly ordered thither, enters upon Public Life; comports himself there like a man who carried his own life in his hand; like a man whose Great Commander's eye was always on him. Not without results. Oliver, well-advanced in years, finds now, by Destiny and his own Deservings, or as he himself better phrased it, by wondrous successive ' Births of Providence,' the Government of England put into his hands. In senate-house and battle-field, in counsel and in action, in private and in public, this man has proved himself a man: England and the voice of God, through waste awful whirlwinds and environments, speaking to his great heart, summon him to assert formally, in the way of solemn Public Fact and as a new piece of English Law, what informally and by Nature's eternal Law needed no asserting, That he, Oliver, was the Ablest-Man of England, the King of England; that he, Oliver, would undertake governing England. His way of making this same ' assertion,' the one way he had of making it, has given rise to immense criticism: but the assertion itself, in what way soever 'made,' is it not somewhat of a solemn one, somewhat of a tremendous one!

And now do but contrast this Oliver with my right honourable friend Sir Jabesh Windbag, Mr. Facing-both-ways, Viscount Mealy-mouth, Earl of Windlestraw, or what other Cagliostro, Cagliostrino, Cagliostraccio, the course of Fortune and Parliamentary Majorities has constitutionally guided to that dignity, any time during these last sorrowful hundred-and-fifty years! Windbag, weak in the faith of a God, which he believes only at Church on Sundays, if even then; strong only in the faith that Paragraphs and Plausibilities bring votes; that Force of Public Opinion, as he calls it, is the primal Necessity of Things, and highest God we have:—Windbag, if we will consider him, has a problem set before him which may be ranged in the impossible class. He is a Columbus minded to sail to the indistinct country of NOWHERE, to the indistinct country of WHITHERWARD, by the *friendship* of those same waste-tumbling Water-Alps and howling waltz of All the Winds; not by conquest of them and in spite of them, but by friendship of them, when once *they* have made up their mind! He is the most original Co-

lumbus I ever saw.   Nay, his problem is not an impossible one:
he will infallibly *arrive* at that same country of NOWHERE; his
indistinct Whitherward will be a *Thither*ward!   In the Ocean
Abysses and Locker of Davy Jones, there certainly enough do he
and *his* ship's company, and all their cargo and navigatings, at last
find lodgment.

Oliver knew that his America lay THERE, Westward Ho;—and
it was not entirely by *friendship* of the Water-Alps, and yeasty
insane Froth-Oceans, that he meant to get thither!   He sailed
accordingly; had compass-card, and Rules of Navigation,—older
and greater than these Froth-Oceans, old as the Eternal God!   Or
again, do but think of this.   Windbag in these his probable five
years of office has to prosper and get Paragraphs: the Paragraphs
of these five years must be his salvation, or he is a lost man; re-
demption nowhere in the Worlds or in the Times discoverable for
him.   Oliver too would like his Paragraphs; successes, popularities in those five years are not undesirable to him: but mark, I
say, this enormous circumstance: *after* these five years are gone
and done, comes an Eternity for Oliver!   Oliver has to appear
before the Most High Judge: the utmost flow of Paragraphs, the
utmost ebb of them, is now, in strictest arithmetic, verily no
matter at all; its exact value *zero;* an account altogether erased!
Enormous;—which a man, in these days, hardly fancies with an
effort!   Oliver's Paragraphs are all done, his battles, division-lists,
successes all summed: and now in that awful unerring Court of
Review, the real question first rises, Whether he has succeeded at
all; whether he has not been defeated miserably forevermore?
Let him come with world-wide *Io-Pæans,* these avail him not.   Let
him come covered over with the world's execrations, gashed with
ignominious death-wounds, the gallows-rope about his neck: what
avails that?   The word is, Come thou brave and faithful; the word
is, Depart thou quack and accursed!

O Windbag, my right honourable friend, in very truth I pity
thee.   I say, these Paragraphs, and low or loud votings of thy
poor fellow-blockheads of mankind, will never guide thee in any enterprise at all.   Govern a country on such guidance?   Thou canst
not make a pair of shoes, sell a pennyworth of tape, on such.   No,
thy shoes are vamped up falsely to meet the market; behold, the
leather only *seemed* to be tanned; thy shoes melt under me to rub-
bishy pulp, and are not veritable mud-defying shoes, but plausible
vendible similitudes of shoes,—thou unfortunate, and I!   O my
right honourable friend, when the Paragraphs flowed in, who was
like Sir Jabesh?   On the swelling tide he mounted; higher, higher,
triumphant, heaven-high.   But the Paragraphs again ebbed out, as

unwise Paragraphs needs must: Sir Jabesh lies stranded, sunk
and forever sinking in ignominious ooze; the Mud-nymphs, and
over-deepening bottomless Oblivion, his portion to eternal time.
' Posterity?' Thou appealest to Posterity, thou? My right honourable friend, what will Posterity do for thee! The voting of Posterity, were it continued through centuries in thy favour, will be
quite inaudible, extra-forensic, without any effect whatever. Posterity can do simply nothing for a man; nor even seem to do
much if the man be not brainsick. Besides, to tell thee truth,
the bets are a thousand to one, Posterity will not hear of thee, my
right honourable friend! Posterity, I have found, has generally
his own Windbags sufficiently trumpeted in all market-places, and
no leisure to attend to ours. Posterity, which has made of Norse
Odin a similitude, and of Norman William a brute monster, what
will or can it make of English Jabesh? O Heavens, ' Posterity!'—

" These poor persecuted Scotch Covenanters," said I to my
inquiring Frenchman, in such stinted French as stood at command, " *ils s'en appelaient à*"—" *A la Postérité,*" interrupted he,
helping me out.—" *Ah, Monsieur, non, mille fois non!* They appealed to the Eternal God; not to Posterity at all! *C'était dif-
férent.*"

CHAPTER XV.

MORRISON AGAIN.

NEVERTHELESS, O Advanced Liberal, one cannot promise thee any
' New Religion,' for some time; to say truth, I do not think we have
the smallest chance of any! Will the candid reader, by way of
closing this Book Third, listen to a few transient remarks on that
subject?

Candid readers have not lately met with any man who had
less notion to interfere with their Thirty-Nine, or other Church-
Articles; wherewith, very helplessly as is like, they may have
struggled to form for themselves some not inconceivable hypothesis about this Universe, and their own Existence there. Super-
stition, my friend, is far from me; Fanaticism, for any *Fanum* likely
to arise soon on this Earth, is far. A man's Church-Articles are
surely articles of price to him; and in these times one has to be
tolerant of many strange ' Articles,' and of many still stranger
' No-articles,' which go about placarding themselves in a very distracted manner,—the numerous long placard-poles, and questionable infirm paste-pots, interfering with one's peaceable thoroughfare sometimes!

Fancy a man, moreover, recommending his fellow men to believe in God, that so Chartism might abate, and the Manchester Operatives be got to spin peaceably! The idea is more distracted than any placard-pole seen hitherto in a public thoroughfare of men! My friend, if thou ever do come to believe in God, thou wilt find all Chartism, Manchester riot, Parliamentary incompetence, Ministries of Windbag, and the wildest Social Dissolutions, and the burning up of this entire Planet, a most small matter in comparison. Brother, this Planet, I find, is but an inconsiderable sandgrain in the continents of Being: this Planet's poor temporary interests, thy interests and my interests there, when I look fixedly into that eternal Light-Sea and Flame-Sea with *its* eternal interests, dwindle literally into Nothing; my speech of it is—silence for the while. I will as soon think of making Galaxies and Star-Systems to guide little herring-vessels by, as of preaching Religion that the Constable may continue possible. O my Advanced-Liberal friend, this new second progress, of proceeding ' to invent God,' is a very strange one! Jacobinism unfolded into Saint-Simonism bodes innumerable blessed things; but the thing itself might draw tears from a Stoic!—As for me, some twelve or thirteen New Religions, heavy Packets, most of them unfranked, having arrived here from various parts of the world, in a space of six calendar months, I have instructed my invaluable friend the Stamped Postman to introduce no more of them, if the charge exceed one penny.

Henry of Essex, duelling in that Thames Island, ' near to Reading Abbey,' had a religion. But was it in virtue of his seeing armed Phantasms of St. Edmund ' on the rim of the horizon,' looking minatory on him? Had that, intrinsically, anything to do with his religion at all? Henry of Essex's religion was the Inner Light or Moral Conscience of his own soul; such as is vouchsafed still to all souls of men;—which Inner Light shone here ' through such intellectual and other media' as there were; producing ' Phantasms,' Kircherean Visual-Spectra, according to circumstances! It is so with all men. The clearer my Inner Light may shine, through the *less* turbid media; the *fewer* Phantasms it may produce,—the gladder surely shall I be, and not the sorrier! Hast thou reflected, O serious reader, Advanced-Liberal or other, that the one end, essence, use of all religion past, present and to come, was this only: To keep that same Moral Conscience or Inner Light of ours alive and shining;—which certainly the ' Phantasms' and the ' turbid media' were not essential for! All religion was here to remind us, better or worse, of what we already know better or worse, of the quite *infinite* difference there is between a Good man and a

Bad; to bid us love infinitely the one, abhor and avoid infinitely the other,—strive infinitely to *be* the one, and not to be the other. 'All religion issues in due Practical Hero-worship.' He that has a soul unasphyxied will never want a religion; he that has a soul asphyxied, reduced to a succedaneum for salt, will never find any religion, though you rose from the dead to preach him one.

But indeed, when men and reformers ask for 'a religion,' it is analogous to their asking, 'What would you have us to do?' and such like. They fancy that their religion too shall be a kind of Morrison's Pill, which they have only to swallow once, and all will be well. Resolutely once gulp down your Religion, your Morrison's Pill, you have it all plain sailing now: you can follow your affairs, your no-affairs, go along money-hunting, pleasure-hunting, dilettanteing, dangling, and miming and chattering like a Dead-Sea Ape: your Morrison will do your business for you. Men's notions are very strange!—Brother, I say there is not, was not, nor will ever be, in the wide circle of Nature, any Pill or Religion of that character. Man cannot afford thee such; for the very gods it is impossible. I advise thee to renounce Morrison; once for all, quit hope of the Universal Pill. For body, for soul, for individual or society, there has not any such article been made. *Non extat.* In Created Nature it is not, was not, will not be. In the void imbroglios of Chaos only, and realms of Bedlam, does some shadow of it hover, to bewilder and bemock the poor inhabitants *there.*

Rituals, Liturgies, Creeds, Hierarchies: all this is not religion; all this, were it dead as Odinism, as Fetishism, does not kill religion at all! It is Stupidity alone, with never so many rituals, that kills religion. Is not this still a World? Spinning Cotton under Arkwright and Adam Smith; founding Cities by the Fountain of Juturna, on the Janiculum Mount; tilling Canaan under Prophet Samuel and Psalmist David, man is ever man; the missionary of Unseen Powers; and great and victorious, while he continues true to his mission; mean, miserable, foiled, and at last annihilated and trodden out of sight and memory, when he proves untrue. Brother, thou art a Man, I think; thou art not a mere building Beaver, or two-legged Cotton-Spider; thou hast verily a Soul in thee, asphyxied or otherwise! Sooty Manchester,—it too is built on the infinite Abysses; overspanned by the skyey Firmaments; and there is birth in it, and death in it;—and it is every whit as wonderful, as fearful, unimaginable, as the oldest Salem or Prophetic City. Go or stand, in what time, in what place we will, are there not Immensities, Eternities over us, around us, in us:

> 'Solemn before us,
> Veiled, the dark Portal,
> Goal of all mortal :—
> Stars silent rest o'er us,
> Graves under us silent!'

Between *these* two great Silences, the hum of all our spinning
cylinders, Trades-Unions, Anti-Corn-Law Leagues and Carlton
Clubs goes on. Stupidity itself ought to pause a little and consider that. I tell thee, through all thy Ledgers, Supply-and-demand
Philosophies, and daily most modern melancholy Business and
Cant, there does shine the presence of a Primeval Unspeakable;
and thou wert wise to recognise, not with lips only, that same!

The Maker's Laws, whether they are promulgated in Sinai
Thunder, to the ear or imagination, or quite otherwise promulgated, are the Laws of God; transcendent, everlasting, imperatively demanding obedience from all men. This, without any
thunder, or with never so much thunder, thou, if there be any
soul left in thee, canst know of a truth. The Universe, I say, is
made by Law; the great Soul of the World is just and not unjust.
Look thou, if thou have eyes or soul left, into this great shoreless
Incomprehensible: in the heart of its tumultuous Appearances,
Embroilments, and mad Time-vortexes, is there not, silent, eternal, an All-just, an All-beautiful; sole Reality and ultimate con-
trolling Power of the whole? This is not a figure of speech; this
is a fact. The fact of Gravitation known to all animals, is not
surer than this inner Fact, which may be known to all men. He
who knows this, it will sink, silent, awful, unspeakable, into his
heart. He will say with Faust: "Who *dare* name HIM?" Most
rituals or 'namings' he will fall in with at present, are like to be
'namings'—which shall be nameless! In silence, in the Eternal
Temple, let him worship, if there be no fit word. Such knowledge,
the crown of his whole spiritual being, the life of his life, let him
keep and sacredly walk by. He has a religion. Hourly and daily,
for himself and for the whole world, a faithful, unspoken, but not
ineffectual prayer rises, "Thy will be done." His whole work on
Earth is an emblematic spoken or acted prayer, Be the will of God
done on Earth,—not the Devil's will, or any of the Devil's servants' wills! He has a religion, this man; an everlasting Loadstar that beams the brighter in the Heavens, the darker here on
Earth grows the night around him. Thou, if thou know not this,
what are all rituals, liturgies, mythologies, mass-chantings, turn-
ings of the rotatory calabash? They are as nothing; in a good
many respects they are as *less*. Divorced from this, getting half-
divorced from this, they are a thing to fill one with a kind of

horror; with a sacred inexpressible pity and fear. The most tragical thing a human eye can look on. It was said to the Prophet, " Behold, I will show thee worse things than these : women weeping to Thammuz." That was the acme of the Prophet's vision,— then as now.

Rituals, Liturgies, Credos, Sinai Thunder: I know more or less the history of these; the rise, progress, decline and fall of these. Can thunder from all the thirty-two azimuths, repeated daily for centuries of years, make God's Laws more godlike to me? Brother, No. Perhaps I am grown to be a man now; and do not need the thunder and the terror any longer! Perhaps I am above being frightened; perhaps it is not Fear, but Reverence alone, that shall now lead me!—Revelations, Inspirations? Yes: and thy own god-created Soul; dost thou not call that a 'revelation?' Who made THEE? Where didst Thou come from? The Voice of Eternity, if thou be not a blasphemer and poor asphyxied mute, speaks with that tongue of thine! *Thou* art the latest Birth of Nature; it is ' the Inspiration of the Almighty' that giveth *thee* understanding! My brother, my brother!—

Under baleful Atheisms, Mammonisms, Joe-Manton Dilettantisms, with their appropriate Cants and Idolisms, and whatsoever scandalous rubbish obscures and all but extinguishes the soul of man,—religion now is; its Laws, written if not on stone tables, yet on the Azure of Infinitude, in the inner heart of God's Creation, certain as Life, certain as Death! I say the Laws are there, and thou shalt not disobey them. It were better for thee not. Better a hundred deaths than yes. Terrible ' penalties' withal, if thou still need ' penalties,' are there for disobeying. Dost thou observe, O redtape Politician, that fiery infernal Phenomenon, which men name FRENCH REVOLUTION, sailing, unlooked-for, unbidden; through thy inane Protocol Dominion:—far-seen, with splendour not of Heaven? Ten centuries will see it. There were Tanneries at Meudon for human skins. And Hell, very truly Hell, had power over God's upper Earth for a season. The cruellest Portent that has risen into created Space these ten centuries: let us hail it, with awestruck repentant hearts, as the voice once more of a God, though of one in wrath. Blessed be the God's-voice; for *it* is true, and Falsehoods have to cease before it! But for that same preternatural quasi-infernal Portent, one could not know what to make of this wretched world, in these days, at all. The deplorablest quack-ridden, and now hunger-ridden, downtrodden Despicability and *Flebile Ludibrium*, of redtape Protocols, rotatory Calabashes, Poor-Law Bastilles: who is there that could think of *its* being fated to continue?—

Penalties enough, my brother! This penalty inclusive of all: Eternal Death to thy own hapless Self, if thou heed no other. Eternal Death, I say,—with many meanings old and new, of which let this single one suffice us here: The eternal impossibility for thee to be aught but a Chimera, and swift-vanishing deceptive Phantasm, in God's Creation;—swift-vanishing, never to reappear: why should *it* reappear! Thou hadst one chance, thou wilt never have another. Everlasting ages will roll on, and no other be given thee. The foolishest articulate-speaking soul now extant, may not he say to himself: "A whole Eternity I waited to be born; and now I have a whole Eternity waiting to see what I will do when born!" This is not Theology, this is Arithmetic. And thou but half-discernest this; thou but half-believest it? Alas, on the shores of the Dead Sea on Sabbath, there goes on a Tragedy!—

But we will leave this of 'Religion;' of which, to say truth, it is chiefly profitable in these unspeakable days to keep silence. Thou needest no 'New Religion;' nor art thou like to get any. Thou hast already more 'religion' than thou makest use of. This day, thou knowest ten commanded duties, seest in thy mind ten things which should be done, for one that thou doest! *Do* one of them; this of itself will show thee ten others which can and shall be done. "But my future fate?" Yes, thy future fate, indeed? Thy future fate, while thou makest *it* the chief question, seems to me—extremely questionable! I do not think it can be good. Norse Odin, immemorial centuries ago, did not he, though a poor Heathen, in the dawn of Time, teach us that for the Dastard there was, and could be, no good fate; no harbour anywhere, save down with Hela, in the pool of Night! Dastards, Knaves, are they that lust for Pleasure, that tremble at Pain. For this world and for the next, Dastards are a class of creatures made to be 'arrested;' they are good for nothing else, can look for nothing else. A greater than Odin has been here. A greater than Odin has taught us—not a greater Dastardism, I hope! My brother, thou must pray for a *soul;* struggle, as with life-and-death energy, to get back thy soul! Know that 'religion' is no Morrison's Pill from without, but a reawakening of thy own Self from within:—and, above all, leave me alone of thy 'religions' and 'new religions' here and elsewhere! I am weary of this sick croaking for a Morrison's-Pill religion; for any and for every such. I want none such; and discern all such to be impossible. The resuscitation of old liturgies fallen dead; much more, the manufacture of new liturgies that will never be alive: how hopeless! Stylitisms, eremite manaticisms and fakeerisms; spasmodic agonistic posture-makings, and narrow, cramped, morbid, if forever noble wrestlings: all this is not a thing desirable to me. It is a thing the world *has* done once,—when its beard was not grown as now!

And yet there is, at worst, one Liturgy which does remain forever unexceptionable: that of *Praying* (as the old Monks did withal) *by Working*. And indeed the Prayer which accomplished itself in special chapels at stated hours, and went not with a man, rising up from all his Work and Action, at all moments sanctifying the same,—what was it ever good for? 'Work is Worship:' yes, in a highly considerable sense,—which, in the present state of all 'worship,' who is there that can unfold! He that understands it well, understands the Prophecy of the whole Future; the last Evangel, which has included all others. *Its* cathedral the Dome of Immensity,—hast thou seen it? coped with the star-galaxies; paved with the green mosaic of land and ocean; and for altar, verily, the Star-throne of the Eternal! Its litany and psalmody the noble acts, the heroic work and suffering, and true heart-utterance of all the Valiant of the Sons of Men. Its choir-music the ancient Winds and Oceans, and deep-toned, inarticulate, but most speaking voices of Destiny and History,—supernal ever as of old. Between two great Silences:

> ' Stars silent rest o'er us,
> Graves under us silent.'

Between which two great Silences, do not, as we said, all human Noises, in the naturallest times, most *preter*-naturally march and roll?—

I will insert this also, in a lower strain, from Sauerteig's *Æsthetische Springwurzeln.* 'Worship?' says he: 'Before that inane 'tumult of Hearsay filled men's heads, while the world lay yet 'silent, and the heart true and open, many things were Worship! 'To the primeval man whatsoever good came, descended on him '(as, in mere fact, it ever does) direct from God; whatsoever duty 'lay visible for him, this a Supreme God had prescribed. To the 'present hour I ask thee, Who else? For the primeval man, in 'whom dwelt Thought, this Universe was all a Temple; Life 'everywhere a Worship.

'What Worship, for example, is there not in mere Washing! 'Perhaps one of the most moral things a man, in common cases, 'has it in his power to do. Strip thyself, go into the bath, or 'were it into the limpid pool and running brook, and there wash 'and be clean; thou wilt step out again a purer and a better man. 'This consciousness of perfect outer pureness, that to thy skin 'there now adheres no foreign speck of imperfection, how it radi-'ates in on thee, with cunning symbolic influences, to thy very

' soul! Thou hast an increase of tendency towards all good things
' whatsoever. The oldest Eastern Sages, with joy and holy grati-
' tude, had felt it so,—and that it was the Maker's gift and will.
' Whose else *is* it? It remains a religious duty, from oldest times,
' in the East.—Nor could Herr Professor Strauss, when I put the
' question, deny that for us at present it is still such here in the
' West! To that dingy fuliginous Operative, emerging from his
' soot-mill, what is the first duty I will prescribe, and offer help
· towards? That he clean the skin of him. *Can* he pray, by any
· ascertained method? One knows not entirely:—but with soap
' and a sufficiency of water, he can wash. Even the dull English
· feel something of this; they have a saying, " Cleanliness is near
· of kin to Godliness :"—yet never, in any country, saw I operative
' men worse washed, and, in a climate drenched with the softest
· cloud - water, such a scarcity of baths !'—Alas, Sauertcig, our
' operative men' are at present short even of potatoes : what ' duty'
can you prescribe to them !

Or let us give a glance at China. Our new friend, the Emperor
there, is Pontiff of three hundred million men; who do all live
and work, these many centuries now; authentically patronised by
Heaven so far; and therefore must have some 'religion' of a kind.
This Emperor-Pontiff has, in fact, a religious belief of certain Laws
of Heaven; observes, with a religious rigour, his ' three thousand
punctualities,' given out by men of insight, some sixty generations
since, as a legible transcript of the same,—the Heavens do seem
to say, not totally an incorrect one. He has not much of a ritual,
this Pontiff-Emperor; believes, it is likest, with the old Monks,
that ' Labour is Worship.' His most public Act of Worship, it
appears, is the drawing solemnly at a certain day, on the green
bosom of our Mother Earth, when the Heavens, after dead black
winter, have again with their vernal radiances awakened her, a
distinct red Furrow with the Plough,—signal that all the Ploughs
of China are to begin ploughing and worshiping ! It is notable
enough. He, in sight of the Seen and Unseen Powers, draws his
distinct red Furrow there; saying, and praying, in mute symbol-
ism, so many most eloquent things !

If you ask this Pontiff, " Who made him? What is to become
of him and us ?" he maintains a dignified reserve ; waves his hand
and pontiff-eyes over the unfathomable deep of Heaven, the
' Tsien,' the azure kingdoms of Infinitude ; as if asking, " Is it
doubtful that we are right *well* made? Can aught that is *wrong* become of us ?"—He and his three hundred millions (it is their chief
' punctuality') visit yearly the Tombs of their Fathers ; each man
the Tomb of his Father and his Mother : alone there, in silence,

with what of 'worship' or of other thought there may be, pauses solemnly each man; the divine Skies all silent over him; the divine Graves, and this divinest Grave, all silent under him; the pulsings of his own soul, if he have any soul, alone audible. Truly it may be a kind of worship! Truly, if a man cannot get some glimpse into the Eternities, looking through this portal,—through what other need he try it?

Our friend the Pontiff-Emperor permits cheerfully, though with contempt, all manner of Buddists, Bonzes, Talapoins and such like, to build brick Temples, on the voluntary principle; to worship with what of chantings, paper-lanterns and tumultuous brayings, pleases them; and make night hideous, since they find some comfort in so doing. Cheerfully, though with contempt. He is a wiser Pontiff than many persons think! He is as yet the one Chief Potentate or Priest in this Earth who has made a distinct systematic attempt at what we call the ultimate result of all religion, ' *Practical* Hero-worship:' he does incessantly, with true anxiety, in such way as he can, search and sift (it would appear) his whole enormous population for the Wisest born among them; by which Wisest, as by born Kings, these three hundred million men are governed. The Heavens, to a certain extent, do appear to countenance him. These three hundred millions actually make porcelain, souchong tea, with innumerable other things; and fight, under Heaven's flag, against Necessity;—and have fewer Seven-Years Wars, Thirty-Years Wars, French-Revolution Wars. and infernal fightings with each other, than certain millions elsewhere have!

Nay, in our poor distracted Europe itself. in these newest times, have there not religious voices risen,—with a religion new and yet the oldest; entirely indisputable to all hearts of men? Some I do know, who did not call or think themselves ' Prophets,' far enough from that; but who were, in very truth, melodious Voices from the eternal Heart of Nature once again: souls forever venerable to all that have a soul. A French Revolution is one phenomenon; as complement and spiritual exponent thereof. a Poet Goethe and German Literature is to me another. The old Secular or Practical World, so to speak, having gone up in fire, is not here the prophecy and dawn of a new Spiritual World, parent of far nobler, wider, new Practical Worlds? A Life of Antique devoutness, Antique veracity and heroism, has again become possible, is again *seen* actual there, for the most modern man. A phenomenon, as quiet as it is, comparable for greatness to no other! ' The great event for the world is, now as always, the arrival in it of a new Wise Man.' Touches there are, be the

Heavens ever thanked, of new Sphere-melody; audible once more,
in the infinite jargoning discords and poor scrannel-pipings of the
thing called Literature;—priceless there, as the voice of new Heavenly Psalms!   Literature, like the old Prayer-Collections of the
first centuries, were it 'well selected from and burnt,' contains
precious things.   For Literature, with all its printing-presses,
puffing-engines and shoreless deafening triviality, *is* yet 'the
Thought of Thinking Souls.' A sacred 'religion,' if you like the
name, does live in the heart of that strange froth-ocean, not wholly
froth, which we call Literature; and will more and more disclose
itself therefrom;—not now as scorching Fire: the red smoky
scorching Fire has purified itself into white sunny Light.   Is not
Light grander than Fire? It is the same element in a state of
purity.

My ingenuous readers, we will march out of this Third Book
with a rhythmic word of Goethe's on our lips; a word which perhaps has already sung itself, in dark hours and in bright, through
many a heart.   To me, finding it devout yet wholly credible and
veritable, full of piety yet free of cant; to me, jóyfully finding much
in it, and joyfully missing so much in it, this little snatch of music, by the greatest German Man, sounds like a stanza in the grand
Road-Song and *Marching-Song* of our great Teutonic Kindred, wending, wending, valiant and victorious, through the undiscovered
Deeps of Time! He calls it *Mason-Lodge*,—not Psalm or Hymn:

> The Mason's ways are
> A type of Existence,
> And his persistence
> Is as the days are
> Of men in this world.
>
> The Future hides in it
> Gladness and sorrow;
> We press still thorow,
> Naught that abides in it
> Daunting us,—onward.
>
> And solemn before us.
> Veiled, the dark Portal,
> Goal of all mortal :—
> Stars silent rest o'er us,
> Graves under us silent.
>
> While earnest thou gazest,
> Comes boding of terror,
> Comes phantasm and error,
> Perplexes the bravest
> With doubt and misgiving.

But heard are the Voices,—
Heard are the Sages,
The Worlds and the Ages:
"Choose well, your choice is
Brief and yet endless:

Here eyes do regard you,
In Eternity's stillness;
Here is all fulness,
Ye brave, to reward you;
Work, and despair not."

BOOK IV.—HOROSCOPE.

CHAPTER I.

ARISTOCRACIES.

To predict the Future, to manage the Present, would not be so impossible, had not the Past been so sacrilegiously mishandled; effaced, and what is worse, defaced! The Past cannot be seen; the Past, looked at through the medium of 'Philosophical History' in these times, cannot even be *not* seen: it is misseen; affirmed to have existed,—and to have been a godless Impossibility. Your Norman Conquerors, true royal souls, crowned kings as such, were vulturous irrational tyrants: your Becket was a noisy egoist and hypocrite; getting his brains spilt on the floor of Canterbury Cathedral, to secure the main chance,—somewhat uncertain how! 'Policy, Fanaticism;' or say 'Enthusiasm,' even 'honest Enthusiasm,'—ah yes, of course:

'The Dog, to gain his private ends,
Went mad, and bit the Man!'—

For in truth, the eye sees in all things 'what it brought with it the means of seeing.' A godless century, looking back on centuries that were godly, produces portraitures more miraculous than any other. All was inane discord in the Past; brute Force bore rule everywhere; Stupidity, savage Unreason, fitter for Bedlam than for a human World! Whereby indeed it becomes sufficiently natural that the like qualities, in new sleeker habiliments, should continue in our time to rule. Millions enchanted in Bastille Workhouses; Irish Widows proving their relationship by typhus-fever: what would you have? It was ever so, or worse. Man's History, was it not always even this: The cookery and eating up of imbecile Dupedom by successful Quackhood; the battle, with various weapons, of vulturous Quack and Tyrant against vulturous Tyrant and Quack? No God was in the Past Time;

s

nothing but Mechanisms and Chaotic Brute-gods :—how shall the poor 'Philosophic Historian,' to whom his own century is all godless, see any God in other centuries ?

Men believe in Bibles, and disbelieve in them: but of all Bibles the frightfullest to disbelieve in is this 'Bible of Universal History.' This is the Eternal Bible and God's-Book, 'which every born man,' till once the soul and eyesight are extinguished in him, 'can and must, with his own eyes, see the God's-Finger writing !' To discredit this, is an *infidelity* like no other. Such infidelity you would punish, if not by fire and faggot, which are difficult to manage in our times, yet by the most peremptory order, To hold its peace till it got something wiser to say. Why should the blessed Silence be broken into noises, to communicate only the like of this ? If the Past have no God's-Reason in it, nothing but Devil's-Unreason, let the Past be eternally forgotten: mention *it* no more ;—we whose ancestors were all hanged, why should we talk of ropes !

It is, in brief, not true that men ever lived by Delirium, Hypocrisy, Injustice, or any form of Unreason, since they came to inhabit this Planet. It is not true that they ever did, or ever will, live except by the reverse of these. Men will again be taught this. Their acted History will then again be a Heroism; their written History, what it once was, an Epic. Nay, forever it is either such, or else it virtually is—Nothing. Were it written in a thousand volumes, the Unheroic of such volumes hastens incessantly to be forgotten; the net content of an Alexandrian Library of Unheroics is, and will ultimately show itself to be, *zero.* ·What man is interested to remember *it ;* have not all men, at all times, the liveliest interest to forget it ?—'Revelations,' if not celestial, then infernal, will teach us that God is; we shall then, if needful, discern without difficulty that He has always been ! The Dryasdust Philosophisms and enlightened Scepticisms of the Eighteenth Century, historical and other, will have to survive for a while with the Physiologists, as a memorable *Nightmare-Dream.* All this haggard epoch, with its ghastly Doctrines, and death's-head Philosophies 'teaching by example' or otherwise, will one day have become, what to our Moslem friends their godless ages are, 'the Period of Ignorance.'

If the convulsive struggles of the last Half-Century have taught poor struggling convulsed Europe any truth, it may perhaps be this as the essence of innumerable others : That Europe requires a real Aristocracy, a real Priesthood, or it cannot continue to exist. Huge French Revolutions, Napoleonisms, then Bourbonisms with their corollary of Three Days, finishing in very unfinal

Louis-Philippisms : all this ought to be didactic! All this may have taught us, That False Aristocracies are insupportable ; that No-Aristocracies, Liberty-and-Equalities are impossible ; that True Aristocracies are at once indispensable and not easily attained.

Aristocracy and Priesthood, a Governing Class and a Teaching Class : these two, sometimes separate, and endeavouring to harmonise themselves, sometimes conjoined as one, and the King a Pontiff-King :—there did no Society exist without these two vital elements, there will none exist. It lies in the very nature of man : you will visit no remotest village in the most republican country of the world, where virtually or actually you do not find these two powers at work. Man, little as he may suppose it, is necessitated to obey superiors. He is a social being in virtue of this necessity ; nay he could not be gregarious otherwise. He obeys those whom he esteems better than himself, wiser, braver ; and will forever obey such ; and even be ready and delighted to do it.

The Wiser, Braver : these, a Virtual Aristocracy everywhere and everywhen, do in all Societies that reach any articulate shape, develop themselves into a ruling class, an Actual Aristocracy, with settled modes of operating, what are called laws and even *private-laws* or privileges, and so forth ; very notable to look upon in this world.—Aristocracy and Priesthood, we say, are sometimes united. For indeed the Wiser and the Braver are properly but one class ; no wise man but needed first of all to be a brave man, or he never had been wise. The noble Priest was always a noble *Aristos* to begin with, and something more to end with. Your Luther, your Knox, your Anselm, Becket, Abbot Samson, Samuel Johnson, if they had not been brave enough, by what possibility could they ever have been wise ?—If, from accident or forethought, this your Actual Aristocracy have got discriminated into Two Classes, there can be no doubt but the Priest Class is the more dignified ; supreme over the other, as governing head is over active hand. And yet in practice again, it is likeliest the reverse will be found arranged ;—a sign that the arrangement is already vitiated ; that a split is introduced into it, which will widen and widen till the whole be rent asunder.

In England, in Europe generally, we may say that these two Virtualities have unfolded themselves into Actualities, in by far the noblest and richest manner any region of the world ever saw. A spiritual Guideship, a practical Governorship, fruit of the grand conscious endeavours, say rather of the immeasurable unconscious instincts and necessities of men, have established themselves ; very strange to behold. Everywhere, while so much has been forgotten, you find the King's Palace, and the Viceking's Castle, Mansion,

Manorhouse; till there is not an inch of ground from sea to sea but has both its King and Viceking, long due series of Vicekings, its Squire, Earl, Duke or whatever the title of him,—to whom you have given the land that he may govern you in it.

More touching still, there is not a hamlet where poor peasants congregate, but by one means and another a Church-Apparatus has been got together,—roofed edifice, with revenues and belfries; pulpit, reading-desk, with Books and Methods: possibility, in short, and strict prescription, That a man stand there and speak of spiritual things to men. It is beautiful;—even in its great obscuration and decadence, it is among the beautifullest, most touching objects one sees on the Earth. This Speaking Man has indeed, in these times, wandered terribly from the point; has alas, as it were totally lost sight of the point: yet, at bottom, whom have we to compare with him? Of all public functionaries boarded and lodged on the Industry of Modern Europe, is there one worthier of the board he has? A man even professing, and never so languidly making still some endeavour, to save the souls of men: contrast him with a man professing to do little but shoot the partridges of men! I wish he could find the point again, this Speaking One; and stick to it with tenacity, with deadly energy; for there is need of him yet! The Speaking Function, this of Truth coming to us with a living voice, nay in a living shape, and as a concrete practical exemplar: this, with all our Writing and Printing Functions, has a perennial place. Could he but find the point again,—take the old spectacles off his nose, and looking up discover, almost in contact with him, what the *real* Satanas, and soul-devouring, world-devouring *Devil*, now is! Original Sin and such like are bad enough, I doubt not: but distilled Gin, dark Ignorance, Stupidity, dark Corn-Law, Bastille and Company, what are they! *Will* he discover our new real Satan, whom he has to fight; or go on droning through his old nose-spectacles about old extinct Satans; and never see the real one, till he *feel* him at his own throat and ours? That is a question, for the world! Let us not intermeddle with it here.

Sorrowful, phantasmal as this same Double Aristocracy of Teachers and Governors now looks, it is worth all men's while to know that the purport of it is and remains noble and most real. Dryasdust, looking merely at the surface, is greatly in error as to those ancient Kings. William Conqueror, William Rufus or Redbeard, Stephen Curthose himself, much more Henry Beauclerc and our brave Plantagenet Henry. the life of these men was not a vulturous Fighting; it was a valorous Governing,—to which occasionally Fighting did, and alas must yet, though far seldomer now, superadd itself as an accident, a distressing impedimental adjunct. The fighting too was indispensable, for ascertaining who had the might over whom, the right over whom. By much hard fighting, as we once said, 'the unrealities, beaten into dust, flew gradually off;' and left the plain reality and fact, "Thou stronger than I; thou wiser than I; thou king, and subject I," in a somewhat clearer condition.

Truly we cannot enough admire, in those Abbot-Samson and William-Conqueror times, the arrangement they had made of their Governing Classes. Highly interesting to observe how the sincere insight, on their part, into what did, of primary necessity, behove to be accomplished, had led them to the way of accomplishing it, and in the course of time to get it accomplished! No imaginary Aristocracy would serve their turn; and accordingly they attained a real one. The Bravest men, who, it is ever to be repeated and remembered, are also on the whole the Wisest, Strongest, everyway Best, had here, with a respectable degree of accuracy, been got selected; seated each on his piece of territory, which was lent him, then gradually given him, that he might govern it. These Vicekings, each on his portion of the common soil of England, with a Head King over all, were a ' Virtuality perfected into an Actuality' really to an astonishing extent.

For those were rugged stalwart ages; full of earnestness, of a rude God's-truth :—nay, at any rate, their *quilting* was so unspeakably *thinner* than ours ; Fact came swiftly on them, if at any time they had yielded to Phantasm ! ' The Knaves and Dastards' had to be ' arrested' in some measure ; or the world, almost within year and day, found that it could not live. The Knaves and Dastards accordingly were got arrested. Dastards upon the very throne had to be got arrested, and taken off the throne,—by such methods as there were ; by the roughest method, if there chanced to be no smoother one ! Doubtless there was much harshness of operation, much severity ; as indeed government and surgery are often somewhat severe. Gurth born thrall of Cedric, it is like, got cuffs as often as pork-parings, if he misdemeaned himself ; but Gurth did belong to Cedric : no human creature then went about connected with nobody ; left to go his ways into Bastilles or worse, under *Laissez-faire ;* reduced to prove his relationship by dying of typhus-fever !—Days come when there is no King in Israel, but every man is his own king, doing that which is right in his own eyes ;—and tarbarrels are burnt to ' Liberty,' ' Tenpound Franchise' and the like, with considerable effect in various ways !—

That Feudal Aristocracy, I say, was no imaginary one. To a

respectable degree, its *Jarls*, what we now call Earls, were *Strong-Ones* in fact as well as etymology; its Dukes *Leaders;* its Lords *Law-wards*. They did all the Soldiering and Police of the country, all the Judging, Law-making, even the Church-Extension; whatsoever in the way of Governing, of Guiding and Protecting could be done. It was a Land Aristocracy; it managed the Governing of this English People, and had the reaping of the Soil of England in return. It is, in many senses, the Law of Nature, this same Law of Feudalism;—no right Aristocracy but a Land one! The curious are invited to meditate upon it in these days. Soldiering, Police and Judging, Church-Extension, nay real Government and Guidance, all this was actually *done* by the Holders of the Land in return for their Land. How much of it is now done by them; done by anybody? Good Heavens, "Laissez-faire. Do ye nothing, eat your wages and sleep," is everywhere the passionate half-wise cry of this time; and they will not so much as do nothing, but must do mere Corn-Laws! We raise Fifty-two millions, from the general mass of us, to get our Governing done, —or, alas, to get ourselves persuaded that it is done: and the ' peculiar burden of the Land' is to pay, not all this, but to pay, as I learn, one twenty-fourth part of all this. Our first Chartist Parliament, or Oliver *Redivivus*, you would say, will know where to lay the new taxes of England!—Or, alas, taxes? If we made the Holders of the Land pay every shilling still of the expense of Governing the Land, what were all that? The Land, by mere hired Governors, cannot be got governed. You cannot hire men to govern the Land: it is by a mission not contracted for in the Stock-Exchange, but felt in their own hearts as coming out of Heaven, that men can govern a Land. The mission of a Land Aristocracy is a *sacred* one, in both the senses of that old word. The footing it stands on, at present, might give rise to thoughts other than of Corn-Laws !—

But truly a ' Splendour of God,' as in William Conqueror's rough oath, did dwell in those old rude veracious ages; did inform, more and more, with a heavenly nobleness, all departments of their work and life. Phantasms could not yet walk abroad in mere Cloth Tailorage; they were at least Phantasms ' on the rim of the horizon,' pencilled there by an eternal Light-beam from within. A most ' practical' Hero-worship went on, unconsciously or half-consciously, everywhere. A Monk Samson, with a maximum of two shillings in his pocket, could, without ballot-box, be made a Viceking of, being seen to be worthy. The difference between a good man and a bad man was as yet felt to be, what it forever is, an immeasurable one. Who *durst* have elected a Pandarus Dogdraught, in those days, to any office, Carlton Club, Senatorship, or place whatsoever? It was felt that the arch Satanas and no other had a clear right of property in Pandarus; that it were better for you to have no hand in Pandarus, to keep out of Pandarus his neighbourhood! Which is, to this hour, the mere fact; though for the present, alas, the forgotten fact. I think they were comparatively blessed times those, in their way! 'Violence,' 'war,' 'disorder:' well, what is war, and death itself, to such a perpetual life-in-death, and 'peace, peace where there is no peace!' Unless some Hero-worship, in its new appropriate form, can return, this world does not promise to be very habitable long.

Old Anselm, exiled Archbishop of Canterbury, one of the purest-minded 'men of genius,' was travelling to make his appeal to Rome against King Rufus,—a man of rough ways, in whom the 'inner Lightbeam' shone very fitfully. It is beautiful to read, in Monk Eadmer, how the Continental populations welcomed and venerated this Anselm, as no French population now venerates Jean-Jacques or giant-killing Voltaire; as not even an American population now venerates a Schnüspel the distinguished Novelist! They had, by phantasy and true insight, the intensest conviction that a God's Blessing dwelt in this Anselm,—as is my conviction too. They crowded round, with bent knees and enkindled hearts, to receive his blessing, to hear his voice, to see the light of his face. My blessings on them and on him!—But the notablest was a certain necessitous or covetous Duke of Burgundy, in straitened circumstances we shall hope,—who reflected that in all likelihood this English Archbishop, going towards Rome to appeal, must have taken store of cash with him to bribe the Cardinals. Wherefore he of Burgundy, for his part, decided to lie in wait and rob him. 'In an open space of a wood,' some 'wood' then green and growing, eight centuries ago, in Burgundian Land,—this fierce Duke, with fierce steel followers, shaggy, savage, as the Russian bear, dashes out on the weak old Anselm; who is riding along there, on his small quiet-going pony; escorted only by Eadmer and another poor Monk on ponies; and, except small modicum of roadmoney, not a gold coin in his possession. The steelclad Russian bear emerges, glaring:. the old white-bearded man starts not,—paces on unmoved, looking into him with those clear old earnest eyes, with that venerable sorrowful time-worn face; of whom no man or thing need be afraid, and who also is afraid of no created man or thing. The fire-eyes of his Burgundian Grace meet these clear eye-glances, convey them swift to his heart: he bethinks him that probably this feeble, fearless, hoary Figure has in it something of the Most High God; that probably he shall be damned if he meddle with it,—that, on the whole, he had better not. He plunges, the rough savage, from his war-horse, down to his knees; embraces the feet of old Anselm: he too begs his blessing; orders men to escort him, guard him from being robbed, and under dread penalties see him safe on his way. *Per os Dei*, as his Majesty was wont to ejaculate!

Neither is this quarrel of Rufus and Anselm, of Henry and Becket, uninstructive to us. It was, at bottom, a great quarrel. For, admitting that Anselm was full of divine blessing, he by no means included in him all forms of divine blessing :—there were far other forms withal, which he little dreamed of; and William Redbeard was unconsciously the representative and spokesman of these. In truth, could your divine Anselm, your divine Pope Gregory have had their way, the results had been very notable. Our Western World had all become a European Thibet, with one Grand Lama sitting at Rome; our one honourable business that of singing mass, all day and all night. Which would not in the least have suited us! The Supreme Powers willed it not so.

It was as if King Redbeard unconsciously, addressing Anselm, Becket and the others, had said : " Right Reverend, your Theory of the Universe is indisputable by man or devil. To the core of our heart we feel that this divine thing, which you call Mother Church, does fill the whole world hitherto known, and is and shall be all our salvation and all our desire. And yet—and yet—Behold, though it is an unspoken secret, the world is *wider* than any of us think, Right Reverend! Behold, there are yet other immeasurable Sacrednesses in this that you call Heathenism, Secularity! On the whole I, in an obscure but most rooted manner, feel that I cannot comply with you. Western Thibet and perpetual mass-chanting,—No. I am, so to speak, in the family-way; with child, of I know not what,—certainly of something far different from this! I have—*Per os Dei*, I have Manchester Cotton-trades, Bromwicham Iron-trades, American Commonwealths, Indian Empires, Steam Mechanisms and Shakspeare Dramas, in my belly; and cannot do it, Right Reverend!"—So accordingly it was decided: and Saxon Becket spilt his life in Canterbury Cathedral, as Scottish Wallace did on Tower-Hill,.and as generally a noble man and martyr has to do,—not for nothing; no, but for a divine something, other than *he* had altogether calculated. We will now quit this of the hard, organic, but limited Feudal Ages: and glance timidly into the immense Industrial Ages, as yet all inorganic, and in a quite pulpy condition, requiring desperately to harden themselves into some organism!

Our Epic having now become *Tools and the Man*, it is more than usually impossible to prophesy the Future. The boundless Future does lie there, predestined, nay already extant though unseen; hiding, in its Continents of Darkness, 'gladness and sorrow:' but the supremest intelligence of man cannot prefigure much of it:—the united intelligence and effort of All Men in all coming generations, this alone will gradually prefigure it, and figure and form it into a seen fact! Straining our eyes hitherto, the utmost effort of intelligence sheds but some most glimmering dawn, a little way into its dark enormous Deeps: only huge outlines loom uncertain on the sight; and the ray of prophecy, at a short distance, expires. But may we not say, here as always, Sufficient for the day is the evil thereof! To shape the whole Future is not our problem; but only to shape faithfully a small part of it, according to rules already known. It is perhaps possible for each of us, who will with due earnestness inquire, to ascertain clearly what he, for his own part, ought to do: this let him, with true heart, do, and continue doing. The general issue will, as it has always done, rest well with a Higher Intelligence than ours.

One grand 'outline,' or even two, many earnest readers may perhaps, at this stage of the business, be able to prefigure for themselves,—and draw some guidance from. One prediction, or even two, are already possible. For the Life-tree Igdrasil, in all its new developments, is the selfsame world-old Life-tree: having found an element or elements there, running from the very roots of it in Hela's Realms, in the Well of Mimer and of the Three Nornas or TIMES, up to this present hour of it in our own hearts, we conclude that such will have to continue. A man has, in his own soul, an Eternal; can read something of the Eternal there, if he will look! He already knows what will continue; what cannot, by any means or appliance whatsoever, be made to continue!

One wide and widest 'outline' ought really, in all ways, to be becoming clear to us; this namely: That a 'Splendour of God,' in one form or other, will have to unfold itself from the heart of these our Industrial Ages too; or they will never get themselves 'organised;' but continue chaotic, distressed, distracted evermore, and have to perish in frantic suicidal dissolution. A second 'outline' or prophecy, narrower, but also wide enough, seems not less certain: That there will again *be* a King in Israel; a system of Order and Government; and every man shall, in some measure, see himself constrained to do that which is right in the King's eyes. This too we may call a sure element of the Future; for this too is of the Eternal;—this too is of the Present, though hidden from most; and without it no fibre of the Past ever was. An actual new Sovereignty. Industrial Aristocracy, real not imaginary Aristocracy, is indispensable and indubitable for us.

But what an Aristocracy; on what new, far more complex and cunningly devised conditions than that old Feudal fighting one! For we are to bethink us that the Epic verily is not *Arms and the Man*, but *Tools and the Man*,—an infinitely wider kind of Epic. And again we are to bethink us that men cannot now be bound to men by *brass-collars*,—not at all: that this brass-collar method, in all figures of it, has vanished out of Europe forevermore! Huge Democracy, walking the streets everywhere in its Sack Coat, has asserted so much; irrevocably, brooking no reply! True enough, man *is* forever the 'born thrall' of certain men, born master of certain other men, born equal of certain others, let him acknowledge the fact or not. It is unblessed for him when he cannot acknowledge this fact; he is in the chaotic state, ready to perish, till he do get the fact acknowledged. But no man is, or can henceforth be, the brass-collar thrall of any man; you will have to bind him by other, far nobler and cunninger methods. Once for all, he is to be loose of the brass-collar, to have a scope *as* wide as his faculties now are:—will he not be all the usefuller to you, in that new state? Let him go abroad as a trusted one, as a free one; and return home to you with rich earnings at night! Gurth could only tend pigs; this one will build cities, conquer waste worlds. —How, in conjunction with inevitable Democracy, indispensable Sovereignty is to exist: certainly it is the hugest question ever heretofore propounded to Mankind! The solution of which is work for long years and centuries. Years and centuries, of one knows not what complexion;—blessed or unblessed, according as they shall, with earnest valiant effort, make progress therein, or, in slothful unveracity and dilettantism, only talk of making progress. For either progress therein, or swift and ever swifter progress towards dissolution, is henceforth a necessity.

It is of importance that this grand reformation were begun; that Corn-Law Debatings and other jargon, little less than delirious in such a time, had fled far away, and left us room to begin! For the evil has grown practical, extremely conspicuous; if it be not seen and provided for, the blindest fool will have to feel it ere long. There is much that can wait; but there is something also that cannot wait. With millions of eager Working Men imprisoned in 'Impossibility' and Poor-Law Bastilles, it is time that some means of dealing with them were trying to become 'possible!' Of the Government of England, of all articulate-speaking functionaries, real and imaginary Aristocracies, of me and of thee, it is imperatively demanded, "How do you mean to manage these men? Where are they to find a supportable existence? What is to become of them,—and of you!"

CHAPTER II.

BRIBERY COMMITTEE.

In the case of the late Bribery Committee, it seemed to be tho conclusion of the soundest practical minds that Bribery could not be put down; that Pure Election was a thing we had seen the last of, and must now go on without, as we best could. A conclusion not a little startling; to which it requires a practical mind of some seasoning to reconcile yourself at once! It seems, then, we are henceforth to get ourselves constituted Legislators not according to what merit we may have, or even what merit we may seem to have, but according to the length of our purse, and our frankness, impudence and dexterity in laying out the contents of the same. Our theory, written down in all books and law-books, spouted forth from all barrel-heads, is perfect purity of Tenpound Franchise, absolute sincerity of question put and answer given;—and our practice is irremediable bribery; irremediable, unpunishable, which you will do more harm than good by attempting to punish! Once more, a very startling conclusion indeed; which, whatever the soundest practical minds in Parliament may think of it, invites all British men to meditations of various kinds.

A Parliament, one would say, which proclaims itself elected and eligible by bribery, tells the Nation that is governed by it a piece of singular news. Bribery: have we reflected what bribery is? Bribery means not only length of purse, which is neither qualification nor the contrary for legislating well; but it means dishonesty, and even impudent dishonesty;—brazen insensibility to lying and to making others lie; total oblivion, and flinging overboard, for the nonce, of any real thing you can call veracity, morality; with dextrous putting on the cast-clothes of that real thing, and strutting about in them! What Legislating can you get out of a man in that fatal situation? None that will profit much, one would think! A Legislator who has left his veracity lying on the door-threshold, he, why verily he—ought to be sent out to seek it again!

Heavens, what an improvement, were there once fairly in Downing-street an Election-Office opened, with a Tariff of Boroughs! Such and such a population, amount of property-tax, ground-rental,

extent of trade; returns two Members, returns one Member, for so
much money down: Ipswich so many thousands, Nottingham so
many,—as they happened, one by one, to fall into this new Downing-street Schedule A! An incalculable improvement, in comparison: for now at least you have it fairly by length of purse, and
leave the dishonesty, the impudence, the unveracity all handsomely aside. Length of purse and desire to be a Legislator ought
to get a man into Parliament, not *with*, but if possible *without* the
unveracity, the impudence and the dishonesty! Length of purse
and desire, these are, as intrinsic qualifications, correctly equal to
zero; but they are not yet *less* than zero,—as the smallest addition of that latter sort will make them!

And is it come to this? And does our venerable Parliament
announce itself elected and eligible in this manner? Surely such
a Parliament promulgates strange horoscopes of itself. What is
to become of a Parliament elected or eligible in this manner?
Unless Belial and Beelzebub have got possession of the throne of
this Universe, such Parliament is preparing itself for new Reform-
bills. We shall have to try it by Chartism, or any conceivable *ism*,
rather than put up with this! There is already in England ' religion' enough to get six hundred and fifty-eight Consulting Men
brought together who do *not* begin work with a lie in their mouth.
Our poor old Parliament, thousands of years old, is still good for
something, for several things;—though many are beginning to ask,
with ominous anxiety, in these days: For what thing? But for
whatever thing and things Parliament be good, indisputably it
must start with other than a lie in its mouth! On the whole, a
Parliament working with a lie in its mouth, will have to take itself
away. To no Parliament or thing, that one has heard of, did this
Universe ever long yield harbour on that footing. At all hours of
the day and night, some Chartism is advancing, some armed Cromwell is advancing, to apprise such Parliament: " Ye are no Parliament. In the name of God,—go!"

In sad truth, once more, how is our whole existence, in these
present days, built on Cant, Speciosity, Falsehood, Dilettantism;
with this one serious Veracity in it: Mammonism! Dig down
where you will, through the Parliament-floor or elsewhere, how infallibly do you, at spade's depth below the service, come upon this
universal *Liars*-rock substratum! Much else is ornamental; true
on barrel-heads, in pulpits, hustings, Parliamentary benches; but
this is forever true and truest: " Money does bring money's worth;
Put money in your purse." Here, if nowhere else, is the human
soul still in thorough earnest; sincere with a prophet's sincerity:
and ' the Hell of the English,' as Sauerteig said, ' is the infinite

terror of Not getting on, especially of Not making money.' With results!

To many persons the horoscope of Parliament is more interesting than to me: but surely all men with souls must admit that sending members to Parliament by bribery is an infamous solecism; an act entirely immoral, which no man can have to do with, more or less, but he will soil his fingers more or less. No Carlton Clubs, Reform Clubs, nor any sort of clubs or creatures, or of accredited opinions or practices, can make a Lie Truth, can make Bribery a Propriety. The Parliament should really either punish and put away Bribery, or legalise it by some Office in Downing-street. As I read the Apocalypses, a Parliament that can do neither of these things is not in a good way.—And yet, alas, what of Parliaments and their Elections? Parliamentary Elections are but the topmost ultimate outcome of an electioneering which goes on at all hours, in all places, in every meeting of two or more men. It is *we* that vote wrong, and teach the poor ragged Freemen of Boroughs to vote wrong. We pay respect to those worthy of no respect.

Is not Pandarus Dogdraught a member of select clubs, and admitted into the drawingrooms of men? Visibly to all persons he is of the offal of Creation; but he carries money in his purse, due lacker on his dog-visage, and it is believed will not steal spoons. The human species does not with one voice, like the Hebrew Psalmist, 'shun to sit' with Dogdraught, refuse totally to dine with Dogdraught; men called of honour are willing enough to dine with him, his talk being lively, and his champagne excellent. We say to ourselves, "The man is in good society,"—others have already voted for him; why should not I? We *forget* the indefeasible right of property that Satan has in Dogdraught,—we are not afraid to be near Dogdraught! It is we that vote wrong; blindly, nay. with falsity prepense! It is we that no longer know the difference between Human Worth and Human Unworth; or feel that the one is admirable and alone admirable, the other detestable, damnable! How shall *we* find out a Hero and Viceking Samson with a maximum of two shillings in his pocket? We have no chance to do such a thing. We have got out of the Ages of Heroism, deep into the Ages of Flunkeyism,—and must return or die. What a noble set of mortals are we, who, because there is no Saint Edmund threatening us at the rim of the horizon, are not afraid to be whatever, for the day and hour, is smoothest for us!

And now, in good sooth, why should an indigent discerning Freeman give his vote without bribes? Let us rather honour the poor man that he does discern clearly wherein lies, for him, the

true kernel of the matter. What is it to the ragged grimy Freeman
of a Tenpound-Franchise Borough, whether Aristides Rigmarole
Esq. of the Destructive, or the Hon. Alcides Dolittle of the Conservative Party be sent to Parliament;—much more, whether the
two-thousandth part of them be sent, for that is the amount of his
faculty in it? Destructive or Conservative, what will either of
them destroy or conserve of vital moment to this Freeman? Has
he found either of them care, at bottom, a sixpence for him or his
interests, or those of his class or of his cause, or of any class or
cause that is of much value to God or to man? Rigmarole and
Dolittle have alike cared for themselves hitherto; and for their
own clique, and self-conceited crotchets,—their greasy dishonest
interests of pudding, or windy dishonest interests of praise; and
not very perceptibly for any other interest whatever. Neither Rigmarole nor Dolittle will accomplish any good or any evil for this
grimy Freeman, like giving him a five-pound note, or refusing to
give it him. It will be smoothest to vote according to value received. That is the veritable fact; and he indigent, like others
that are not indigent, acts conformably thereto.

Why, reader, truly, if they asked thee or me, Which way we
meant to vote?—were it not our likeliest answer: Neither way!
I, as a Tenpound Franchiser, will receive no bribe; but also I will
not vote for either of these men. Neither Rigmarole nor Dolittle
shall, by furtherance of mine, go and make laws for this country.
I will have no hand in such a mission. How dare I! If other
men cannot be got in England, a totally other sort of men, different as light is from dark, as star-fire is from street-mud, what
is the use of votings, or of Parliaments in England? England
ought to resign herself; there is no hope or possibility for England. If England cannot get her Knaves and Dastards 'arrested,'
in some degree, but only get them 'elected,' what is to become of
England?

I conclude, with all confidence, that England will verily have
to put an end to briberies on her Election Hustings and elsewhere,
at what cost soever;—and likewise that we, Electors and Eligibles,
one and all of us, for our own behoof and hers, cannot too soon
begin, at what cost soever, to put an end to *bribeabilities* in ourselves. The death-leprosy, attacked in this manner, by purifying
lotions from without and by rallying of the vital energies and
purities from within, will probably abate somewhat! It has otherwise no chance to abate.

CHAPTER III.

THE ONE INSTITUTION.

WHAT our Government can do in this grand Problem of the Working Classes of England? Yes, supposing the insane Corn-Laws totally abolished, all speech of them ended, and 'from ten to twenty years of new possibility to live and find wages' conceded us in consequence: What the English Government might be expected to accomplish or attempt towards rendering the existence of our Labouring Millions somewhat less anomalous, somewhat less impossible, in the years that are to follow those · ten or twenty,' if either 'ten' or 'twenty' there be?

It is the most momentous question. For all this of the Corn-Law Abrogation, and what can follow therefrom, is but as the shadow on King Hezekiah's Dial: the shadow has gone back twenty years; but will again, in spite of Free-Trades and Abrogations, travel forward its old fated way. With our present system of individual Mammonism, and Government by Laissez-faire, this Nation cannot live. And if, in the priceless interim, some new life and healing be not found, there is no second respite to be counted on. The shadow on the Dial advances thenceforth without pausing. What Government can do? This that they call 'Organising of Labour' is, if well understood, the Problem of the whole Future, for all who will in future pretend to govern men. But our first preliminary stage of it, How to deal with the Actual Labouring Millions of England? this is the imperatively pressing Problem of the Present, pressing with a truly fearful intensity and imminence in these very years and days. No Government can longer neglect it: once more, what can our Government do in it?

Governments are of very various degrees of activity: some, altogether Lazy Governments, in 'free countries' as they are called, seem in these times almost to profess to do, if not nothing, one knows not at first what. To debate in Parliament, and gain majorities; and ascertain who shall be. with a toil hardly second to Ixion's, the Prime Speaker and Spoke-holder. and keep the Ixion's-Wheel going, if not forward, yet round? Not altogether so:— much, to the experienced eye, is not what it seems! Chancery and certain other Law-Courts seem nothing: yet in fact they are, the worst of them, something: chimneys for the devilry and contention of men to escape by;—a very considerable something! Parliament too has its tasks, if thou wilt look; fit to wear out the

lives of toughest men. The celebrated Kilkenny Cats, through
their tumultuous congress, cleaving the ear of Night, could they
be said to do nothing? Hadst thou been of them, thou hadst
seen! The feline heart laboured, as with steam up — to the bursting point; and death-doing energy nerved every muscle: they had
a work there; and did it! On the morrow, two tails were found
left, and peaceable annihilation; a neighbourhood *delivered* from
despair.

Again, are not Spinning-Dervishes an eloquent emblem, significant of much? Hast thou noticed him, that solemn-visaged Turk,
the eyes shut; dingy wool mantle circularly hiding his figure; —
bell-shaped; like a dingy bell set spinning on the *tongue* of it? By
centrifugal force the dingy wool mantle heaves itself; spreads more
and more, like upturned cup widening into upturned saucer: thus
spins he, to the praise of Allah and advantage of mankind, fast
and faster, till collapse ensue, and sometimes death! —

A Government such as ours, consisting of from seven to eight
hundred Parliamentary Talkers, with their escort of Able Editors
and Public Opinion; and for head, certain Lords and Servants of
the Treasury, and Chief Secretaries and others, who find themselves
at once Chiefs and No-Chiefs, and often commanded rather than
commanding, — is doubtless a most complicate entity, and none of
the alertest for getting on with business! Clearly enough, if the
Chiefs be not self-motive and what we call men, but mere patient
lay-figures without self-motive principle, the Government will not
move anywhither; it will tumble disastrously, and jumble, round
its own axis, as for many years past we have seen it do.—And yet
a self-motive man who is not a lay-figure, place him in the heart of
what entity you may, will make it move more or less! The absurd-
est in Nature he will make a little *less* absurd, he. The unwieldiest
he will make to move;—that is the use of his existing there. He
will at least have the manfulness to depart out of it, if not; to say:
"I cannot move in thee, and be a man; like a wretched drift-log
dressed in man's clothes and minister's clothes, doomed to a lot
baser than belongs to man, I will not continue with thee, tumbling
aimless on the Mother of Dead Dogs here:—Adieu!"

For, on the whole, it is the lot of Chiefs everywhere, this same.
No Chief in the most despotic country but was a Servant withal;
at once an absolute commanding General, and a poor Orderly-Ser-
geant, ordered by the very men in the ranks, — obliged to collect
the vote of the ranks too, in some articulate or inarticulate shape,
and weigh well the same. The proper name of all Kings is Minister, Servant. In no conceivable Government can a lay-figure get
forward! *This* Worker, surely he above all others has to 'spread

out his Gideon's Fleece,' and collect the monitions of Immensity; the poor Localities, as we said, and Parishes of Palace-yard or elsewhere, having no due monition in them. A Prime Minister, even here in England, who shall dare believe the heavenly omens, and address himself like a man and hero to the great dumb-struggling heart of England; and speak out for it, and act out for it, the God's-Justice it is writhing to get uttered and perishing for want of,—yes, he too will see awaken round him, in passionate burning all-defiant loyalty, the heart of England, and such a 'support' as no Division-List or Parliamentary Majority was ever yet known to yield a man! Here as there, now as then, he who can and dare trust the heavenly Immensities, all earthly Localities are subject to him. We will pray for such a Man and First-Lord;—yes, and far better, we will strive and incessantly make ready, each of us, to be worthy to serve and second such a First-Lord! We shall then be as good as sure of his arriving; sure of many things, let him arrive or not.

Who can despair of Governments that passes a Soldier's Guard-house, or meets a redcoated man on the streets! That a body of men could be got together to kill other men when you bade them: this, *a priori*, does it not seem one of the impossiblest things? Yet look, behold it: in the stolidest of Donothing Governments, that impossibility is a thing done. See it there, with buff-belts, red coats on its back; walking sentry at guardhouses, brushing white breeches in barracks; an indisputable palpable fact. Out of gray Antiquity, amid all finance-difficulties, *scaccarium*-tallies, ship-moneys, coat-and-conduct moneys, and vicissitudes of Chance and Time, there; down to the present blessed hour, it is.

Often, in these painfully decadent and painfully nascent Times, with their distresses, inarticulate gaspings and 'impossibilities;' meeting a tall Lifeguardsman in his snow-white trousers, or seeing those two statuesque Lifeguardsmen in their frowning bearskins, pipe-clayed buckskins. on their coal-black sleek-fiery quadrupeds, riding sentry at the Horse-Guards,—it strikes one with a kind of mournful interest, how, in such universal down-rushing and wrecked impotence of almost all old institutions, this oldest Fighting Institution is still so young! Fresh-complexioned, firm-limbed, six feet by the standard, this fighting-man has verily been got up, and can fight. While so much has not yet got into being; while so much has gone gradually out of it, and become an empty Semblance or Clothes-suit; and highest king's-cloaks, mere chimeras parading under them so long, are getting unsightly to the

T

earnest eye, unsightly, almost offensive, like a costlier kind of scarecrow's-blanket,—here still is a reality!

The man in horsehair wig advances, promising that he will get me 'justice:' he takes me into Chancery Law-Courts, into decades, half-centuries of hubbub, of distracted jargon; and does *get* me— disappointment, almost desperation; and one refuge: that of dismissing him and his 'justice' altogether out of my head. For I have work to do; I cannot spend my decades in mere arguing with other men about the exact wages of my work: I will work cheerfully with no wages, sooner than with a ten-years gangrene or Chancery Lawsuit in my heart! He of the horsehair wig is a sort of failure; no substance, but a fond imagination of the mind. He of the shovel-hat, again, who comes forward professing that he will save my soul—O ye Eternities, of him in this place be absolute silence!—But he of the red coat, I say, is a success and no failure! He will veritably, if he get orders, draw out a long sword and kill me. No mistake there. He is a fact and not a shadow. Alive in this Year Forty-three, able and willing to do *his* work. In dim old centuries, with William Rufus, William of Ipres, or far earlier, he began; and has come down safe so far. Catapult has given place to cannon, pike has given place to musket, iron mail-shirt to coat of red cloth, saltpetre ropematch to percussion cap; equipments, circumstances have all changed, and again changed: but the human battle-engine, in the inside of any or of each of these, ready still to do battle, stands there, six feet in standard size. There are Pay-Offices, Woolwich Arsenals, there is a Horse-Guards, War-Office, Captain-General; persuasive Sergeants, with tap of drum, recruit in market-towns and villages;—and, on the whole, I say, here is your actual drilled fighting-man; here are your actual Ninety-thousand of such, ready to go into any quarter of the world and fight!

Strange, interesting, and yet most mournful to reflect on. Was this, then, of all the things mankind had some talent for, the one thing important to learn well, and bring to perfection; this of successfully killing one another? Truly you have learned it well, and carried the business to a high perfection. It is incalculable what, by arranging, commanding and regimenting, you can make of men. These thousand straight-standing firmset individuals, who shoulder arms, who march, wheel, advance, retreat; and are, for your behoof, a magazine charged with fiery death, in the most perfect condition of potential activity: few months ago, till the persuasive sergeant came, what were they? Multiform ragged losels, runaway apprentices, starved weavers, thievish valets; an entirely broken population, fast tending towards the treadmill. But the persuasive sergeant came; by tap of drum enlisted, or formed lists of them, took heartily to drilling them;—and he and you have made them this! Most potent, effectual for all work whatsoever, is wise planning, firm combining and commanding among men. Let no man despair of Governments who looks on these two sentries at the Horse-Guards, and our United-Service Clubs! I could conceive an Emigration Service, a Teaching Service, considerable varieties of United and Separate Services, of the due thousands strong, all effective as this Fighting Service is; all doing *their* work, like it;—which work, much more than fighting, is henceforth the necessity of these New Ages we are got into! Much lies among us, convulsively, nigh desperately *struggling to be born.*

But mean Governments, as mean-limited individuals do, have stood by the physically indispensable; have realised that and nothing more. The Soldier is perhaps one of the most difficult things to realise; but Governments, had they not realised him, could not have existed: accordingly he is here. O Heavens, if we saw an army ninety-thousand strong, maintained and fully equipt, in continual real action and battle against Human Starvation, against Chaos, Necessity, Stupidity, and our real ' natural enemies,' what a business were it! Fighting and molesting not ' the French,' who, poor men, have a hard enough battle of their own in the like kind, and need no additional molesting from us; but fighting and incessantly spearing down and destroying Falsehood, Nescience, Delusion, Disorder, and the Devil and his Angels! Thou thyself, cultivated reader, hast done something in that alone true warfare; but, alas, under what circumstances was it? Thee no beneficent drill-sergeant, with any effectiveness, would rank in line beside thy fellows; train, like a true didactic artist, by the wit of all past experience, to do thy soldiering; encourage thee when right, punish thee when wrong, and everywhere with wise word-of-command say, Forward on this hand, Forward on that! Ah, no: thou hadst to learn thy small-sword and platoon exercise where and how thou couldst; to all mortals but thyself it was indifferent whether thou shouldst ever learn it. And the rations, and shilling a day, were they provided thee,—reduced as I have known brave Jean-Pauls, learning their exercise, to live on ' water *without* the bread?' The rations; or any furtherance of promotion to corporalship, lance-corporalship, or due cat-o'-nine tails, with the slightest reference to thy deserts, were not provided. Forethought, even as of a pipe-clayed drill-sergeant, did not preside over thee. To corporalship, lance-corporalship, thou didst attain; alas, also to the halberts and cat: but thy rewarder and punisher seemed blind as the Deluge: neither lance-corporalship, nor even drummer's cat, because both appeared delirious, brought thee due profit.

It was well, all this, we know;—and yet it was not well! Forty soldiers, I am told, will disperse the largest Spitalfields mob: forty to ten-thousand, that is the proportion between drilled and undrilled. Much there is which cannot yet be organised in this world; but somewhat also which can, somewhat also which must. When one thinks, for example, what Books are become and becoming for us, what Operative Lancashires are become; what a Fourth Estate, and innumerable Virtualities not yet got to be Actualities are become and becoming,—one sees Organisms enough in the dim huge Future; and ' United Services' quite other than the redcoat one; and much, even in these years, struggling to be born!

Of Time-Bill, Factory-Bill and other such Bills the present Editor has no authority to speak. He knows not, it is for others than he to know, in what specific ways it may be feasible to interfere, with Legislation, between the Workers and the Master-Workers;—knows only and sees, what all men are beginning to see, that Legislative interference, and interferences not a few are indispensable; that as a lawless anarchy of supply-and-demand, on market-wages alone, this province of things cannot longer be left. Nay interference has begun: there are already Factory Inspectors, —who seem to have no *lack* of work. Perhaps there might be Mine-Inspectors too:—might there not be Furrowfield Inspectors withal, and ascertain for us how on seven and sixpence a week a human family does live! Interference has begun; it must continue, must extensively enlarge itself, deepen and sharpen itself. Such things cannot longer be idly lapped in darkness, and suffered to go on unseen: the Heavens do see them; the curse, not the blessing of the Heavens is on an Earth that refuses to see them.

Again, are not Sanitary Regulations possible for a Legislature? The old Romans had their Ædiles; who would, I think, in direct contravention to supply-and-demand, have rigorously seen rammed up into total abolition many a foul cellar in our Southwarks, Saint-Gileses, and dark poison-lanes; saying sternly, " Shall a Roman man dwell there?" The Legislature, at whatever cost of consequences, would have had to answer, " God forbid!"—The Legislature, even as it now is, could order all dingy Manufacturing Towns to cease from their soot and darkness; to let in the blessed sunlight, the blue of Heaven, and become clear and clean; to burn their coal-smoke, namely, and make flame of it. Baths, free air, a wholesome temperature, ceilings twenty feet high, might be ordained, by Act of Parliament, in all establishments licensed as Mills. There are such Mills already extant;—honour to the builders of them! The Legislature can say to others: Go ye and do likewise; better if you can.

Every toiling Manchester, its smoke and soot all burnt, ought it not, among so many world-wide conquests, to have a hundred acres or so of free greenfield, with trees on it, conquered, for its little children to disport in; for its all-conquering workers to take a breath of twilight air in? You would say so! A willing Legislature could say so with effect. A willing Legislature could say very many things! And to whatsoever 'vested interest,' or such like, stood up, gainsaying merely, " I shall lose profits,"—the willing Legislature would answer, " Yes, but my sons and daughters will gain health, and life, and a soul."—" What is to become of our Cotton-trade?" cried certain Spinners, when the Factory Bill was proposed; " What is to become of our invaluable Cotton-trade?" The Humanity of England answered stedfastly: " Deliver me these rickety perishing souls of infants, and let your Cotton-trade take its chance. God Himself commands the one thing; not God especially the other thing. We cannot have prosperous Cotton-trades at the expense of keeping the Devil a partner in them!"—

Bills enough, were the Corn-Law Abrogation Bill once passed, and a Legislature willing! Nay this one Bill, which lies yet un-enacted, a right Education Bill, is not this of itself the sure parent of innumerable wise Bills,—wise regulations, practical methods and proposals, gradually ripening towards the state of Bills? To irradiate with intelligence, that is to say, with order, arrangement and all blessedness, the Chaotic, Unintelligent: how, except by educating, *can* you accomplish this? That thought, reflection, ar-ticulate utterance and understanding be awakened in these indivi-dual million heads, which are the atoms of your Chaos: there is no other way of illuminating any Chaos! The sum-total of intelli-gence that is found in it, determines the extent of order that is possible for your Chaos,—the feasibility and rationality of what your Chaos will dimly demand from you, and will gladly obey when proposed by you! It is an exact equation; the one accu-rately measures the other.—If the whole English People, during these 'twenty years of respite,' be not educated, with at least schoolmaster's educating, a tremendous responsibility, before God and men, will rest somewhere! How dare any man, especially a man calling himself minister of God, stand up in any Parliament or place, under any pretext or delusion, and for a day or an hour forbid God's Light to come into the world, and bid the Devil's Darkness continue in it one hour more! For all light and science,

under all shapes, in all degrees of perfection, is of God; all darkness, nescience, is of the Enemy of God. ' The schoolmaster's
creed is somewhat awry?' Yes, I have found few creeds entirely
correct; few light-beams shining *white*, pure of admixture: but of
all creeds and religions now or ever before known, was not that of
thoughtless thriftless Animalism, of Distilled Gin, and Stupor and
Despair, unspeakably the least orthodox? We will exchange *it*
even with Paganism, with Fetishism; and, on the whole, must exchange it with something.

An effective ' Teaching Service' I do consider that there must
be; some Education Secretary, Captain-General of Teachers, who
will actually contrive to get us *taught*. Then again, why should
there not be an ' Emigration Service,' and Secretary, with adjuncts,
with funds, forces, idle Navy-ships, and ever-increasing apparatus;
in fine an *effective system* of Emigration; so that, at length, before
our twenty years of respite ended, every honest willing Workman
who found England too strait, and the ' Organisation of Labour'
not yet sufficiently advanced, might find likewise a bridge built to
carry him into new Western Lands, there to ' organise' with more
elbow-room some labour for himself? There to be a real blessing,
raising new corn for us, purchasing new webs and hatchets from
us; leaving us at least in peace;—instead of staying here to be a
Physical-Force Chartist, unblessed and no blessing! Is it not
scandalous to consider that a Prime Minister could raise within
the year, as I have seen it done, a Hundred and Twenty Millions
Sterling to shoot the French; and we are stopt short for want of
the hundredth part of that to keep the English living? The bodies
of the English living, and the souls of the English living:—these
two ' Services,' an Education Service and an Emigration Service,
these with others will actually have to be organised!

A free bridge for Emigrants: why, we should then be on a par
with America itself, the most favoured of all lands that have no
government; and we should have, besides, so many traditions and
mementos of priceless things which America has cast away. We
could proceed deliberately to ' organise Labour,' not doomed to
perish unless we effected it within year and day;—every willing
Worker that proved superfluous, finding a bridge ready for him.
This verily will have to be done; the Time is big with this. Our
little Isle is grown too narrow for us; but the world is wide enough
yet for another Six Thousand Years. England's sure markets will
be among new Colonies of Englishmen in all quarters of the Globe.
All men trade with all men, when mutually convenient; and are
even bound to do it by the Maker of men. Our friends of China,
who guiltily refused to trade, in these circumstances,—had we not

to argue with them, in cannon-shot at last, and convince them that
they ought to trade! 'Hostile Tariffs' will arise, to shut us out;
and then again will fall, to let us in: but the Sons of England,
speakers of the English language were it nothing more, will in all
times have the ineradicable predisposition to trade with England.
Mycale was the *Pan-Ionion*, rendezvous of all the Tribes of Ion, for
old Greece: why should not London long continue the *All-Saxon-
home*, rendezvous of all the 'Children of the Harz-Rock,' arriving,
in select samples, from the Antipodes and elsewhere, by steam
and otherwise, to the 'season' here!—What a Future; wide as the
world, if we have the heart and heroism for it,—which, by Heaven's blessing, we shall:

> 'Keep not standing fixed and rooted,
> Briskly venture, briskly roam;
> Head and hand, where'er thou foot it,
> And stout heart are still at home.
>
> In what land the sun does visit,
> Brisk are we, whate'er betide:
> To give space for wandering is it
> That the world was made so wide.'[1]

Fourteen hundred years ago, it was by a considerable 'Emigration
Service,' never doubt it, by much enlistment, discussion and apparatus, that we ourselves arrived in this remarkable Island,—and
got into our present difficulties among others!

It is true the English Legislature, like the English People, is
of slow temper; essentially conservative. In our wildest periods
of reform, in the Long Parliament itself, you notice always the
invincible instinct to hold fast by the Old; to admit the *minimum*
of New; to expand, if it be possible. some old habit or method,
already found fruitful, into new growth for the new need. It is
an instinct worthy of all honour; akin to all strength and all wisdom. The Future hereby is not dissevered from the Past, but
based continuously on it; grows with all the vitalities of the Past,
and is rooted down deep into the beginnings of us. The English
Legislature is entirely repugnant to believe in 'new epochs.' The
English Legislature does not occupy itself with epochs; has, indeed, other business to do than looking at the Time-Horologe and
hearing it tick! Nevertheless new epochs do actually come; and
with them new imperious peremptory necessities; so that even an
English Legislature has to look up, and admit, though with reluctance, that the hour has struck. The hour having struck, let us
not say 'impossible:'—it will have to be possible! 'Contrary to

[1] Goethe, *Wilhelm Meister.*

the habits of Parliament, the habits of Government?' Yes: but did any Parliament or Government ever sit in a Year Forty-three before? One of the most original, unexampled years and epochs; in several important respects, totally unlike any other! For Time, all-edacious and all-feracious, does run on: and the Seven Sleepers, awakening hungry after a hundred years, find that it is not their old nurses who can now give them suck!

For the rest, let not any Parliament, Aristocracy, Millocracy, or Member of the Governing Class, condemn with much triumph this small specimen of 'remedial measures;' or ask again, with the least anger, of this Editor, What is to be done, How that alarming problem of the Working Classes is to be managed? Editors are not here, foremost of all, to say How. A certain Editor thanks the gods that nobody pays him three hundred thousand pounds a year, two hundred thousand, twenty thousand, or any similar sum of cash for saying How;—that his wages are very different, his work somewhat fitter for him. An Editor's stipulated work is to apprise *thee* that it must be done. The 'way to do it,'— is to try it, knowing that thou shalt die if it be not done. There is the bare back, there is the web of cloth; thou shalt cut me a coat to cover the bare back, thou whose trade it is. 'Impossible?' Hapless Fraction, dost thou discern Fate there, half unveiling herself in the gloom of the future, with her gibbet-cords, her steel-whips, and very authentic Tailor's Hell; waiting to see whether it is 'possible?' Out with thy scissors, and cut that cloth or thy own windpipe!

CHAPTER IV.

CAPTAINS OF INDUSTRY.

If I believed that Mammonism with its adjuncts was to continue henceforth the one serious principle of our existence, I should reckon it idle to solicit remedial measures from any Government, the disease being insusceptible of remedy. Government can do much, but it can in no wise do all. Government, as the most conspicuous object in Society, is called upon to give signal of what shall be done; and, in many ways, to preside over, further, and command the doing of it. But the Government cannot do, by all its signalling and commanding, what the Society is radically indisposed to do. In the long-run every Government is the exact symbol of its People, with their wisdom and unwisdom; we have to say, Like People like Government.—The main substance of this immense Problem of Organising Labour, and first of all of Managing the Working Classes, will, it is very clear, have to be solved by those who stand practically in the middle of it; by those who themselves work and preside over work. Of all that can be enacted by any Parliament in regard to it, the germs must already lie potentially extant in those two Classes, who are to obey such enactment. A Human Chaos *in* which there is no light, you vainly attempt to irradiate by light shed *on* it: order never can arise there.

But it is my firm conviction that the 'Hell of England' will *cease* to be that of 'not making money;' that we shall get a nobler Hell and a nobler Heaven! I anticipate light *in* the Human Chaos, glimmering, shining more and more; under manifold true signals from without That light shall shine. Our deity no longer being Mammon,—O Heavens, each man will then say to himself: "Why such deadly haste to make money? I shall not go to Hell, even if I do not make money! There is another Hell, I am told!" Competition, at railway-speed, in all branches of commerce and work will then abate :—good felt-hats for the head, in every sense, instead of seven-feet lath-and-plaster hats on wheels, will then be discoverable! Bubble-periods, with their panics and commercial crises, will again become infrequent; steady modest industry will take the place of gambling speculation. To be a noble Master, among noble Workers, will again be the first ambition with some few; to be a rich Master only the second. How the Inventive Genius of England, with the whirr of its bobbins and billy-rollers shoved somewhat into the backgrounds of the brain, will contrive and devise, not cheaper produce exclusively, but fairer distribution of the produce at its present cheapness! By degrees, we shall again have a Society with something of Heroism in it, something of Heaven's Blessing on it; we shall again have, as my German friend asserts, 'instead of Mammon-Feudalism with un-'sold cotton-shirts and Preservation of the Game, noble just In-'dustrialism and Government by the Wisest!'

It is with the hope of awakening here and there a British man to know himself for a man and divine soul, that a few words of parting admonition, to all persons to whom the Heavenly Powers have lent power of any kind in this land, may now be addressed. And first to those same Master-Workers, Leaders of Industry; who stand nearest, and in fact powerfullest, though not most prominent, being as yet in too many senses a Virtuality rather than an Actuality.

The Leaders of Industry, if Industry is ever to be led, are virtually the Captains of the World; if there be no nobleness in

them, there will never be an Aristocracy more.   But let the Captains of Industry consider : once again, are they born of other
clay than the old Captains of Slaughter; doomed forever to be no
Chivalry, but a mere gold-plated *Doggery*,—what the French well
name *Canaille*, ' Doggery' with more or less gold carrion at its
disposal ?   Captains of Industry are the true Fighters, henceforth
recognisable as the only true ones : Fighters against Chaos, Necessity and the Devils and Jötuns ; and lead on Mankind in that
great, and alone true, and universal warfare ; the stars in their
courses fighting for them, and all Heaven and all Earth saying
audibly, Well done ! Let the Captains of Industry retire into
their own hearts, and ask solemnly, If there is nothing but vulturous hunger, for fine wines, valet reputation and gilt carriages,
discoverable there ?   Of hearts made by the Almighty God I will
not believe such a thing.   Deep-hidden under wretchedest godforgetting Cants, Epicurisms, Dead-Sea Apisms ; forgotten as under foullest fat Lethe mud and weeds, there is yet, in all hearts
born into this God's-World, a spark of the Godlike slumbering.
Awake, O nightmare sleepers; awake, arise, or be forever fallen !
This is not playhouse poetry; it is sober fact.   Our England, our
world cannot live as it is.   It will connect itself with a God again,
or go down with nameless throes and fire-consummation to the
Devils.   Thou who feelest aught of such a Godlike stirring in
thee, any faintest intimation of it as through heavy-laden dreams,
follow *it*, I conjure thee.   Arise, save thyself, be one of those that
save thy country.

Bucaniers, Chactaw Indians, whose supreme aim in fighting
is that they may get the scalps, the money, that they may amass
scalps and money : out of such came no Chivalry, and never will !
Out of such came only gore and wreck, infernal rage and misery ;
desperation quenched in annihilation.   Behold it, I bid thee, behold there, and consider !   What is it that thou have a hundred
thousand-pound bills laid up in thy strong-room, a hundred scalps
hung up in thy wigwam ?   I value not them or thee.   Thy scalps
and thy thousand-pound bills are as yet nothing, if no nobleness
from within irradiate them ; if no Chivalry, in action, or in embryo
ever struggling towards birth and action, be there.

Love of men cannot be bought by cash-payment; and without
love, men cannot endure to be together.   You cannot lead a Fighting World without having it regimented, chivalried : the thing,
in a day, becomes impossible; all men in it, the highest at first,
the very lowest at last, discern consciously, or by a noble instinct,
this necessity.   And can you any more continue to lead a Working World unregimented, anarchic ?   I answer, and the Heavens

and Earth are now answering, No! The thing becomes not 'in a day' impossible; but in some two generations it does. Yes, when fathers and mothers, in Stockport hunger-cellars, begin to eat their children, and Irish widows have to prove their relationship by dying of typhus-fever; and amid Governing 'Corporations of the Best and Bravest,' busy to preserve their game by 'bushing,' dark millions of God's human creatures start up in mad Chartisms, impracticable Sacred-Months, and Manchester Insurrections;—and there is a virtual Industrial Aristocracy as yet only half-alive, spell-bound amid money-bags and ledgers; and an actual Idle Aristocracy seemingly near dead in somnolent delusions, in trespasses and double-barrels; 'sliding,' as on inclined-planes, which every new year they *soap* with new Hansard's-jargon under God's sky, and so are 'sliding' ever faster, towards a 'scale' and balance-scale whereon is written *Thou art found Wanting:*—in such days, after a generation or two, I say, it does become, even to the low and simple, very palpably impossible! No Working World, any more than a Fighting World, can be led on without a noble Chivalry of Work, and laws and fixed rules which follow out of that,—far nobler than any Chivalry of Fighting was. As an anarchic multitude on mere Supply-and-demand, it is becoming inevitable that we dwindle in horrid suicidal convulsion, and self-abrasion, frightful to the imagination, into *Chactaw* Workers. With wigwams and scalps,—with palaces and thousand-pound bills; with savagery, depopulation, chaotic desolation! Good Heavens, will not one French Revolution and Reign of Terror suffice us, but must there be two? There will be two if needed; there will be twenty if needed; there will be precisely as many as are needed. The Laws of Nature will have themselves fulfilled. That is a thing certain to me.

Your gallant battle-hosts and work-hosts, as the others did, will need to be made loyally yours; they must and will be regulated, methodically secured in their just share of conquest under you;—joined with you in veritable brotherhood, sonhood, by quite other and deeper ties than those of temporary day's wages! How would mere redcoated regiments, to say nothing of chivalries, fight for you, if you could discharge them on the evening of the battle, on payment of the stipulated shillings,—and they discharge you on the morning of it! Chelsea Hospitals, pensions, promotions, rigorous lasting covenant on the one side and on the other, are indispensable even for a hired fighter. The Feudal Baron, much more,—how could he subsist with mere temporary mercenaries round him, at sixpence a day; ready to go over to the other side, if sevenpence were offered? He could not have subsisted;—and his noble instinct saved him from the necessity of even trying! The Feudal Baron had a Man's Soul in him; to which anarchy, mutiny, and the other fruits of temporary mercenaries, were intolerable: he had never been a Baron otherwise, but had continued a Chactaw and Bucanier. He felt it precious, and at last it became habitual, and his fruitful enlarged existence included it as a necessity, to have men round him who in heart loved him; whose life he watched over with rigour yet with love; who were prepared to give their life for him, if need came. It was beautiful; it was human! Man lives not otherwise, nor can live contented, anywhere or anywhen. Isolation is the sum-total of wretchedness to man. To be cut off, to be left solitary: to have a world alien, not your world; all a hostile camp for you; not a home at all, of hearts and faces who are yours, whose you are! It is the frightfullest enchantment; too truly a work of the Evil One. To have neither superior, nor inferior, nor equal, united manlike to you. Without father, without child, without brother. Man knows no sadder destiny. ' How is each of us,' exclaims Jean Paul, ' so lonely in the wide bosom of the All!' Encased each as in his transparent ' ice-palace;' our brother visible in his, making signals and gesticulations to us;—visible, but forever unattainable: on his bosom we shall never rest, nor he on ours. It was not a God that did this; no!

Awake, ye noble Workers, warriors in the one true war: all this must be remedied. It is you who are already half-alive, whom I will welcome into life; whom I will conjure in God's name to shake off your enchanted sleep, and live wholly! Cease to count scalps, gold-purses; not in these lies your or our salvation. Even these, if you count only these, will not long be left. Let bucaniering be put far from you; alter, speedily abrogate all laws of the bucaniers, if you would gain any victory that shall endure. Let God's justice, let pity, nobleness and manly valour, with more gold-purses or with fewer, testify themselves in this your brief Life-transit to all the Eternities, the Gods and Silences. It is to you I call; for ye are not dead, ye are already half-alive: there is in you a sleepless dauntless energy, the prime-matter of all nobleness in man. Honour to you in your kind. It is to you I call: ye know at least this, That the mandate of God to His creature man is: Work! The future Epic of the World rests not with those that are near dead, but with those that are alive, and those that are coming into life.

Look around you. Your world-hosts are all in mutiny, in confusion, destitution; on the eve of fiery wreck and madness! They will not march farther for you, on the sixpence a day and supply-

and-demand principle: they will not; nor ought they, nor can they. Ye shall reduce them to order, begin reducing them. To order, to just subordination; noble loyalty in return for noble guidance. Their souls are driven nigh mad; let yours be sane and ever saner. Not as a bewildered bewildering mob; but as a firm regimented mass, with real captains over them, will these men march any more. All human interests, combined human endeavours, and social growths in this world, have, at a certain stage of their development, required organising: and Work, the grandest of human interests, does now require it.

God knows, the task will be hard: but no noble task was ever easy. This task will wear away your lives, and the lives of your sons and grandsons: but for what purpose, if not for tasks like this, were lives given to men? Ye shall cease to count your thousand-pound scalps, the noble of you shall cease! Nay the very scalps, as I say, will not long be left if you count only these. Ye shall cease wholly to be barbarous vulturous Chactaws, and become noble European Nineteenth-Century Men. Ye shall know that Mammon, in never such gigs and flunkey 'respectabilities,' is not the alone God; that of himself he is but a Devil, and even a Brute-god.

Difficult? Yes, it will be difficult. The short-fibre cotton; that too was difficult. The waste cotton-shrub, long useless, disobedient, as the thistle by the wayside,—have ye not conquered it; made it into beautiful bandana webs; white woven shirts for men; bright-tinted air-garments wherein flit goddesses? Ye have shivered mountains asunder, made the hard iron pliant to you as soft putty: the Forest-giants, Marsh-jötuns bear sheaves of golden grain; Ægir the Sea-demon himself stretches his back for a sleek highway to you, and on Firehorses and Windhorses ye career. Ye are most strong. Thor red-bearded, with his blue sun-eyes, with his cheery heart and strong thunder-hammer, he and you have prevailed. Ye are most strong, ye Sons of the icy North, of the far East,—far marching from your rugged Eastern Wildernesses, hitherward from the gray Dawn of Time! Ye are Sons of the *Jötun*-land; the land of Difficulties Conquered. Difficult? You must try this thing. Once try it with the understanding that it will and shall have to be done. Try it as ye try the paltrier thing, making of money' I will bet on you once more, against all Jötuns, Tailor-gods, Double-barrelled Law-wards, and Denizens of Chaos whatsoever!

CHAPTER V.

PERMANENCE.

STANDING on the threshold, nay as yet outside the threshold, of a 'Chivalry of Labour,' and an immeasurable Future which it is to fill with fruitfulness and verdant shade; where so much has not yet come even to the rudimental state, and all speech of positive enactments were hazardous in those who know this business only by the eye,—let us here hint at simply one widest universal principle, as the basis from which all organisation hitherto has grown up among men, and all henceforth will have to grow: The principle of Permanent Contract instead of Temporary.

Permanent not Temporary:—you do not hire the mere red-coated fighter by the day, but by the score of years! Permanence, persistence is the first condition of all fruitfulness in the ways of men. The 'tendency to persevere,' to persist in spite of hindrances, discouragements and 'impossibilities:' it is this that in all things distinguishes the strong soul from the weak; the civilised burgher from the nomadic savage,—the Species Man from the Genus Ape! The Nomad has his very house set on wheels; the Nomad, and in a still higher degree the Ape, are all for 'liberty;' the privilege to flit continually is indispensable for them. Alas, in how many ways, does our humour, in this swift-rolling self-abrading Time, show itself nomadic, apelike; mournful enough to him that looks on it with eyes! This humour will have to abate; it is the first element of all fertility in human things, that such 'liberty' of apes and nomads do by freewill or constraint abridge itself, give place to a better. The civilised man lives not in wheeled houses. He builds stone castles, plants lands, makes lifelong marriage-contracts;—has long-dated hundred-fold possessions, not to be valued in the money-market; has pedigrees, libraries, law-codes; has memories and hopes, even for this Earth, that reach over thousands of years. Lifelong marriage-contracts: how much preferable were year-long or month-long—to the nomad or ape!

Month-long contracts please me little, in any province where there can by possibility be found virtue enough for more. Month-long contracts do not answer well even with your house-servants; the liberty on both sides to change every month is growing very apelike, nomadic;—and I hear philosophers predict that it will alter, or that strange results will follow: that wise men, pestered with nomads, with unattached ever-shifting spies and enemies

rather than friends and servants, will gradually, weighing substance against semblance, with indignation, dismiss such, down
almost to the very shoeblack, and say, "Begone; I will serve myself rather, and have peace!" Gurth was hired for life to Cedric,
and Cedric to Gurth. O Anti-Slavery Convention, loud-sounding
long-eared Exeter-Hall—But in thee too is a kind of instinct towards justice, and I will complain of nothing. Only black Quashee
over the seas being once sufficiently attended to, wilt thou not
perhaps open thy dull sodden eyes to the 'sixty-thousand valets
'in London itself who are yearly dismissed to the streets, to be
'what they can, when the season ends;'—or to the hungerstricken,
pallid, *yellow*-coloured 'Free Labourers' in Lancashire, Yorkshire,
Buckinghamshire, and all other shires! These Yellow-coloured,
for the present, absorb all my sympathies: if I had a Twenty Millions, with Model-Farms and Niger Expeditions, it is to these that
I would give it! Quashee has already victuals, clothing; Quashee
is not dying of such despair as the yellow-coloured pale man's.
Quashee, it must be owned, is hitherto a kind of blockhead. The
Haiti Duke of Marmalade, educated now for almost half a century,
seems to have next to no sense in him. Why, in one of those Lancashire Weavers, dying of hunger, there is more thought and
heart, a greater arithmetical amount of misery and desperation,
than in whole gangs of Quashees. It must be owned, thy eyes are
of the sodden sort; and with thy emancipations, and thy twenty-
millionings and long-eared clamourings, thou, like Robespierre
with his pasteboard *Etre Suprême*, threatenest to become a bore to
us: *Avec ton Etre Suprême tu commences m'embêter!*—

In a Printed Sheet of the assiduous, much-abused, and truly
useful Mr. Chadwick's, containing queries and responses from far
and near, as to this great question, 'What is the effect of Education on working-men, in respect of their value as mere workers?'
the present Editor, reading with satisfaction a decisive unanimous verdict as to Education, reads with inexpressible interest this
special remark, put in by way of marginal incidental note, from a
practical manufacturing Quaker, whom, as he is anonymous, we
will call Friend Prudence. Prudence keeps a thousand workmen;
has striven in all ways to attach them to him; has provided con-
versational soirées; play-grounds, bands of music for the young
ones; went even 'the length of buying them a drum:' all which
has turned out to be an excellent investment. For a certain person, marked here by a black stroke, whom we shall name Blank,
living over the way,—he also keeps somewhere about a thousand
men; but has done none of these things for them, nor any other

thing, except due payment of the wages by supply-and-demand. Blank's workers are perpetually getting into mutiny, into broils and coils: every six months, we suppose, Blank has a strike; every one month, every day and every hour, they are fretting and obstructing the shortsighted Blank; pilfering from him, wasting and idling for him, omitting and committing for him. "I would not," says Friend Prudence, "exchange my workers for his *with seven thousand pounds to boot*."[1]

Right, O honourable Prudence; thou art wholly in the right: Seven thousand pounds even as a matter of profit for this world, nay for the mere cash-market of this world! And as a matter of profit not for this world only, but for the other world and all worlds, it outweighs the Bank of England!—Can the sagacious reader descry here, as it were the outmost inconsiderable rock-ledge of a universal rock-foundation, deep once more as the Centre of the World, emerging so, in the experience of this good Quaker, through the Stygian mud-vortexes and general Mother of Dead Dogs, whereon, for the present, all swags and insecurely hovers, as if ready to be swallowed?

Some Permanence of Contract is already almost possible; the principle of Permanence, year by year, better seen into and elaborated, may enlarge itself, expand gradually on every side into a system. This once secured, the basis of all good results were laid. Once permanent, you do not quarrel with the first difficulty on your path, and quit it in weak disgust; you reflect that it cannot be quitted, that it must be conquered, a wise arrangement fallen on with regard to it. Ye foolish Wedded Two, who have quarrelled, between whom the Evil Spirit has stirred up transient strife and bitterness, so that 'incompatibility' seems almost nigh, ye are nevertheless the Two who, by long habit, were it by nothing more, do best of all others suit each other: it is expedient for your own two foolish selves, to say nothing of the infants, pedigrees and public in general, that ye agree again; that ye put away the Evil Spirit, and wisely on both hands struggle for the guidance of a Good Spirit!

The very horse that is permanent, how much kindlier do his rider and he work, than the temporary one, hired on any hack principle yet known! I am for permanence in all things, at the earliest possible moment, and to the latest possible. Blessed is he that continueth where he is. Here let us rest, and lay out seedfields; here let us learn to dwell. Here, even here, the orchards that we plant will yield us fruit; the acorns will be wood and

[1] Report on the Training of Pauper Children (1841), p. 18.

pleasant umbrage, if we wait. How much grows everywhere, if we do but wait! Through the swamps we will shape causeways, force purifying drains; we will learn to thread the rocky inaccessibilities; and beaten tracks, worn smooth by mere travelling of human feet, will form themselves. Not a difficulty but can transfigure itself into a triumph; not even a deformity but, if our own soul have imprinted worth on it, will grow dear to us. The sunny plains and deep indigo transparent skies of Italy are all indifferent to the great sick heart of a Sir Walter Scott: on the back of the Apennines, in wild spring weather, the sight of bleak Scotch firs, and snow-spotted heath and desolation, brings tears into his eyes.[1]

O unwise mortals that forever change and shift, and say, Yonder, not Here! Wealth richer than both the Indies lies everywhere for man, if he will endure. Not his oaks only and his fruit-trees, his very heart roots itself wherever he will abide;—roots itself, draws nourishment from the deep fountains of Universal Being! Vagrant Sam-Slicks, who rove over the Earth doing 'strokes of trade,' what wealth have they? Horseloads, shiploads of white or yellow metal: in very sooth, what *are* these? Slick rests nowhere, he is homeless. He can build stone or marble houses; but to continue in them is denied him. The wealth of a man is the number of things which he loves and blesses, which he is loved and blessed by! The herdsman in his poor clay shealing, where his very cow and dog are friends to him, and not a cataract but carries memories for him, and not a mountain-top but nods old recognition: his life, all encircled as in blessed mother's-arms, is it poorer than Slick's with the ass-loads of yellow metal on his back? Unhappy Slick! Alas, there has so much grown nomadic, apelike, with us: so much will have, with whatever pain, repugnance and 'impossibility,' to alter itself, to fix itself again,—in some wise way, in any not delirious way!

A question arises here: Whether, in some ulterior, perhaps some not far-distant stage of this 'Chivalry of Labour,' your Master-Worker may not find it possible, and needful, to grant his Workers permanent *interest* in his enterprise and theirs? So that it become, in practical result, what in essential fact and justice it ever is, a joint enterprise; all men, from the Chief Master down to the lowest Overseer and Operative, economically as well as loyally concerned for it?—Which question I do not answer. The answer, near or else far, is perhaps, Yes;—and yet one knows the difficulties. Despotism is essential in most enterprises; I am

[1] Lockhart's *Life of Scott*.

U

told, they do not tolerate 'freedom of debate' on board a Seventy-four! Republican senate and *plebiscita* would not answer well in Cotton-Mills. And yet observe there too: Freedom, not nomad's or ape's Freedom, but man's Freedom; this is indispensable. We must have it, and will have it! To reconcile Despotism with Freedom:—well, is that such a mystery? Do you not already know the way? It is to make your Despotism *just*. Rigorous as Destiny; but just too, as Destiny and its Laws. The Laws of God: all men obey these, and have no 'Freedom' at all but in obeying them. The way is already known, part of the way;—and courage and some qualities are needed for walking on it!

CHAPTER VI.

THE LANDED.

A MAN with fifty, with five hundred, with a thousand pounds a day, given him freely, without condition at all,—on condition, as it now runs, that he will sit with his hands in his pockets and do no mischief, pass no Corn-Laws or the like,—he too, you would say, is or might be a rather strong Worker! He is a Worker with such tools as no man in this world ever before had. But in practice, very astonishing, very ominous to look at, he proves not a strong Worker;—you are too happy if he will prove but a No-worker, do nothing, and not be a Wrong-worker.

You ask him, at the year's end: "Where is your three-hundred thousand pound; what have you realised to us with that?" He answers, in indignant surprise: "Done with it? Who are you that ask? I have eaten it: I and my flunkeys, and parasites, and slaves two-footed and four-footed, in an ornamental manner; and I am here alive by it; *I* am realised by it to you!"—It is, as we have often said, such an answer as was never before given under this Sun. An answer that fills me with boding apprehension, with foreshadows of despair. O stolid Use-and-wont of an atheistic Half-century, O Ignavia, Tailor-godhood, soul-killing Cant, to what passes art thou bringing us!—Out of the loud-piping whirlwind, audibly to him that has ears, the Highest God is again announcing in these days: "Idleness shall not be." God has said it, man cannot gainsay.

Ah, how happy were it, if he this Aristocrat Worker would, in like manner, see *his* work and do it! It is frightful seeking another to do it for him. Guillotines, Meudon Tanneries, and half-a-million men shot dead, have already been expended in that business; and it is yet far from done. This man too is something; nay he is a great thing. Look on him there: a man of manful aspect; something of the 'cheerfulness of pride' still lingering in him. A free air of graceful stoicism, of easy silent dignity sits well on him; in his heart, could we reach it, lie elements of generosity, self-sacrificing justice, true human valour. Why should he, with such appliances, stand an incumbrance in the Present; perish disastrously out of the Future! From no section of the Future would we lose these noble courtesies, impalpable yet all-controlling; these dignified reticences, these kingly simplicities; —lose aught of what the fruitful Past still gives us token of, memento of, in this man. Can we not save him:—can he not help us to save him! A brave man he too; had not undivine Ignavia, Hearsay, Speech without meaning,—had not Cant, thousandfold Cant within him and around him, enveloping him like choke-damp, like thick Egyptian darkness, thrown his soul into asphyxia, as it were extinguished his soul; so that he sees not, hears not, and Moses and all the Prophets address him in vain.

Will he awaken, be alive again, and have a soul; or is this death-fit very death? It is a question of questions, for himself and for us all! Alas, is there no noble work for this man too? Has he not thickheaded ignorant boors; lazy, enslaved farmers; weedy lands? Lands! Has he not weary heavy-laden ploughers of land; immortal souls of men, ploughing, ditching, day-drudging; bare of back, empty of stomach, nigh desperate of heart; and none peaceably to help them but he, under Heaven? Does he find, with his three hundred thousand pounds, no noble thing trodden down in the thoroughfares, which it were godlike to help up? Can he do nothing for his Burns but make a Gauger of him; lionise him, bedinner him, for a foolish while; then whistle him down the wind, to desperation and bitter death?—His work too is difficult, in these modern, far-dislocated ages. But it may be done; it may be tried;—it must be done.

A modern Duke of Weimar, not a god he either, but a human duke, levied, as I reckon, in rents and taxes and all incomings whatsoever, less than several of our English Dukes do in rent alone. The Duke of Weimar, with these incomings, had to govern, judge, defend, everyway administer *his* Dukedom. He does all this as few others did: and he improves lands besides all this, makes river-embankments, maintains not soldiers only but Universities and Institutions;—and in his Court were these four men: Wieland, Herder, Schiller, Goethe. Not as parasites, which was impossible; not as table-wits and poetic Katerfeltoes; but as noble Spiritual Men working under a noble Practical Man.

Shielded by him from many miseries; perhaps from many short-comings, destructive aberrations. Heaven had sent, once more, heavenly Light into the world; and this man's honour was that he gave it welcome. A new noble kind of Clergy, under an old but still noble kind of King! I reckon that this one Duke of Weimar did more for the Culture of his Nation than all the Eng-lish Dukes and *Duces* now extant, or that were extant since Henry the Eighth gave them the Church Lands to eat, have done for theirs!—I am ashamed, I am alarmed for my English Dukes: what word have I to say?

If our Actual Aristocracy, appointed 'Best-and-Bravest,' will be wise, how inexpressibly happy for us! If not,—the voice of God from the whirlwind is very audible to me. Nay, I will thank the Great God, that He has said, in whatever fearful ways, and just wrath against us, "Idleness shall be no more!" Idleness? The awakened soul of man, all but the asphyxied soul of man, turns from it as from worse than death. It is the life-in-death of Poet Coleridge. That fable of the Dead-Sea Apes ceases to be a fable. The poor Worker starved to death is not the saddest of sights. He lies there, dead on his shield; fallen down into the bosom of his old Mother; with haggard pale face, sorrow-worn, but stilled now into divine peace, silently appeals to the Eternal God and all the Universe,—the most silent, the most eloquent of men.

Exceptions,—ah yes, thank Heaven, we know there are excep-tions. Our case were too hard, were there not exceptions, and partial exceptions not a few, whom we know, and whom we do not know. Honour to the name of Ashley,—honour to this and the other valiant Abdiel, found faithful still; who would fain, by work and by word, admonish their Order not to rush upon destruction! These are they who will, if not save their Order, postpone the wreck of it;—by whom, under blessing of the Upper Powers, 'a ' quiet euthanasia spread over generations, instead of a swift tor-' ture-death concentred into years,' may be brought about for many things. All honour and success to these. The noble man can still strive nobly to save and serve his Order;—at lowest, he can remember the precept of the Prophet: " Come out of her, my peo-ple ; come out of her !"

To sit idle aloft, like living statues, like absurd Epicurus'-gods, in pampered isolation, in exclusion from the glorious fateful bat-tlefield of this God's-World: it is a poor life for a man, when all Upholsterers and French-Cooks have done their utmost for it !— Nay, what a shallow delusion is this we have all got into, That any man should or can keep himself apart from men, have 'no business' with them, except a cash-account 'business!' It is the silliest tale a distressed generation of men ever took to telling one another. Men cannot live isolated: we *are* all bound together, for mutual good or else for mutual misery, as living nerves in the same body. No highest man can disunite himself from any lowest. Consider it. Your poor 'Werter blowing out his distracted existence because Charlotte will not have the keeping thereof:' this is no peculiar phasis; it is simply the highest expression of a phasis traceable wherever one human creature meets another! Let the meanest crookbacked Thersites teach the supremest Agamemnon that he actually does not reverence him, the supremest Agamemnon's eyes flash fire responsive; a real pain, and partial insanity, has seized Agamemnon. Strange enough: a many-counselled Ulysses is set in motion by a scoundrel-blockhead; plays tunes, like a barrel-organ, at the scoundrel-blockhead's touch,— has to snatch, namely, his sceptre-cudgel, and weal the crooked back with bumps and thumps! Let a chief of men reflect well on it. Not in having 'no business' with men, but in having no unjust business with them, and in *having* all manner of true and just business, can either his or their blessedness be found possible, and this waste world become, for both parties, a home and peopled garden.

Men do reverence men. Men do worship in that 'one temple of the world,' as Novalis calls it, the Presence of a Man! Hero-worship, true and blessed, or else mistaken, false and accursed, goes on everywhere and everywhen. In this world there is one godlike thing, the essence of all that was or ever will be of godlike in this world: the veneration done to Human Worth by the hearts of men. Hero-worship, in the souls of the heroic, of the clear and wise,—it is the perpetual presence of Heaven in our poor Earth: when it is not there, Heaven is veiled from us; and all is under Heaven's ban and interdict, and there is no worship, or worth-ship, or worth or blessedness in the Earth any more!—

Independence, 'lord of the lion-heart and eagle-eye,'—alas, yes, he is one we have got acquainted with in these late times: a very indispensable one, for spurning off with due energy innumerable sham-superiors, Tailor-made: honour to him, entire success to him! Entire success is sure to him. But he must not stop there, at that small success, with his eagle-eye. He has now a second far greater success to gain: to seek out his real superiors, whom not the Tailor but the Almighty God has made superior to him, and see a little what he will do with these! Rebel against these also? Pass by with minatory eagle-glance, with calm-sniffing mockery, or even without any mockery or sniff, when these present themselves? The lion-hearted will never dream of such a thing. Forever far be it from him! His minatory eagle-glance will veil itself in softness of the dove: his lion-heart will become a lamb's; all its just indignation changed into just reverence, dissolved in blessed floods of noble humble love, how much heavenlier than any pride, nay, if you will, how much prouder! I know him, this lion-hearted, eagle-eyed one; have met him, rushing on, 'with bosom bare,' in a very distracted dishevelled manner, the times being hard;—and can say, and guarantee on my life, That in him is no rebellion; that in him is the reverse of rebellion, the needful preparation for obedience. For if you do mean to obey God-made superiors, your first step is to sweep out the Tailor-made ones; order them, under penalties, to vanish, to make ready for vanishing!

Nay, what is best of all, he cannot rebel, if he would. Superiors whom God has made for us we cannot order to withdraw! Not in the least. No Grand-Turk himself, thickest-quilted tailor-made Brother of the Sun and Moon can do it: but an Arab Man, in cloak of his own clouting; with black beaming eyes, with flaming sovereign-heart direct from the centre of the Universe; and also, I am told, with terrible 'horse-shoe vein' of swelling wrath in his brow, and lightning (if you will not have it as light) tingling through every vein of him,—he rises; says authoritatively: "Thickest-quilted Grand-Turk, tailor-made Brother of the Sun and Moon, No:—*I* withdraw not; thou shalt obey me or withdraw!" And so accordingly it is: thickest-quilted Grand-Turks and all their progeny, to this hour, obey that man in the remarkablest manner; preferring *not* to withdraw.

O brother, it is an endless consolation to me, in this disorganic, as yet so quack-ridden, what you may well call hag-ridden and hell-ridden world, to find that disobedience to the Heavens, when they send any messenger whatever, is and remains impossible. It cannot be done; no Turk grand or small can do it. 'Show the 'dullest clodpole,' says my invaluable German friend, 'show the 'haughtiest featherhead, that a soul higher than himself is here; 'were his knees stiffened into brass, he must down and worship.'

———

CHAPTER VII.

THE GIFTED.

YES, in what tumultuous huge anarchy soever a Noble human Principle may dwell and strive, such tumult is in the way of being calmed into a fruitful sovereignty. It is inevitable. No Chaos can continue chaotic with a soul in it. Besouled with earnest human Nobleness, did not slaughter, violence and fire-eyed fury, grow into a Chivalry; into a blessed Loyalty of Governor and Governed? And in Work, which is of itself noble, and the only true fighting, there shall be no such possibility? Believe it not; it is incredible; the whole Universe contradicts it. Here too the Chactaw Principle will be subordinated; the Man Principle will, by degrees, become superior, become supreme.

I know Mammon too; Banks-of-England, Credit-Systems, world-wide possibilities of work and traffic; and applaud and admire them. Mammon is like Fire; the usefullest of all servants, if the frightfullest of all masters! The Cliffords, Fitzadelms and Chivalry Fighters 'wished to gain victory,' never doubt it: but victory, unless gained in a certain spirit, was no victory; defeat, sustained in a certain spirit, was itself victory. I say again and again, had they counted the scalps alone, they had continued Chactaws, and no Chivalry or lasting victory had been. And in Industrial Fighters and Captains is there no nobleness discoverable? To them, alone of men, there shall forever be no blessedness but in swollen coffers? To see beauty, order, gratitude, loyal human hearts around them, shall be of no moment; to see fuliginous deformity, mutiny, hatred and despair, with the addition of half-a-million guineas, shall be better? Heaven's blessedness not there; Hell's cursedness, and your half-million bits of metal, a substitute for that! Is there no profit in diffusing Heaven's blessedness, but only in gaining gold?—If so, I apprise the Mill-owner and Millionnaire, that he too must prepare for vanishing; that neither is *he* born to be of the sovereigns of this world; that he will have to be trampled and chained down in whatever terrible ways, and brass-collared safe, among the born thralls of this world! We cannot have *Canailles* and Doggeries that will not make some Chivalry of themselves: our noble Planet is impatient of such; in the end, totally intolerant of such!

For the Heavens, unwearying in their bounty, do send other souls into this world; to whom yet, as to their forerunners, in Old Roman, in Old Hebrew and all noble times, the omnipotent guinea is, on the whole, an impotent guinea. Has your half-dead avaricious Corn-Law Lord, your half-alive avaricious Cotton-Law Lord, never seen one such? Such are, not one, but several; are, and will be, unless the gods have doomed this world to swift dire ruin. These are they, the elect of the world; the born champions, strong men, and liberatory Samsons of this poor world: whom the poor Delilah-world will not always shear of their strength and eyesight, and set to grind in darkness at *its* poor gin-wheel! Such souls are, in these days, getting somewhat out of humour with the world. Your very Byron, in these days, is at least driven mad; flatly refuses fealty to the world. The world with its injustices, its golden brutalities, and dull yellow guineas, is a disgust to such souls: the ray of Heaven that is in them does at least predoom them to be very miserable here. Yes:—and yet all misery is faculty misdirected, strength that has not yet found its way. The black whirlwind is mother of the lightning. No *smoke*, in any sense, but can become flame and radiance! Such soul, once graduated in Heaven's stern University, steps out superior to your guinea.

Dost thou know, O sumptuous Corn-Lord, Cotton-Lord, O mutinous Trades-Unionist, gin-vanquished, undeliverable; O much-enslaved World,—this man is not a slave with thee! None of thy promotions is necessary for him. His place is with the stars of Heaven: to thee it may be momentous, to thee it may be life or death, to him it is indifferent, whether thou place him in the lowest hut, or forty feet higher at the top of thy stupendous high tower, while here on Earth. The joys of Earth that are precious, they depend not on thee and thy promotions. Food and raiment, and, round a social hearth, souls who love him, whom he loves: these are already his. He wants none of thy rewards; behold also, he fears none of thy penalties. Thou canst not answer even by killing him: the case of Anaxarchus thou canst kill; but the self of Anaxarchus, the word or act of Anaxarchus, in no wise whatever. To this man death is not a bugbear; to this man life is already as earnest and awful, and beautiful and terrible, as death.

Not a May-game is this man's life; but a battle and a march, a warfare with principalities and powers. No idle promenade through fragrant orange-groves and green flowery spaces, waited on by the choral Muses and the rosy Hours: it is a stern pilgrimage through burning sandy solitudes, through regions of thick-ribbed ice. He walks among men; loves men, with inexpressible soft pity,—as they *cannot* love him: but his soul dwells in solitude, in the uttermost parts of Creation. In green oases by the palm-tree wells, he rests a space; but anon he has to journey forward, escorted by the Terrors and the Splendours, the Arch-demons and Archangels. All Heaven, all Pandemonium are his escort. The stars keen-glancing, from the Immensities, send tidings to him; the graves, silent with their dead, from the Eter-nities. Deep calls for him unto Deep.

Thou, O World, how wilt thou secure thyself against this man? Thou canst not hire him by thy guineas; nor by thy gibbets and law-penalties restrain him. He eludes thee like a Spirit. Thou canst not forward him, thou canst not hinder him. Thy penalties, thy poverties, neglects, contumelies: behold, all these are good for him. Come to him as an enemy; turn from him as an un-friend; only do not this one thing,—infect him not with thy own delusion: the benign Genius, were it by very death, shall guard him against this!—What wilt thou do with him? He is above thee, like a god. Thou, in thy stupendous three-inch pattens, art under him. He is thy born king, thy conqueror and supreme lawgiver: not all the guineas and cannons, and leather and pru-nella, under the sky can save thee from him. Hardest thick-skinned Mammon-world, ruggedest Caliban shall obey him, or become not Caliban but a cramp. Oh, if in this man, whose eyes can flash Heaven's lightning, and make all Calibans into a cramp, there dwelt not, as the essence of his very being, a God's justice, human Nobleness, Veracity and Mercy,—I should tremble for the world. But his strength, let us rejoice to understand, is even this: The quantity of Justice, of Valour and Pity that is in him. To hypocrites and tailored quacks in high places, his eyes are lightning; but they melt in dewy pity softer than a mother's to the downpressed, maltreated; in his heart, in his great thought, is a sanctuary for all the wretched. This world's improvement is forever sure.

'Man of Genius?' Thou hast small notion, meseems, O Me-cænas Twiddledee, of what a Man of Genius is. Read in thy New Testament and elsewhere,—if, with floods of mealymouthed inanity, with miserable froth-vortices of Cant now several centu-ries old, thy New Testament is not all bedimmed for thee. *Canst* thou read in thy New Testament at all? The Highest Man of Genius, knowest thou him; Godlike and a God to this hour? His crown a Crown of Thorns? Thou fool, with *thy* empty God-hoods, Apotheoses *edgegilt;* the Crown of Thorns made into a poor jewel-room crown, fit for the head of blockheads; the bearing of the Cross changed to a riding in the Long-Acre Gig! Pause in thy mass-chantings, in thy litanyings, and Calmuck prayings by machinery; and pray, if noisily, at least in a more human manner. How with thy rubrics and dalmatics, and clothwebs and cobwebs, and with thy stupidities and grovelling baseheartedness, hast thou hidden the Holiest into all but invisibility!—

'Man of Genius:' O Mecænas Twiddledee, hast thou any notion what a Man of Genius is? Genius is 'the inspired gift of God.' It is the clearer presence of God Most High in a man. Dim, potential in all men; in this man it has become clear, actual. So says John Milton, who ought to be a judge; so answer him the Voices of all Ages and all Worlds. Wouldst thou commune with such a one? *Be* his real peer then: does that lie in thee? Know thyself and thy real and thy apparent place, and know him and his real and his apparent place, and act in some noble conformity with all that. What! The star-fire of the Empyrean shall eclipse itself, and illuminate magic-lanterns to amuse grown children? He, the god-inspired, is to twang harps for thee, and blow through scrannel-pipes, to soothe thy sated soul with visions of new, still wider Eldorados, Houri Paradises, richer Lands of Cockaigne? Brother, this is not he; this is a counterfeit, this twangling, jangling, vain, acrid, scrannel-piping man. Thou dost well to say with sick Saul, "It is naught, such harping!"—and in sudden rage, to grasp thy spear, and try if thou canst pin such a one to the wall. King Saul was mistaken in his man, but thou art right in thine. It is the due of such a one: nail him to the wall, and leave him there. So ought copper shillings to be nailed on counters; copper geniuses on walls, and left there for a sign!—

I conclude that the Men of Letters too may become a 'Chivalry,' an actual instead of a virtual Priesthood, with result immeasurable, —so soon as there is nobleness in themselves for that. And, to a certainty, not sooner! Of intrinsic Valetisms you cannot, with whole Parliaments to help you, make a Heroism. Doggeries never so gold-plated, Doggeries never so escutcheoned, Doggeries never so diplomaed, bepuffed, gas-lighted, continue Doggeries, and must take the fate of such.

CHAPTER VIII.

THE DIDACTIC.

CERTAINLY it were a fond imagination to expect that any preaching of mine could abate Mammonism; that Bobus of Houndsditch will love his guineas less, or his poor soul more, for any preaching of mine! But there is one Preacher who does preach with effect, and gradually persuade all persons: his name is Destiny, is Divine Providence, and his Sermon the inflexible Course of Things. Experience does take dreadfully high school-wages; but he teaches like no other!

I revert to Friend Prudence the good Quaker's refusal of 'seven thousand pounds to boot.' Friend Prudence's practical conclusion will, by degrees, become that of all rational practical men whatsoever. On the present scheme and principle, Work cannot continue. Trades' Strikes, Trades' Unions, Chartisms; mutiny, squalor, rage and desperate revolt, growing ever more desperate, will go on their way. As dark misery settles down on us, and our refuges of lies fall in pieces one after one, the hearts of men, now at last serious, will turn to refuges of truth. The eternal stars shine out again, so soon as it is dark *enough*.

Begirt with desperate Trades' Unionism and Anarchic Mutiny, many an Industrial *Law-ward*, by and by, who has neglected to make laws and keep them, will be heard saying to himself: "Why have I realised five hundred thousand pounds? I rose early and sat late, I toiled and moiled, and in the sweat of my brow and of my soul I strove to gain this money, that I might become conspicuous, and have some honour among my fellow-creatures. I wanted them to honour me, to love me. The money is here, earned with my best lifeblood: but the honour? I am encircled with squalor, with hunger, rage, and sooty desperation. Not honoured, hardly even envied; only fools and the flunkey-species so much as envy me. I am conspicuous,—as a mark for curses and brickbats. What good is it? My five hundred scalps hang here in my wigwam: would to Heaven I had sought something else than the scalps; would to Heaven I had been a Christian Fighter, not a Chactaw one! To have ruled and fought not in a Mammonish but in a Godlike spirit; to have had the hearts of the people bless me, as a true ruler and captain of my people; to have felt my own heart bless me, and that God above instead of Mammon below was blessing me,—this had been something. Out of my sight, ye beggarly five hundred scalps of banker's-thousands: I will try for something other, or account my life a tragical futility!"

Friend Prudence's 'rock-ledge,' as we called it, will gradually disclose itself to many a man; to all men. Gradually, assaulted from beneath and from above, the Stygian mud-deluge of Laissez-faire, Supply-and-demand, Cash-payment the one Duty, will abate on all hands; and the everlasting mountain-tops, and secure rock-foundations that reach to the centre of the world, and rest on Nature's self, will again emerge, to found on, and to build on. When Mammon-worshipers here and there begin to be God-worshipers, and bipeds-of-prey become men, and there is a Soul felt once more in the huge-pulsing elephantine mechanic Animalism of this Earth, it will be again a blessed Earth.

"Men cease to regard money?" cries Bobus of Houndsditch: "What else do all men strive for? The very Bishop informs me that Christianity cannot get on without a minimum of Four thousand five hundred in its pocket. Cease to regard money? That will be at Doomsday in the afternoon!"—O Bobus, my opinion is somewhat different. My opinion is, that the Upper Powers have not yet determined on destroying this Lower World. A respectable, ever-increasing minority, who do strive for something higher than money, I with confidence anticipate; ever-increasing, till there be a sprinkling of them found in all quarters, as salt of the Earth once more. The Christianity that cannot get on without a minimum of Four thousand five hundred, will give place to something better that can. Thou wilt not join our small minority, thou? Not till Doomsday in the afternoon? Well; *then*, at least, thou wilt join it, thou and the majority in mass!

But truly it is beautiful to see the brutish empire of Mammon cracking everywhere; giving sure promise of dying, or of being changed. A strange, chill, almost ghastly dayspring strikes up in Yankeeland itself: my Transcendental friends announce there, in a distinct, though somewhat lankhaired, ungainly manner, that the Demiurgus Dollar is dethroned; that new unheard-of Demiurgus-ships, Priesthoods, Aristocracies, Growths and Destructions, are already visible in the gray of coming Time. Chronos is dethroned by Jove; Odin by St. Olaf: the Dollar cannot rule in Heaven forever. No; I reckon, not. Socinian Preachers quit their pulpits in Yankeeland, saying, "Friends, this is all gone to coloured cobweb, we regret to say!"—and retire into the fields to cultivate onion-beds, and live frugally on vegetables. It is very notable. Old godlike Calvinism declares that its old body is now fallen to tatters, and done; and its mournful ghost, disembodied, seeking new embodiment, pipes again in the winds;—a ghost and spirit as yet, but heralding new Spirit-worlds, and better Dynasties than the Dollar one.

Yes, here as there, light is coming into the world; men love not darkness, they do love light. A deep feeling of the eternal nature of Justice looks out among us everywhere,—even through the dull eyes of Exeter Hall; an unspeakable religiousness struggles, in the most helpless manner, to speak itself, in Puseyisms and the like. Of our Cant, all condemnable, how much is not condemnable without pity; we had almost said, without respect! The inarticulate worth and truth that is in England goes down yet to the Foundations.

Some ' Chivalry of Labour,' some noble Humanity and practical Divineness of Labour, will yet be realised on this Earth. Or why *will;* why do we pray to Heaven, without setting our own shoulder to the wheel? The Present, if it will have the Future accomplish, shall itself commence. Thou who prophesiest, who believest, begin thou to fulfil. Here or nowhere, now equally as at any time! That outcast help-needing thing or person, trampled down under vulgar feet or hoofs, no help ' possible' for it, no prize offered for the saving of it,—canst not thou save it, then, without prize? Put forth thy hand, in God's name; know that ' impossible,' where Truth and Mercy and the everlasting Voice of Nature order, has no place in the brave man's dictionary. That when all men have said " Impossible," and tumbled noisily elsewhither, and thou alone art left, then first thy time and possibility have come. It is for thee now; do thou that, and ask no man's counsel, but thy own only and God's. Brother, thou hast possibility in thee for much: the possibility of writing on the eternal skies the record of a heroic life. That noble downfallen or yet unborn ' Impossibility,' thou canst lift it up, thou canst, by thy soul's travail, bring it into clear being. That loud inane Actuality, with millions in its pocket, too ' possible' that, which rolls along there, with quilted trumpeters blaring round it, and all the world escorting it as mute or vocal flunkey,—escort it not thou; say to it, either nothing, or else deeply in thy heart: " Loud-blaring Nonentity, no force of trumpets, cash, Long-Acre art, or universal flunkeyhood of men, makes thee an Entity; thou art a *No*entity, and deceptive Simulacrum, more accursed than thou seemest. Pass on in the Devil's name, unworshiped by at least one man, and leave the thoroughfare clear!"

Not on Ilion's or Latium's plains; on far other plains and places henceforth can noble deeds be now done. Not on Ilion's plains; how much less in Mayfair's drawingrooms! Not in victory over poor brother French or Phrygians; but in victory over Frost-jötuns, Marsh-giants, over demons of Discord, Idleness, Injustice, Unreason, and Chaos come again. None of the old Epics is longer possible. The Epic of French and Phrygians was comparatively a small Epic: but that of Flirts and Fribbles, what is that? A thing that vanishes at cock-crowing,—that already begins to scent the morning air! Game-preserving Aristocracies, let them ' bush' never so effectually, cannot escape the Subtle Fowler. Game seasons will be excellent, and again will be indifferent, and by and by they will not be at all. The Last Partridge of England, of an England where millions of men can get no corn to eat, will be shot and ended. Aristocracies with

beards on their chins will find other work to do than amuse themselves with trundling-hoops.

But it is to you, ye Workers, who do already work, and are as
grown men, noble and honourable in a sort, that the whole world
calls for new work and nobleness. . Subdue mutiny, discord, wide-
spread despair, by manfulness, justice, mercy and wisdom. Chaos
is dark, deep as Hell; let light be, and there is instead a green
flowery World. O, it is great, and there is no other greatness.
To make some nook of God's Creation a little fruitfuller, better,
more worthy of God; to make some human hearts a little wiser,
manfuller, happier,—more blessed, less accursed! It is work for
a God. Sooty Hell of mutiny and savagery and despair can, by
man's energy, be made a kind of Heaven; cleared of its soot, of
its mutiny, of its need to mutiny; the everlasting arch of Heaven's
azure overspanning *it* too, and its cunning mechanisms and tall
chimney-steeples, as a birth of Heaven; God and all men looking
on it well pleased.

Unstained by wasteful deformities, by wasted tears or heart's-
blood of men, or any defacement of the Pit, noble fruitful Labour,
growing ever nobler, will come forth,—the grand sole miracle of
Man; whereby Man has risen from the low places of this Earth,
very literally, into divine Heavens. Ploughers, Spinners, Builders; Prophets, Poets, Kings; Brindleys and Goethes, Odins and
Arkwrights; all martyrs, and noble men, and gods · are of one
grand Host; immeasurable; marching ever forward since the Beginnings of the World. The enormous, all-conquering, flame-
crowned Host, noble every soldier in it; sacred, and alone noble.
Let him who is not of it hide himself; let him tremble for himself.
Stars at every button cannot make him noble; sheaves of Bath-
garters, nor bushels of Georges; nor any other contrivance but
manfully enlisting in it, valiantly taking place and step in it. O
Heavens, will he not bethink himself; he too is so needed in the
Host! It were so blessed, thrice-blessed, for himself and for us
all! In hope of the Last Partridge, and some Duke of Weimar
among our English Dukes, we will be patient yet a while.

> ' The Future hides in it
> Gladness and sorrow;
> We press still thorow,
> Naught that abides in it
> Daunting us,—onward.'

SUMMARY OF CHARTISM.

———

CHAP. I. *Condition-of-England Question.*

CONDITION and disposition of the Working Classes: The Chartist Petition. 'Chartism' a new name for a thing which has had many names. Why Parliament throws no light on this dark question: Collective Folly of a Nation. Rights and Mights: Submission to the inevitable. Working-Class discontent. (p. 3).

CHAP. II. *Statistics.*

Statistic-Society Reports: Tables beautifully reticulated, but which hold no knowledge. Conclusive facts only separable from inconclusive by a head that understands and knows. Condition-of-England question, a most complex concrete matter: What constitutes the well-being of a man. Thrift decreasing, and almost gone. (p. 8).

CHAP. III. *New Poor-Law.*

Refusal of out-door relief, the one recipe for the woes of England: Not a very noble method. Merely to let everything and everybody well alone, a chief social principle false and damnable, if ever aught was. The Poor-Law Amendment Act, a *half*-truth, and preliminary of good. He that will not work according to his faculty, let him perish according to his necessity. Supervisal by the Central Government. The claim of the poor labourer, something quite other than that 'Statute of the Forty-third of Elizabeth.' (p. 11).

CHAP. IV. *Finest Peasantry in the World.*

The poor man seeking for *work*, yet unable to find it. Irish perennial starvation: The Irish National character degraded, disordered. English injustice to Ireland. Circuitous, yet stern retribution: England invaded by Irish destitution. (p. 16).—English labourers approximating more and more to the condition of the Irish competing with them: Labour disturbed and superseded by Mechanism. *Laissez-faire*, applied to horses, or to poor ignorant peasants. Mere wages no index of well-being in the working man. A world, not a home, but a dingy prison-house of reckless unthrift and rancorous rebellion. (20).

Chap. V. *Rights and Mights.*

Not what a man outwardly has or wants, that constitutes the happiness or misery of him: The feeling of *injustice*, the one intolerability to all men: Revenge. (p. 23).—No conquest ever became permanent, which did not prove itself beneficial to the conquered: Romans; old Norman Nobles. The Wise man the only strong man. The grand question as to the condition of our Working Men. Of lower classes so related to upper, happy nations are not made. The French Revolution not yet completed: Bankruptcy of Speciosity and Imposture. Glory to God, our Europe was not to die but to live! (24).—The rights of man, little worth ascertaining in comparison to the mights, or practical availabilities, of man: How his notions of his 'rights' vary according to place and time. An Ideal of Right, in all men, and procedures of men: Nothing unjust can continue in this world. (29).

Chap. VI. *Laissez-faire.*

The principle of *Let-alone* applied to English affairs: Church, Aristocracy, Fact. Under what tragic conditions *Laissez-faire* becomes a reasonable cry. Inalienable 'right' of the ignorant to be guided by the wiser. True meaning of Democracy. (p. 31).—An Aristocracy a corporation of the Best and Bravest. Priesthoods, and the one question concerning them: How France cast its benighted Priesthood into destruction: The British Reader's self-complacent yet futile solacement. Cash-Payment the sole nexus of man to man. Protection of *property:* What *is* property? The Ideal, and the poor imperfect Actual. Nothing, not a reality, ever got men to pay bed and board to it long. (34).

Chap. VII. *Not Laissez-faire.*

Better relations between Upper and Under Classes. The preliminary of all good, to know that a work must actually be done. Habits of Parliament for a century back. Parliament with its privileges is strong; but Necessity and the Laws of Nature are stronger. Cash-Payment; and so many things that cash will not pay. (p. 39).

Chap. VIII. *New Eras.*

A new Practice indispensable in every New Era. Sauerteig on the Eras of England. Romans dead out; English are come in. Hengst and Horsa mooring on the mud-beach of Thanet. Six centuries of obscure endeavour: A stormy spring-time, if ever there was one for a Nation. Might and Right do differ frightfully from hour to hour; but give them centuries, they are found to be identical. The land of Britain. Normans and Saxons originally of one stock. (p. 42).—Two grand tasks in World-History assigned to this English People. Rights, everywhere, correctly-articulated *mights*. A real House of Commons come decisively into play: Material and spiritual accumulations and growths of England. (46).—New England: The little ship Mayflower of Delft-Haven. The Elizabethan Era a spiritual flower-time. Manchester; its squalor and despair not forever inseparable from it. Richard Arkwright; James Watt. Our greatest benefactors walk daily among us, shrouded in darkness. All *new* things, unexpected, unforeseen; yet not unexpected by Supreme Power. (48).

Chap. IX. *Parliamentary Radicalism.*

Where the great masses of men are tolerably right, all is right; where they are not right, all is wrong. Claim of the Free Working-man to be raised to a level with the Working Slave: A Do-nothing Guidance, in a Do-something world. English notion of ' Suffrage.' Reform Ministries, with their Benthamee formulas, barren as the east wind: Ultra-radicalism, not of the Benthamee sort. Obedience the primary duty of man: Recognised or not, a man *has* his superiors, a regular Hierarchy above him. (p. 54).

Chap. X. *Impossible.*

'What are we to do?'—No good comes of men who have 'impossible' too often in their mouths. Paralytic Radicalism. Two things, great things, might be done. (p. 57).—Education: The grand ' seedfield of Time' is man's, and we give it him not. Consequences of neglect. Intellect or insight: Twenty-four million intellects, awakened into action. Difficulties occasioned by ' Religion:' Cast-iron Parsons: In order to teach religion, the one needful thing to find a man who *has* religion. What a real Prime-Minister of England *might* do towards educating the people. (59).—Emigration; the one remedy for ' over-population.' Malthusian controversies: ' Preventive check:' Infanticide by ' painless extinction.' What a black, godless, waste-struggling world, in this once merry England, do such things betoken! (64).

SUMMARY OF PAST AND PRESENT.

BOOK I.—PROEM.

CHAP. I. *Midas.*

THE condition of England one of the most ominous ever seen in this world: Full of wealth in every kind, yet dying of inanition. Workhouses, in which no work can be done. Destitution in Scotland. Stockport Assizes. (p. 71).—England's unprofitable success: Human faces glooming discordantly on one another. Midas longed for gold, and the gods gave it him. (74).

CHAP. II. *The Sphinx.*

The grand unnamable Sphinx-riddle, which each man is called upon to solve. Notions of the foolish concerning justice and judgment. Courts of Westminster, and the general High Court of the Universe. The one strong thing, the just thing, the true thing. (p. 75).—A noble Conservatism, as well as an ignoble. In all battles of men each fighter, in the end, prospers according to his right: Wallace of Scotland. (79).—Fact and Semblance. What is Justice? As many men as there are in a Nation who can *see* Heaven's Justice, so many are there who stand between it and perdition. (80).

CHAP. III. *Manchester Insurrection.*

Peterloo not an unsuccessful Insurrection. Governors who wait for Insurrection to instruct them, getting into the fatallest courses. Unspeakable County Yeomanry. Poor Manchester operatives, and their huge inarticulate question: Unhappy Workers, unhappier Idlers, of this actual England! (p. 81).—Fair day's-wages for fair day's-work: Milton's 'wages;' Cromwell's. Pay to each man what he has earned and done and deserved; what more have we to ask?—Some not *in*supportable approximation indispensable and inevitable. (85).

CHAP. IV. *Morrison's Pill.*

A state of mind worth reflecting on. No Morrison's Pill for curing the maladies of Society: Universal alteration of regimen and way of life: Vain jargon giving place to some genuine Speech again. (p. 88).—If we walk according to the Law of this Universe, the Law-Maker will befriend us; if not, not. Quacks, sham heroes, the one bane of the world. Quack and Dupe, upper side and under of the selfsame substance. (89).

CHAP. V. *Aristocracy of Talent.*

All misery the fruit of unwisdom: Neither with individuals nor with Nations is it fundamentally otherwise. Nature in late centuries universally supposed to be dead; but now everywhere asserting herself to be alive and miraculous. The guidance of this country not sufficiently wise. (p. 91).—Aristocracy of Talent, or government by the Wisest, a dreadfully difficult affair to get started. The true *eye* for talent; and the flunkey eye for respectabilities, warm garnitures and larders dropping fatness: Bobus and Bobissimus. (93).

CHAP. VI. *Hero-worship.*

Enlightened Egoism, never so luminous, not the rule by which man's life can be led: A *soul*, different from a stomach in any sense of the word. Hero-worship, done differently in every different epoch of the world. Reform, like Charity, must begin at home. ' Arrestment of the knaves and dastards,' beginning by arresting our own poor selves out of that fraternity. (p. 96).—The present Editor's purpose to himself full of hope. A Loadstar in the eternal sky: A glimmering of light, for here and there a human soul. (98).

BOOK II.—THE ANCIENT MONK.

CHAP. I. *Jocelin of Brakelond.*

How the Centuries stand lineally related to each other. The one Book not permissible, the kind that has nothing in it. Jocelin's ' Chronicle,' a private Boswellean Notebook, now seven centuries old. How Jocelin, from under his monk's cowl, looked out on that narrow section of the world in a really *human* manner: A wise simplicity in him; a *veracity* that goes deeper than words. Jocelin's Monk-Latin; and Mr. Rokewood's editorial helpfulness and fidelity. (p. 101).—A veritable Monk of old Bury St. Edmunds worth attending to. This England of ours, of the year 1200: Cœur-de-Lion: King Lackland, and his thirteenpenny mass. The poorest historical Fact, and the grandest imaginative Fiction. (104).

CHAP. II. *St. Edmundsbury.*

St. Edmund's Bury, a prosperous brisk Town: Extensive ruins of the Abbey still visible. Assiduous Pedantry, and its rubbish-heaps called ' History.' Another world it was, when those black ruins first saw the sun as walls. At lowest, O dilettante friend, let us know always that it *was* a world. No easy matter to get across the chasm of Seven Centuries: Of all helps, a Boswell, even a small Boswell, the welcomest. (p. 107).

CHAP. III. *Landlord Edmund.*

' Battle of Fornham,' a fact, though a forgotten one. Edmund, Land-

lord of the Eastern Counties: A very singular kind of 'landlord.' How he
came to be 'sainted.' Seen and felt to have done verily a man's part in
this life-pilgrimage of his. How they took up the slain body of their Edmund, and reverently embalmed it. (p. 110).—Pious munificence, ever
growing by new pious gifts. Certain Times do crystallise themselves in
a magnificent manner; others in a rather shabby one. (114).

CHAP. IV. *Abbot Hugo.*

All things have two faces, a light one and a dark: The Ideal has to
grow in the Real, and to seek its bed and board there, often in a very sorry
manner. Abbot Hugo, grown old and feeble. Jew debts, and Jew creditors.
How approximate justice strives to accomplish itself. (p. 115).—In the old
monastic Books, almost no mention whatever of 'personal religion.' A
poor Lord Abbot, all stuck-over with horse-leeches: A 'royal commission
of inquiry,' to no purpose. A monk's first duty, obedience. Magister Samson, Teacher of the Novices. The Abbot's providential death. (117).

CHAP. V. *Twelfth Century.*

Inspectors or Custodiars; the King not in any breathless haste to appoint a new Abbot. Dim and very strange looks that monk-life to us. Our
venerable ancient spinning grandmothers, shrieking, and rushing out with
their distaffs. Lakenheath eels, too slippery to be caught. (p. 119).—How
much is alive in England, in that Twelfth Century; how much not yet
come into life. Feudal Aristocracy; Willelmus Conquestor: Not a steeple-
chimney yet got on end from sea to sea. (121).

CHAP. VI. *Monk Samson.*

Monk-Life and Monk-Religion: A great heaven-high Unquestionability,
encompassing, interpenetrating all human Duties. Our modern Arkwright
Joe-Manton ages: All human dues and reciprocities changed into one great
due of 'cash-payment.' The old monks but a limited class of creatures,
with a somewhat dull life of it. (p. 122).—One Monk of a taciturn nature
distinguishes himself among those babbling ones. A Son of poor Norfolk
parents. Little Samson's awful dream: His poor mother dedicates him
to St. Edmund. He grows to be a learned man, of devout grave nature.
Sent to Rome on business; and returns *too* successful: Method of travelling thither in those days. His tribulations at home: Strange conditions
under which Wisdom has sometimes to struggle with Folly. (124).

CHAP. VII. *The Canvassing.*

A new Abbot to be elected. Even gossip, seven centuries off, has significance. The Prior with Twelve Monks, to wait on his Majesty at Waltham.
An 'election' the one important social act: Given the Man a People choose,
the worth and worthlessness of the People itself is given. (p. 127).

CHAP. VIII. *The Election.*

Electoral methods and manipulations. Brother Samson ready oftenest with some question, some suggestion, that has wisdom in it. The Thirteen off to Waltham, to choose their Abbot: In the solitude of the Convent, Destiny thus big and in her birthtime, what gossiping, babbling, dreaming of dreams! (p. 130).—King Henry II. in his high Presence-chamber. Samson chosen Abbot: The King's royal acceptation. (132).—St. Edmundsbury Monks, without express ballot-box or other winnowing machine. In every Nation and Community, there is at all times *a fittest*, wisest, bravest, best. Human Worth and human Worthlessness. (134).

CHAP. IX. *Abbot Samson.*

The Lord Abbot's arrival at St. Edmundsbury: The selfsame Samson, yesterday a poor mendicant, this day finds himself a *Dominus Abbas* and mitred Peer of Parliament. (p. 135).—Depth and opulence of true social vitality in those old barbarous ages. True Governors go about under all manner of disguises now as then. Genius, Poet; what these words mean. George the Third, head charioteer of England; and Robert Burns, gauger of ale in Dumfries. (136).—How Abbot Samson found a Convent all in dilapidation. His life-long harsh apprenticeship to governing, namely obeying. First get your Man; all is got. Danger of blockheads. (138).

CHAP. X. *Government.*

Beautiful, how the chrysalis governing-soul, shaking off its dusty slough and prison, starts forth winged, a true royal soul!—One first labour, to institute a strenuous review and radical reform of his economics. Wheresoever Disorder may stand or lie, let it have a care; here is a man that has declared war with it. (p. 140).—In less than four years the Convent Debts are all liquidated; and the harpy Jews banished from St. Edmundsbury. New life springs beneficent everywhere: Spiritual rubbish as little tolerated as material. (142).

CHAP. XI. *The Abbot's Ways.*

Reproaches, open and secret, of ingratitude, unsociability: Except for 'fit men' in all kinds, hard to say for whom Abbot Samson had much favour. Remembrance of benefits. (p. 143).—An eloquent man, but intent more on substance than on ornament. A just clear heart the basis of all true talent. One of the justest of judges: His invaluable 'talent of silence.' The kind of people he liked worst. Hospitality and stoicism. (144). —The country, in those days, still dark with noble wood and umbrage: How the old trees gradually died out, no man heeding it. Monachism itself, so rich and fruitful once, now all rotted into *peat*. Devastations of four-footed cattle and Henry-the-Eighths. (146).

CHAP. XII. *The Abbot's Troubles.*

The troubles of Abbot Samson, more than tongue can tell. Not the spoil of victory, only the glorious toil of battle, can be theirs who really govern. An insurrection of the Monks: Behave better, ye remiss Monks, and thank Heaven for such an Abbot. (p. 147).—Worn down with incessant toil and tribulation: Gleams of hilarity too; little snatches of encouragement granted even to a Governor. How my Lord of Clare, coming to claim his undue 'debt,' gets a Rowland for his Oliver. A Life of Literature; noble and ignoble. (149).

CHAP. XIII. *In Parliament.*

Confused days of Lackland's usurpation, while Cœur-de-Lion was away: Our brave Abbot took helmet himself, excommunicating all who should favour Lackland. King Richard a captive in Germany. (p. 151).—St. Edmund's Shrine not meddled with: A Heavenly Awe overshadowed and encompassed, as it still ought and must, all earthly Business whatsoever. (152).

CHAP. XIV. *Henry of Essex.*

How St. Edmund punished terribly, yet with mercy: A Narrative, significant of the Time. Henry Earl of Essex, standard-bearer of England: No right reverence for the Heavenly in Man. A traitor or a coward. Solemn Duel, by the King's appointment. An evil Conscience doth make cowards of us all. (p. 153).

CHAP. XV. *Practical-Devotional.*

A Tournament proclaimed and held in the Abbot's domain, in spite of him. Roystering young dogs brought to reason. The Abbot a man that generally remains master at last: The importunate Bishop of Ely outwitted. A man that dare abide King Richard's anger, with justice on his side. Thou brave Richard, thou brave Samson! (p. 156).—The basis of Abbot Samson's life, truly religion. His zealous interest in the Crusades. The great antique heart, like a child's in its simplicity, like a man's in its earnest solemnity and depth. His comparative silence as to his religion, precisely the healthiest sign of him and it. Methodism, Dilettantism, Puseyism. (159).

CHAP. XVI. *St. Edmund.*

Abbot Samson built many useful, many pious edifices: All ruinous, incomplete things, an eye-sorrow to him. Rebuilding the great Altar: A glimpse of the glorious Martyr's very Body. What a scene; how far vanished from us, in these unworshiping ages of ours! The manner of men's Hero-worship, verily the innermost fact of their existence, determining all the rest. (p. 162).—On the whole, who knows how to reverence the Body of Man?—Abbot Samson, at the culminating point of his existence: Our real-phantasmagory of St. Edmundsbury plunges into the bosom of the Twelfth Century again, and all is over. (166).

CHAP. XVII. *The Beginnings.*

Formulas, the very skin and muscular tissue of a Man's Life: Living Formulas, and dead. Habit the deepest law of human nature. A pathway through the pathless. Nationalities. Pulpy infancy, kneaded, baked into any form you choose: The Man of Business; the hard-handed Labourer; the genus Dandy. No mortal out of the depths of Bedlam, but lives by Formulas. (p. 168).—The hosts and generations of brave men, Oblivion has swallowed: Their crumbled dust, the soil our life-fruit grows on. Invention of Speech; Forms of Worship; Methods of Justice. This English Land, here and now, the summary of what was wise, and noble, and accordant with God's Truth, in all the generations of English Men. The thing called 'Fame.' (170).

BOOK III.—THE MODERN WORKER.

CHAP. I. *Phenomena.*

How men have 'forgotten God;' taken the Fact of this Universe as it *is not;* God's Laws, become a Greatest-Happiness Principle, a Parliamentary Expediency. Man has lost the *soul* out of him, and begins to find the want of it. (p. 177).—The old Pope of Rome, with his stuffed dummy to do the kneeling for him. Few men that worship by the rotatory Calabash, do it in half so great, frank or effectual a way. (178).—Our Aristocracy, no longer able to *do* its work; and not in the least conscious that it has any work to do. The Champion of England 'lifted into his saddle.' The Hatter in the Strand, mounting a huge lath-and-plaster Hat. Our noble ancestors have fashioned for us, in how many thousand senses, a 'life-road;' and we their sons, are madly, literally enough, 'consuming the way.' (180).

CHAP. II. *Gospel of Mammonism.*

Heaven and Hell, often as the words are on our tongue, got to be fabulous or semi-fabulous for most of us. The real 'Hell' of the English. Cash-payment, *not* the sole or even chief relation of human beings. Practical Atheism, and its despicable fruits. (p. 183).—One of Dr. Alison's melancholy facts: A poor Irish Widow in the Lanes of Edinburgh, *proving* her sisterhood. Until we get a human *soul* within us, all things are *impossible*: Infatuated geese, with feathers and without. (186).

CHAP. III. *Gospel of Dilettantism.*

Mammonism at least works; but 'Go gracefully idle in Mayfair,' what does or can that mean?—Impotent, insolent Donothingism in Practice, and Saynothingism in Speech. No man now speaks a plain word: Insincere Speech, the prime material of insincere Action. (p. 188).—Moslem parable of Moses and the Dwellers by the Dead Sea: The Universe *become* a Humbug, to the Apes that thought it one. (189).

CHAP. IV. *Happy.*

All work, noble; and every noble crown a crown of thorns. Man's pitiful pretension to be what he calls 'happy :' His Greatest-Happiness Principle fast becoming a rather unhappy one. Byron's large audience. A philosophical Doctor: A disconsolate Meat-jack, gnarring and creaking with rust and work. (p. 190).—The only 'happiness' a brave man ever troubled himself much about, the happiness to get his work done. (192).

CHAP. V. *The English.*

With all thy theoretic platitudes, what a depth of practical sense in thee, great England! A dumb people, who can do great acts, but not describe them. The noble Warhorse, and the Dog of Knowledge: The freest utterances not by any means the best. (p. 193).—The done Work, much more than the spoken Word, an epitome of the man. The Man of Practice, and the Man of Theory: Ineloquent Brindley. The English, of all Nations, the stupidest in speech, the wisest in action: Sadness and seriousness: Unconsciously this great Universe is great to them. The Silent Romans. John Bull's admirable insensibility to Logic. (194).—All great Peoples conservative. The English Ready-Reckoner a Solecism in Eastcheap. Berserkir-rage. Truth and Justice alone *capable* of being 'conserved.' Bitter indignation engendered by the Corn-Laws in every just English heart. (197).

CHAP. VI. *Two Centuries.*

The 'Settlement' of the year 1660, one of the mournfullest that ever took place in this land of ours. The true end of Government, to guide men in the way they should go: The true good of this life, the portal of infinite good in the life to come. Oliver Cromwell's body hung on the Tyburn-gallows; the type of Puritanism found futile, inexecutable, execrable. The Spiritualism of England, for two godless centuries, utterly forgettable: Her practical Material Work alone memorable. (p. 200).—Bewildering obscurations and impediments: Valiant Sons of Toil enchanted, by the million, in their Poor-Law Bastille. Giant Labour, yet to be King of this Earth. (202).

CHAP. VII. *Over-Production.*

An idle Governing Class addressing its Workers with an indictment of 'Over-production.' Duty of justly apportioning the Wages of Work done. A game-preserving Aristocracy, guiltless of producing or apportioning anything. Owning the soil of England. (p. 203).—The Working Aristocracy, steeped in ignoble Mammonism: The Idle Aristocracy, with its yellow parchments and pretentious futilities. (205).

CHAP. VIII. *Unworking Aristocracy.*

Our Land the *Mother* of us all: No true Aristocracy but must possess the Land. Men talk of 'selling' Land: Whom it belongs to. Our much-

consuming Aristocracy : By the law of their position bound to furnish guidance and governance. Mad and miserable Corn-Laws. (p. 206).—The Working Aristocracy, and its terrible New-Work : The Idle Aristocracy, and its horoscope of despair. (208).—A High Class without duties to do, like a tree planted on precipices. In a valiant suffering for others, not in a slothful making others suffer for us, did nobleness ever lie. The Pagan Hercules ; the Czar of Russia. (210).—Parchments, venerable and not venerable. Benedict the Jew, and his usuries. No Chapter on the Corn-Laws : The Corn-Laws too mad to have a Chapter. (211).

CHAP. IX. *Working Aristocracy.*

Many things for the Working Aristocracy, in their extreme need, to consider. A National Existence supposed to depend on 'selling cheaper' than any other People. Let inventive men try to invent a little how cotton at its present cheapness could be somewhat justlier divided. Many 'impossibles' will have to become possible. (p. 212).—Supply-and-demand : For what noble work was there ever yet any audible 'demand' in that poor sense ? (215).

CHAP. X. *Plugson of Undershot.*

Man's philosophies usually the 'supplement of his practice :' Symptoms of social death. Cash-Payment : The Plugson Ledger, and the Tablets of Heaven's Chancery, discrepant exceedingly. (p. 216).—All human things do require to have an Ideal in them. How murderous Fighting became a 'glorious Chivalry.' Noble devout-hearted Chevaliers. Ignoble Bucaniers and Chactaw Indians : Howel Davies. Napoleon flung out, at last, to St. Helena ; the latter end of him sternly compensating for the beginning. (218).—The indomitable Plugson, as yet a Bucanier and Chactaw. William Conqueror and his Norman followers. Organisation of Labour : Courage, there are yet many brave men in England ! (220).

CHAP. XI. *Labour.*

A perennial nobleness, and even sacredness in Work. Significance of the Potter's Wheel. Blessed is he who has found his Work ; let him ask no other blessedness. (p. 223).—A brave Sir Christopher, and his Paul's Cathedral : Every noble work, at first 'impossible.' Columbus, royallest Sea-king of all : A depth of Silence, deeper than the Sea ; a Silence unsoundable ; known to God only. (224).

CHAP. XII. *Reward.*

Work is Worship : Labour, wide as the Earth, has its summit in Heaven. One monster there is in the world, the idle man. (p. 226).—' Fair day's-wages for a fair day's-work,' the most unrefusable demand. The 'wages' of every noble Work, in Heaven or else Nowhere : The brave man has to *give* his Life away. He that works, bodies forth the form of Things

Unseen. Strange mystic affinity of Wisdom and Insanity: All Work, in its degree, a making of Madness sane. (228).—Labour not a devil, even when encased in Mammonism: The unredeemed ugliness, a slothful People. The vulgarest Plugson of a Master-Worker, not a man to strangle by Corn-Laws and Shotbelts. (231).

Chap. XIII. *Democracy.*

Man must actually have his debts and earnings a little better paid by man. At no time was the lot of the dumb millions of toilers so entirely unbearable as now. Sisterhood, brotherhood, often forgotten; but never before so expressly denied. Mungo Park and his poor Black Benefactress. (p. 233).—Gurth born thrall of Cedric the Saxon: Liberty, a Divine thing; but 'liberty to die by starvation' not so divine. Nature's Aristocracies. William Conqueror, a resident House-Surgeon provided by Nature for her beloved English People. (235).—Democracy, the despair of finding Heroes to govern us, and contented putting up with the want of them. The very Tailor unconsciously symbolising the reign of Equality. Wherever ranks do actually exist, strict division of costumes will also be enforced. (237).— Freedom from oppression, an indispensable yet most insignificant portion of Human Liberty. A *best path* does exist for every man; a thing which, here and now, it were of all things *wisest* for him to do. Mock Superiors and Real Superiors. (239).

Chap. XIV. *Sir Jabesh Windbag.*

Oliver Cromwell, the remarkablest Governor we have had for the last five centuries or so: No volunteer in Public Life, but plainly a balloted soldier: The Government of England put into his hands. (p. 242).—Windbag, weak in the faith of a God; strong only in the faith that Paragraphs and Plausibilities bring votes. Five years of popularity or unpopularity; and *after* those five years, an Eternity. Oliver has to appear before the Most High Judge: Windbag, appealing to 'Posterity.' (243).

Chap. XV. *Morrison again.*

New Religions: This new stage of progress, proceeding 'to invent God,' a very strange one indeed. (p. 245).—Religion, the Inner Light or Moral Conscience of a man's soul. Infinite difference between a Good man and a Bad. The great Soul of the World, just and not unjust: Faithful, unspoken, but not ineffectual 'prayer.' Penalties: The French Revolution; cruellest Portent that has risen into created Space these ten centuries. Man needs no 'New Religion;' nor is like to get it: Spiritual Dastardism, and sick folly. (246).—One Liturgy which does remain forever unexceptionable, that of *Praying by Working.* Sauerteig on the symbolic influences of Washing. Chinese Pontiff-Emperor and his significant 'punctualities.' (250).—Goethe and German Literature. The great event for the world, now as always, the arrival in it of a new Wise Man. Goethe's *Mason-Lodge.* (253).

BOOK IV.—HOROSCOPE.

CHAP. I. *Aristocracies.*

To predict the Future, to manage the Present, would not be so impossible, had not the Past been so sacrilegiously mishandled : A godless century, looking back to centuries that were godly. (p. 257).—A new real Aristocracy and Priesthood. The noble Priest always a noble *Aristos* to begin with, and something more to end with. Modern Preachers, and the *real* Satanas that now is. Abbot-Samson and William-Conqueror times. The mission of a Land Aristocracy, a *sacred* one, in both senses of that old word. Truly a 'Splendour of God' did dwell in those old rude veracious ages. Old Anselm travelling to Rome, to appeal against King Rufus. Their quarrel at bottom a great quarrel. (258).—The boundless Future, predestined, nay already extant though unseen. Our Epic, not *Arms and the Man*, but *Tools and the Man ;* an infinitely wider kind of Epic. Important that our grand Reformation were begun. (265).

CHAP. II. *Bribery Committee.*

Our theory, perfect purity of Tenpound Franchise; our practice, irremediable bribery. Bribery, indicative not only of length of purse, but of brazen dishonesty: Proposed improvements. A Parliament, starting with a lie in its mouth, promulgates strange horoscopes of itself. (p. 267).— Respect paid to those worthy of no respect: Pandarus Dogdraught. The indigent discerning Freeman ; and the kind of men he is called upon to vote for. (269).

CHAP. III. *The one Institution.*

The 'Organisation of Labour,' if well understood, the Problem of the whole Future. Governments of various degrees of utility. Kilkenny Cats; Spinning-Dervishes; Parliamentary Eloquence. A Prime-Minister who would dare believe the heavenly omens. (p. 271).—Who can despair of. Governments, that passes a Soldier's Guard-house?—Incalculable what, by arranging, commanding and regimenting, can be made of men. Organisms enough in the dim huge Future; and 'United Services' quite other than the redcoat one. (273).—Legislative interference between Workers and Master-Workers increasingly indispensable. Sanitary Reform : People's Parks : A right Education Bill, and effective Teaching Service. Free bridge for Emigrants : England's sure markets, among her Colonies. London, the *All-Saxon-Home*, rendezvous of all the 'Children of the Harz-Rock.' (276).—The English essentially conservative : Always the invincible instinct to hold fast by the Old, to admit the *minimum* of New. Yet new epochs do actually come ; and with them new peremptory necessities. A certain Editor's stipulated work. (279).

CHAP. IV. *Captains of Industry.*

Government can do much, but it can in nowise do all. Fall of Mammon: To be a noble Master among noble Workers, will again be the first ambition with some few. (p. 280).—The Leaders of Industry, virtually the Captains of the World: Doggeries and Chivalries. Isolation, the sum-total of wretchedness to man. All social growths in this world have required organising; and Work, the grandest of human interests, does now require it. (281).

CHAP. V. *Permanence.*

The 'tendency to persevere,' to persist in spite of hindrances, discouragements and 'impossibilities,' that which distinguishes the Species Man from the Genus Ape. Month-long contracts, and Exeter-Hall purblindness. A practical manufacturing Quaker's care for his workmen. (p. 286).—Blessing of Permanent Contract: Permanence in all things, at the earliest possible moment, and to the latest possible. Vagrant Sam-Slicks. The wealth of a man the number of things he loves and blesses, which he is loved and blessed by. (288).—The Worker's *interest* in the enterprise with which he is connected. How to reconcile Despotism with Freedom. (289).

CHAP. VI. *The Landed.*

A man with fifty, with five hundred, with a thousand pounds a day, given him freely, without condition at all, might be a rather strong Worker: The sad reality, very ominous to look at. Will he awaken, be alive again; or is this death-fit very death?—Goethe's Duke of Weimar. Doom of Idleness. (p. 290).—To sit idle aloft, like absurd Epicurus'-gods, a poor life for a man. Independence, 'lord of the lion-heart and eagle-eye:' Rejection of sham Superiors, the needful preparation for obedience to *real* Superiors. (292).

CHAP. VII. *The Gifted.*

Tumultuous anarchy, calmed by noble effort into fruitful sovereignty. Mammon like Fire, the usefullest of servants, if the frightfullest of masters. Souls to whom the omnipotent guinea is, on the whole, an impotent guinea: Not a May-game is this man's life; but a battle and stern pilgrimage: God's justice, human Nobleness, Veracity and Mercy, the essence of his very being. (p. 295).—What a man of Genius is. The Highest 'Man of Genius.' Genius, the clearer presence of God Most High in a man. Of intrinsic Valetisms you cannot, with whole Parliaments to help you, make a Heroism. (297).

CHAP. VIII. *The Didactic.*

One preacher who does preach with effect, and gradually persuade all persons. Repentant Captains of Industry: A Chactaw Fighter, become a Christian Fighter. (p. 298).—Doomsday in the afternoon. The 'Christianity' that cannot get on without a minimum of Four-thousand-five-hundred, will give place to something better that can. Beautiful to see the brutish empire of Mammon cracking everywhere: A strange, chill, almost ghastly dayspring in Yankeeland itself. Here as there, Light is coming into the world. Whoso believes, let him begin to fulfil: 'Impossible,' where Truth and Mercy and the everlasting Voice of Nature order, can have no place in the brave man's dictionary. (300).—Not on Ilion's or Latium's plains; on far other plains and places henceforth can noble deeds be done. The last Partridge of England shot and ended: Aristocracies with beards on their chins. O, it is great, and there is no other greatness: To make some nook of God's Creation a little fruitfuller; to make some human hearts a little wiser, manfuller, happier: It is work for a God! (301).

INDEX.

CHARTISM.

ARISTOCRACY, ominous condition of our, 31, 39, 54; an Aristocracy a corporation of the Best and Bravest, 34; old Feudal Aristocracies, 36, 38.

Arkwright, Richard, historical importance of, 51.

Battle, all, misunderstanding, 6.

Bede, Venerable, 44.

Berserkir-rage, deep-hidden in the Saxon heart, 19.

Burns, 16, 37.

Cash-payment, 36, 41.

Celts, the, 44.

Chartism, 3, 26, 32; the history of Chartism not mysterious, 54.

Church, the, and what it might be, 31; 'church' done by machinery, 61.

Clive, Robert, 52.

Conquest, no, permanent if altogether unjust, 24.

Conscience, 48.

Constitution, the English, 46, 49.

Cromwell, 34, 48.

Democracy, true meaning of, 33.

Dupes and Impostors, 28.

Education, 59, 62.

Eighteenth Century, 40; Industrial victories of, 50.

Elizabethan Era, 50.

Emigration, 64.

England, Condition-of-, question, 3, 10; England guilty towards Ireland, 16, 18; Eras of England, 42-53; whose the proprietorship of England, 45; two tasks assigned, 46; education of, 62; over-population, 64.

Europe, modern revolutionary, 27; over-crowded, 67.

Evil, manfully fronted, 58.

French Revolution, the, not yet completed, 26; French Convention, 33; Priesthood destroyed, 35.

Gin, the most authentic demon in our times, 22.

Girondins, the, 56.

Glasgow Thugs, 4, 22, 26.

Hengst and Horsa, 43.

Horse, the, willing to work can find food and shelter, 16; Laissez-faire applied to horses, 21.

Ideals, 38.

Idleness, doom of, 13.

Ignorant, right of the, to be guided by the Wise, 33.

Impossible, not a good word to have often in the mouth, 57. See New.

Industrialisms, English, 46.

Injustice the one thing utterly intolerable, 23, 25; nothing unjust can continue in this world, 30, 38.

Intellects, twenty-four million, awakened into action, 60.

Ireland, tragic mismanagement of, 16; Irish National character degraded, 17; England invaded by Irish destitution, 18.

Johnson, Samuel, 41.

Kings and Slaves, 16.

Laissez-faire, 13; applied to horses, 21; as good as done its part in many provinces, 31, 67; when a reasonable cry, 32.

Magna Charta, 46.

Malthusian controversies, 65.

Manchester, its squalor and despair not forever inseparable from it, 50; once organic, a blessing instead of an affliction, 64.

Mayflower, sailing of the, 48.

Mechanism disturbing labour, 21.

Might and Right, 7, 29, 44. See Rights.

Necessity, submission to, 7, 24.

New, growth of the, 35; New Eras, 42; all new things strange and unexpected. 50.

Norman Nobles, 24; Normans and Saxons originally of one stock, 45.

PAST AND PRESENT.

Printed in Great Britain
by Amazon.co.uk, Ltd.,
Marston Gate.